Quiet Water

NEW YORK

AMC's Canoe and Kayak Guide to the State's
Best Ponds, Lakes, and Easy Rivers

3RD EDITION

JOHN HAYES & ALEX WILSON

AMC is a nonprofit organization, and sales of AMC Books fund our mission of protecting the Northeast outdoors. If you appreciate our efforts and would like to become a member or make a donation to AMC, visit outdoors.org, call 800-372-1758, or contact us at Appalachian Mountain Club, 10 City Square, Boston, MA 02129.

outdoors.org/books-maps

Distributed by National Book Network

Front cover photograph of Upper Saranac Lake © Stephen Ritchie, Creative Commons on Flickr
Back cover photograph of Lows Lake © Alex Wilson
Title page photo: A view of Lake Lila from a trail that extends above the lake
Interior photographs © John Hayes and Alex Wilson
Cartography by Siobhan Hayes 3rd Edition; Vanessa Gray 2nd Edition; Ian Duncan 1st Edition
Pen-and-ink drawings by Marrin Robinson
Book design by Eric Edstam

Library of Congress Cataloging-in-Publication Data

Names: Hayes, John, 1944- author. | Wilson, Alex, 1955- author.
Title: Quiet water New York : AMC's canoe and kayak guide to the state's best ponds, lakes, and easy rivers / John Hayes, Alex Wilson.
Description: Third edition. | Boston, Massachusetts : Appalachian Mountain Club Books, [2021] | Includes index. | Summary: "AMC's guide to New York's best quiet water canoe and kayak paddling, covering 157 of the best ponds, lakes, and easy rivers, from Long Island to Buffalo"-- Provided by publisher.
Identifiers: LCCN 2020057096 (print) | LCCN 2020057097 (ebook) | ISBN 9781628421125 (trade paperback) | ISBN 9781628421132 (epub) | ISBN 9781628421149 (mobi)
Subjects: LCSH: Canoes and canoeing--New York (State)--Guidebooks. | Lakes--New York (State)--Guidebooks. | Ponds--New York (State)--Guidebooks. | New York (State)--Guidebooks.
Classification: LCC GV776.N7 H39 2021 (print) | LCC GV776.N7 (ebook) | DDC 797.122/409747--dc23
LC record available at https://lccn.loc.gov/2020057096
LC ebook record available at https://lccn.loc.gov/2020057097

The paper used in this publication meets the minimum requirements of the American National Standard for Information Sciences-Permanence of Paper for Printed Library Materials, ANSI Z39.48-1984. ∞

Interior pages and cover are printed on responsibly harvested paper stock certified by The Forest Stewardship Council®, an independent auditor of responsible forestry practices. Printed in the United States of America, using vegetable-based inks.

FSC www.fsc.org MIX Paper from responsible sources FSC® C005010

5 4 3 2 1   21 22 23 24 25

Quiet Water

NEW YORK

AMC's Canoe and Kayak Guide to the State's
Best Ponds, Lakes, and Easy Rivers

3RD EDITION

JOHN HAYES & ALEX WILSON

Appalachian Mountain Club Books
Boston, Massachusetts

LOCATOR MAP: NEW YORK

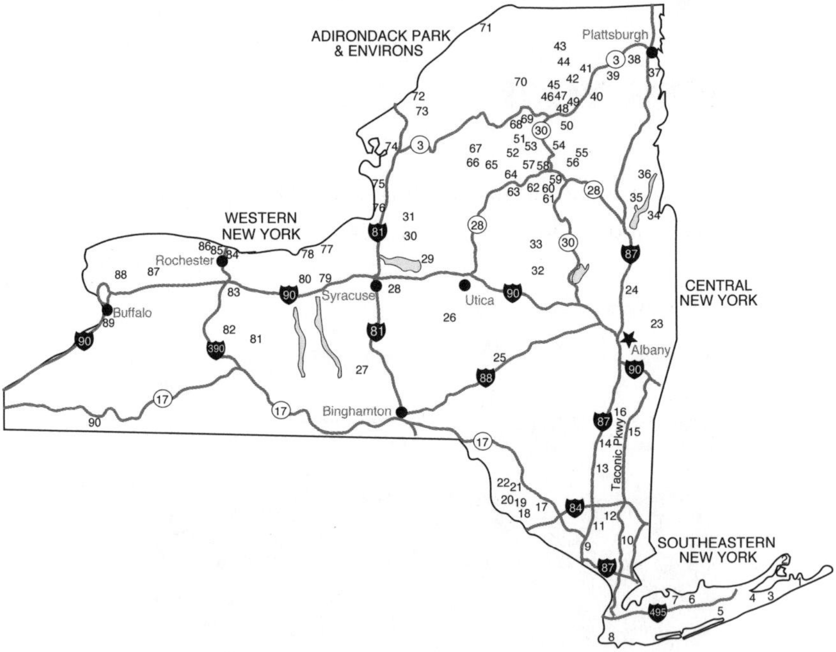

Numbers on map correspond to trips; for a complete list, see Contents, beginning on page vii.

MAP LEGEND

Tent site

Lean-to

Picnic area

Campground

Boat access

Parking area

Marsh

Peak

Dam

Divided highway

State highway

Paved road

Less-traveled road

Rough dirt road

Foot path

Carry path

Railroad tracks

River

Stream

arrow indicates direction of flow

Contents

SECTION 2: CENTRAL NEW YORK

SECTION 3: ADIRONDACK PARK AND ENVIRONS

SECTION 4: WESTERN NEW YORK

NATURE ESSAYS

Facing page: Co-author Alex Wilson portaging his canoe and gear along the rough gravel road that leads into Third Lake, one of the Essex Chain Lakes in Adirondack Park.

MOILLE

At-a-Glance Trip Planner

TRIP #	TRIP	PAGE	ACCESS LOCATION	AREA/ ONE-WAY LENGTH
SOUTHEASTERN NEW YORK				
1	Accabonac Harbor	2	East Hampton	390 acres
2	Hallock Bay (Long Beach Bay) and Little Bay	6	Southold	680 acres
3	Sebonac Creek	9	Southampton	530 acres
4	Flanders Bay Tributaries and Peconic River	13	Riverhead, Southampton	
5	Carmans River	17	Brookhaven	4.5 miles
6	Stony Brook Harbor	21	Smithtown	940 acres
7	Nissequogue River	24	Smithtown	5.5 miles
8	Jamaica Bay Wildlife Refuge	27	Brooklyn, Queens	9,155 acres

NOTES

[1] MPH or HP limit
[2] few motorboats
[3] no personal watercraft

ESTIMATED TIME	HIKING TRAILS Y/N	SWIMMING Y/N	MOTORBOATS Y/N	TRIP TYPE
4 hours	Y	N	Y	short-grass salt marsh estuary
5 hours	Y	Y	Y	long-grass salt marsh estuary
all day	Y	N	Y	long-grass salt marsh estuary
all day, multiday	N	N	Y	tidal estuary below Riverhead; impounded, slow-flowing river above
4 hours	Y	N	Y[2]	tidal estuary below Route 27, impounded river above; no development
5 hours	N	N	Y	tidal estuary, islands, protected coves; mud flats at low tide
5 hours	N	N	Y[2]	tidal estuary, islands, and oxbows; extensive mud flats at low tide
all day, multiday	Y	N	Y	large salt marsh estuary; many islands and protected bays, nature trails

TRIP #	TRIP	PAGE	ACCESS LOCATION	AREA/ ONE-WAY LENGTH
9	Harriman State Park Lakes	31	Haverstraw, Tuxedo, Woodbury	8 lakes, 36 to 310 acres
10	Mohansic Lake and Crom Pond	46	Yorktown	107 acres, 30 acres
11	Constitution Marsh	49	Philipstown	270 acres
12	Canopus Lake and Stillwater Pond	53	Kent	104 acres
13	Chodikee Lake	57	Esopus, Lloyd	63 acres, 2.5 miles
14	Tivoli Marshes—North Bay	60	Red Hook	1,468 acres
15	Lake Taghkanic and Rudd Pond	63	Gallatin, Northeast	104 acres, 66 acres
16	Catskill Creek and RamsHorn Marsh	67	Catskill	3 creeks, 6.5 miles
17	Basher Kill	70	Mamakating	1,920 acres
18	Rio Reservoir	73	Deer Park, Forestburg, Lumberland	435 acres
19	Mongaup Falls Reservoir	76	Forestburg, Lumberland	130 acres
20	Cliff Lake	78	Bethel, Highland, Lumberland	200 acres
21	Toronto Reservoir	84	Bethel	834 acres
22	Lake Superior	87	Bethel	188 acres
CENTRAL NEW YORK				
23	Grafton Lakes and Dunham Reservoir	92	Grafton	5 ponds, 19 to 113 acres

NOTES

[1] MPH or HP limit

[2] few motorboats

[3] no personal watercraft

ESTIMATED TIME	HIKING TRAILS Y/N	SWIMMING Y/N	MOTORBOATS Y/N	TRIP TYPE
all day, multiday	Y	Y	N	Eight small ponds and lakes, nature trails
3 hours	Y	Y	N	small recreational lake and small marshy pond; nature trails
3 hours	Y	N	N	tidal marsh
3 hours	Y	Y	N	small ponds
4 hours	N	N	N	small lake with swampy inlet and outlet streams
4 hours	N	N	N	tidal, freshwater marshlands with shrubs; no development
2 hours	Y	Y	Y	small, recreation-oriented ponds
5 hours	N	N	Y[2]	tidal, freshwater rivers, marshland with trees; little development
5 hours	Y	N	N	large, shallow marsh
3 hours	N	N	N	deep, narrow reservoir
2 hours	N	N	N	small, shallow reservoir with some marshy areas
3 hours	Y	N	N	small reservoir
4 hours	Y	N	Y[3]	reservoir
4 hours	N	Y	N	shallow, marshy, weedy pond
6 hours	Y	Y	Y	small, shallow ponds

TRIP #	TRIP	PAGE	ACCESS LOCATION	AREA/ ONE-WAY LENGTH
24	Fish Creek (Saratoga Lake)	95	Saratoga, Saratoga Springs	11 miles
25	Susquehanna River	99	Milford	366 acres, 10 miles
26	Sangerfield River (Ninemile Swamp)	103	Brookfield, Hamilton	4 miles (one way)
27	Dryden Lake	106	Dryden	106 acres
28	Old Erie Canal	109	De Witt, Manlius	2.5 miles or 5.5 miles
29	Fish Creek to Oneida Lake	113	Vienna	9 miles
30	Gifford Lake/West Branch Fish Creek	119	Amboy, Williamstown	6 miles
31	Salmon River Reservoir	122	Orwell, Redfield	2,660 acres
ADIRONDACK PARK & ENVIRONS				
32	Canada Lake and West Lake	128	Caroga, Stratford	554 acres
33	Sacandaga River West Branch	131	Arietta	8 miles
34	South Bay	135	Dresden, Fort Ann, Whitehall	1,100 acres
35	Lake George Northwest Bay	139	Bolton	2 miles, plus large bay
36	Putnam Pond	143	Ticonderoga	185 acres
37	Ausable Marsh	146	Ausable, Peru	6 miles
38	Davis Lake and Salmon River	150	Peru, Schuyler Falls	60 acres, 1 mile
39	Taylor Pond	154	Black Brook	803 acres

NOTES

[1] MPH or HP limit
[2] few motorboats
[3] no personal watercraft

ESTIMATED TIME	HIKING TRAILS Y/N	SWIMMING Y/N	MOTORBOATS Y/N	TRIP TYPE
3–4 hours, each section	N	N	Y	slow-flowing stream
6 hours	N	N	Y[2]	slow-flowing stream through farmland and woodlot
3 hours	N	N	N	swampy stream
2 hours	Y	N	N	small, shallow, weed-filled pond
4 hours	Y	N	N	shallow former canal
6 hours	N	N	N	wide, shallow, slow-flowing stream
5 hours	N	N	N	marshy, slow-flowing creek
all day	N	N	Y[2]	large reservoir and marshy inlet stream
5 hours	N	N	Y	deep lakes
all day	N	N	N	river and connected small ponds
4 hours	N	N	Y[2]	large, shallow lake with marshy bays and inlets
4 hours	Y	N	Y	shallow brook emptying into relatively small bay on huge lake
3 hours	Y	N	Y[2]	shallow pond with marshy coves
4 hours	N	N	N	marshes and slow-flowing rivers
3 hours	N	N	N	small, shallow lake; narrow, slow-flowing stream
4 hours	Y	N	Y[2]	deep oligotrophic lake

TRIP #	TRIP	PAGE	ACCESS LOCATION	AREA/ ONE-WAY LENGTH
40	Moose Pond	157	St. Armand	140 acres
41	Lake Kushaqua and Rainbow Lake	160	Brighton, Franklin	588 acres, 377 acres, 3 miles
42	Osgood Pond, Jones Pond, and Osgood River	166	Brighton	508 acres, 170 acres, 1.5 and 3 miles
43	Deer River Flow and Horseshoe Pond	169	Duane	500 acres
44	Osgood River and Meacham Lake	173	Brighton, Duane	1,203 acres, 6 miles
45	St. Regis Lakes and Spitfire Lake	177	Brighton, Harrietstown	711 acres, 365 acres, 254 acres
46	St. Regis Canoe Area	181	Santa Clara	many ponds from 43 to 455 acres
47	Fish Creek Loops	194	Santa Clara	many ponds from 43 to 491 acres
48	Middle Saranac Lake	200	Harrietstown, Santa Clara	1,193 acres
49	Lower Saranac Lake	204	Harrietstown	2,214 acres
50	Raquette River	207	Harrietstown	10 miles
51	Lows Lake (Bog River Flow)	211	Clifton, Colton, Long Lake, Piercefield	2,845 acres

NOTES

[1] MPH or HP limit
[2] few motorboats
[3] no personal watercraft

ESTIMATED TIME	HIKING TRAILS Y/N	SWIMMING Y/N	MOTORBOATS Y/N	TRIP TYPE
3 hours	Y	N	Y[2]	small, deep, oligotrophic pond
all day	Y	Y	Y[2]	extensive interconnected lakes and river
5 hours	Y	N	Y[2]	interconnected ponds and river
5 hours	Y	N	Y[2]	shallow, marshy pond surrounded by northern boreal forest
3 hours, all day	Y	Y	Y	large lake, marshy stream, northern boreal forest
all day, multiday	Y	N	Y2	lakes with many islands and coves
all day, multiday	Y	Y	N	small- to medium-sized ponds connected by short carries, surrounded by northern boreal forest
all day, multiday	Y	Y	N	ponds, some connected by streams, surrounded by forest
5 hours	Y	N	Y	large lake with marshy coves and outlet stream
all day	Y	N	Y	large lake with many islands, deep coves, and two adjacent ponds
all day	Y	N	Y[2]	slow-flowing, marshy river
all day, multiday	Y	N	Y[2]	long, narrow, shallow, marshy lake

TRIP #	TRIP	PAGE	ACCESS LOCATION	AREA/ ONE-WAY LENGTH
52	Lake Lila	221	Long Lake	1,490 acres plus miles of streams
53	Little Tupper Lake, Round Lake, and Rock Pond	224	Long Lake	2,300 acres, 800 acres, 282 acres
54	Long Lake	229	Long Lake	3,904 acres
55	Harris Lake and Rich Lake	233	Newcomb	310 acres, 342 acres, plus creeks
56	Essex Chain Lakes	239	Long Lake, Minerva, Newcomb	12 lakes, largest 262 acres
57	Forked Lake	244	Arietta, Long Lake	1,248 acres plus connecting streams
58	Blue Mountain, Eagle, and Utowana Lakes and Marion River	247	Indian Lake	1,220 acres, 10 miles
59	Lake Durant and Rock Pond	253	Indian Lake	330 acres
60	Cedar River Flow	256	Lake Pleasant	710 acres, many miles of inlet streams
61	Indian Lake	260	Indian Lake, Lake Pleasant	4,255 acres
62	Eighth Lake (Fulton Chain)	264	Inlet	320 acres
63	Limekiln Lake	270	Inlet, Ohio	457 acres
64	Moss Lake	273	Webb	115 acres

NOTES

[1] MPH or HP limit
[2] few motorboats
[3] no personal watercraft

ESTIMATED TIME	HIKING TRAILS Y/N	SWIMMING Y/N	MOTORBOATS Y/N	TRIP TYPE
all day, multiday	Y	N	N	shallow wilderness lake
all day, multiday	Y	N	N	interconnected lakes with marshy inlets and coves
all day, multiday	Y	N	Y[2]	long, wide lake with coves, islands, and inlet streams
5 hours, all day	Y	N	Y[2]	small lakes with extensive marshes and access to the upper Hudson River
all day, multiday	Y	N	N	connected small lakes with extensive marshes, wooded shorelines
6 hours, all day	Y	N	Y[2]	long, large lake
all day, multiday	Y	Y	Y	large lake; long narrow connecting lakes; slow-flowing river
4 hours	Y	N	Y	long, shallow, marshy lake and pond
4 hours, multiday	Y	N	Y[2]	shallow, weed-filled lake and slow-flowing river
all day, multiday	Y	N	Y	huge, deep lake
2 hours, all day	N	N	Y[2]	small lake in a valley
4 hours	Y	Y	Y	oligotrophic lake with marshy inlet stream
2 hours	Y	N	N	small, shallow, marshy lake and outlet stream

TRIP #	TRIP	PAGE	ACCESS LOCATION	AREA/ ONE-WAY LENGTH
65	Stillwater Reservoir	276	Webb	6,195 acres
66	Beaver River Canoe Route	280	Croghan, Watson, Webb	6 reservoirs, largest 294 acres; 10 miles
67	Long Pond, Round Pond, and Oswegatchie River West Branch	286	Croghan	146 acres, 1.5 miles
68	Oswegatchie River	290	Fine	13 miles
69	Cranberry Lake	294	Clifton, Colton, Fine	6,995 acres
70	Five Falls, Rainbow Falls, and Blake Falls Reservoirs	298	Colton, Parishville	106 acres, 739 acres, 642 acres
71	Coles Creek	308	Louisville, Waddington	680 acres
WESTERN NEW YORK				
72	Crooked Creek	312	Alexandria, Hammond	7 miles
73	Red Lake and Indian River	315	Theresa	366 acres, 5 miles
74	Black River Bay	319	Brownsville, Hounsfield	1,350 acres
75	Lakeview Wildlife Management Area—North and South Colwell Ponds, Goose Pond, Floodwood Pond, and Lakeview Pond	322	Ellisburg	3,461 acres
76	Deer Creek Marsh	327	Richland	1,771 acres, 2.5 miles
77	Sterling Valley Creek/The Pond	331	Sterling	7 miles
78	East Bay	334	Huron	290 acres, 6 miles

NOTES

1 MPH or HP limit
2 few motorboats
3 no personal watercraft

ESTIMATED TIME	HIKING TRAILS Y/N	SWIMMING Y/N	MOTORBOATS Y/N	TRIP TYPE
all day, multiday	N	N	Y	very large, shallow reservoir
all day, multiday	N	Y	Y[2]	interconnected small lakes with portages
5 hours	Y	N	Y[2]	small ponds and slow-flowing, marshy river
all day, multiday	Y	N	N	twisting wilderness stream through northern boreal forest
all day, multiday	Y	Y	Y	large, shallow lake
all day	Y	Y	Y	wooded reservoirs
all day	N	N	Y[2]	shallow, marshy, dammed-up creek
all day	N	Y	Y[2]	shallow, marshy creek
5 hours	N	N	Y[2]	winding, slow-flowing river and small lake
4 hours, all day	N	N	Y[2]	shallow, marshy bay
5 hours, all day	Y	N	N	shallow, marshy ponds; small, wooded streams
3 hours	Y	N	N	shallow, slow-flowing creek
5 hours	Y	Y	Y[2]	shallow, marshy streams
4 hours	N	N	Y[2]	shallow, marshy creeks

TRIP #	TRIP	PAGE	ACCESS LOCATION	AREA/ ONE-WAY LENGTH
79	Seneca River (Howland Island)	338	Conquest	10 mile loop
80	Clyde River	342	Galen	10.5 miles
81	West River	345	Italy	3.5 miles
82	Hemlock Lake and Canadice Lake	348	Canadice, Conesus, Livonia	1,800 acres, 650 acres
83	Mendon Ponds	352	Mendon	120 acres, 30 acres
84	Genesee River Gorge	356	Rochester	4 miles
85	Buck Pond	358	Greece	550 acres
86	Salmon Creek and West Creek	364	Greece, Parma	6 miles
87	Oak Orchard Creek	367	Alabama, Shelby	6 miles
88	Tonawanda Creek	370	Amherst, Clarence, Lockport, Newstead, Pendleton, Royalton	20 miles
89	Buffalo River	373	Buffalo, West Seneca	6 miles
90	Allegheny Reservoir	378	Coldspring, Elko, South Valley	12,000 acres

NOTES

[1] MPH or HP limit

[2] few motorboats

[3] no personal watercraft

ESTIMATED TIME	HIKING TRAILS Y/N	SWIMMING Y/N	MOTORBOATS Y/N	TRIP TYPE
5 hours	Y	N	Y[2]	shallow, slow-flowing river
5 hours	Y	N	N	small, shallow stream
4 hours	Y	N	Y[2]	slow-flowing stream through a wide swamp
all day	Y	N	Y[2]	deep, long, water-supply reservoirs
2 hours	Y	N	N	small, shallow ponds
3 hours	N	N	Y	wide, deep, slow-flowing river
3 hours	N	N	Y[2]	cattail swamp
3 hours	N	N	Y[2]	shallow, marshy creeks
5 hours	Y	N	N	shallow, marshy, slow-flowing stream
all day	N	N	Y[2]	slow-flowing stream
half day, all day	N	N	Y	slow-flowing, industrial, channelized, polluted river undergoing ecological restoration
all day	Y	N	Y	large reservoir

Foreword

Let's get one thing straight. If, as a paddler, you have a yen for exploits on the Upper Hudson and the Colorado's Grand Canyon, if the more challenging the waters the more you are satisfied, if, in short, heroism is your aim, this book is not for you. It is a book not for heroes who seek to dominate the natural world but for pilgrims who seek it humbly for understanding and harmony. *Quiet Water: New York* is a handbook for natural history as well as a practical guide to getting there. It will open your eyes to the richness of perception that awaits the casual paddler on New York State's lakes, ponds, and flatwater streams. The authors are competent guides. Alex Wilson is a naturalist and writer of three other quietwater guidebooks. John Hayes is a retired professor of biochemistry and environmental science and a leader of natural-history field trips. You may not have their luck of spotting four bald eagles at once, adults and fledglings, at a nest on Deer River Flow. But there is a good chance that they will draw your attention to cavorting river otters; to the spectacular flight of the peregrine falcon; to damselflies leaping off the landing pads of floating vegetation as your boat glides by; to the intricate mechanism by which carnivorous plants—sundew, pitcher, and bladderwort—feed on insects. And in the forever-wild forests of the Adirondacks and Catskills, Wilson and Hayes will assist in transporting you back to an early time on this continent.

—Paul Jamieson

Author of *Adirondack Canoe Waters: North Flow*

Preface

The first edition of *Quiet Water: New York* was the fourth in a series that includes guides to New Hampshire and Vermont; Massachusetts, Connecticut, and Rhode Island; Maine; and New Jersey and eastern Pennsylvania. Alex Wilson started the series in 1992 with the New Hampshire and Vermont guide, then followed with the southern New England guide in 1993. John Hayes co-authored the Maine guide with Alex in 1995, followed by the New York guide in 1996. He became co-author, again with Alex, of subsequent editions of the other guides.

We took the opportunity in the second and third New York editions to add new material, including seven new trips: Little Tupper Lake; Sacandaga River West Branch; Jamaica Bay; Tivoli Marshes; Catskill Creek and RamsHorn Marsh; Buffalo River; and Essex Chain Lakes. We also eliminated the sections on Massawepie and Grass Creek and on South Pond because of difficult access, and we eliminated Morningside Lake because of its small size and heavy recreational use.

The third edition has 90 trips covering over 200 bodies of water.

Because descriptions inevitably go out of date, we also rechecked all bodies of water to ensure that new development had not crowded the shores; revised directions to reflect new road names; and added GPS coordinates to access points. When possible, we avoided bodies of water with substantial development, but the larger worry was the effect of personal motorized watercraft and high-speed boating on safety, the quietwater experience, and the environment.

Introduction

Quiet waters—lakes, ponds, estuaries, and slow-flowing streams—receive much less attention than whitewater rivers. If you seek the adrenaline rush of paddling cascading rivers, plenty of excellent resources exist, but this is not one of them. New York offers outstanding paddling opportunities. Indeed, many people think that the lakes, ponds, and rivers of New York's Adirondack Park offer the finest canoeing and kayaking in the Northeast. Although few places in the United States surpass the wildness of Adirondack lakes and meandering flows, New York offers many other outstanding paddling destinations. From the tidal estuaries of Long Island to the historic Erie Canal in the central part of the state to the wild and marshy inlet creeks of Lake Ontario, tremendous paddling exists near and far—places just right for a several-day expedition or for a half day of paddling near home.

The peaceful solitude of out-of-the-way lakes and ponds lures us to quietwater paddling. This guide will lead you to wood ducks swimming through early morning mists. You will round a bend in a winding inlet channel to encounter the playful antics of river otters or feel the thrill of spotting moose—mouths full of pondweeds—as they repopulate the northern part of the state. White pines towering above crystal-clear ponds will help you imagine what this region's forests looked like centuries ago while you listen to the loon's haunting wail wafting off the water as afternoon settles into dusk.

With quietwater paddling, you can focus on *being* there instead of *getting* there. You don't need a lot of fancy high-tech equipment, although a light canoe or kayak makes portaging over beaver dams much easier. Binoculars and field guides to fauna and flora are the most important gear—after boats, paddles, and personal flotation devices (PFDs).

This guide will lead you to a body of water and describe why you might want to paddle it. We tried to include places with abundant wildlife or extensive marshlands or beautiful scenery; most entries have all three. We hope that our research will allow you to spend your valuable time paddling instead of driving around for hours, trying to find elusive accesses. We designed the *Quiet Water* series for paddlers of all experience levels, to help you better enjoy the Northeast's wonderful water resources.

THE SELECTION PROCESS

This guide includes only a small percentage of New York's lakes, ponds, estuaries, and slow-flowing streams. In the selection process, we looked for great scenery; limited development; few motorboats and personal watercraft; a varied shoreline with lots of coves and inlets to explore; and interesting plants, animals, and geologic formations.

We included a variety of water types: big lakes and rivers for longer excursions, and protected ponds and marshes for when you have limited time or when weather conditions preclude paddling larger bodies of water. To make the book as useful as possible, we paid particular attention to lakes and ponds in more populated regions, even though many more-remote locations in northern New York better fit our standards for ideal paddling.

We asked people in the out-of-doors about the best places to paddle; we consulted DeLorme's *New York Atlas & Gazetteer;* we bought other books about paddling, including the superb guides from the Adirondack Mountain Club (see Further Reading); and we systematically searched the 850-plus U.S. Geological Survey (USGS) 7.5-minute topographic maps of New York.

Although we tried to include the very best places to paddle, we doubtless missed some excellent locations. If you have suggestions for other lakes, ponds, and streams to consider for future editions, please write to Alex Wilson (alex@atwilson.com).

SAFETY, EQUIPMENT, AND TECHNIQUE

We all long to glide on mist-filled, mirror-smooth surfaces of quiet ponds at daybreak. But if you spend any time paddling lakes and tidal rivers, you will also encounter far less tranquil conditions. Swift estuary tides, coupled with wind, can make conditions dangerous. On larger bodies of water, strong winds can arise quickly, whipping up 2- to 4-foot waves in no time—waves big enough to swamp an open boat. If you capsize in cold water even a moderate distance from shore, hypothermia—a cooling of the body's core that can lead to mental and physical collapse—can set in quickly. If you reach a particular lake and find it dangerously windy, choose a more protected body of water or go hiking instead.

Safety First

All Northeast states require each boater to carry a U.S. Coast Guard–approved (Type I, II, or III) personal flotation device (PFD). A good PFD keeps a person's face above water, even if that person has lost consciousness. A foam- or kapok-filled PFD will also keep you warmer in cold water.

Children 12 and younger must wear their PFDs at all times. Adult PFDs are not acceptable for children—if they are too large, they might slip off. New York law also requires all occupants of recreational watercraft less than 21 feet in length to wear PFDs between November 1 and May 1. We strongly recommend that you wear a PFD *at all times* regardless of the written rules, especially when paddling with children. If you do not normally wear a PFD when you paddle, at least don it in windy conditions, when crossing large lakes, or when you may encounter substantial motorboat wakes. It could save your life.

You should also bring along a waterproof first-aid kit. The best kit is one you assemble yourself. Make sure that it has bandages and moleskin for blisters, an antihistamine for allergic reactions, sunscreen, an extra hat, a pain reliever, and any special medications you might require.

As for clothing, plan for the unexpected. Even with a sunny-day forecast, a shower can appear by afternoon. On trips of more than a few hours, we bring along rain gear and dry clothes in a waterproof stuff sack as a matter of course. Along with rain arriving unexpectedly, temperatures can drop quickly, especially in spring or fall, making conditions ripe for hypothermia. Avoid wearing cotton. Lightweight nylon or polypropylene clothing dries more quickly than cotton, and wool retards heat loss even when wet, whereas cotton does not. Remember that heads lose heat faster than torsos. Bring a hat.

Also, bring a whistle, which you may need to summon help. The sound of a whistle travels farther than the sound of a human voice, especially in windy conditions. Bring enough food to maintain your energy level, and carry 1 liter of water for short trips and 2 or more liters for long trips. Avoid shallow, marshy waters during waterfowl-hunting season. For hunting season dates, check the New York Department of Environmental Conservation website: dec.ny.gov/outdoor/28888.html.

Other safety tips include:

- Get off the water during lightning storms; lightning usually strikes the highest object in the vicinity. When you're in a boat on a lake, that means you.

- Know what to do if you capsize—and have experience doing it.
- Avoid dehydration by drinking plenty of liquids.
- Avoid areas with a lot of high-speed boating.
- Check the weather forecast before going out.
- If appropriate, check times of low and high tides.

Equipment

For quietwater paddling, avoid high-performance racing or tippy whitewater canoes and kayaks. Rent or borrow a boat before buying; selection will be easier with a little experience. Whether you prefer a canoe or kayak, look for a model with good initial and secondary stability. A boat with good initial stability and poor secondary stability will tip slowly, but once it starts, it may keep going. The best canoes for lakes and ponds have a keel or shallow V-shaped hull, and the bottoms are fairly flat from bow to stern. This helps them track in a straight line, even in a breeze. Kayaks perform extremely well in rough water, particularly if equipped with a foot-operated rudder and a sprayskirt to keep from taking on water.

If you yearn for out-of-the-way paddles requiring portages, get a Kevlar (strong, lightweight carbon fiber) boat if you can afford it. We paddle a rugged, high-capacity, 18-foot, 4-inch Mad River Lamoille canoe that weighs just 60 pounds; a 15-foot, 9-inch Mad River Independence solo canoe that weighs less than 40 pounds; a 14-foot Wenonah Wigeon kayak that weighs 38 pounds; and a 14-foot Wilderness Systems Tchaika kayak that weighs 32 pounds. (These older boats have been replaced by newer, similar models.) If you plan to paddle alone, consider a sea kayak or a solo canoe in which you sit (or kneel) close to the boat's center. You will find paddling a well-designed solo canoe far easier than paddling a two-seater by yourself. The touring or sea kayak—with its long, narrow design, low profile to the wind, and two-bladed paddling style—is faster and more efficient to paddle than a canoe.

A padded portage yoke in place of the center thwart (a crosswise, left-to-right strut) on a canoe is essential if you plan on doing much carrying. With unpadded yokes, wear a life vest with padded shoulders when carrying. Attach a rope—called a painter—to the bow so that you can secure the boat when you stop for lunch, line it up or down a stream, and—if the need ever arises—grab onto it in an emergency. We have some embarrassing stories about not using a painter. Wind can cause Kevlar boats to disappear very quickly, and it's not fun to watch your canoe or kayak bobbing away in a stiff wind!

Choose light, comfortable paddles. For canoeing, we use a relatively short (48- or 50-inch), laminated, bent-shaft paddle. The paddle, a composite of various woods to give it strength, has a synthetic tip to protect the blade. Straight-shaft paddles work well, but bent-shaft paddles are more efficient because the downward force converts more directly into forward thrust. Always carry at least one spare paddle per group, particularly on longer trips, in case you break a paddle or a porcupine gets hold of one.

Paddling Technique

On a quiet pond, does it matter if you use the proper J stroke, the sweep stroke, or the draw? No. Learning some of these strokes, however, can make paddling more relaxing and enjoyable. We watch lots of novices zigzagging along, frantically switching sides, shouting orders fore and aft. People have told us about marriage counseling sessions devoted to paddling technique!

If you are new to the sport and want to learn canoeing or kayaking techniques, buy a book or participate in a paddling workshop, such as those offered by the Appalachian Mountain Club (see outdoors.org/outdoor-activities/paddle), equipment retailers, and boat manufacturers. See Appendix B (page 391) for some recommended books on canoeing and kayaking.

Start out on small ponds. Practice paddling into, with, and across the wind. On a warm day, close to shore, with your PFD on and others to help you if needed, practice capsizing. Intentionally tipping your boat will give you an idea of how easily it can upend. Try to get back into the boat away from shore.

Bailing water out of a kayak while treading water is impossible. Use a hand pump—either a boat-mounted permanent one or a portable one. Two people should be able to right a canoe, bailing most of the water out. (Keep a bailer *fastened* to a thwart.) Getting back in the boat is another story. Try climbing in simultaneously from opposite sides. If that doesn't work, grab onto the boat on opposite sides, and kick your way to shore. Good luck!

PADDLING WITH KIDS

When canoeing with kids, keep calm and try to make it fun. Even though you may be plenty warm from paddling, children can get cold while sitting in the boat. Remember that everyone should wear PFDs at all times, and PFDs will help keep children warm. Kids also need protection from sun and biting insects. Watch for signs of discomfort. Set up a cozy place where youngsters can sleep; after the initial excitement of paddling fades, a gently rolling canoe often makes children drowsy, especially near the end of a long day. Also, for lengthy excursions, make sure to bring a waterproof sack with dry clothes for everyone.

New York law requires that children wear life vests (PFDs) in boats. We recommend that everyone wear a PFD when paddling.

How to Use This Book

For each trip, we provide a list of basic information, a map, directions, and a short description of what you'll see.

TRIP INFORMATION

At the start of each trip description, we include location, DeLorme and USGS map references, area covered by the trip, an estimate of time required for a leisurely paddle, habitat type (i.e., type of environment you will encounter), types of game fish, predominant animals and kinds of vegetation you should expect to see, public campgrounds, contact details, and notes about development or hazards to avoid. For information on private campgrounds, see the extensive lists in the DeLorme atlas.

Choose larger bodies of water and longer rivers when you have more time and a good weather forecast. Under windy conditions, opt for smaller waterways. Most entries include substantial shallow-water marshlands.

Note that although we list fish species for each destination, specific or general advisories against eating caught fish from all bodies of water exist, particularly for pregnant and nursing women and for children. Advisories do not apply to stocked hatchery fish. General and specific advisories are in Appendix C. Fishing licenses may be obtained from sporting goods stores or on the Department of Environmental Conservation website. Children younger than 16 do not need a license.

MAPS

We recommend that you use the most recent edition of DeLorme's *New York Atlas & Gazetteer*, available at bookstores, outdoor retailers, and garmin.com. We key each entry to the DeLorme atlas, which divides the state into 107 detailed 10-by-14-inch maps at 1:127,000 scale. The maps include most—but not all—access locations, campsites, road names, campgrounds, parks, and other pertinent information. (Note: Older versions of DeLorme's New York atlas had a 150,000:1 scale and different page numbering.) We also include maps that we drew for each location, using U.S. Geological Survey (USGS) topographic maps to outline waterways and some roads and natural features. For more detail, refer to the 7.5-minute, 1:24,000-scale USGS topographic maps listed with each trip.

GETTING THERE

We give directions from the nearest city or major highway to the access, providing distances between points, with the cumulative distance given in parentheses. We assume you will use a detailed highway map, such as DeLorme's atlas. We also include Global Positioning System (GPS) coordinates, with latitude and longitude values reported in degrees and minutes. If it's more convenient to use degrees as one number, just divide the minutes by 60 to get a decimal. For example, to convert 41° 1.107′, divide 1.107 minutes by 60 minutes per degree to get 0.01845°. Then add this decimal to 41° to get 41.01845°. You can use these coordinates on your cell phone to get directions to an access. For example, if you enter 41° 1.107′ N and the corresponding longitude, 72° 8.725′ W, into the search function on the iPhone Maps app or Google Maps app (as *41 1.107'n 72 8.725'w* or as *41.01845n 72.14542w*), you'll get directions to the Accabonac Harbor access.

WHAT YOU'LL SEE

The trip descriptions, each a few paragraphs long, give details about the area's natural features. Those details include birds, animals, and plants you will likely see and, in some cases, prominent geologic landmarks. Bringing field guides to birds, plants, and animals—along with waterproof binoculars—would be a great help in identifying and enjoying what you see.

Happy paddling!

Stewardship and Conservation

Diverse wetlands—among the richest, most readily accessible ecosystems—provide wonderful opportunities for paddlers to learn about nature. You can visit crystal-clear mountain ponds, slow-flowing rivers, and interesting bog habitats. You can observe hundreds of species of birds; dozens of mammal, turtle, and snake species; and hundreds of plant and insect species. Some quite rare species, such as a delicate bog orchid or a family of otters, provide a real treat. But even ordinary plants and animals lead to exciting discoveries and can provide hours of enjoyment.

In essays separate from the trip descriptions, we describe a few interesting plants and animals you might encounter on your journeys. The essays and accompanying pen-and-ink illustrations by Marrin Robinson appear throughout the book. We hope this additional information will enhance your own observations.

DO WE REALLY WANT TO TELL PEOPLE ABOUT THE BEST PLACES?

People have asked us how we could, in good conscience, tell others about remote, pristine, unspoiled places. After all, increased visitation would make these locations less idyllic. After spending many an hour grappling with this difficult issue as we paddled along, we concluded that people who experience wild, remote areas firsthand will come to value them and will build support for their protection.

New York's diverse wetlands—lakes, ponds, rivers and streams, wooded swamps, bogs, fens, freshwater marshes, salt marshes, brackish marshes, and floodplains—cover 2.4 million acres, or 7 percent, of New York's surface area. In contrast, Maine, a state with only 57 percent of New York's area, has 5 million acres of wetlands (25 percent of its area). Although Maine has lost comparatively little of its wetlands, New York has lost as much as 60 percent of its nonlake and river wetlands since 1780.

Wetlands perform extremely important functions, including recharging groundwater, helping control floods, supporting fishing and waterfowl hunting, and providing habitats for hundreds of species, including many that are rare and endangered. Even low-impact uses, such as canoeing and kayaking, can substantially affect fragile marsh habitat. Paddling can disturb nesting loons and eagles, rare turtles, and delicate bog orchids. Canoes or kayaks can carry invasive plants and other harmful organisms from one body of water to another. Be sure to clean off your boat before you visit other water bodies.

You can go even farther than the adage "Take only photographs, leave only footprints." Carry a trash bag and clean up after less thoughtful individuals. If each of us did the same, we would all enjoy more attractive places to paddle. Motorboat users tend to have a bad reputation when it comes to leaving trash; paddlers should strive for the opposite reputation, which could come in handy when seeking restrictions on high-impact resource use.

For information on low-impact camping and other uses of fragile habitats, see *Soft Paths: Enjoying the Wilderness without Harming It*, by Rich Brame and David Cole (4th edition, Stackpole Books, 2011). Also, visit the website of Leave No Trace (lnt.org), an organization dedicated to teaching people how to minimize their outdoor impact. (See page xxxix for more on the Leave No Trace ethic.)

Besides reducing our impact on the environment, we can actively work to protect the fragile populations of bald eagle, osprey, otter, loon, and other wildlife. If we want to preserve these species and their habitats for future generations, we must demand that elected and appointed officials make wildlife preservation and ecosystem protection a higher priority. We can also join conservation organizations—such as AMC, Adirondack Mountain Club, Sierra Club, The Nature Conservancy, New York Audubon, and many others—so that when those organizations speak about preserving the environment, their voices carry the weight of tens of thousands of like-minded members.

PUBLIC ACCESS

Private land abuts many waterways. To ensure continued access, please respect this property. Never camp or picnic on private land without permission. In many places, adjacent landowners also own the riverbed or lakebed, which means, for example, that even if you may paddle there, you may not have the right to fish there.

New York's Department of Environmental Conservation has done a good job of providing public access to state waterways, either by establishing conservation easements or by outright land and water purchase. There are two particular areas worthy of discussion: Adirondack Park and Long Island.

Adirondack Park

Private inholdings—much of it owned by paper companies—have kept some lakes and waterways in Adirondack Park off-limits. Paul Jamieson, who wrote the foreword to this book, was for 60 years a strong advocate for increased water access. Recently, the state has made great progress, procuring access to an outstanding resource in Little Tupper Lake, part of Whitney Park. The state's purchase in 1999 of 29,000 acres of Champion International Paper lands and the acquisition of conservation easements on an additional 110,000 acres gives paddlers access to substantial portions of Deer River, Grass South Branch, and Onion River, as well as Oswegatchie West Branch, the main and east branches of Saint Regis River, and Quebec Brook, including Madawaska Flow.

In 2004, International Paper sold conservation easements to the state on all of its 257,000 acres of park holdings, protecting an additional 9 percent of the park. Despite these recent successes, and even though a 1998 Court of Appeals decision (*Adirondack League Club, Inc., v. Sierra Club, et al.*) established rights to paddle navigable waterways, many still remain off-limits. The salient parts of the decision, allowing portages on private land:

> [I]n order to circumvent these occasional obstacles, the right to navigate carries with it the incidental privilege to make use, when absolutely necessary, of the bed and banks, including the right to portage on riparian lands. . . . On the other hand, any use of private riverbeds or banks that is not strictly incidental to the right to navigate gives rise to an action for trespass.

The section that extends navigability to recreational uses:

> In line with these modern circumstances and our precedents, we are satisfied that recreational use should be part of the navigability analysis.

However, more than twenty years after the highest New York court decision, we could not gain access to Little Forked Lake from Forked Lake because of a locked gate across the wide connecting waterway. Unfortunately, the court decision does not apply to ponds at the upper ends of waterways.

Long Island

This situation differs materially from that in the Adirondacks in that paddlers have always had access to the best paddling locations on Long Island—but it comes at an increasingly steep price for nonresidents. As a nonresident, if you took a weeklong tour of Long Island, paddling once on each of the locations in this book, it would cost you hundreds of dollars in access and parking fees. Is it reasonable to charge someone who will paddle a body of water only once in a season $150 for that privilege? We must prod the Department of Environmental Conservation to put in more public accesses on Long Island.

Public Campgrounds

Within Adirondack Park and throughout New York, the state maintains hundreds of campgrounds and camping areas for public enjoyment. Campgrounds charge modest fees, and some camping areas—particularly in Adirondack and Catskill parks—are free. Because fragile vegetation around lakes and ponds can easily suffer damage from heavy use, we recommend camping in designated areas only. For a complete listing, see Appendix A.

LEAVE NO TRACE

Leave No Trace™ Center for Outdoor Ethics | LNT.org

The Appalachian Mountain Club (AMC) is a national education partner of the Leave No Trace Center for Outdoor Ethics. The center is an international nonprofit organization dedicated to responsible enjoyment and active stewardship of the outdoors by all people, worldwide. The organization teaches children and adults vital skills to minimize their impact when they're outdoors. Leave No Trace (LNT) is the most widely accepted outdoor ethics program used today on public lands across the nation by all types of outdoor recreationists. LNT unites five federal land management agencies—U.S. Forest Service, National Park Service, Bureau of Land Management, Army Corps of Engineers, and U.S. Fish and Wildlife Service—with manufacturers, outdoor retailers, user groups, educators, organizations such as AMC, and individuals.

THESE SEVEN PRINCIPLES GUIDE THE LEAVE NO TRACE ETHIC:

Plan Ahead and Prepare. Know the terrain and any regulations applicable to the area you're planning to visit, and be prepared for extreme weather or other emergencies. This will enhance your enjoyment and ensure that you've chosen an appropriate destination. Small groups have less impact on resources and on the experiences of other backcountry visitors.

Travel and Camp on Durable Surfaces. Travel and camp on established trails and campsites, rock, gravel, dry grasses, or snow. Good campsites are found, not made. Camp at least 200 feet from lakes and streams, and focus activities on areas where vegetation is absent. In pristine areas, disperse use to prevent the creation of campsites and trails.

Dispose of Waste Properly. Pack it in, pack it out. Inspect your camp for trash or food scraps. Deposit solid human waste in cat holes dug 6 to 8 inches deep, at least 200 feet from water, camps, and trails. Pack out toilet paper and hygiene products. To wash yourself or your dishes, carry water 200 feet from streams or lakes and use small amounts of biodegradable soap. Scatter strained dishwater.

Leave What You Find. Cultural or historical artifacts, as well as natural objects such as plants and rocks, should be left as found.

Minimize Campfire Impacts. Cook on a stove. Use established fire rings, fire pans, or mound fires. If you build a campfire, keep it small and use dead sticks found on the ground.

Respect Wildlife. Observe wildlife from a distance. Feeding animals alters their natural behavior. Protect wildlife from your food by storing rations and trash securely.

Be Considerate of Other Visitors. Be courteous, respect the quality of other visitors' backcountry experience, and let nature's sounds prevail.

AMC is a national provider of the Leave No Trace Master Educator course. AMC offers this five-day course, designed especially for outdoor professionals and land managers, as well as the shorter two-day Leave No Trace Trainer course, at locations throughout the Northeast.

For Leave No Trace information and materials, contact the Leave No Trace Center for Outdoor Ethics, P.O. Box 997, Boulder, CO 80306; 800-332-4100 or 302-442-8222; lnt.org. For a schedule of AMC Leave No Trace courses, see outdoors.org/education/lnt.

1 | SOUTHEASTERN NEW YORK

This region provides 22 nearby paddling opportunities for about 14 million New Yorkers. Eight large bodies of water on Long Island—starting with Jamaica Bay Wildlife Refuge, right next to JFK Airport, and ending with Accabonac Harbor, all the way out in East Hampton—provide southeastern New York with outstanding paddling resources. You could spend many, many hours exploring these tide-influenced bays and rivers.

Outside of Long Island, many small lakes, ponds, and streams nestle within scenic state parks or are protected reservoirs. For example, Harriman State Park, just a little northwest of the I-87 Tappan Zee Bridge over the Hudson River, hosts eight small ponds. Although none are very large, you would have to paddle about 20 miles to circumnavigate all of their shores.

Three more bodies of water—Constitution Marsh, Tivoli Marshes, and Catskill Creek—empty into the Hudson River under its tidal influence. If you enjoy paddling through large marshlands, these offer a great opportunity. We also love Basher Kill, the largest freshwater wetlands in southeastern New York, a Delaware River tributary that lies in the shadow of the Shawangunk Mountains.

1 | Accabonac Harbor

Because The Nature Conservancy, state of New York, and town of East Hampton protect much of the land surrounding Accabonac Harbor, it provides a great place to study the salt marsh ecosystem. Look for sea lavender and glasswort plants here, along with an assortment of egrets, herons, plovers, gulls, and raptors.

Location: East Hampton
Maps: *New York Atlas & Gazetteer*, Map 115: B7, C7; USGS Gardiners Island West
Area: 390 acres (high tide), maximum depth 6 feet
Time: 4 hours
Habitat Type: Short-grass salt marsh estuary
Fish and Shellfish: Bluefish, flounder, razor clam, scallop, whelk (see fish advisories, Appendix C)
Camping and Trails: Appendix A (32, 122, 127); trails, The Nature Conservancy, nature.org
Take Note: Tides, tide-forecast.com; free parking on road shoulder; $100 annual nonresident launch area parking fee, easthamptonvillage.org

GETTING THERE

From Route 27/Main Street in East Hampton, turn left (north) on Accabonac Road. Go 3.8 miles, and turn left on Old Stone Highway. Go 0.2 mile (4.0 miles), and turn right on Landing Lane (free parking on road shoulder). (41° 1.107′ N, 72° 8.725′ W)

WHAT YOU'LL SEE

Accabonac Harbor and East Harbor extend roughly 2 miles north to south but offer 8 miles of shoreline to explore, including two principal islands. With limited development, the whole area—rich with fauna and flora and protected by The Nature Conservancy, town, and state—exudes wildness.

One might suspect that all salt marshes are pretty much the same. Not true. Accabonac Harbor's salt marsh ecosystem differs dramatically from the one at nearby Sebonac Creek. Although tall *Spartina alterniflora*—commonly known as salt marsh cordgrass—dominates most of the estuaries described in this guide, the much shorter *Spartina patens*, or saltmeadow cordgrass, dominates

TRIP 1: ACCABONAC HARBOR

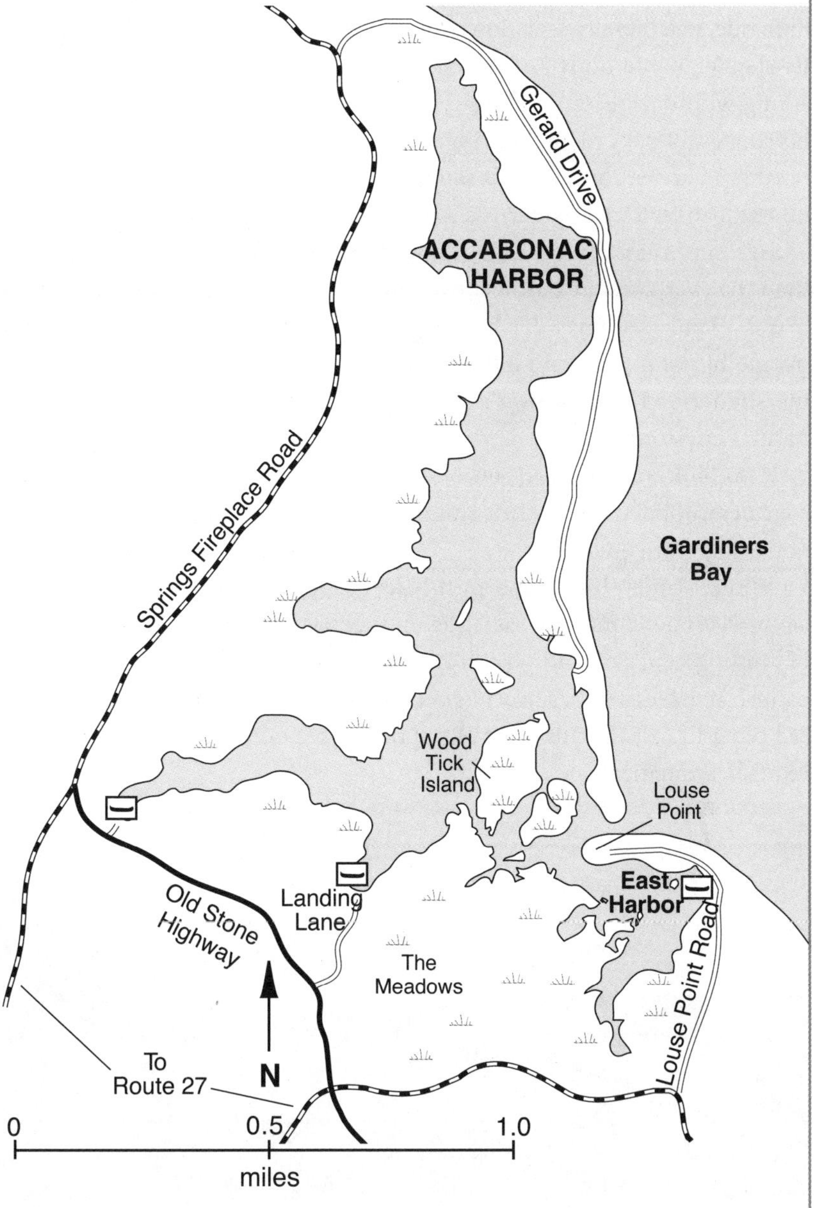

Accabonac Harbor. The shorter plants—just 8 inches high—give the marsh a more diminutive feel.

Even at midtide, you can see out over the marsh for a great distance. At high tide, you literally look down on it. We could see a great egret a mile away, its slender white body prominent against the marsh's greens and browns. Along with dozens of great egrets, we saw great blue herons, snowy egrets, herring gull flocks madly picking at some sort of prey in the marsh, ospreys, northern harriers, and various sandpipers, including lesser yellowlegs feeding on mudbanks. Rare least terns and threatened piping plovers nest here.

In some areas, sea lavender (*Limonium carolinianum*) seems even denser than the ever-present saltmeadow cordgrass. One of the most beautiful salt marsh plants, sea lavender blooms in July with masses of diminutive pale purple blossoms. People have removed this plant from vast areas of salt marsh to use in dried flower arrangements—please enjoy sea lavender in its natural environment.

Also look for glasswort, an odd plant with no obvious leaves and thick, succulent, jointed stems. In autumn, glasswort turns a deep red, making it noticeable from quite a distance.

White, scarlet, black, and post oaks occupy much of the higher ground, along with pignut hickory, sassafras, and sumac, a lot of it overlaid with a tangle of grape, greenbrier, and poison ivy vines. Look for the deep green foliage of eastern red cedar (*Juniperus virginiana*) among the deciduous trees. Eastern red cedar has small whitish or bluish berrylike cones, ruddy-brown bark, and reddish, aromatic wood.

Herring gulls take flight over a *Spartina patens* salt marsh.

High tide floods *Spartina patens* in Accabonac Harbor.

At the harbor's southern end, the Meadows forms the marsh's wildest and most attractive area. From Landing Road, paddle between Wood Tick Island and the Meadows, snaking toward East Harbor. At high tide, the mosquito-control ditches become accessible. Built in the 1930s and 1940s, most of these ditches remain after more than 60 years, reflecting the permanence of our changes to the salt marsh. People still debate the effectiveness of this past practice.

Development intrudes on East Harbor's eastern side and on much of the main harbor's northern end. For a change of pace, from the north end of East Harbor, cross the dunes and explore the ocean side. To the south, the quite dramatic Accabonac Cliffs rise from the sea. You could also explore a Nature Conservancy trail between Springs Fireplace Road and Accabonac Harbor.

2 | Hallock Bay (Long Beach Bay) and Little Bay

Hallock Bay, relatively free of development and bordered on the south by Orient Beach State Park, offers about 10 miles of shoreline to explore, much of it covered with salt marsh cordgrass. Ospreys abound, and you're likely to spot northern harriers, egrets, shorebirds, and lots more. A prickly pear cactus with special adaptations to avoid freeze damage can be found here.

Location: Southold
Maps: *New York Atlas & Gazetteer*, Map 114: A5; USGS Orient
Area: 680 acres, maximum depth 6 feet
Time: 5 hours
Habitat Type: Long-grass salt marsh estuary
Fish and Shellfish: Razor clam, scallop, striped bass, whelk (see fish advisories, Appendix C)
Camping and Trails: Appendix A (33, 124); trails, Orient Beach State Park, parks.ny.gov/parks/106/details
Information: Orient Point-New London ferry, longislandferry.com, 860-443-5281 (New England), 631-323-2525 (Long Island)
Take Note: Tides, tide-forecast.com; Narrow River Road parking permit, nonresident $12 daily, $100 annual, 631-765-1800

GETTING THERE

Narrow River Road Access. From the junction of Routes 25 and 48 north of Greenport, go 4.6 miles east on Route 25/Main Road, and turn right on Platt Road. Go 0.8 mile (5.4 miles), and continue straight on Narrow River Road. Go 0.1 mile (5.5 miles) to the access on the left (parking permit required). (41° 8.242′ N, 72° 16.957′ W)

If coming from the Orient Point ferry, go 2.3 miles west on Route 25/Main Road, and turn left on Narrow River Road. Go 1.1 miles (3.4 miles) to the access on the left.

Orient Beach State Park Access. From the junction of Routes 25 and 48, go 7.6 miles to the park entrance on the right (0.3 mile west of the ferry). (41° 9.276′ N, 72° 14.747′ W)

TRIP 2: HALLOCK BAY (LONG BEACH BAY) AND LITTLE BAY

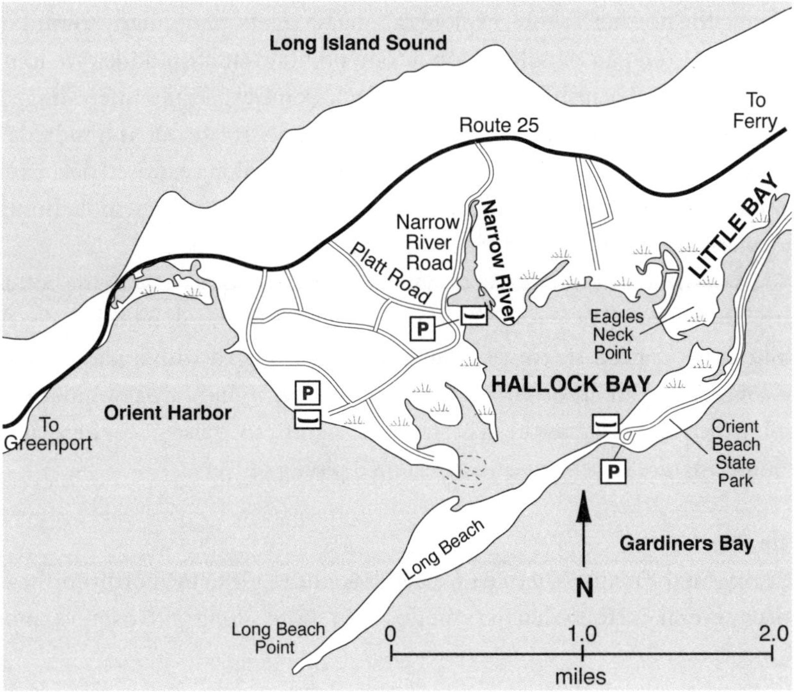

WHAT YOU'LL SEE

Hallock Bay

Just minutes from the New London–Orient Point ferry terminus, Hallock Bay offers excellent paddling. Little development intrudes on this area, and currents remain modest (except at the harbor's mouth). On a mid-October trip, we watched three skeins of migrating snow geese, momentarily distracting us from the deep reds of oaks, bright orange-reds of sumac, and spots of red glasswort in the salt marsh.

Hallock Bay offers plenty of opportunities for salt marsh exploration. From the access, paddle "upriver" (north), passing through thick stands of salt marsh cordgrass (*Spartina alterniflora*). Although the tide submerges this dominant plant twice daily, it has developed mechanisms to survive high salt concentrations, and it plays a critical role in this ecosystem, providing habitat for young striped bass and other species.

At low tide, note the thick clusters of ribbed mussel along the *Spartina* base. This species is not commercially harvested—perhaps explaining its profusion.

Patches of *Phragmites*—a very tall grass displacing *Spartina* in some areas of the Northeast—grow on slightly higher ground. Farther from shore, you will see black locust, sumac, wild cherry, white and scarlet oak, and eastern red cedar.

Along the northern shore, explore salt marsh inlets, particularly toward the eastern end. You can paddle a loop at one point, even at midtide. We found the branching inlet just west of Eagles Neck Point especially interesting. As we neared an exposed mudbank, a frenzy of activity broke out as hundreds of critters—appropriately called ghost crabs—skittered along exposed peat banks and scurried down their three-quarter-inch holes. We got our best look through binoculars, sneaking up quietly to within about a dozen feet.

On a calm day, the bay's exceptionally clear water allows views of the bottom nearly throughout. We got a good look at whelks crawling along, while dozens of blue crabs danced sideways—one that we challenged with a paddle had a foot-long claw span. Just south of the Narrow River mouth, we saw quite a few small striped bass. Eelgrass beds of statewide significance also occur here, along with nesting rare least terns and threatened piping plovers.

Little Bay

Little Bay, on the map's eastern end, extends about a mile to the north-northeast. We saw several northern harriers on this wild shore, along with ospreys (more

Early morning light reflects salt marsh cordgrass (*Spartina alterniflora*).

than a dozen nesting platforms dot the bay), Canada geese, great and snowy egrets, greater yellowlegs, cormorants, and common loons. In fall, notice the groundsel (*Baccharis halimifolia*) near the north end. From a distance, it appears covered with bushy white blooms, but these are actually cottony tufts (technically, pappi) that aid in seed dispersal.

Orient Beach State Park

Orient Beach State Park covers the entire 357-acre southeastern shore of Hallock and Little bays. It has remained in public hands since 1774, when the residents preserved it forever by written agreement. In October 1929, the owners deeded the land to the state for the park, which offers picnicking and swimming, along with hiking among rare plant communities, including blackjack oak (*Quercus marilandica*), a 69-acre eastern red cedar forest (*Juniperus virginiana*), and eastern prickly pear cactus (*Opuntia humifusa*). Among the 1,800 or so species of prickly pear, *O. humifusa* exhibits a rare adaptation: special chemicals in its pads keep them safe from freeze damage, allowing it to range as far north as Ontario, Canada.

---

3 | Sebonac Creek

Sebonac Creek and connected bodies of water may offer the finest paddling on Long Island. Salt marsh cordgrass dominates the shoreline of these highly productive waters. Look for ospreys, northern harriers, herons, egrets, shorebirds, ducks, and geese.

Location: Southampton
Maps: *New York Atlas & Gazetteer*, Map 114: D3; USGS Southampton
Area: 530 acres, maximum depth 16 feet (Scallop Pond)
Time: All day
Habitat Type: Long-grass salt marsh estuary
Fish and Shellfish: Razor clam, scallop, striped bass, whelk (see fish advisories, Appendix C)
Camping: Appendix A (33, 122, 123, 124, 125, 126)
Information: Canoe and kayak rentals, transportation at the Peconic Paddler, thepeconicpaddler.com

TRIP 3: SEBONAC CREEK

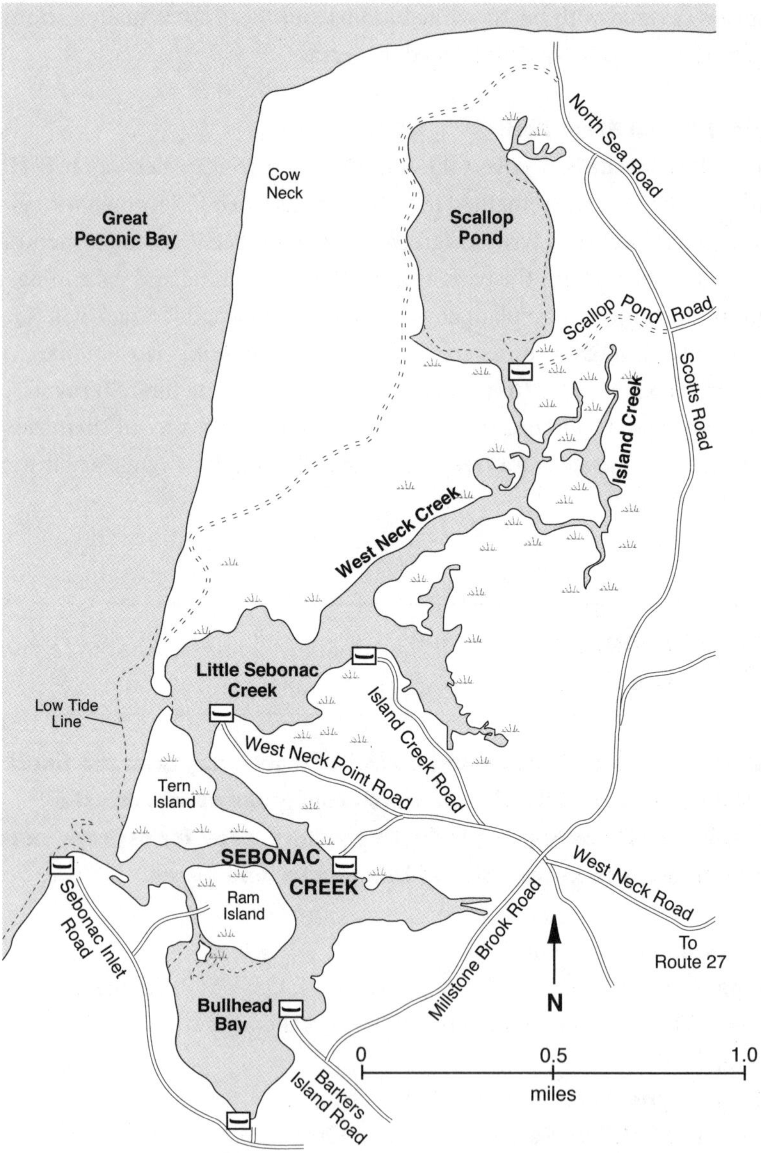

Take Note: Tides, tide-forecast.com; West Neck Road ramp use permit required, Town of Southampton, southamptontownny.gov, 631-287-5740; avoid during duck hunting season

GETTING THERE

West Neck Road Accesses. From the junction of Routes 27 and 52/Sandy Hollow Road north of Southampton, go 0.9 mile north on Route 52, and turn left on Route 38/North Sea Road. Turn immediately left on West Neck Road, and go 1.2 miles (2.1 miles) to the junction with Millstone Brook Road. Continue across to one of the three accesses on the map. The farthest south access has a $150 annual nonresident ramp fee. (40° 55.036′ N, 72° 25.757′ W)

Scallop Pond Access. From the junction of Millstone Brook Road and West Neck Road, go 1.3 miles north on Millstone Brook Road/Scotts Road to the Scallop Pond Road access on the left (high clearance recommended). (40° 56.130′ N, 72° 25.792′ W)

WHAT YOU'LL SEE

The contiguous waters of Sebonac Creek, Bullhead Bay, Little Sebonac Creek, West Neck Creek, Island Creek, and Scallop Pond provide a wonderful paddling opportunity, perhaps the best on Long Island. Manageable in size yet extensive enough for lots of exercise, these waters can keep you occupied all day, exploring the nooks and crannies. We paddled more than 10 miles and did not explore every creek, let alone the dozens of mosquito-control ditches, many of which are accessible at high tide.

Salt marsh cordgrass (*Spartina alterniflora*) dominates the entire shoreline of this estuary. One of the few plants able to survive regular saltwater flooding, much of it is submerged at high tide and reemerges at low tide. This cordgrass evolved to fill an important ecological niche, and it indeed thrives in the salt marsh environment.

On higher ground not flooded by the twice-daily high tides, you will see a much shorter cousin, *Spartina patens*, along with such plants as sea lavender and glasswort. In autumn, the bright red glasswort stands out markedly amid the browns and yellows of other vegetation. Thick clusters of ribbed mussel and masses of reddish-brown seaweed grow beneath the salt marsh's raised plain.

A thick oak woods stands back from the shore; white oak dominates, but you will also see scarlet oak and may come across black, post, and scrub oak. Pignut hickory, beech, black gum (which turns crimson in early fall), sassafras, and black cherry add variety to the tree species mix.

Bird life fills the estuary, including great blue and green herons, great and snowy egrets, hundreds of black ducks, pied-billed grebes, greater yellowlegs, kingfishers, ospreys, northern harriers, and the ever-present herring gulls—to mention a few. Note that hunters also know about the many ducks here. Keep your eye out for deer, fox, mink, and otter, as well.

Mink live near water and can be spotted by attentive paddlers.

Little development intrudes on the estuary except on Little Sebonac Creek and Bullhead Bay. Many houses there represent architectural statements, and we enjoyed examining them as we passed. The estuary's northern sections remain wilder and more remote, although Scallop Pond sports a few houses.

Little Sebonac Creek's eastern extension and Island Creek's extensive winding channels provide a wonderful paddling experience, where you can feel truly alone; even on a windy day, you can find protected areas to escape rougher water. Along Island Creek, you get a real feel for the marsh—the wide, flat plain of grass seems almost like a sea, surrounded by oak forest on higher ground.

On Island Creek's northern extension, watch for a mansion on the right, a colonial-style house set well back from the water. Within a few hours of high tide, you can paddle north, past the house. The channel looks as if it will peter out as you pass a gazebo, but it winds around, passes under a footbridge, and continues at least another quarter-mile until vegetation swallows it.

Scallop Pond, a large oval at the estuary's northern end, extends for two-thirds of a mile. A narrow band of salt marsh cordgrass surrounds it, but trees extend much closer to the water here. A very prominent mansion and its associated buildings lend a dramatic feel to this area. From a distance, what appears to be a large boathouse is visible on the waterside, but this turns out to be a curving concrete wall with windows that backs up to the water—creating what must be a very unusual space inside.

Just past the mansion, a narrow passageway leads to another, much smaller salt marsh. One might be able to paddle (carefully) through this channel—almost a tunnel of wooden posts—but on the day we visited, the wind blew a gale, and we could not get into the channel without being bashed against the sides by waves.

When you paddle back into Little Sebonac Creek, take out up near the cut at the creek's western end, and cross over the narrow band of dunes to go for a walk on a fairly wild section of Peconic Bay shoreline. Moving north toward Cow Neck, you will find lots of shells and colorful stones.

You can easily paddle around Ram Island, passing under its access road bridge. Although you might explore some marshy islands just south, we found Bullhead Bay less interesting than the marsh north of Ram Island. The bay backs up on a huge golf course with a road right along the western shore.

4 | Flanders Bay Tributaries and Peconic River

Flanders Bay provides access to several small scenic streams and ponds, but beware of strong winds on the bay itself. When it's windy, stick to the Peconic River, which is also a great place to paddle. Look for ospreys, herons, egrets, ducks, and geese, as well as white-tailed deer.

Location: Riverhead, Southampton
Maps: *New York Atlas & Gazetteer*, Map 113: B10 and Map 114: D1, D2; USGS Mattituck, Riverhead
Time: All day or multiday
Habitat Type: Tidal estuary below Riverhead; impounded, slow-flowing river above

TRIP 4: FLANDERS BAY TRIBUTARIES AND PECONIC RIVER

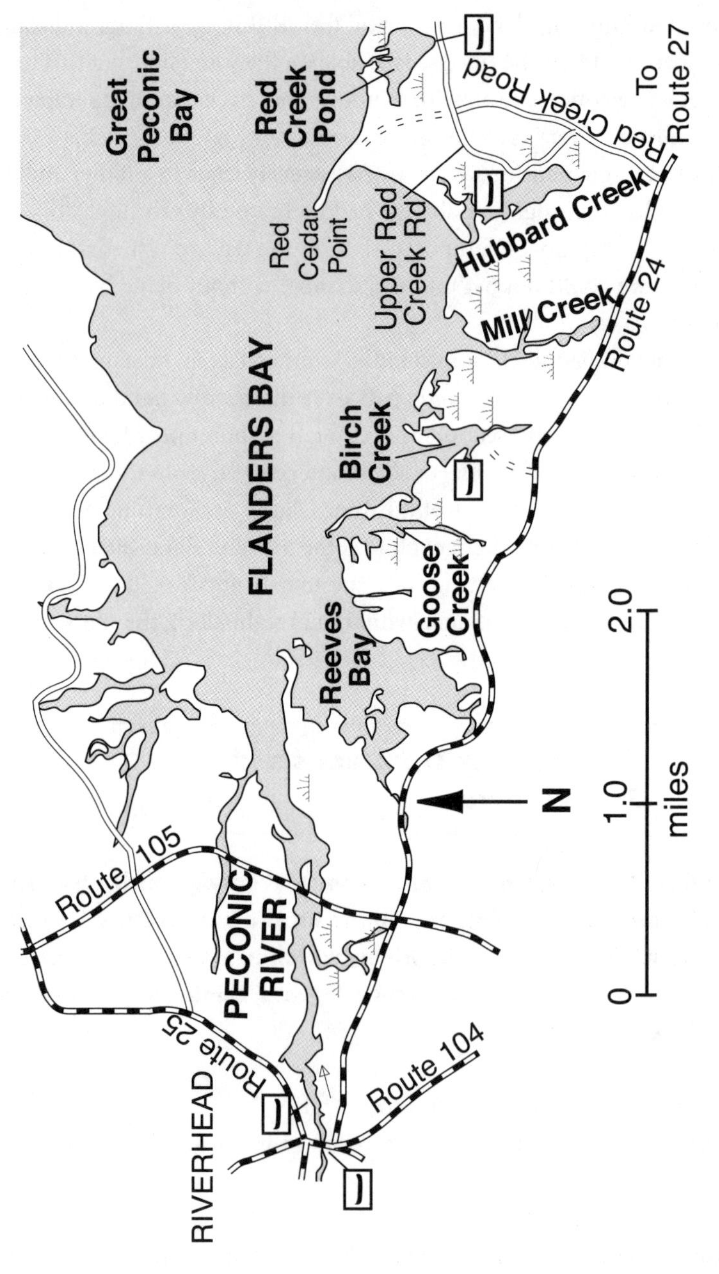

Fish and Shellfish: Razor clam, scallop, striped bass, whelk (see fish advisories, Appendix C; see specific advisory for Peconic Bay, health.ny.gov/environmental/outdoors/fish/health_advisories)
Camping: Appendix A (33, 123, 124, 125, 126, 129, 131)
Information: Canoe and kayak rentals, transportation at the Peconic Paddler, thepeconicpaddler.com
Take Note: Tides, tide-forecast.com; novice paddlers should avoid Flanders and Peconic bays under windy conditions; always wear a personal flotation device (PFD)

GETTING THERE

Birch Creek Access. From Route 104/Riverleigh Avenue in Riverhead, go 4.0 miles east on Route 24, turn left on Birch Creek Road, and go 0.4 mile (4.4 miles) to the access. (40° 54.300′ N, 72° 35.518′ W)

Hubbard Creek Access. From Route 104/Riverleigh Avenue, go 5.3 miles east on Route 24, and turn left on Red Creek Road. Go 0.6 mile (5.9 miles), turn left on Upper Red Creek Road, and go 0.4 mile (6.3 miles) to the access on the left by an old building. Carry 175 feet to the water. (40° 54.087′ N, 72° 33.822′ W)

Red Creek Pond Access. From the junction of Route 24 and Red Creek Road, go 1.7 miles on Red Creek Road to the access on the left. (40° 54.516′ N, 72° 33.076′ W)

Riverhead Access. From I-495, Exit 71, go about 4 miles on Route 24 to Riverhead. Access on Peconic Avenue at the Peconic Paddler or just across the river at a public access (under development as of publication). (40° 54.935′ N, 72° 39.773′ W)

WHAT YOU'LL SEE

Flanders Bay Tributaries

Although dangerous on a windy day, large Flanders Bay offers several tributaries with superb paddling. We recommend three creeks: Hubbard, Mill, and Birch. Hubbard Creek's islands, deep twisting coves, and winding salt marsh channels provide the most interesting paddling. When breezes blow on the bay, this sheltered creek provides a quiet retreat from the world—although you have to carry your boat a little way to get to it.

Birch Creek provides the closest access to Mill Creek. Red Creek Pond also has an access, although you would have to paddle around Red Cedar Point, which we don't recommend under windy conditions. You can also paddle from

Riverhead across Reeves Bay to reach these undeveloped areas. We suggest using sea kayaks with sprayskirts when paddling on the bays.

Salt marsh cordgrass (*Spartina alterniflora*) dominates the salt marshes and tidal inlets on Flanders Bay. This grass can survive—and indeed requires—regular flooding by salt water. In centuries past, Long Island settlers harvested this grass as winter feed for livestock.

Paddling here in autumn, we saw lots of black ducks, a half-dozen mute swans, an osprey hovering in search of fish, and an assortment of songbirds preparing for fall migration. In the creeks, the shallow, mucky bottoms could leave you high and, unfortunately, not very dry at low tide.

A thick woods of oak and pitch pine occurs on higher ground. Early settlers used pitch pine—the only common pine with three-needle clusters—for making charcoal and fence posts, and they tapped the trees for sap, which they made into turpentine and resin. Among the deciduous trees, white and scarlet oaks seem to be most common. Also look for groundsel and bayberry, with its highly scented leaves.

Peconic River—Downstream

Launching in Riverhead, you can explore about 2 miles of river before reaching Flanders Bay. A little tributary on the south side, just west of the Route 105

Black ducks, along with many other species, nest and feed in the marshes along the Flanders Bay tributaries.

bridge, offers very pleasant salt marsh exploration. The north side of the bay suffers from quite a bit of development, and we do not recommend paddling there.

Peconic River—Upstream

You can also enjoy fine paddling on a one-way, 8-mile trip along the Peconic River farther west, from Connecticut Avenue in Manorville to Riverhead. If you are considering this, be sure to check with the Peconic Paddler, a local outfitter, about river conditions.

The Peconic River—the longest river on Long Island and one of the most popular paddling locations—flows entirely with freshwater west of the dam at Riverhead. Winding through woodland, farmland, old cranberry bog impoundments, and a few industry backyards, some narrow sections have moderate current but no rapids; other sections flow through broad marshes. You must carry over several dams and roads. The Peconic Paddler rents canoes and kayaks, and even if you do not rent anything, the outfitter will ferry you and your boat to the access in Manorville for a modest fee.

5 | Carmans River

This wild waterway flows through Wertheim National Wildlife Refuge, making it the least developed of Long Island's major rivers. Look for ospreys, herons, egrets, wood and black ducks, deer, and muskrat among a wide variety of trees and shrubs.

Location: Brookhaven
Maps: *New York Atlas & Gazetteer*, Map 113: C8; USGS Bellport
Length: 4.5 miles one way (lower section)
Time: 4 hours (lower section)
Habitat Type: Tidal estuary below Route 27, impounded river above; no development
Fish: Flounder, pickerel, striped bass, brown and rainbow trout (see fish advisories, Appendix C)
Camping and Trails: Appendix A (31, 33, 124, 129, 130, 131, 132); trails, Wertheim National Wildlife Refuge, fws.gov/refuge/wertheim

TRIP 5: CARMANS RIVER

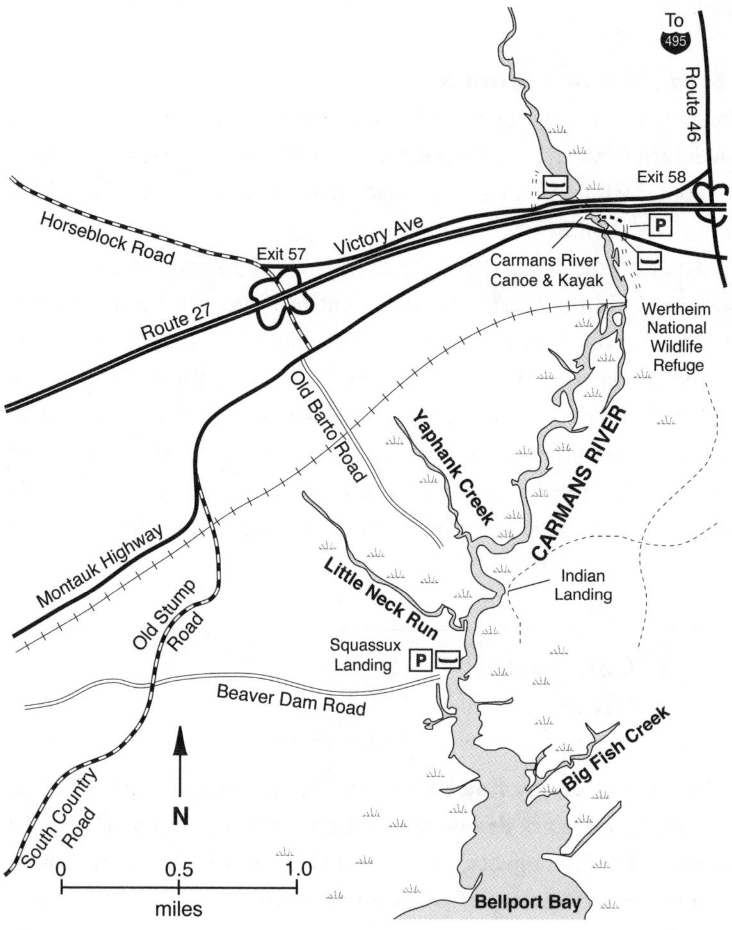

Information: Canoe and kayak rentals, transportation at Carmans River Canoe & Kayak, carmansriverkayak.com
Take Note: Tides, tide-forecast.com

GETTING THERE

Squassux Landing Access. From Route 27, Exit 57, go 0.3 mile west (right) on Montauk Highway (Route 80), and turn left on Old Stump Road. Go 1.4 miles (1.7 miles), turn left on Beaver Dam Road, and go 0.2 mile (1.9 miles) to the access. (40° 46.438′ N, 72° 53.799′ W)

Montauk Highway Access. From I-495, Exit 68, go south on William Floyd Parkway (Route 46) to Montauk Highway (Route 80). Turn right (west), and go 0.9 mile to the access on the right, several feet past the Smith Road traffic light. Carry your boat about 250 yards to the river. (40° 48.046′ N, 72° 52.851′ W)

Upper Carmans River Access. Use Carmans River Canoe & Kayak services on Carmans River, just west of the Montauk Highway bridge. (40° 48.087′ N, 72° 53.103′ W)

WHAT YOU'LL SEE

Lower Carmans River

Carmans River and its surrounding marsh represent one of the last undeveloped estuaries on Long Island. The wildest and most pristine of the island's four major rivers—the others are Nissequogue, Connetquot, and Peconic—it offers fantastic paddling and wildlife observing. The lower tidal section meanders 4.5 miles from Route 27 to Bellport Bay through 2,550-acre Wertheim National Wildlife Refuge.

Phragmites (common reed) lines the banks in some areas, its tall, plumed stalks swaying in the breeze, along with two species of cordgrass, *Spartina alterniflora* and *S. cynosuroides*. Although not far from major highways and development, you can immerse yourself in wildness here.

The tributaries Little Neck Run, Yaphank Creek, and Big Fish Creek invite exploration—at least at high tide. On these streams, you gradually leave the *Phragmites*-dominated marshland, encountering much more variety—Atlantic white cedar, black gum, and pitch pine, for example. We saw lots of wood ducks here, along with herons, ospreys, and a snapping turtle.

In the shallow water, crabs skitter sideways while huge carp wallow in the mud. We spotted two Virginia rails foraging for insects and crustaceans in the mud amid *Phragmites* stems. This elusive, well-camouflaged bird sports a fairly long, down-curved bill and very long toes for support on soft mud. We also saw common goldeneyes, double-crested cormorants, mallards, and common loons—perhaps having just returned to the coast from the Adirondacks. (Although the loon spends most of its life in salt water, it breeds only in freshwater.)

In late summer, look for the dramatic blooms of swamp mallow (*Hibiscus moscheutos* subspecies *palustris*), a relative of the hollyhock. We saw several plants with beautiful pink, five-petaled roselike flowers about 5 inches across.

A trail leaves from Indian Landing, on the eastern shore, providing an opportunity to explore the refuge's higher ground on foot. Unless the tide is clearly receding, be sure to tie up your boat.

Maples and other deciduous trees replace salt marsh vegetation at the north end of Carmans River's tidal portion.

Upper Carmans River

Carmans River Canoe & Kayak operates trips on the upper Carmans River, above the Route 27 dam, which has a very different character from the tidal river below. This 5-mile stretch of freshwater meanders slowly through woodland and marshy areas. For a fee, the outfitter will shuttle you and your boat to the upper end, allowing you to paddle downriver to South Haven Park, just north of Route 27.

6 | Stony Brook Harbor

Although strong tides sometimes make it a challenge, we believe this harbor is well worth exploring, especially the southern part and West Meadow Creek. Look for ospreys, least terns, herons, egrets, ducks, and geese. You'll also see thick, deciduous woodlands with stands of a variety of large trees.

Location: Smithtown
Maps: *New York Atlas & Gazetteer*, Map 112: A4, A5, B4, B5; USGS Saint James
Area: 940 acres (high tide)
Time: 5 hours
Habitat Type: Tidal estuary, islands, protected coves; mud flats at low tide
Fish: Flounder, striped bass (see fish advisories, Appendix C)
Camping: Appendix A (31, 33, 128, 129, 130, 131, 132)
Take Note: Tides, tide-forecast.com; because of strong tides, always wear a personal flotation device (PFD); inexperienced paddlers should avoid this harbor

GETTING THERE

Stony Brook Village Access. From I-495, go 3.8 miles north on Route 111, and veer right on Route 25A. Go 5.0 miles (8.8 miles), and continue straight on Main Street. Go 0.5 mile (9.3 miles), and turn left on Shore Road. Go 0.2 mile (9.5 miles) to the access by the yacht club. (40° 55.256′ N, 73° 8.991′ W)

Harbor Road Access. There seems to be no prohibition against launching from Harbor Road, although parking is limited. (40° 53.618′ N, 73° 10.110′ W)

TRIP 6: STONY BROOK HARBOR

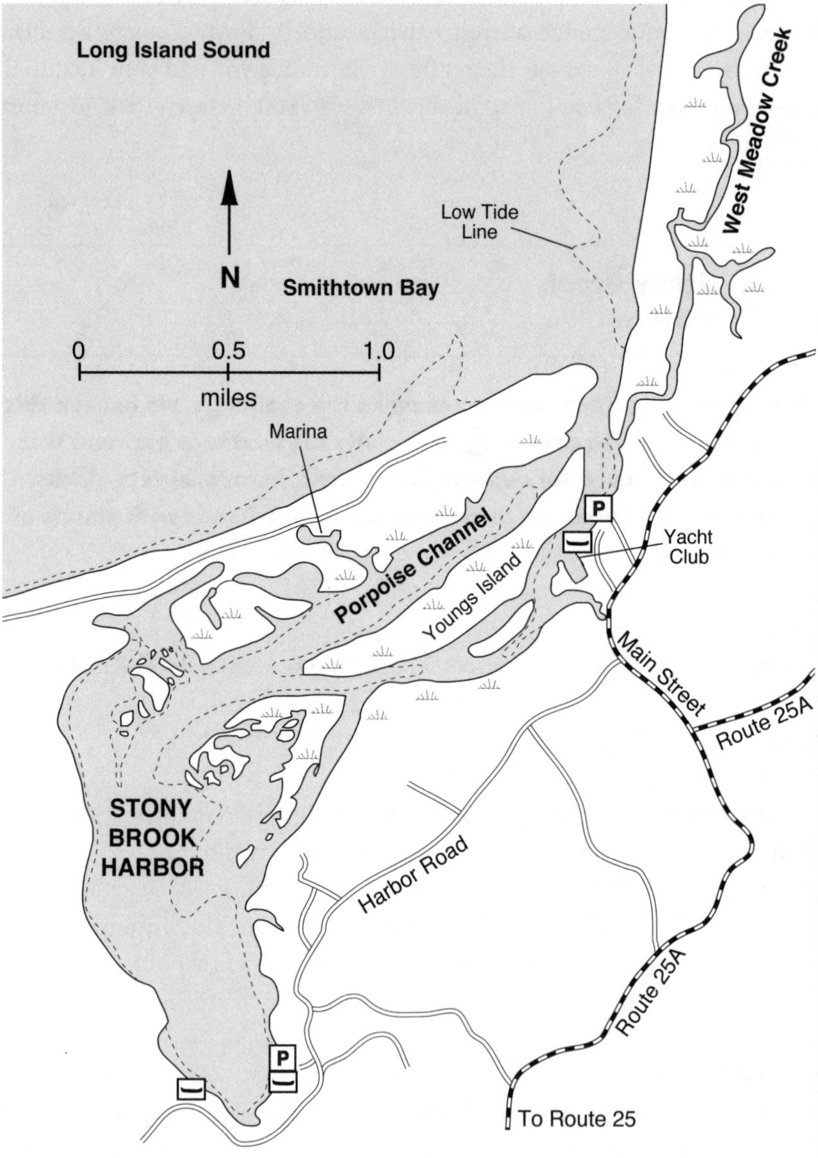

WHAT YOU'LL SEE

Located along Long Island's north shore on Smithtown Bay, Stony Brook Harbor provides a superb example of tidal estuary. Six-foot-tall salt marsh cordgrass (*Spartina alterniflora*) dominates the harbor, including the entire shoreline and numerous islands. Throughout the Atlantic seaboard, thousands of tidal acres contain salt marsh cordgrass as almost the only vascular plant. Low tide exposes vast mussel shoals and high peat banks, reducing the open water by about half. At high tide, only the upper cordgrass portions wave back and forth with the current and the wakes of passing boats.

Great blue and green herons and great and snowy egrets congregate here in large numbers. Both types of egrets boast a full plumage of snow-white feathers, but the great egret is bigger. It also has a yellow bill that distinguishes it from the snowy egret, which has a black bill. Both have black legs, but the snowy egret has yellow feet. Near the turn of the twentieth century, hunters nearly extirpated these birds in this country, harvesting their gorgeous breeding-season plumes to be used in women's high fashion.

The double-crested cormorant, an ungainly bird that often stands with wings outstretched to dry in the sun, occurs here in great numbers. Its rear-set, webbed feet help it swim through water, hunting for fish. Because the bird spends so much time underwater, its wings waterlog and need to dry before it takes to the air—quite a laborious process even with dry wings.

Watch for least terns—the smallest and most graceful members of the tern family—particularly along the northeastern end of Youngs Island. The island remains off-limits to protect the nesting colony.

Where the harbor bends south—our favorite section—you can weave through the cordgrass islands, but only at high tide. Beyond the cordgrass, thick deciduous woodlands cling to the hills. Huge white oaks and black birches, along with black locust, sassafras, beech, and black walnut, interrupt the manicured lawns of the estates that overlook the water.

Tides can make traveling near the Long Island Sound outlet difficult. Current at the harbor mouth may be so strong that you cannot paddle against it. Start out on an incoming tide to explore the cordgrass islands around high tide, and then ride the outgoing tide back through the more southern channel to the access—avoiding the main Porpoise Channel and currents near the mouth altogether. Only at high tide can you circumnavigate Youngs Island and avoid dealing with strong current on one side or the other. We really had to work to make our way southwest along this channel back to the access with the tide going out. To explore West Meadow Creek without a lot of extra effort, paddle north on the incoming or high tide and back south at high tide or after the tide has turned.

7 | Nissequogue River

Nissequogue River is an outstanding paddling resource, but don't expect to explore alone on nice summer days. Look for ospreys, herons, ducks, geese, and mute swans. We saw large concentrations of double-crested cormorants and egrets. Threatened least terns nest here. Besides acres of salt marsh cordgrass, you will see large swaths of a variety of deciduous trees back from shore.

Location: Smithtown
Maps: *New York Atlas & Gazetteer*, Map 112: B4; USGS Central Islip, Saint James
Length: 5.5 miles one way
Time: 5 hours round trip
Habitat Type: Tidal estuary, islands, and oxbows; extensive mud flats at low tide
Fish: Flounder, striped bass; brook, brown, and rainbow trout above Route 25 bridge (see fish advisories, Appendix C)
Camping: Appendix A (31, 33, 128, 129, 130, 131, 132)
Information: Canoe and kayak rentals, transportation at Nissequogue River Canoe & Kayak Rentals, canoerentals.com; Bob's Canoe Rental, canoerentalslongisland.com; Nissequogue River State Park, parks.ny.gov/parks/110
Take Note: Tides, tide-forecast.com

GETTING THERE

Nissequogue River State Park Access. From I-495, Exit 53, go 6.0 miles north on Sunken Meadow Parkway to Exit SM4E. Go east 2.2 miles (8.2 miles) on Pulaski Road/Old Dock Road, and turn right on Saint Johnland Road. Go 0.4 mile (8.6 miles) to the park entrance on the left. (40° 53.755′ N, 73° 14.134′ W)

Paul T. Given County Park Access. Access on the south at the junction of Routes 25 and 25A in Smithtown. (40° 51.478′ N, 73° 12.592′ W)

WHAT YOU'LL SEE

New York State designated the Nissequogue a Scenic and Recreational River in 1982, and it remains almost totally undeveloped and one of Long Island's most popular paddling locations. Outfitters rent boats and provide shuttle service,

TRIP 7: NISSEQUOGUE RIVER

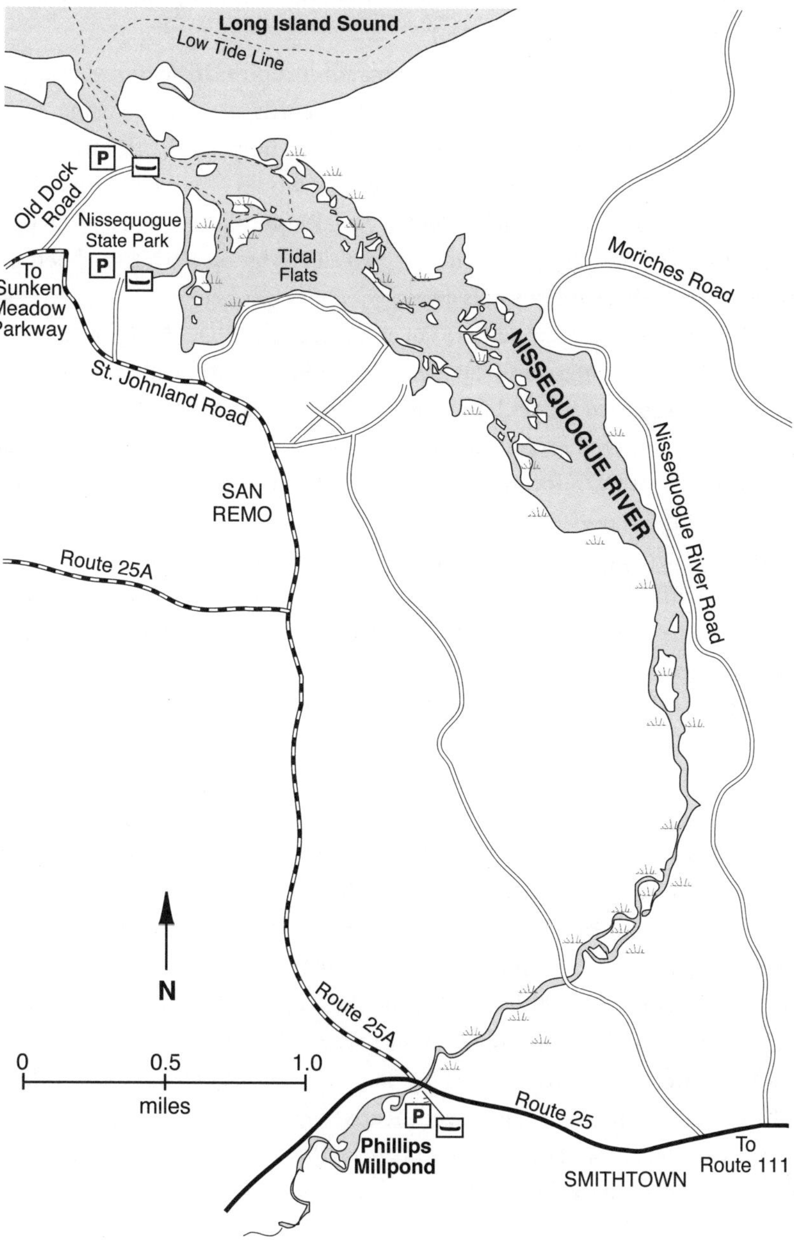

making it easy to paddle downstream on an outgoing tide or upstream on an incoming tide. The modest current would not prevent an up-and-back trip, except near the river's mouth, although you might want to shuttle if you have to deal with both current and wind.

Nissequogue River bristles with salt marsh cordgrass (*Spartina alterniflora*). Among the few tidal salt marsh plants, this cordgrass thrives using several important adaptations, including maintaining high salt concentrations to counteract the osmotic forces of salt water that would otherwise dehydrate the plant. *Spartina* also secretes a concentrated salt solution through special pores; as water evaporates, crystals form, giving the cordgrass a whitish sheen until the next tide washes the crystals away.

Early Northeast coastal settlers cut and dried *Spartina alterniflora* as winter livestock feed. The marshes provided spawning habitat for many marine fish species that supplied a livelihood for generations of coastal families. But this environment suffered ecological havoc from the 1940s until the 1970s, caused by intense use of DDT for mosquito control. The ospreys you see here provide evidence of the ecosystem's gradual recovery.

You will see many egrets and herons. In one spot, we saw a group of trees dripping with almost 100 egrets. Cormorants covered another tree farther upriver. Kingfishers flew from snag to snag, emitting their rattling calls. Both common and least terns—the latter a threatened species in New York—nest near the river mouth; the least tern colony constitutes supposedly the largest on Long Island.

Spartina islands and the river shoreline offer hours of exploration at high tide—much less time at low tide. Passageways may extend around an island or reach a dead end. In places, channels have gradually closed in, leaving narrow, sinewy, mazelike creeks that wind among the islands.

The river exhibits a pronounced salt-concentration gradient; the farther south you go, the less saline the water. Near the Route 25 bridge, the water runs fresh to brackish, with cattail, arrowhead, sweet flag, alder, winterberry, and sweet pepperbush lining the bank. Trees include red maple, black gum, black walnut, and sassafras. Look for *Spartina cynosuroides*, or big cordgrass, with its distinctive spreading seed heads. *Phragmites* also grows here and then mixes with *Spartina alterniflora* farther north. Near the sound, *S. alterniflora* dominates.

8 | Jamaica Bay Wildlife Refuge

As you paddle the protected waters among the islands, expect to see rafts of birds, including herons, egrets, gulls, cormorants, shorebirds, ospreys, and more. Hundreds of species nest here or pass through during migration. Because wind can affect this big water, always wear your personal flotation device (PFD).

Location: Brooklyn, Queens
Maps: *New York Atlas & Gazetteer*, Map 117: A6, A7; USGS Brooklyn, Coney Island, Far Rockaway, Jamaica
Area: 9,155 acres in wildlife refuge
Time: All day or multiday
Habitat Type: Large salt marsh estuary; many islands and protected bays, nature trails
Fish: Flounder, striped bass, other saltwater species (see fish advisories, Appendix C; see specific advisory, health.ny.gov/environmental/outdoors/fish/health_advisories)
Camping: Appendix A (31, 128, 135)
Information: Jamaica Bay Wildlife Refuge, nyharborparks.org/visit-parks, nps.gov/gate/planyourvisit/thingstodojamaicabay.htm; Sebago Canoe Club, sebagocanoeclub.org
Take Note: For tide information, visit saltwatertides.com. Select New York; 4. Long Island South Shore, Shinnecock Inlet to Mill Basin; Jamaica Bay; Beach Channel (bridge). Always wear your PFD here.

GETTING THERE

Jamaica Bay Wildlife Refuge Visitor Center Access. From the north and east, follow signs to JFK Airport. From the Van Wyck Expressway, I-678, Exit 1W, go 0.5 mile west, and merge onto Route 27/Conduit Avenue. Go 0.1 mile (0.6 mile), and merge onto Belt Parkway. Go 1.9 miles (2.5 miles) to Exit 17S, Cross Bay Boulevard. Go 3.6 miles (6.1 miles) south on Cross Bay Boulevard to the visitor center on the right. (40° 37.033′ N, 73° 49.440′ W)

Cross Bay Boulevard Access. After crossing North Channel Bridge, park on the left or right, where you can launch nonmotorized boats. (40° 38.285′ N, 73° 49.940′ W)

TRIP 7: NISSEQUOGUE RIVER

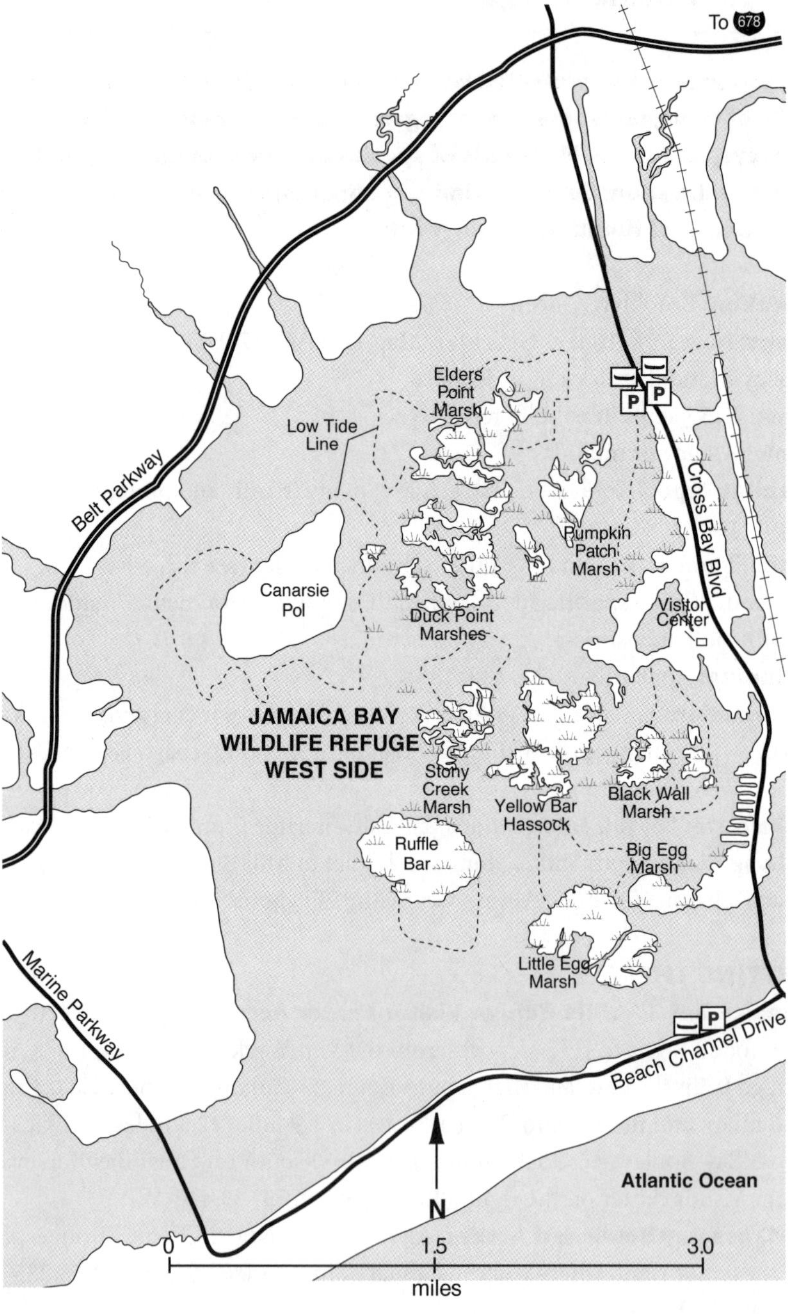

TRIP 7: NISSEQUOGUE RIVER

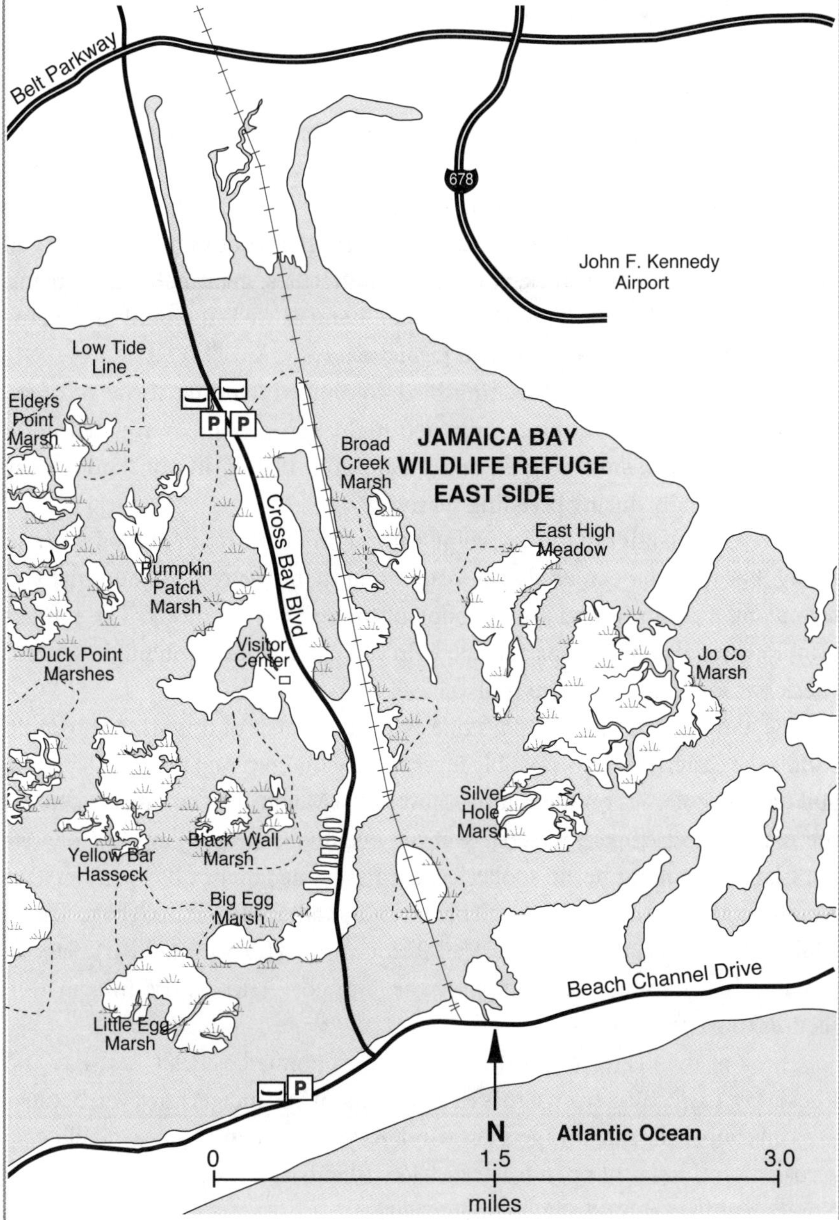

Rockaway Access. Continue past the visitor center. After the tollbooths, go right on Beach Channel Drive, following signs for Riis Park. Access is on the right in 0.5 mile, just after the Beach Channel High School tennis courts. (40° 35.066′ N, 73° 49.736′ W)

WHAT YOU'LL SEE

Huge Jamaica Bay, part of Gateway National Recreation Area, supports an extraordinary number of birds, including waterfowl and shorebirds, that nest or winter there or stop over during migration. At least 332 species have been recorded in the Jamaica Bay environs. The bay supports one of two laughing gull nesting colonies in New York. A variety of butterflies, mammals, amphibians, and reptiles—including sea turtles—reside here, as well. It would take many days to fully explore this wonderful resource.

Several islands support nesting bird colonies, including those of green heron, tricolored heron, black-crowned night heron, yellow-crowned night heron, glossy ibis, snowy egret, and great egret. Please do not land on any islands, especially during breeding season.

Dozens of islands dot the bay, some natural, some the result of dredging and filling. Because you can easily get lost among them, we recommend that you take along a compass and a photocopy of the map in this book. The refuge's visitor center also sells maps and can help you get oriented. You might want to check out some of the nature trails as well.

The main question: How does one explore a marsh of this size? You could paddle the eastern section, possibly investigating the common tern and laughing gull nesting colonies on the multi-island Jo Co Marsh. You could also explore the more island-choked western section, eventually heading up to Canarsie Pol Island to look for heron rookeries. For first-time Jamaica Bay paddlers, we recommend going out with experienced hands, perhaps from the Sebago Canoe Club or the Hudson River Watertrail Association. The National Park Service provides boats and guided tours; see the "nps.gov" URL in the Information section above for reservations.

Check at the visitor center for other access points besides Cross Bay and Rockaway. Launching from Cross Bay presents an advantage, however, because you can choose the side that gets less wind. As you might imagine, wind blowing across several miles of open water and low islands can whip up sizable waves. Novice paddlers should avoid Jamaica Bay.

9 | Harriman State Park Lakes

These eight small wooded ponds, close to New York City, abound in wildlife. Expect to see ducks, geese, beavers, and lots of white-tailed deer. We saw a red fox and a few otters. It's best to visit before June 15 or after Labor Day. If you paddle here in summer, aim for weekdays to avoid the crowds.

Location: Haverstraw, Tuxedo, Woodbury
Maps: *New York Atlas & Gazetteer*, Map 107: C10, D10 and Map 108: C1, D1; USGS Popolopen Lake, Sloatsburg, Thiells; free park map, avenzamaps.com
Area: 47,000 acres in park; Lake Sebago, 310 acres; Lake Tiorati, 294 acres; Lake Kanawauke, 170 acres; Lake Skannatati, 36 acres; Little Long Pond, 56 acres; Lake Stahahe, 86 acres; Silvermine Lake, 84 acres; Lake Welch, 205 acres
Time: All day or multiday
Habitat Type: Eight small ponds and lakes, nature trails
Fish: Largemouth and smallmouth bass, pickerel, brook trout (see fish advisories, Appendix C)
Camping: Appendix A (38, 39) (on-site, and at the Stephen & Betsy Corman AMC Harriman Outdoor Center)
Information: Sebago Canoe Club, sebagocanoeclub.org, maintains facilities on Lake Sebago.
Take Note: Gasoline motors prohibited; paddling April 1 to November 30, permit required; boating regulations: parks.ny.gov/documents/parks/SilverMinePalisadesBoatingInformation.pdf

GETTING THERE

From Palisades Interstate Parkway, Exit 18, follow Seven Lakes Drive southwest. From I-87, Exit 15A, turn left (north) on Route 17. Go 2.5 miles, and turn right (northeast) on Seven Lakes Drive.

Lake Sebago Access. From Palisades Interstate Parkway, go 9.6 miles southwest on Seven Lakes Drive to the access on the right. From Route 17, go 4.2 miles northeast on Seven Lakes Drive to the access on the left. (41° 11.855′ N, 74° 7.987′ W)

TRIP 9: HARRIMAN STATE PARK LAKES

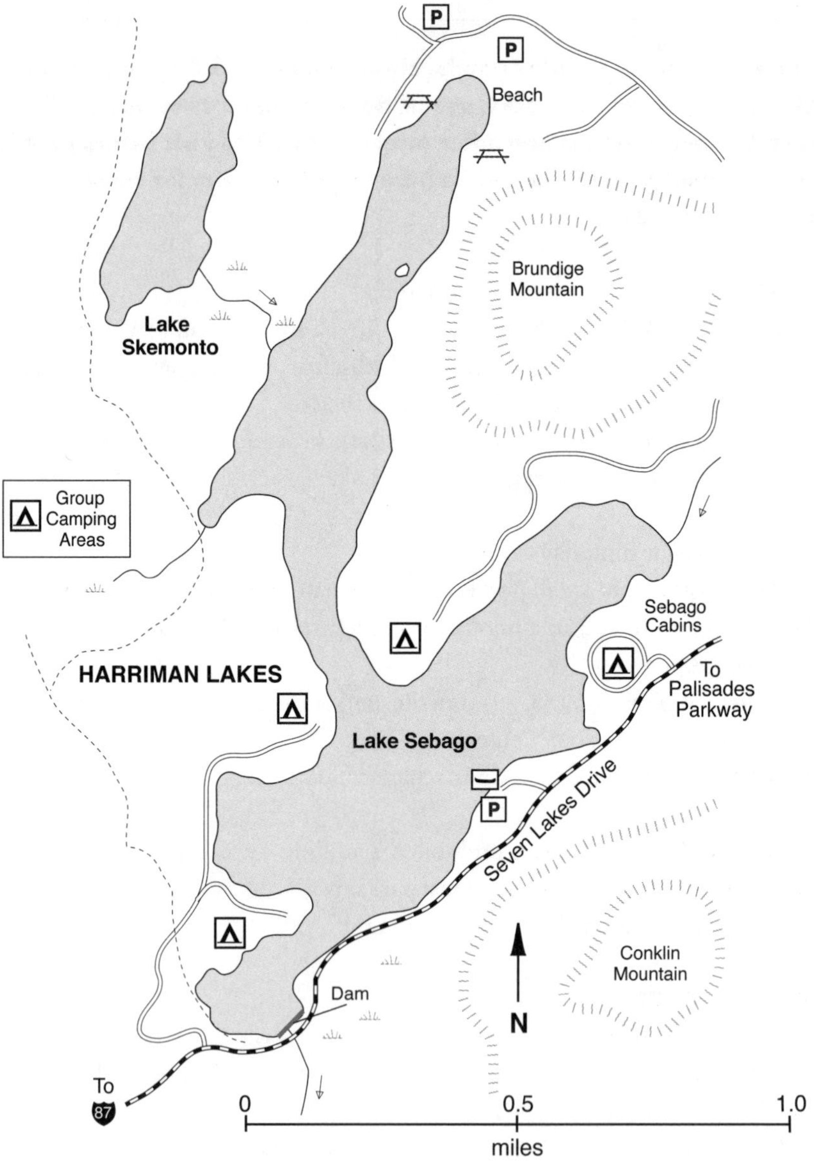

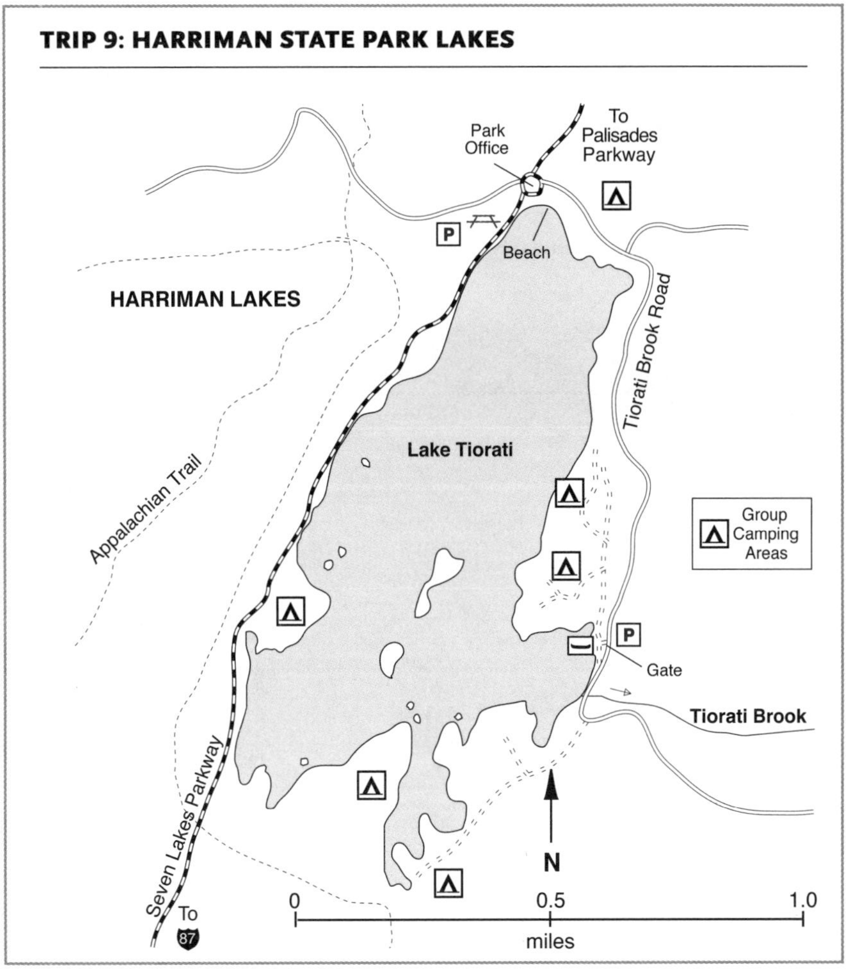

Lake Tiorati Access. At the junction of Seven Lakes Drive and Route 106, go north 3.2 miles on Seven Lakes Drive to Tiorati Circle, and bear right on Tiorati Brook Road. Go 1.1 miles (4.3 miles) to the access on the right. (41° 15.740′ N, 74° 5.106′ W)

TRIP 9: HARRIMAN STATE PARK LAKES

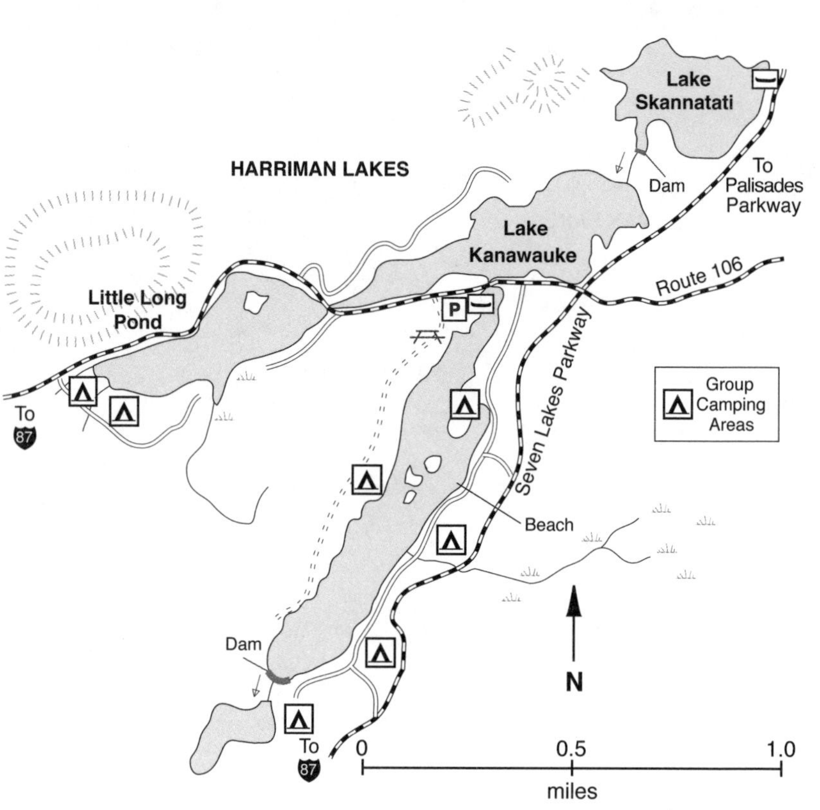

Lake Kanawauke Access. At the junction of Seven Lakes Drive and Route 106, go 0.4 mile west on Route 106 to the access on the left. (41° 14.055′ N, 74° 7.987′ W)

Lake Skannatati Access. At the junction of Seven Lakes Drive and Route 106, go 0.8 mile northeast on Seven Lakes Drive to the access on the left. (41° 11.855′ N, 74° 6.990′ W)

TRIP 9: HARRIMAN STATE PARK LAKES

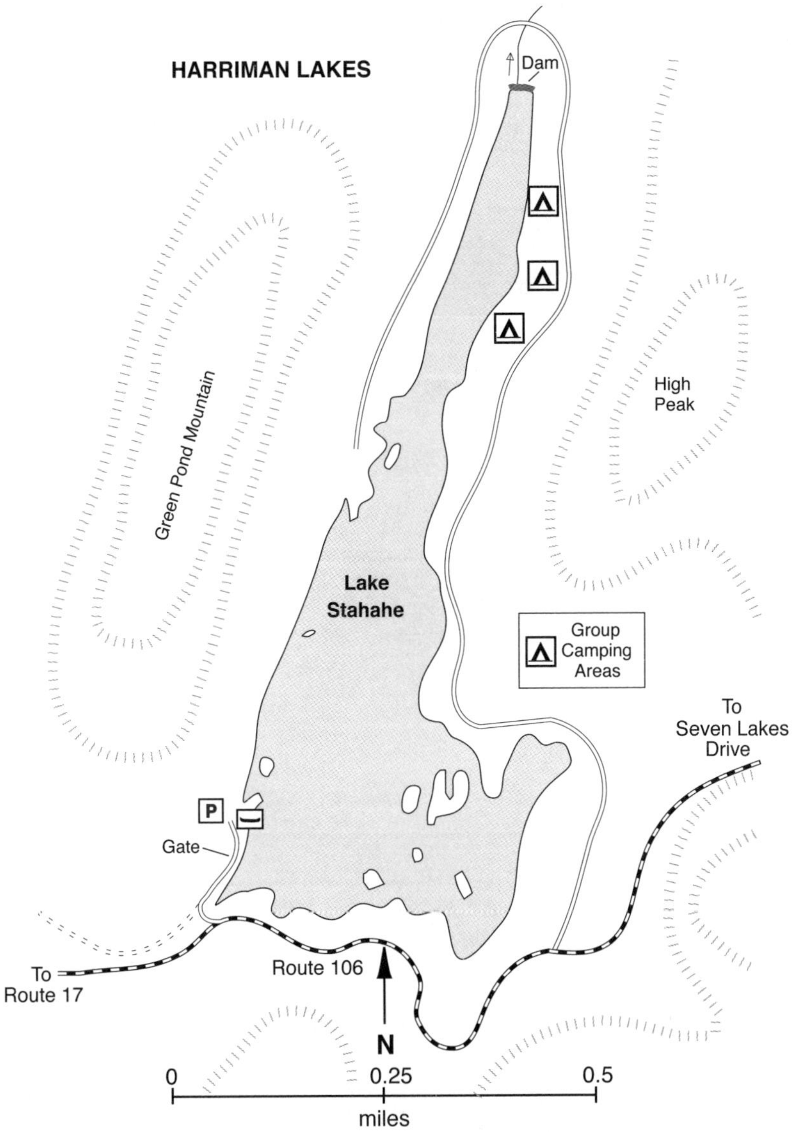

Lake Stahahe Access. At the junction of Seven Lakes Drive and Route 106, go 3.9 miles west on Route 106, and turn right on the access road. (41° 13.989′ N, 74° 9.912′ W)

TRIP 9: HARRIMAN STATE PARK LAKES

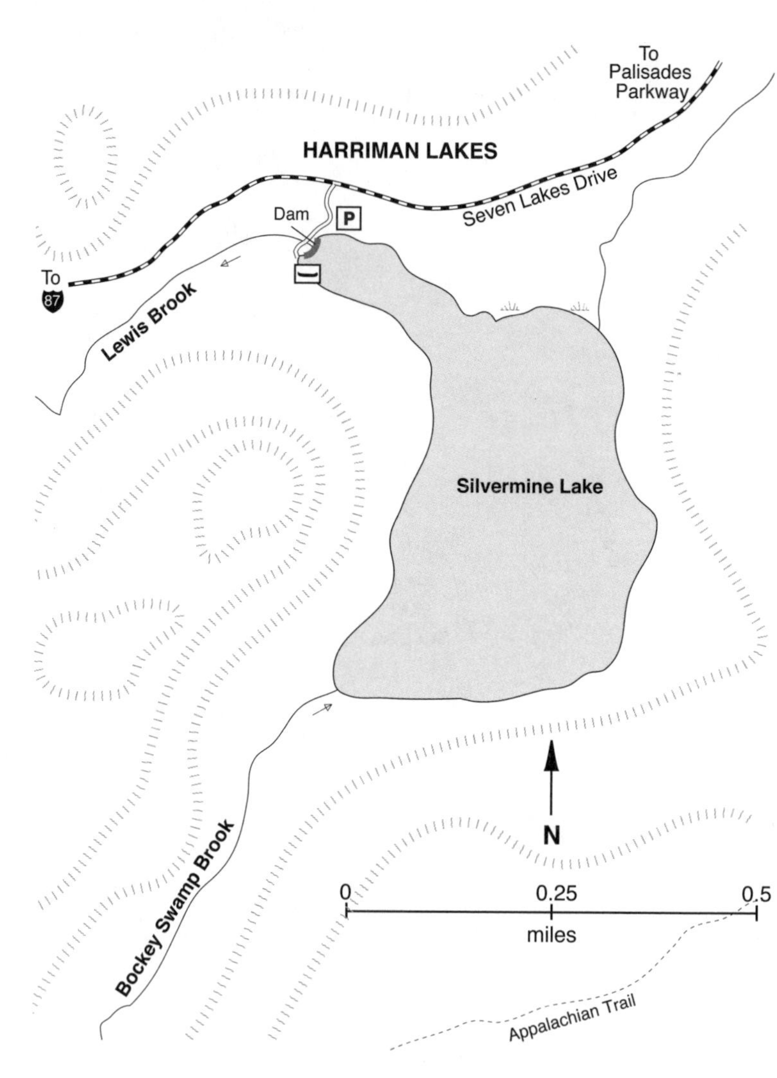

Silvermine Lake Access. From Tiorati Circle, go 2.2 miles northeast on Seven Lakes Drive, and turn right into the Silvermine picnic area. Cross the small bridge to unload your boat; park in the parking lot. (41° 17.729′ N, 74° 3.569′ W)

TRIP 9: HARRIMAN STATE PARK LAKES

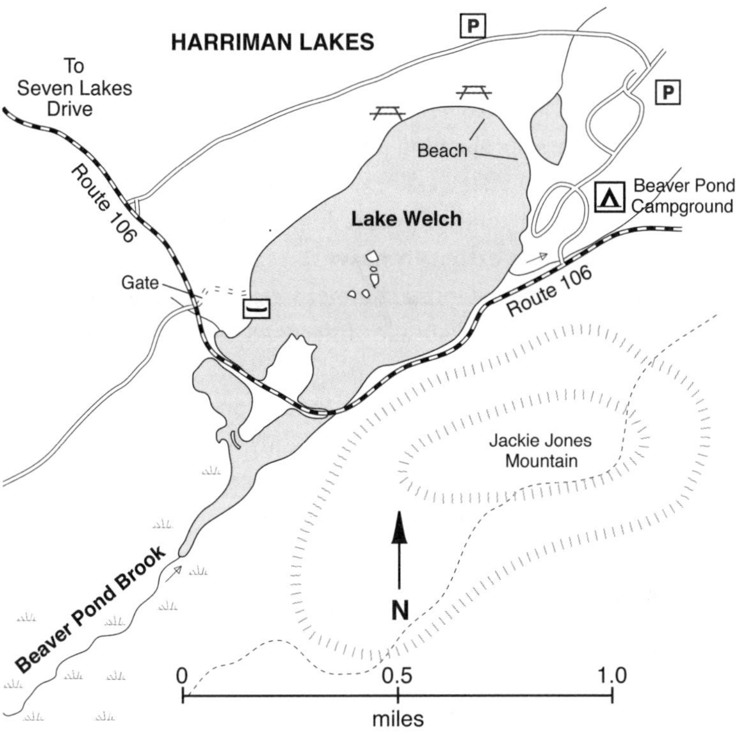

Lake Welch Access. At the junction of Seven Lakes Drive and Route 106, go 1.7 miles east on Route 106, and turn left on the access road (watch carefully, it's easy to miss). (41° 13.932′ N, 74° 4.962′ W)

WHAT YOU'LL SEE

Just north of the New Jersey border and only about 45 minutes from New York City, the lakes of Harriman State Park provide a remarkable surprise of fine paddling close to the city. It took us two days of exploration to visit the eight bodies of water described here, paddling more than 20 miles, most of it at a very slow pace to maximize wildlife viewing.

Harriman State Park forms the largest parcel of land managed by the Palisades Interstate Park Commission, which owns more than 100,000 acres in New York and New Jersey. In the late 1800s, quarrying began to leave serious scars on the Hudson's scenic west bank; the cliffs and the rubble beneath them provided ideal stone for constructing New York's brownstones and for producing concrete aggregate. The New Jersey Federation of Women's Clubs fought for legislation to protect the cliffs, resulting in the establishment of the Palisades Interstate Park Commission in 1900. Andrew H. Green, founder of the American Scenic and Historic Preservation Society, sponsored a similar effort in New York. Harriman State Park was born in 1910 with the donation of 10,000 acres of land to New York State from Mary Harriman—with the stipulation that the state abandon plans to build Sing Sing Prison on land that is now Bear Mountain State Park.

Because nearly 14 million people live within an hour's drive, the park sometimes suffers from extremely heavy recreational use, although most come here for hiking. During a typical summer weekend, hundreds of boats vie for space on some lakes. The Palisades Interstate Park Commission sells about 3,000 boating permits annually.

If you can, paddle here before mid-June or after Labor Day. In fact, three of the bodies of water are open to boating only during these times. Also, visit on weekdays; on a gorgeous Monday in mid-October—with trees in their full autumn splendor—we had the place to ourselves!

Lake Sebago

Sebago, the park's largest lake, boasts 6 miles of shoreline that offer splendid paddling. The widest portion of the lake extends in a northeast-southwest orientation, and a long arm extends to the north from its midpoint.

Massive slabs of granite and gneiss, a metamorphic rock, extend down into the water in places, some carpeted with mosses and polypody fern. Thick stands of mountain laurel, spectacular when in bloom in June, grow along the banks. Highbush blueberries also grow in profusion here, so in August, you may want to bring along a container and pick some for your pancakes.

Sebago's surrounding woodland includes mostly deciduous trees: oak (white, chestnut, scarlet, and red), beech, hickory, black birch, white ash, sugar maple, black locust, witch hazel, and American chestnut. Once one of the most abundant and economically important trees in the Northeast, the chestnut succumbed to the chestnut blight in the early 1900s. Saplings still sprout from rootstock, but these typically die after reaching 20 or 30 feet. We saw clumps of struggling saplings and hope someday a blight-resistant strain will reclaim its place in our eastern forests.

The open woodland invites exploration. You can explore from shore or hike some of the 200 miles of trails—including the Appalachian Trail—that extend throughout the park. We saw lots of deer browsing along the shore, a beaver, mallards, and a loon during a late-afternoon paddle around the lake in mid-October.

Recreational facilities include an extensive swimming beach at the lake's northern tip, along with two picnic areas, playgrounds, ball fields, and rowboat rentals. Several group camping and cabin locations are scattered around the southern section.

Lake Tiorati

The second-largest body of water in the park, located near its middle, Lake Tiorati perches at the highest elevation of waterways you can paddle. Also one of the most beautiful, with numerous wooded islands just south of the center, Tiorati—which means "skylike" in Algonkin—was created in 1914 by the damming of 40-acre Cedar Pond and 15-acre Little Clear Pond, which raised the water level by 17 feet and flooded 200 acres of swampland.

The southern shore stands out as our favorite part, with many coves, inlets, and islands to explore, along with a couple of beaver lodges. Look for beavers—the largest of North America's rodents—early in the morning or at dusk. At dusk, we have sometimes paddled right up to one, usually hearing a loud slap of the tail as it plunges into the water's depths.

In the shallows south of the large islands, notice the extensive beds of underwater vegetation. By midsummer, long, bushy tassels of coontail and

A lone white pine towers over the predominantly oak woods around Lake Tiorati.

milfoil reach toward the surface. In the right light, these extraordinary plants—their feathery stems seeming to sparkle in captured light—stand out brightly against the much darker lake bottom. One can easily confuse these native species with the invasive Eurasian watermilfoil, which has taken over some New York lakes and the nearby Hudson River. Fanwort and several species of bladderwort also grow here, providing important habitat for bass and pickerel.

Oak dominates the forests, although you will see more pine and hemlock here than on most other bodies of water in the park. In many places, massive rock outcroppings reach down into the water.

Unfortunately, roads nearly surround the lake—Seven Lakes Drive passes along the entire western shore, and the less-traveled Tiorati Brook Road traces two-thirds of the eastern shore. Considerable recreational development also encroaches on the lake, including group camping sites, picnic areas, a swimming beach, and the park office.

Lake Kanawauke, Lake Skannatati,and Little Long Pond

Before 1915, only Little Long Pond existed here. Damming Stony Brook at the southern tip of the present lake created Lake Kanawauke—"place of much water." Lake Skannatati, meaning "the other side," was not formed until 1947.

Lake Kanawauke and Little Long Pond

To reach Kanawauke's northern section and Little Long Pond (the only waters accessible during most of the summer), you have to paddle under the Route 106 arched stone bridge from the Lake Kanawauke access.

A large stand of red pine overlooks Kanawauke's eastern end, alongside the oak-dominated woodland found throughout the park. At the northeastern tip's inlet stream, you can tie up your boat and walk along the creek to Lake Skannatati through a gorgeous woodland where gnarled tree trunks rising from massive rock outcroppings evoke an almost magical feeling.

Visiting here off-season, you can explore Kanawauke's southern section. About halfway down, just below a cove extending back to the north, you can paddle among an attractive group of islands. But refrain from getting out on them—doing so might harm the vegetation and disturb wildlife.

Despite the group camping sites and the road along Little Long Pond's northern shore, we found this the most interesting of the three connected ponds. A very attractive island cluster greets you as you paddle into the pond, and across the way, exposed rock faces provide a delightful vista. Just east of the islands, a shallow, stumpy area contains lots of floating vegetation and wildlife. Look for the small purple flowers of aquatic bladderwort here, along with American white waterlily, yellow pondlily, and water shield. Also, watch for great blue herons, mallards, ring-necked ducks, pied-billed grebes, red-tailed hawks, and beavers. As we paddled along the pond's southern shore into a small marshy area, we spooked about a dozen wood ducks getting ready for fall migration.

Lake Skannatati

Despite its small size, we love paddling Skannatati. With no group camping areas, it's quieter than the other waterways. The shallow western end remains our favorite, where the coves and outlet arm take paddlers away from the road. Some spectacular rock outcroppings here drip with ferns, and others sport moss-filled cracks, resembling massive road maps.

Igneous granite or metamorphic gneisses and schists form most of the park's exposed bedrock, although Storm King granite—a coarse-grained gray rock highly resistant to weathering—forms Bear Mountain to the east. The Bear Mountain Trailside Museum at the Palisades Interstate Parkway terminus contains information on the area's geology.

In the northern cove and along the western end of Skannatati, look for carnivorous sundews on moss-covered logs by the water's edge and on grassy hummocks. Keep an eye out as well for leatherleaf—a plant frequently associated with bogs and northern fens—with its small, leathery leaves and bell-like, early season white flowers.

Lake Stahahe

The narrow northern end of this mile-long lake has lots of cabins and group camping sites, but these should be mostly empty during the time of year that you can paddle on Stahahe. Even so, the southern end offers more interesting paddling, with lots of islands to explore and shallow marshy areas, rich in fauna and flora.

Near dusk on an October day, we watched an otter for about a half hour as it fished—or perhaps just frolicked—in the shallows. We also saw a small flock of Canada geese. Deer browsed everywhere along the shore—obviously fairly tame and too familiar with the presence of people. We also saw a beautiful red fox just south of the lake near Route 106.

Silvermine Lake

With no development, Silvermine Lake sees somewhat fewer visitors than other Harriman lakes. Created in 1934 by a dam on Bockey Swamp Brook that flooded a beaver swamp, the lake still has a marshy feel, and its vegetation is quite different from that found in and around other park lakes.

A large stand of tamarack grows near the northeastern end, and thick clumps of alder, willow, red maple, red osier dogwood, sweet pepperbush, gray birch, and common reed (*Phragmites*)—all common marsh plants—line the northern shore. A dense oak-beech-maple forest—more typical of the region—rises from the water's southern edge. Submerged aquatic vegetation fills the relatively shallow lake, and various waterlilies cover the arm to the northwest.

We saw lots of mallards and Canada geese; turkey vultures and red-tailed hawks soared overhead. Though we didn't climb up the steep slope of the ski area near the access, it looked as if there would be a great view to the north.

Lake Welch

Of all the park's waterways, Lake Welch remains our favorite. The main part of the lake does not appeal because of its large, oval shape, and a gigantic swimming beach dominates the northeast end—although we did see a flock of ruddy ducks and several Canada geese during a mid-October paddle. But we love the southwest arm and Beaver Pond Brook.

Paddle southeast from the access and around a would-be island now connected by Route 106. After crossing under the road, paddle southwest, away from the cacophony of the beach and cars. As the lake narrows and becomes

A monarch butterfly sucks nectar from late-season asters in preparation for its long migration to Mexico.

rocky, expect a scratch or two. Ease your way into the marshy Beaver Pond Brook inlet, leaving rocks behind and entering a wild, magical area.

True to the brook's name, we quickly came upon a beaver lodge in the broad outlet. Although hard to gauge distance here, we paddled at least a half-mile along this highly twisted, slow-flowing brook as it meandered through a *Phragmites* and red maple swamp. In places, the channel grew so narrow and the curves so tight that it became a challenge to squeak through. The farther we went, the shallower the water. Eventually, sand replaced mucky bottom, and a downed log blocked our way. Fortunately, we found a place where—with some difficulty—we could turn around. If you plan to use a kayak, bring a breakdown paddle; a two-bladed paddle would be out of the question along this creek.

Beaver Pond Brook teems with wildlife. We saw songbirds galore in the thick shrubs and grasses. Paddling back, after the brook widened out, we noticed movement and spotted a young otter making its way along the bank. Obviously hunting, it crawled over, slithered around, and swam under tree roots and grass hummocks hanging out over the water. Watching this otter—with no sign of other people anywhere—we reveled in the fact that New York City lay only an hour away.

On the way back north toward the Route 106 bridge, paddle into the narrow channel heading to the left (northwest) that leads to another part of the lake. Although within view of Route 106, this area felt quite wild. Immediately upon entering the cove, we spotted an osprey that took off with a half-eaten fish in its talons.

SNAPPING TURTLE: HIDDEN DWELLER OF THE POND

The snapping turtle—New York's most common species of turtle, even more common than the painted turtle—inhabits almost every beaver pond, millpond, lake, marsh, and slow-moving stream in the Northeast. Hundreds live in some bodies of water, but you would not know it. Even if you spend quite a bit of time paddling, you'll rarely see this large reptile. Unlike its sun-loving cousin, the painted turtle, the snapping turtle prefers pond-bottom depths and rarely basks in the sun. The photo here shows an obvious exception.

You can easily recognize a snapping turtle (*Chelydra serpentina*), especially out of water. A long, spiny-ridged tail and very large head relative to body size give it away. The young have a distinct ridge on the top shell (carapace), although on a large adult, the surface may have worn smooth. On the underside, the bottom shell (plastron) bears a cross-like shape. Mature snapping turtles can grow quite large, much larger than any other Northeast turtle. The carapace can reach a length of 20 inches (an overall length, nose to tail, of more than 3 feet), and a snapping turtle can weigh more than 60 pounds.

When paddling relatively clear, shallow water, we occasionally see a snapping turtle underwater or on a bank above a pond or slow-moving river—probably en route to another nearby body of water or, perhaps, a female preparing to lay a clutch of eggs. Snapping turtles may travel a great distance in search of a suitable nesting site—one marked individual went 16 kilometers round-trip. Our usual glimpse, though, as we paddle along is just the triangular nose sticking out of the water.

Many people fear snapping turtles—and we admit to a bit of concern when two large specimens chased one another just inches beneath our boat in a shallow pond—but they really pose no harm *as long as they remain in the water.* Even in the unlikely event that one bites a swimmer's toe, it quickly lets go, realizing that the quarry is more than it can handle. In the water, snappers avoid human contact. Watch out for a snapping turtle on land, though. It lashes out with lightning speed when feeling threatened. With its massive jaw muscles and razor-sharp beak, a large snapper exerts more than 400 pounds of force per square inch—enough to easily sever a finger.

The species has existed for at least 80 million years, and most scientists believe it to be the oldest North American reptile. As in all turtles, its rib cage and vertebrae have evolved into a bony carapace and plastron. Although the carapace provides armored protection, the small plastron offers almost no safeguard for the snapping turtle's underside, leaving it vulnerable to leeches. The animal sometimes leaves the water to rid itself of this parasite.

Most Northeast turtle species hibernate for long periods, but we sometimes see the relatively cold-resistant snapping turtle swimming beneath the ice, although in northern New York, it typically hibernates in the bottom mud for at least a while during the dead of winter. When idle underwater, it does not need to breathe air. Special surfaces in its rear cloacal cavity extract oxygen from the water, much like gills. When active, however, it needs more oxygen and must surface for air—providing the quiet paddler an opportunity to catch a glimpse.

Omnivore and opportunist, the snapping turtle dines on a wide range of animals and plants, including fish, frogs, salamanders, occasional ducklings and loon chicks, dead animals, and aquatic plants. A snapper can kill anything its size or smaller, but it seems to prefer the easy meal. A superb sense of smell helps it to scavenge for dead animals. The snapping turtle literature recounts a story of an American Indian who helped find drowning victims by using a snapping turtle on a long leash. When released into the water, the turtle unerringly headed for the decomposing corpse and latched onto it with its strong jaws. The turtle's handler then slowly reeled it in—corpse and all.

A mature female leaves the water in late spring or early summer to lay eggs. She digs a hole, typically deposits from 20 to 30 (rarely, up to 80) eggs the size of Ping-Pong balls, and then covers the hole. Some lay eggs in two or more holes or may even dig several false holes to mislead predators, which take a heavy toll on snapping turtle clutches. The eggs usually hatch in the fall, some 70 to 100 days after laying (depending on temperature), and the inch-long hatchlings make a beeline for the water—often as raccoons, birds, and other predators try to gobble them up.

As with many turtle species, nest temperature determines sex. Several studies found that at very cool or very warm temperatures, the embryos all developed into females, while intermediate temperatures produced males. Within most nests, temperature varies with location, so both males and females develop.

The snapping turtle population in New York remains secure—unlike that of most other turtles. This species seems to tolerate current levels of environmental pollution and can even live in highly polluted marshy areas in cities. Traffic crushes fewer snappers than it does more terrestrial turtles.

Some people regard snapper meat highly, however, resulting in heavy trapping in certain areas.

If you come across a snapping turtle on land, avoid the temptation to deliver it to the nearest body of water. Chances are pretty good that it's a female; she knows where to head to lay her eggs and does not need assistance in this endeavor.

10 | Mohansic Lake and Crom Pond

This lake and pond in Franklin D. Roosevelt State Park draw anglers and recreational paddlers, but most people come to swim in the park's gigantic pool and hike the trails. Make sure you paddle back into Crom Pond where you will find more seclusion and see more wildlife, including ducks, geese, rabbits, and deer.

Location: Yorktown
Maps: *New York Atlas & Gazetteer*, Map 108: C4; USGS Mohegan Lake
Area: Mohansic Lake, 107 acres; Crom Pond, 30 acres
Time: 3 hours
Habitat Type: Small recreational lake and small marshy pond; nature trails
Fish: Largemouth bass, pickerel (see fish advisories, Appendix C)
Camping and Trails: Appendix A (37, 38, 39, 45); trails, Franklin D. Roosevelt State Park, parks.ny.gov/parks/148/details.aspx
Take Note: An annual $30 fee provides access to Taconic region lakes and ponds

GETTING THERE

From I-287, go about 16 miles north on the Taconic Parkway, and exit at Franklin D. Roosevelt State Park. Stay right at each junction to reach the access. (41° 16.997′ N, 73° 49.081′ W)

WHAT YOU'LL SEE

Franklin D. Roosevelt State Park, one of several parks along the scenic Taconic Parkway, contains both Mohansic Lake and connected Crom Pond. Paddling here means contending with road noise from the parkway.

TRIP 10: MOHANSIC LAKE AND CROM POND

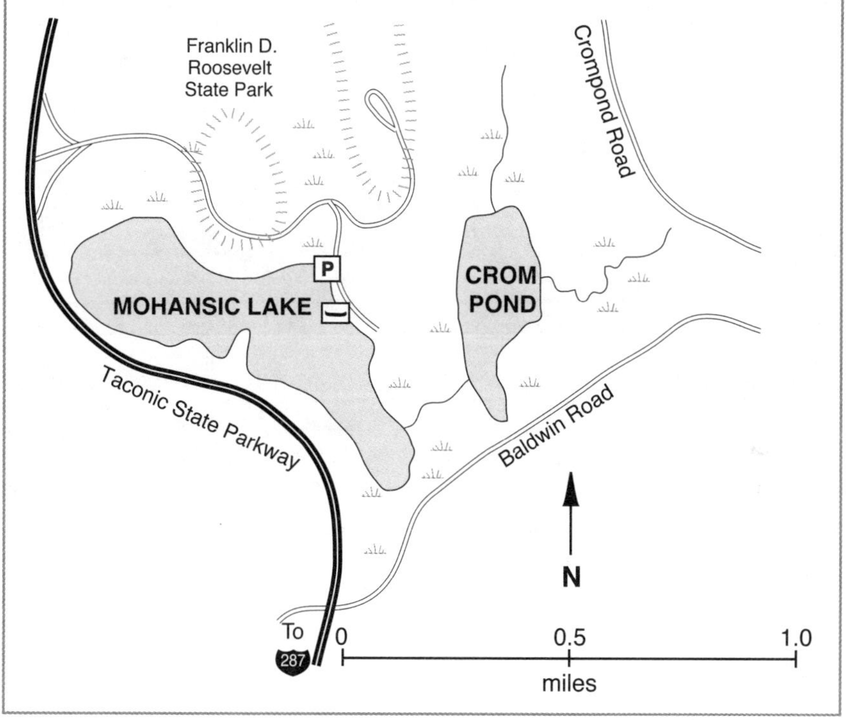

FDR Park attracts few boaters, especially in the off-season. Most people come for other types of recreation: swimming in one of the largest pools in the United States, hiking on an extensive network of trails, biking in summer, and cross-country skiing and ice-skating in winter. Dubious at first about paddling, given the road noise, we became converts after visiting Crom Pond, a wilderness retreat where traffic sounds just barely impinge.

A huge flock of tame Canada geese begged for food at the access, ignoring signs that said both Do Not Feed Wildlife and No Swimming in the Lake. Tame cottontails munched the grass, and pied-billed grebes swam about in thick aquatic vegetation. A flock of coots also worked to keep the abundant aquatic plants in check, seemingly to no avail, while a lone cormorant surveyed the scene from an exposed rock out in the middle of Mohansic Lake.

We left behind the access, with its large beeches, weeping willows, sugar maples, big-tooth aspens, and unfed geese, and headed for Crom Pond. On our way south to the connector, the sheer volume of white and yellow waterlilies impressed us. Their flat leaves, floating on the water's surface, covered the entire

A female ruddy duck—one of the smallest North American ducks—paddles about the surface of Crom Pond during fall migration.

southern cove. The large trees near the access gave way to shrubby shoreline that included dwarf red maple and black gum.

As we paddled the connector, ducks scurried into the tiny channels back under the shrubbery, and a pied-billed grebe dove for cover. Shrubs and dwarf red maple dominated, with buttonbush, dwarf willow, and purple loosestrife growing in profusion, along with winterberry and lesser amounts of several other common shrubs.

Two anglers in a rowboat tried their luck casting for bass along the northern shore, while eight ruddy ducks paddled about. As we drew near, we could see that the male ducks already sported winter plumage. These unusually small ducks—also called stifftails—have short tails that often point straight up, revealing a bright white rump. Males in breeding plumage have reddish necks, backs, and sides; a black head with large white face patch; and a bright blue bill—quite a sight to behold! In keeping with their strange visage, in spring, males putt-putt around in little circles and figure-eights, using those stiff tails as rudders, trying to attract female attention; this perhaps does not look comical to female ruddy ducks.

Because these birds usually nest on small ponds, paddlers rarely see them, except in migration. Eventually, this group decided that we had approached too close and dove for cover; they typically dive rather than fly when danger approaches.

Having surveyed all we could, reluctantly we paddled back to Mohansic Lake, where we found the geese still unsuccessfully panhandling. Given their robust size, it seems they usually find a more responsive crowd. As we left the park near dusk and drove northward on the Taconic heading back to Vermont, the deer that like to dodge cars emerged. We had not even gotten onto the parkway when several deer appeared, browsing roadside shrubs. In gathering darkness, our headlights frequently caught their eyeshine. We had to stop abruptly more than a few times to avoid hitting them, although we did not see any dead along the road. The drivers who travel this route regularly must maintain quite a bit of caution. Frankly, nowhere else in our travels throughout New York can we remember seeing such a large population of deer.

11 | Constitution Marsh

Constitution Marsh, protected by the National Audubon Society, is a great place to study New York's flora and fauna. Twice-a-day, tide-induced flooding brings nutrients into the marsh, causing plants to grow rapidly. In turn, the plants provide food for a wide variety of animals. Expect to see mute swans, ducks, geese, kingfishers, and lots more. Paddle here only around high tide.

Location: Philipstown
Maps: *New York Atlas & Gazetteer*, Map 108: B2; USGS West Point
Area: 270 acres
Time: 3 hours
Habitat Type: Tidal marsh
Camping and Trails: Appendix A (37, 38, 39, 45); trails, Constitution Marsh Audubon Center and Sanctuary, constitution.audubon.org
Take Note: No motors; tides, tidesandcurrents.noaa.gov

GETTING THERE

From the south, go north on Route 9 through Peekskill, and turn left on Routes 6 and 202 (Bear Mountain Highway). Turn right (north) off Routes 6 and 202 on Route 9D.

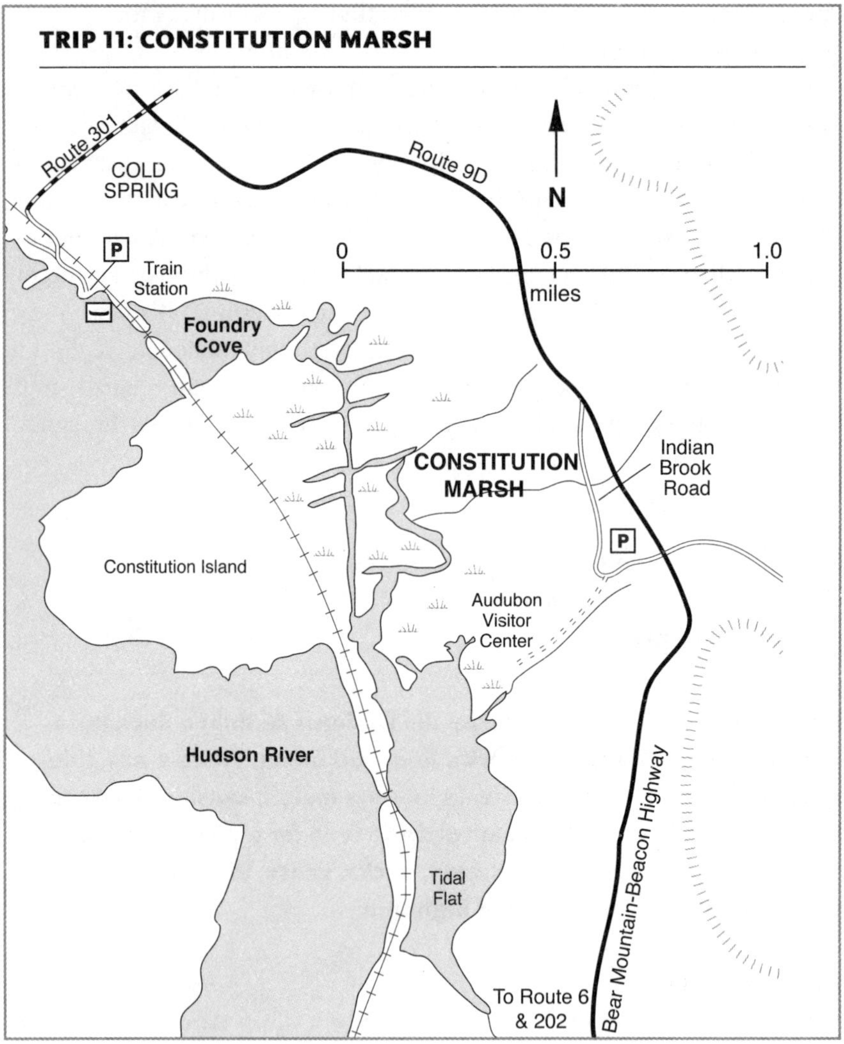

From I-87, take Route 6, cross the Bear Mountain Bridge, and turn left (north) on Route 9D.

Train Station Access. At the junction of Routes 9D and 301, turn left, and go to the end of the street. Turn left on Lunn Terrace, and turn immediately right to cross a bridge. At the T, turn left, and go through the station parking lot to the end. Lower your boat down over the rocks into the Hudson River. A ramp is near the station. (41° 24.888′ N, 73° 57.489′ W)

Audubon Society Visitor Center Access. At the junction of Routes 9D and 301, go south 1.4 miles on Route 9D, and turn diagonally right on narrow, easy-to-miss Indian Brook Road. Go 0.4 mile (1.8 miles) to the parking lot. To avoid being towed, do not park along the road. Hike the half-mile down to the visitor center. (41° 24.255′ N, 73° 56.056′ W)

WHAT YOU'LL SEE

Constitution Marsh, owned by the National Audubon Society, includes forests, streams, and tidal marshes, making it a wonderful location to take children to learn about the natural world. Three nature trails weave through the 270-acre sanctuary: one teaches tree identification, one leads to an ancient rock shelter built by native people, and one allows close inspection of the marsh via a 700-foot boardwalk. An archaeological dig has dated native people occupation back at least 5,000 years.

Audubon naturalists also run guided canoe trips into the marsh for groups of up to fifteen adults; programs for schoolchildren accommodate as many as 25 students, along with adult assistants. Unfortunately, you cannot paddle your own boat out from the visitor center. An alternate entrance to the marsh exists, however. You can launch from the Cold Spring train station parking lot and paddle about a half-mile through Foundry Cove into the marsh's northern reaches. Because you can travel the marsh only for about two hours either side of high tide, be sure to call the visitor center and ask about tides or use tide tables.

From the Cold Spring station lot access, paddle downstream for a few hundred feet and pass under the railroad bridge. From there, head due east for

Cormorants spread their wings to dry them after diving in pursuit of fish.

the very back of Foundry Cove, where outgoing tides drain Constitution Marsh through a wide passageway.

On our visit, as we entered Foundry Cove, flocks of mallards and black ducks and five mute swans greeted us. Three of the swans spilled out of the EPA Superfund restoration site at the back of Foundry Cove. We eyeballed them pretty carefully but could discern no extra appendages or other mutations. The ducks and the other two swans had the good sense to stay out of this area.

Up close, the swans—5 feet from beak tip to tail end—dwarfed the 2-foot-long ducks, especially in bulk. An Old World import, wild populations of mute swans have expanded along the East Coast from Maine to the Carolinas.

We paddled back through acres of narrow-leaved cattails. Large deciduous trees line the marsh's eastern edge and populate Constitution Island, which juts out into the Hudson. As we gazed out over the marsh and up the surrounding bluffs and hillsides, we noticed large, isolated homes overlooking this beautiful scene through glorious fall foliage.

The Audubon Society says that the 154-mile tidal stretch of the Hudson from New York City to Troy represents the only major American river still functioning as a complete ecosystem. Despite pollution and development, the Hudson has not lost a single fish species. It produces huge populations of striped bass, shad, blue crabs, and other species, all of which depend on tidal marshes for food.

We recommend that you walk the sanctuary trails and, using the excellent guidebook, study the 39 species of trees and shrubs described. We found interesting information about several tree species. For example, the last Ice Age nearly exterminated the black locust. Early settlers, however, transplanted it from its last holdout in Appalachian valleys to all over the East and Midwest. Settlers used black locust for many products; today, people still use it to make split-rail fences because of its tremendous durability. Locust also can substitute for pressure-treated wood, which is made rot resistant by impregnating it with environmental toxins. We urge you to visit here, to paddle, to walk the trails, and to talk to the staff. We especially urge you to bring children to this special place.

12 | Canopus Lake and Stillwater Pond

Because Clarence Fahnestock State Park is so accessible to New York's large population center and because the Appalachian Trail courses through the woods on Canopus Lake's west side, we prefer to paddle here in spring and fall. Look for Canada geese, wild turkeys, and woodland birds. A further draw in spring is the huge stands of mountain laurel putting on an electric bloom in May.

Location: Kent
Maps: *New York Atlas & Gazetteer*, Map 108: A3, A4; USGS Oscawana Lake
Area: 104 acres; park area 14,086 acres
Time: 3 hours
Habitat Type: Small ponds
Fish: Largemouth bass, pickerel, brook and rainbow trout (see fish advisories, Appendix C)
Camping and Trails: Appendix A (45) (on-site); trails, Clarence Fahnestock State Park, parks.ny.gov/parks/133
Take Note: No motors; annual $30 fee provides access to Taconic region lakes and ponds

GETTING THERE

From the Taconic Parkway, go 1.0 mile south on Route 301 to the access on the right. Limited parking is available across the road. (41° 27.434′ N, 73° 49.892′ W)

WHAT YOU'LL SEE

Canopus Lake

Within Clarence Fahnestock State Park, Canopus Lake offers a wonderful paddling opportunity, especially in the off-season. Although the park prohibits gasoline motors, believe it or not, the lake can become overrun with rowboats, canoes, and kayaks, especially on sunny summer weekends. Three reasons account for this: the Appalachian Trail, which skirts the lake's western edge, draws hikers; the park contains a popular campground; and the Taconic Parkway runs through the park, providing easy accessibility to literally millions of recreation-starved downstate city dwellers.

Even though we had to share the lake with other boaters, we loved paddling here, given its small, protected nature and incredible beauty. Lovely tall hemlocks

TRIP 12: CANOPUS LAKE AND STILLWATER POND

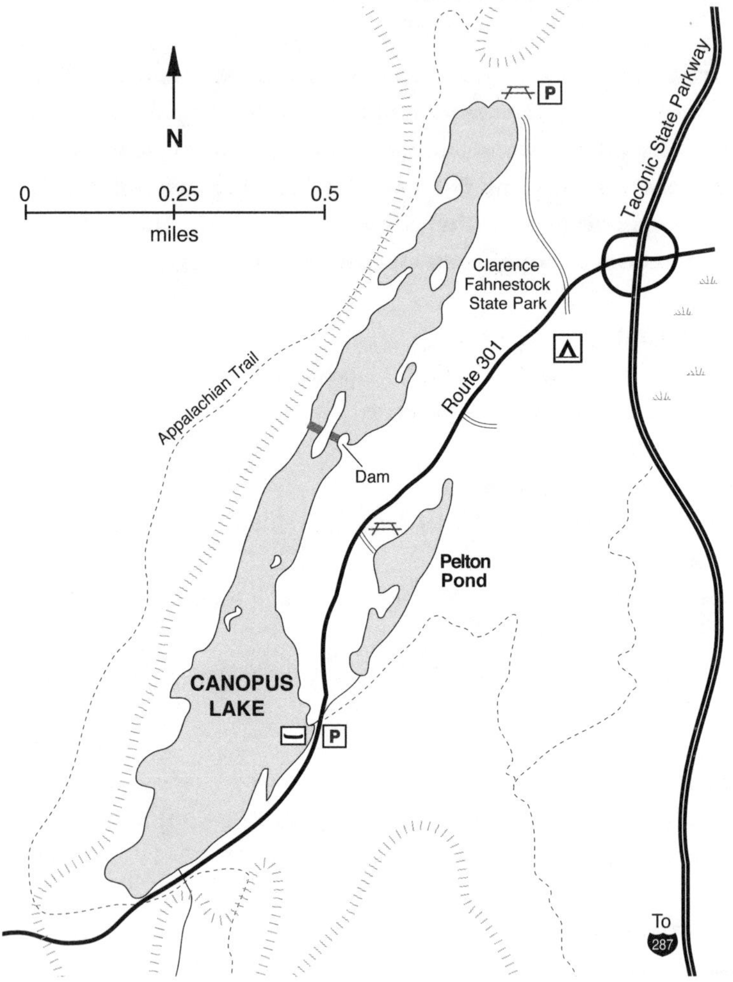

dominate the rocky hillside across from the access, and their lacy leaves droop out over the shores, especially on the upper lake. But the real attraction remains the understory's tree-sized mountain laurel. A showy evergreen member of the heath family—which includes leatherleaf, bog rosemary, sheep laurel, and blueberry—mountain laurel, like most heaths, prefers acidic soil. Blooming in late May, the gorgeous clusters of pink-to-white flowers present a perfect pollen trap for honeybees. The ten stamens of each flower press tightly

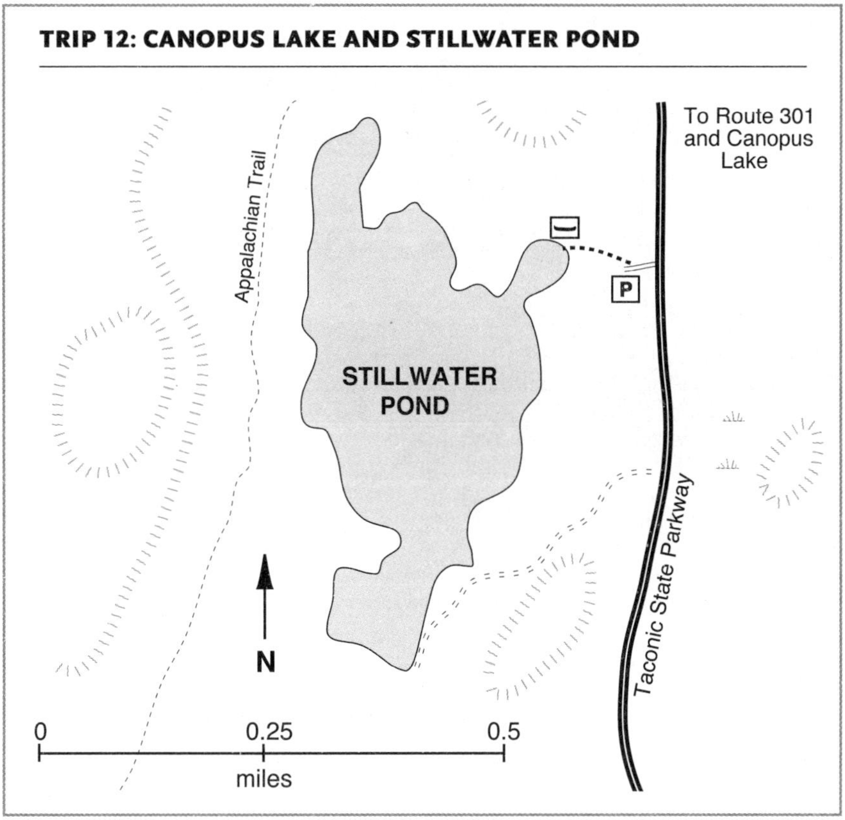

against the petals. When a bee lands on a flower seeking nectar, the stamens spring out, dusting the bee with pollen to be carried on to the next flower for cross-pollination.

The twisted tops of oak, beech, and yellow birch dominate the hillsides, providing cover for the Appalachian Trail. After leaving the park, the trail heads northeast, eventually entering Connecticut in northern Fairfield County on the way to its northern terminus in Maine's Baxter State Park.

Many smooth granite boulders dot Canopus Lake's surface; unfortunately, the park does not allow swimming on the lower part of the lake. The lake's upper portion is off-limits to boating during swimming season; when we paddled here in April, we carried up over the dam that separates the lake's two halves. Stay to the right for the carry.

In April, a pair of Canada geese nested on the south end of a tiny island near the east shore, just where the lower lake starts to narrow. The bird sitting on the nest hunkered down, trying to look invisible, as we quietly paddled by. (Signs tell visitors not to feed the geese, which probably have gotten quite tame

Early season anglers try their luck for smallmouth bass.

over the years.) In addition, we saw several other species of birds, all of them newly arrived migrants thinking about nesting: eastern phoebes, robins, turkey vultures, flickers, and barn swallows. We also saw wild turkeys.

Stillwater Pond

To gain access, you need to show your boat permit at the park office. A huge tulip tree, 3 feet in diameter, grows along the path to the water. This member of the magnolia family—with its large, waxy yellow treetop flowers—is at the northern extension of its range here. Smooth, gray-barked sweet birch trees (*Betula lenta*) also grow along the path. Scratch off some bark from a branch, and note the sweet aroma of wintergreen. You can use this characteristic to distinguish sweet birch from the similar river birch (*Betula nigra*), which lacks this odor.

Along the shore in several places we spotted the heavily serrated 9-inch leaves of American chestnut. This magnificent tree, once a codominant species in the Appalachians, its nuts an important food source for wildlife, has nearly died out because of the inadvertent introduction of chestnut blight, a fungus that gets under the bark. Stump sprouts, such as the ones we saw, rarely live long enough to flower before the disease fells them. The stumps still sprout because the soft, resinous wood resists decay. That quality made the wood useful for railroad ties and split-rail fences; many chestnut split-rail fences still survive after many decades.

13 | Chodikee Lake

At just 63 acres, Chodikee Lake is quite small. When we paddle here, we spend our time in the inlet and outlet streams, reveling in the huge amount of birdlife that we encounter. Look for osprey, kestrel, raven, bluebird, red-bellied woodpecker, and waterfowl. The best time to visit is in spring during high water.

Location: Esopus, Lloyd
Maps: *New York Atlas & Gazetteer*, Map 103: B7; USGS Hyde Park
Area and Length: 63 acres; stream length 2.5 miles one way
Time: 4 hours
Habitat Type: Small lake with swampy inlet and outlet streams
Fish: Largemouth bass (see fish advisories, Appendix C; see specific advisory, health.ny.gov/environmental/outdoors/fish/health_advisories)
Camping: Appendix A (45, 47)
Take Note: Gasoline motors prohibited; paddling is better during spring high water

GETTING THERE

From Poughkeepsie, cross the Hudson River on Route 44, and turn right on Route 9W. Go 2.3 miles, and turn left on Route 299. Go 1.3 miles (3.6 miles), and turn right on Chodikee Lake Road. Go 1.0 mile (4.6 miles) to a T, turn left, and go 0.9 mile (5.5 miles) to the access on the right. (41° 46.245′ N, 73° 59.304′ W)

From I-87, Exit 18, go 3.8 miles east on Route 299, turn left on Chodikee Lake Road, and proceed as above.

WHAT YOU'LL SEE

We first paddled Chodikee Lake in spring before the mosquitoes hatched out of the extensive marshes surrounding the lake and before more than an occasional angler plied the waters. We found an idyllic site, an extraordinary wildlife paradise free from insects and people that would later appear in large numbers. We have returned to this lake and its streams many times.

The plaintive calls of spring peepers, the chatter of chipmunks, and the mournful cry of doves greeted us at the access, and as we looked out over the lake from the end of the dock, two mute swans drifted slowly by. These Eurasian imports, larger than our native swans at 5 feet from bill to tail tip, continue to

TRIP 13: CHODIKEE LAKE

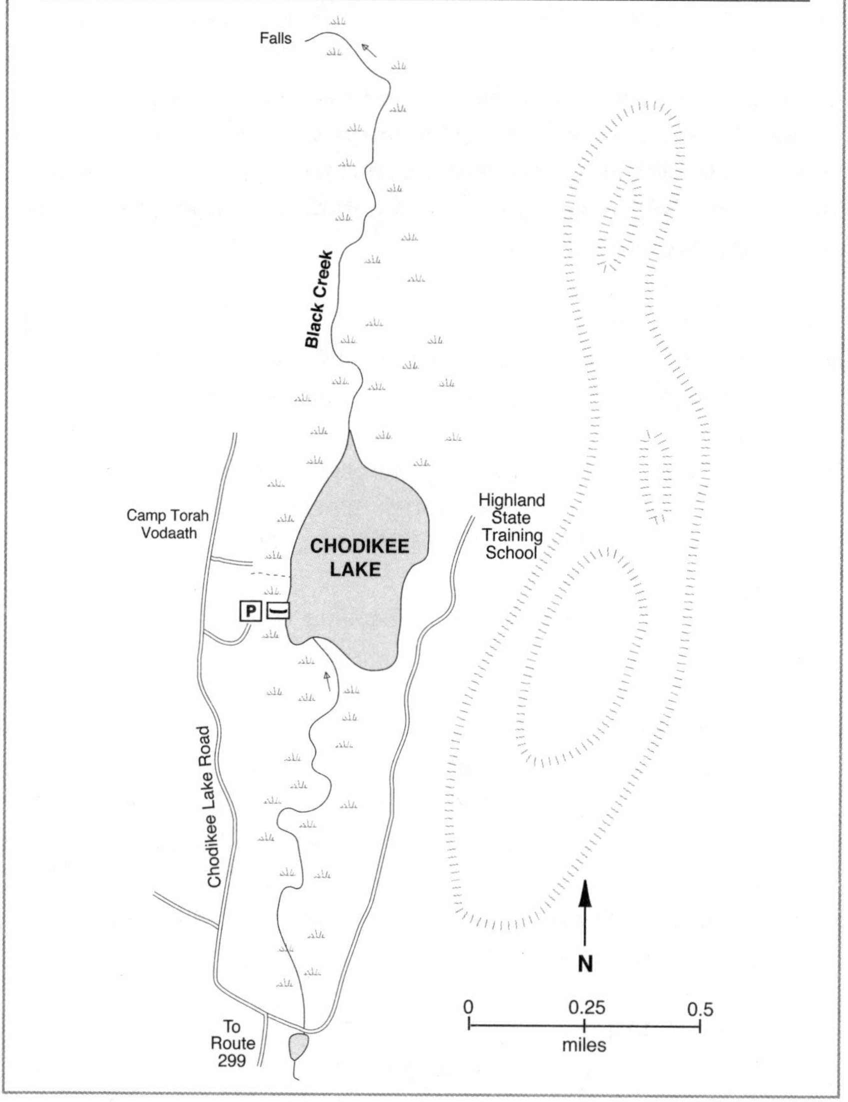

spread along the eastern seaboard from Maine to the Carolinas. They often swim with their necks held in a graceful S-shaped curve. We distinguish them from native swans by their orange-yellow bills with a black knob at the top.

Chodikee Lake overflows with wildlife habitat, boasting acres of dead and dying trees, meandering streams on the north and south ends, extensive wooded swamps, and stands of cattails and other marsh vegetation. At times of high water, you can paddle the south creek upstream to the road and the north creek downstream to a series of small waterfalls—and encounter a prodigious amount of wildlife along the way.

Flickers and red-bellied woodpeckers have carved out holes in hundreds of dead trees, providing nests for themselves and for other cavity nesters, including wood ducks, kestrels, bluebirds, and tree swallows. On our first visit, hundreds of tree swallows cruised the water, scooping up early emerging insects; we saw several kestrels and many bluebirds. The red-bellied woodpecker used to reach the northern extension of its range in southern New York but has moved north as the climate warms. Distinguish it from the flicker by the large red patch on the back and top of the red-bellied woodpecker's head and the alternating black and white stripes on the back—a so-called ladder-back.

But the ducks provided the real attraction. We saw many gorgeously colored wood ducks—especially in the northern stream's wooded swamp—hundreds of green-winged teal, quite a few mallards, and some black ducks. Several pairs of geese, which nest quite early compared with other waterfowl, hunkered down over their nests on rotting stumps, incubating their eggs just a foot or two above the water.

At the outflow stream's northern end, a hemlock canopy draped over beautiful rock formations. Both times we paddled here in spring—six years apart—in the shade of the hemlocks, a phoebe pair nested in a natural cavity in a vertical rock face where the stream narrowed and tumbled gently over rockfalls, the land posted against further travel.

A Canada goose eyes us as we glide by.

14 | Tivoli Marshes— North Bay

North Bay of Tivoli Marshes stands out as an extraordinary paddling resource. Highly productive because of twice-daily tidal nutrient influxes, the lush vegetation provides great habitat for a variety of species, including muskrat and waterfowl and other marsh birds. You may also see beavers here.

Location: Red Hook
Maps: *New York Atlas & Gazetteer*, Map 98: D2, D3; USGS Saugerties
Area: 1,468 acres in the wildlife management area
Time: 4 hours
Habitat Type: Tidal, freshwater marshlands with shrubs; no development
Camping and Trails: Appendix A (46, 47, 48, 49, 115, 119, 121); trails, Tivoli Bays Wildlife Management Area and Research Reserve, dec.ny.gov/lands/92370.html
Take Note: No motors; novice paddlers should avoid the railroad bridges and the Hudson River and always wear personal flotation devices (PFDs); tides, tidesandcurrents.noaa.gov

GETTING THERE

From I-87, Exit 21, go east on Route 23 across the Hudson River, and turn right (south) on Route 9G. From the junction with Route 78, go south on Route 9G for 0.6 mile, and turn right on Kidd Lane. Go 0.5 mile (1.1 miles) west on Kidd Lane, turn left, and go 0.9 mile downhill (2.0 miles) to the access. (42° 2.331′ N, 73° 54.871′ W)

WHAT YOU'LL SEE

North Bay of Tivoli Marshes, part of the Hudson River National Estuarine Research Reserve, contains one of the most scenic and ecologically productive Hudson marshes. Looking out over the broad expanse of marsh as the sun sets over 1,100-foot-high Indian Head, Overlook, and High Peak mountains in the Catskills is awe-inspiring. We highly recommend this wonderful paddling destination, especially at midtide to high tide. Hundreds of passageways penetrate through all sections of the marsh, but many become inaccessible at lower tide levels.

TRIP 14: TIVOLI MARSHES—NORTH BAY

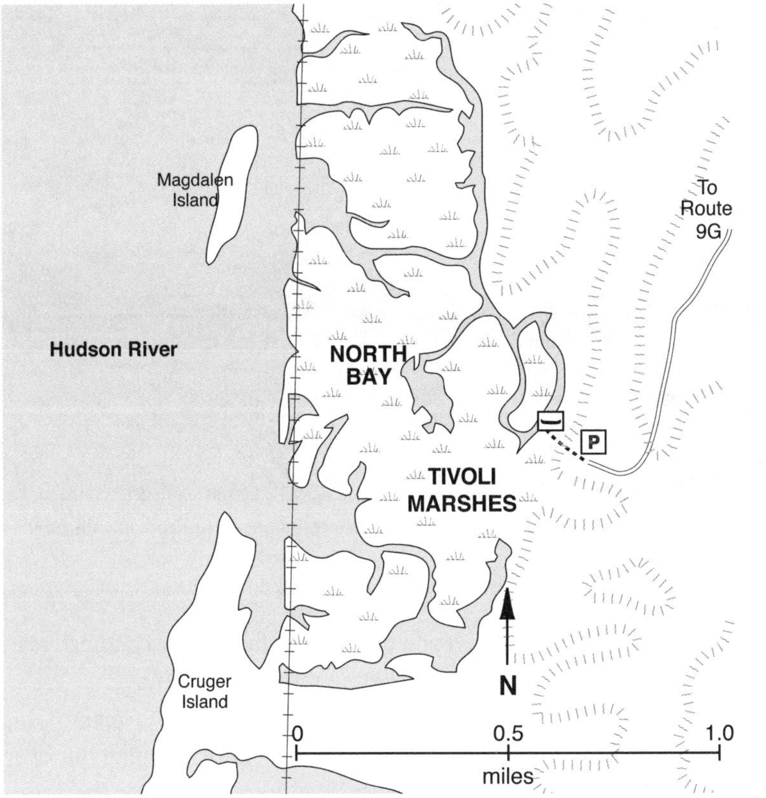

How did we come to be looking out over the marsh at sunset? We got lost—over and over again. We decided to paddle a counterclockwise circuit, heading north from the access. After inspecting a few dead-end channels filled with pickerelweed, we had little trouble making our way across the marsh's northern end to the railroad embankment. We simply followed the outgoing tide to the more northern of two bridges that connect the marsh with the Hudson.

However, after heading south along the railroad embankment—investigating the profuse growth of swamp rose, jewelweed, grape, and Virginia creeper along the way—we tried to complete the circuit by heading inland. Time and again, what looked like promising passages turned out to be labyrinthine, pickerelweed-filled, carbon copy dead-ends. After several hours of trying—and truly enjoying the sunset—we made our way back to the access. The only two waterways that lead back to the access that we could find are at the north

Beautiful swamp rose grows in profusion along the shores of many New York marshy ponds and streams.

and at about the midway point. If you do explore the marsh's southern reaches, head back north by the embankment before returning inland.

Besides the dwarf red maple that occupies some of the marsh's higher hummocks, any trees found here hug the eastern shore, hanging out over the channel that runs north from the access. Hemlock interrupts the primarily mixed deciduous woodland. Out in the open swamp, large patches of wild rice, yellow pondlily, and arrowhead grow among the abundant pickerelweed. Narrow-leaved cattail occurs in profusion, providing nesting habitat for marsh wrens, but red-winged blackbirds rule. We watched songbirds scatter as a sharp-shinned hawk glided by low on silent wings. Expect to see waterfowl here as well, especially during migration.

Although we wanted to explore the Hudson, especially Magdalen and Cruger islands, squeaking under the bridges just after high tide looked dicey. While we could have squeezed under the northern bridge, paddling back against the substantial current would not have worked, given the lack of overhead room for hard paddling.

15 | Lake Taghkanic and Rudd Pond

People visit Lake Taghkanic State Park primarily for hiking and camping, but it is also a good place to study trees, especially oaks. We found five species here. We also saw pileated woodpecker, beaver, and deer while paddling. You can camp at either Lake Taghkanic or Rudd Pond.

Location: Gallatin, Northeast
Maps: *New York Atlas & Gazetteer*, Map 98: C5, C6 and Map 99: E7; USGS Ancram, Millerton
Area: Lake Taghkanic, 104 acres; Rudd Pond, 66 acres; park, 1,600 acres
Time: 2 hours (for both bodies of water)
Habitat Type: Small, recreation-oriented ponds
Fish: Largemouth bass, pickerel (see fish advisories, Appendix C)
Camping and Trails: Appendix A (46, 48) (on-site); trails, Lake Taghkanic State Park, parks.ny.gov/parks/38/details.aspx
Take Note: No motors; annual $30 fee provides access to Taconic region lakes and ponds

GETTING THERE

Lake Taghkanic Access. From I-84, go 41.3 miles north on the Taconic Parkway, and turn right on Lake Taghkanic Road. Go to East Beach; when the main road goes left, continue straight to the parking lot. (42° 5.437′ N, 73° 42.002′ W)

Rudd Pond Access. From Lake Taghkanic, go southeast on Route 82 to Ancramdale, and turn left on Route 3. Where Route 3 bears left, go straight on Over Mountain Road. At the fork, go left downhill, and turn right (south) on Route 22. After crossing Dutchess County line, go 0.9 mile, turn left on Route 62, and follow signs to Rudd Pond. Enter the park and pay to use the access, or continue south on Route 22 and put in at the pull-off. (41° 58.682′ N, 73° 30.443′ W)

TRIP 15: LAKE TAGHKANIC AND RUDD POND

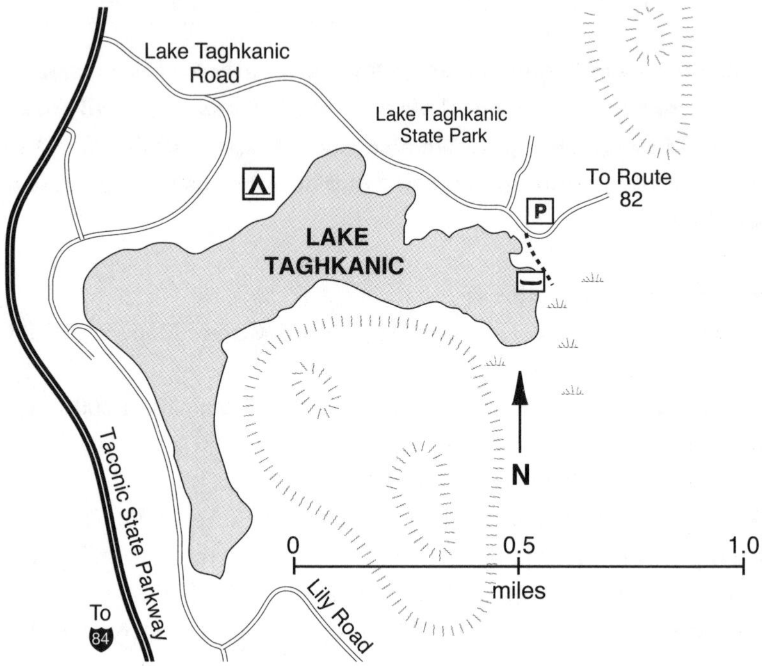

WHAT YOU'LL SEE

Lake Taghkanic

This small but popular park, just off the Taconic Parkway in southern Columbia County, draws many recreation-starved downstaters. A popular picnic and day-use area for swimming, hiking, biking, and boating, it also includes a campground.

We paddled here just before Labor Day as fall colors were starting to creep into the hillsides; people crowded the park, trying to get in that last bit of warm, sunny activity before winter's onslaught. Still, we paddled alone most of the time. The lake's small size means that even a leisurely paddle will only take about an hour, so this park remains mainly recreation and family oriented. It's a great place to teach children about plants and wildlife and, in the protected waters, how to paddle a canoe or kayak.

We especially enjoyed studying the oaks and found five of the twelve species that grow in downstate New York: red, white, scarlet, pin, and chestnut. We did not see the other seven—bur, post, swamp white, chinkapin, bear, southern red, and black—but it would be interesting to try to find all of them.

TRIP 15: LAKE TAGHKANIC AND RUDD POND

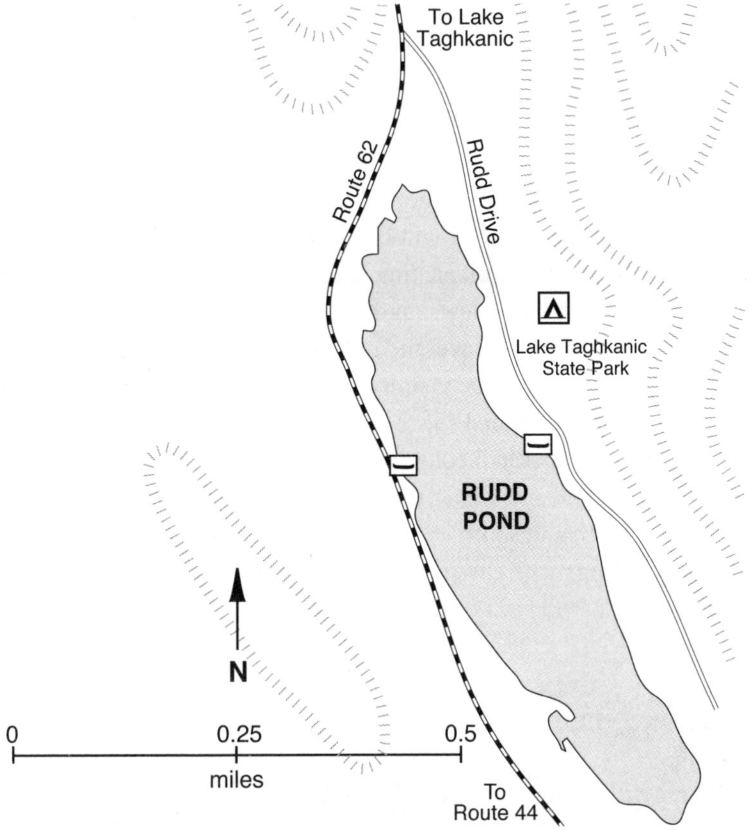

Biologists theorize that oaks evolved millions of years ago in Mexico—which harbors 150 species—and radiated outward. The United States overall has about 50 species, with fewer and fewer as you approach the Northeast. Oaks fall into two major groups, red and white. The main differences: red oak leaf tips have bristles, and white oak leaf tips are rounded; white oak acorns mature in one year, but red oak acorns hang on for two years. Trees usually bear heavy acorn crops on a two- to four-year rotation, and these seeds serve as an important food source for squirrels, wild turkeys, grouse, black bears, deer, wood ducks, and small mammals.

When we paddled here, shoreside black gum trees had started to turn a brilliant scarlet, which they do before other hardwoods begin to turn. We also spotted hickory, northern white cedar, and red and sugar maples, although none of these nearly as frequently as oaks. On the lake's marshy east end, we found large patches of water shield, yellow pondlily, American white waterlily, pickerelweed, purple loosestrife, buttonbush, fanwort, and pondweed. On other trips here, we saw pileated woodpeckers, Baltimore orioles, and beavers.

Rudd Pond

If Lake Taghkanic is too crowded, you can also camp and paddle at Rudd Pond, a much smaller and more out-of-the-way member of the Taconic State Park group near the Connecticut border. Because Route 62 travels down the western shore, paddling here will not be a wilderness experience, but this is a pleasant place for camping, picnicking, and relaxing among towering white pines, spreading weeping willows, and tall black locusts. Oak, paper birch, hickory, tamarack, Norway spruce, and red pine round out the tree population. More so than most areas in the vicinity, this location boasts truly huge trees of all the previously mentioned species. The hillsides forested with deciduous trees glowed brightly with fall colors when we returned to the pond in mid-October—a month and a half later than our first visit.

The marshy north and south ends of Rudd Pond sport a blanket of aquatic vegetation, including pickerelweed, American white waterlily, yellow pondlily, pondweed, cattails, *Phragmites*, purple loosestrife, and more.

Canoes and rowboats share the access on Lake Taghkanic.

16 | Catskill Creek and RamsHorn Marsh

The creeks and marsh described here provide hours of paddling, either along tree-lined shores or back into the depths of the marsh. Expect to see muskrats, beavers, waterfowl, marsh birds, aquatic vegetation, and varied shrubs and trees. You may also see bald eagles and river otters.

Location: Catskill
Maps: *New York Atlas & Gazetteer*, Map 98: B3; USGS Cementon, Hudson South
Length: Catskill Creek, 4 miles; RamsHorn Creek, 1.5 miles; Dubois Creek, 1 mile; all one way
Time: 5 hours
Habitat Type: Tidal, freshwater rivers, marshland with trees; little development
Camping and Trails: Appendix A (46, 49, 115, 117, 119, 121); trails, RamsHorn-Livingston Sanctuary (co-owned by Audubon Society and Scenic Hudson), scenichudson.org/parks/ramshornlivingston
Take Note: Motors at mouth of Catskill Creek; RamsHorn Creek access from Hudson River; novice paddlers should avoid the Hudson and always wear personal flotation devices (PFDs)

GETTING THERE

From I-87, Exit 21, turn left, go 1.7 miles east on Main Street, and veer right for 0.1 mile (1.8 miles) onto Maple Avenue. Go 0.2 mile (2.0 miles), and turn left on West Main Street. Go 0.3 mile (2.3 miles), just past the far end of the Catskill Middle School parking lot on the left. (42° 13.134′ N, 73° 52.105′ W)

WHAT YOU'LL SEE

Starting in the Hudson River town of Catskill, we found three wonderful places to paddle. Paddling left up Catskill Creek, after 1.5 miles you come to a beautiful falls, with water cascading down over a series of broken ledges. We saw flocks of migrating Canada geese in this broad waterway with tree-lined shores. By carrying up through the middle of the creek, you can paddle beyond, farther up Catskill Creek or up Kaaterskill Creek. At the start, we noticed many Norway maples along the banks.

TRIP 16: CATSKILL CREEK AND RAMSHORN MARSH

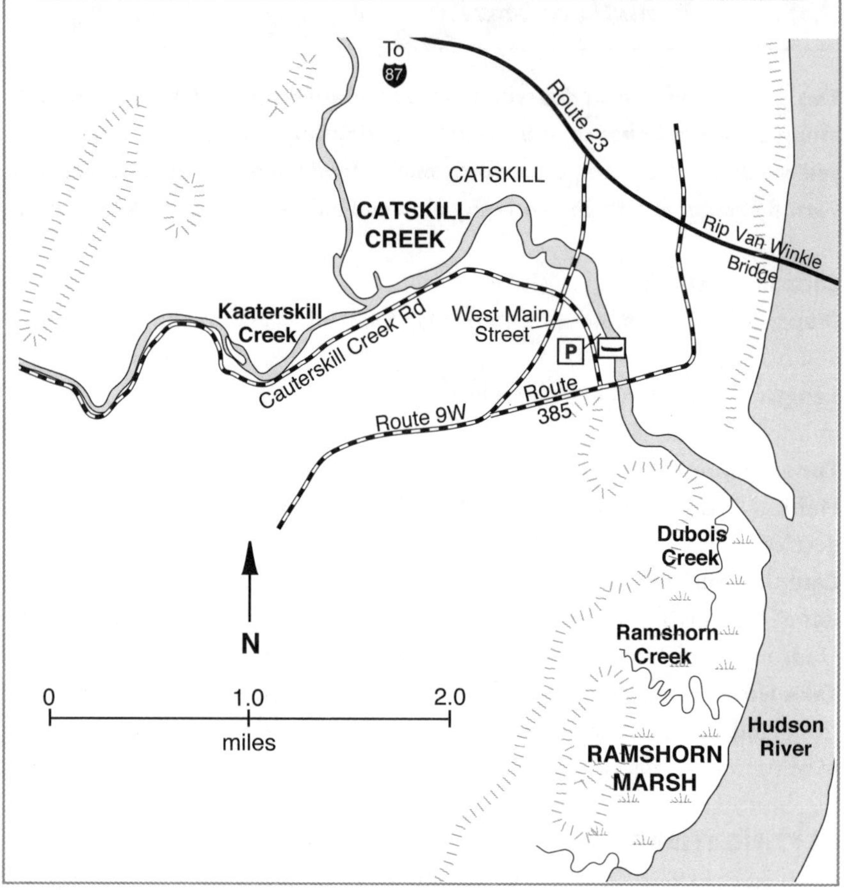

Paddling downstream instead, you pass through a boat basin. In less than a mile, after clearing the last boat dock on the right, turn right into the mouth of Dubois Creek, which penetrates RamsHorn Marsh for about a mile. Along this route, we saw beaver during the day, iris in bloom, arrowhead, alder, dogwood, dwarf red maple, and myriad other shrubs. The creek starts out wide and gradually narrows; near the end, we had to pull ourselves under overhanging branches as we winched our boats around tight turns.

Back out on the Catskill, you can paddle to its mouth and head downstream on the Hudson, noting the *Phragmites* and cattails growing along the marshy shore on the right. About three-quarters of a mile south of Catskill Creek, turn into RamsHorn Creek, which starts out 50 feet wide and narrows as it proceeds inland. The 612-acre RamsHorn-Livingston Sanctuary, operated by

Flowering dogwood thrives in moist soil.

Scenic Hudson (a land trust) and the National Audubon Society, protects the Hudson River's largest forested tidal swamp. The habitat here mimics that of Dubois Creek, although with a wider and longer waterway.

We saw lots of beaver sign; it probably would be easy to spot them here in the evening. As we paddled back into the marsh's far reaches, exploring the many side channels, wood ducks erupted from the water when we emerged around tight turns. We also saw red-bellied woodpeckers, cedar waxwings, bluebirds, song sparrows, black-capped chickadees, tufted titmice, kingfishers, and great blue herons.

We saw several flocks of yellow-rumped warblers, although other warbler species had already migrated south. Yellow-rumped warblers winter farther north than any other warbler—as far as coastal Maine. Indeed, most warblers winter in the Caribbean or Mexico. The yellow-rumped remains one of the most abundant warblers because it has adapted to a wide array of food sources. Most warblers eat mainly insects and spiders. Some, such as the black-and-white warbler, just glean insects from main branches, while others, such as the American redstart, engage in active flycatching. The yellow-rumped warbler does both, but more importantly, it readily switches diet in winter to abundant bayberries that grow along the coast. It also eats other berries, including poison ivy, viburnum, mountain ash, honeysuckle, and eastern red cedar—and probably lots more.

17 | Basher Kill

The Bashakill Wildlife Management Area protects a huge freshwater marsh, along with hillsides clad in deciduous trees. In this wildlife haven with no motors allowed, you will likely see ducks, geese, bald eagles, ospreys, great blue herons, and many songbirds. You might also find white-tailed deer, beavers, otters, and muskrats.

Location: Mamakating
Maps: *New York Atlas & Gazetteer*, Map 101: E10; USGS Yankee Lake
Area: 1,920 acres (3,107 acres in the wildlife management area)
Time: 5 hours
Habitat Type: Large, shallow marsh; meandering, open channel; no development
Fish: Largemouth bass, pickerel (see fish advisories, Appendix C)
Camping and Trails: Appendix A (37, 38, 39); trails, Bashakill Wildlife Management Area, dec.ny.gov/outdoor/82727.html
Take Note: Gasoline motors prohibited

GETTING THERE

Northern Access. From Route 17, Exit 113, go south on Route 209 for 1.2 miles to the access on the left. We prefer the bisecting bridge or southern accesses, described below. (41° 32.822′ N, 74° 30.801′ W)

Haven Road Bridge Access. From Route 17, Exit 113, go south on Route 209 for 1.9 miles, and turn left on Haven Road. Go 0.3 mile (2.2 miles) to the parking area on the left; launch across the road. (41° 32.262′ N, 74° 31.167′ W) Alternatively, go 0.2 mile (2.4 miles) farther to the bridge (room for two small cars). (41° 32.155′ N, 74° 31.023′ W)

Southern Access. From the bridge, continue 0.4 mile (2.8 miles), and turn right on South Road. Go 1.7 miles (4.5 miles) to the access on the right. (41° 30.999′ N, 74° 32.281′ W)

Waterfall Access. From the southern access, continue 0.5 mile (5.0 miles) south to the waterfall on the left. (41° 30.471′ N, 74° 32.649′ W) Another access is 0.9 mile (5.9 miles) south of the waterfall, where Pine Kill enters. (41° 29.937′ N, 74° 33.157′ W)

TRIP 17: BASHER KILL

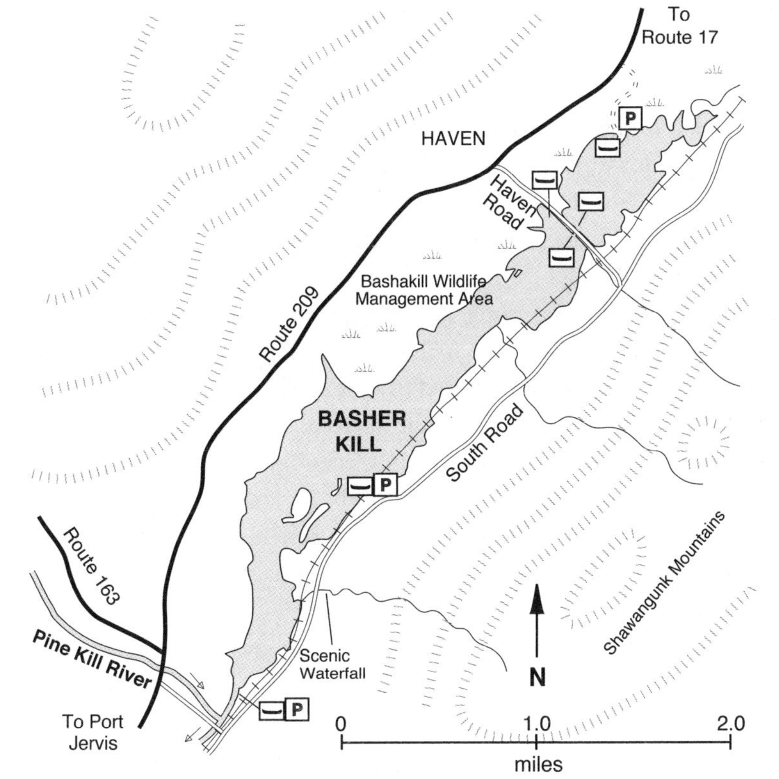

WHAT YOU'LL SEE

For observing wildlife near New York City, nothing beats Sullivan County's Bashakill Wildlife Management Area. The largest freshwater wetland in southeastern New York at 3,107 acres, Bashakill protects the marshland surrounding the Basher Kill River and the habitat of deer, grouse, wild turkey, fox, beaver, muskrat, raccoon, rabbit, skunk, mink, opossum, and waterfowl, particularly wood duck.

The middle section of the Shawangunk Mountains—the northern "Gunks" are famous with rock climbers and hikers—parallels Basher Kill's eastern shore, providing a scenic backdrop for paddlers and hikers alike. The western shore's beautiful hillsides dripped with fall colors in late October, the first time we paddled there. Since then, we have returned in spring to admire dogwood in bloom and in summer to watch ospreys dive for fish. We have seen many deer, muskrats, and wild turkeys, along with a few beavers. In the absence of gasoline motors, you can paddle among the islands and drowned timber for hours in peace. For hiking, we recommend the perimeter trails—one follows the historic Delaware and Hudson (D & H) Canal along the western shore, and the other proceeds over a long-abandoned railroad grade along the eastern shore.

The Department of Environmental Conservation enhances nesting success of three bird species in particular by erecting nesting platforms for osprey and nesting boxes for wood duck and bluebird. In addition to nesting populations, migrating wood ducks stop here to fatten up on acorns and aquatic plants, and flocks of Canada geese from the far north honk from the marsh. In October, at the tail end of songbird migration, in one mixed foraging flock, we saw chipping, white-throated, song, and fox sparrows; dark-eyed juncos, yellow-rumped warblers, a tail-bobbing palm warbler, and ruby-crowned kinglets. We also spotted hermit thrushes, tufted titmice, and eastern phoebes.

Red and white oaks dominate the surrounding high ground, their leaves turning a burnished red in the fall air. Occasional sugar and red maples add orange and red accents, while aspen and birch lend a vibrant yellow against a backdrop of dark green conifers. Besides providing food for wood ducks, oaks and beeches nourish wild turkeys and abundant gray squirrels. Waterlilies and other aquatic plants cover the reservoir's shallow surface, and alien invader purple loosestrife vies with buttonbush and arrowhead to dominate the shallows. Muskrat homes—small vegetation piles—dot the marsh. Along streams, muskrats burrow under roots in soft banks; in an area with abundant food but no banks, they resort to the vegetation piles.

Rising early morning mists reveal clumps of purple loosestrife, an invasive species.

In spring or if recent rains have fallen, a beautiful waterfall tumbles down out of the Shawangunks, cascading over ledges in three drops, through an overhanging canopy of lacy hemlock boughs, flowing into the reservoir's south end. You can easily see it from South Road as you approach.

18 | Rio Reservoir

Long, narrow Rio Reservoir, surrounded by wooded hillsides and rocky shores, can provide exercise for paddlers who travel the reservoir's 3.6-mile length in both directions. Avoid paddling here under windy conditions. Expect to see bald eagles, Canada geese, great blue herons, and underwater Bryozoa colonies here.

Location: Deer Park, Forestburg, Lumberland
Maps: *New York Atlas & Gazetteer*, Map 101: E7 and Map 106: A2; USGS Highland Lake, Pond Eddy
Area: 435 acres
Time: 3 hours
Habitat Type: Deep, narrow reservoir
Fish: Largemouth and smallmouth bass, brown trout (see fish advisories, Appendix C; see specific advisory, health.ny.gov/environmental/outdoors/fish/health_advisories)
Camping: Appendix A (118, 120)
Take Note: Gasoline motors prohibited; on windy days, the gorge funnels wind; open April 1 to November 30

GETTING THERE

From I-84, Exit 1, go 2.2 miles west on Main Street/Route 6, and bear right on Routes 42 and 97, which run together for a few miles. Go 2.7 miles (4.9 miles), and veer right on Route 42. Go 6.1 miles (11.0 miles), and turn left on Old Plank Road. Go 0.7 mile (11.7 miles), and turn left on Rio Dam Road. After 1.2 more miles (12.9 miles), you'll reach the access on the left, just over the dam. (41° 28.679′ N, 74° 45.353′ W) Or put in at the northern access on Plank Road, 2.7 miles (14.4 miles) north of Rio Dam Road. (41° 31.300′ N, 74° 45.659′ W)

TRIP 18: RIO RESERVOIR

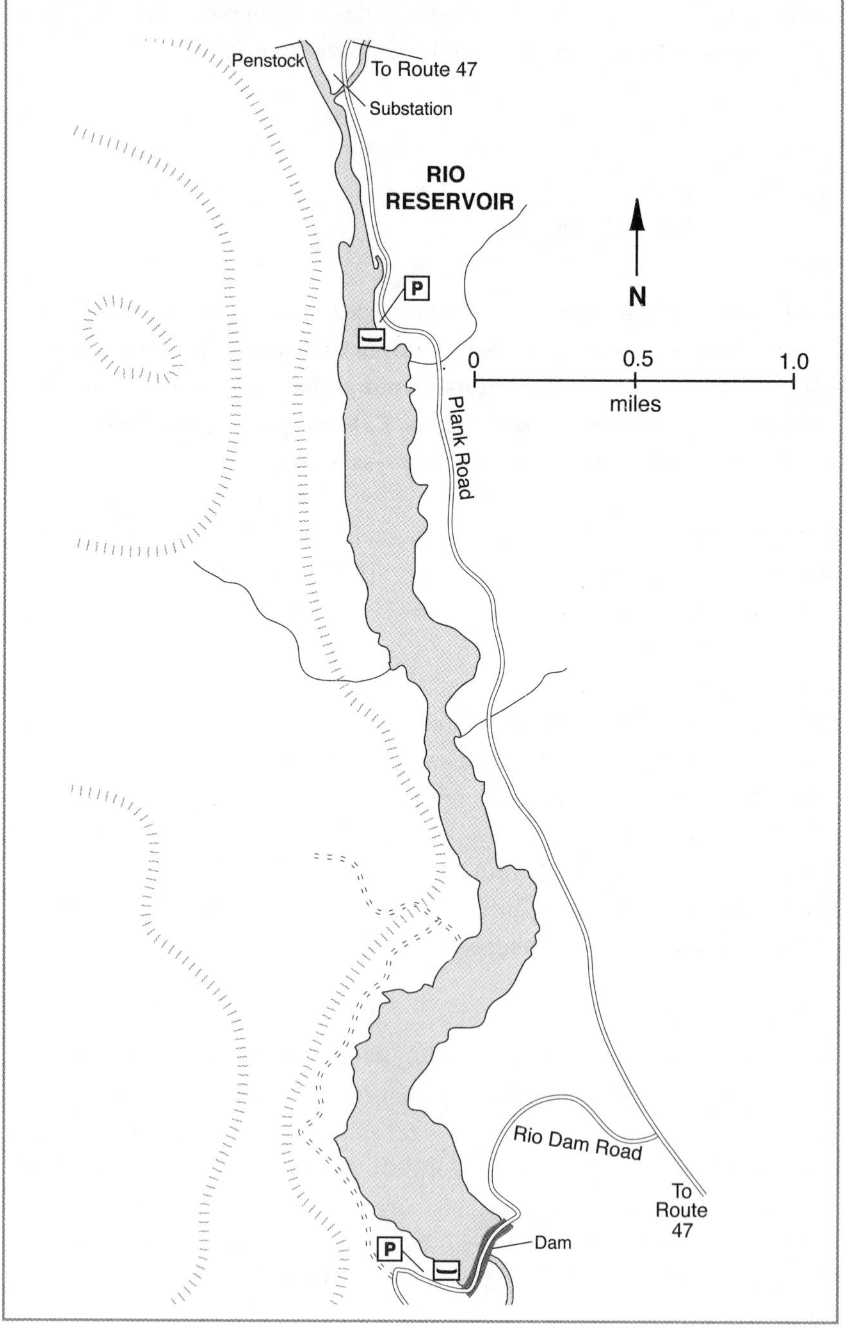

From Route 17, Exit 105A, go 9.6 miles south on Route 42, cross Route 43, and immediately turn right on Mill Road. Go 0.6 mile (10.2 miles), and turn left on Plank Road. Go 1.9 miles (12.1 miles) to the northern access on the right, or 2.7 miles (14.8 miles) farther to Rio Dam Road.

WHAT YOU'LL SEE

Rio (rhymes with "bio") Reservoir, the southernmost of three reservoirs that can be paddled on the Mongaup River near Monticello, New York, lies within the Mongaup Valley Wildlife Management Area, which provides protection for wintering bald eagles (see Mongaup Falls Reservoir, trip 19).

Rio Reservoir extends roughly 3.6 miles north to south, with several sweeping S-curves in the southern half. Maximum width reaches about a third of a mile. On a morning paddle during a sunny Labor Day weekend, only about a half dozen boats plied the water. On spring visits, we saw even fewer visitors.

Rio's exposed outcroppings and fairly uniform rocky shoreline rise steeply from the water, precluding marshy areas. Although hemlock dominates the banks, the hillsides support white pine, beech, black birch, ironwood, sassafras, shagbark hickory, red and sugar maples, and at least four oaks (red, white, chestnut, and scarlet). Although not as dense as on nearby Lake Superior, rhododendron grows in profusion along the shore and should be gorgeous during the late June or early July flowering season. A few weeks earlier, paddlers will be treated to blooming mountain laurel—a shorter, smaller-leaved member of the same heath family.

Look for roundish blobs growing on submerged branches—these Bryozoa, an animal phylum, grow in associated colonies like coral. Most Bryozoa live in salt water, but a few freshwater species--such as the *Pectinatella magnifica* growing here—occur in New York. Each knob on the globular mass represents an individual animal. Hairlike appendages filter food particles out of the water.

We spotted common mergansers, Canada geese, and great blue herons, among other bird species, and we saw some evidence of beavers but not the critters themselves.

From the northern access, you can paddle a little ways north, passing the remains of an old wooden structure for a gas pipeline that used to cross the reservoir. Beyond, the reservoir narrows into a rocky river section with quick water.

19 | Mongaup Falls Reservoir

Bald eagles are the main attraction at Mongaup Falls Reservoir. A pair usually nests here in spring and summer, while sometimes dozens fish here in winter on Mongaup's ice-free water. A variety of fish species inhabit this water, which also draws anglers.

Location: Forestburg, Lumberland
Maps: *New York Atlas & Gazetteer*, Map 101: E7; USGS Highland Lake
Area: 130 acres
Time: 2 hours
Habitat Type: Small, shallow reservoir with some marshy areas
Fish: Largemouth and smallmouth bass, pickerel, brown trout (see fish advisories, Appendix C)
Camping: Appendix A (118, 120)
Take Note: Gasoline motors prohibited; open April 1 to November 30; novice paddlers should avoid the inlet river

GETTING THERE

From I-84, Exit 1, go 2.2 miles west on Main Street/Route 6, and veer right on Routes 42 and 97, which run together for a few miles. Go 2.7 miles (4.9 miles), and turn right on Route 42. Go 11.0 miles (15.9 miles), and turn left on Route 43/Forestburgh Road. In 2.0 miles (17.9 miles), you'll arrive at the access on the left. (41° 33.213′ N, 74° 46.757′ W)

From Route 17, Exit 105A, go 9.6 miles south on Route 42, turn right on Route 43, and follow as above.

Winter Eagle-Watching Area. Go 0.3 mile past the access to the viewing area on the left. (41° 33.297′ N, 74° 47.090′ W)

WHAT YOU'LL SEE

Mongaup Falls Reservoir—a 2-mile-long, dammed-up section of the Mongaup River, upstream from Rio Reservoir (see trip 18)—feels much different from its southern neighbor. We prefer paddling this smaller, shallower body of water on windy days because surrounding hills seem to do a better job of shielding it.

At the reservoir's north end, you can paddle upstream for another half-mile on a usually quiet Mongaup River section. (*Caution*: The river can rise suddenly, carrying vastly more water, turning a relaxing paddle into a more

TRIP 19: MONGAUP FALLS RESERVOIR

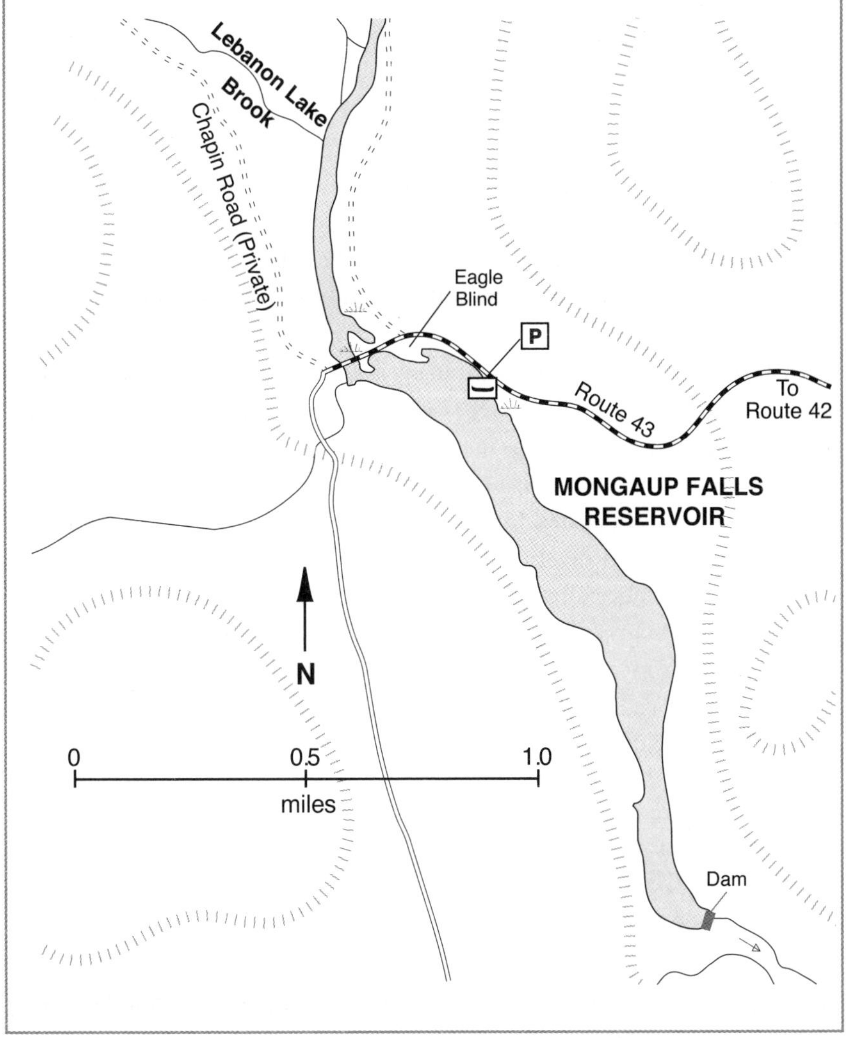

exciting quickwater adventure. When both dam turbines generate power, the flow increases from about 100 cubic feet per second to 1,600 cubic feet per second.) We paddled up to the inlet brook from Lebanon Lake; above there, exposed rocks and rapids blocked our way.

Mongaup Falls offers quite a bit of variety. Marshy areas contain all sorts of wetland plants (pickerelweed, bulrush, and sedge, for example). In the marsh just below the Route 43 bridge, we studied a well-camouflaged green heron before it flew. A few small patches of cattail marsh occur north of the bridge.

On the reservoir's eastern side—heavily wooded, except for a few stretches of marsh—white pine predominates, with oak, maple, beech, and birch mixed in. A few small, well-hidden cabins do not intrude on the wild feeling here.

Along the western shore's high-voltage power-line right of way, open fields extend down to the water's edge. Some fields consist mostly of hay-scented fern, which turns golden brown in early September. Closed gentian, cardinal flower, turtlehead, and false dragonhead grow along here as well, where their feet can remain moist. When a dropping water level exposes new ground during summer, gorgeous cardinal flower often springs up.

We saw Bryozoa colonies on most submerged branches, indicating fairly pure water. If you reach down into the water and touch a globular Bryozoa colony, it feels gelatinous.

In winter, Mongaup Falls draws as many as 150 bald eagles from the Northeast and Canada because the dam keeps water from freezing and the turbines kill some fish, leaving easy pickings for scavengers. An eagle-watching blind at the reservoir's north end allows visitors to observe these majestic creatures without disturbing them. Eagles had historically wintered here, but by the 1960s, the population had fallen drastically because of DDT poisoning. These raptors have made a dramatic comeback in New York, largely the result of a bald eagle reintroduction program begun in the Adirondacks in 1976.

You might also see eagles here during the rest of the year. Several pairs nest in the Mongaup Valley and along the Upper Delaware River. We saw pairs on both Cliff Lake and Toronto Reservoir.

20 | Cliff Lake

This out-of-the-way reservoir attracts few visitors, making it a delightful place to paddle. It's small, but because it's long and relatively narrow, you can paddle more than 4 miles of shoreline. As with other nearby reservoirs, watch for bald eagles; we saw three on our last visit.

Location: Bethel, Highland, Lumberland
Maps: *New York Atlas & Gazetteer*, Map 101: D7; USGS Highland Lake
Area: 200 acres
Time: 3 hours
Habitat Type: Small reservoir

TRIP 20: CLIFF LAKE

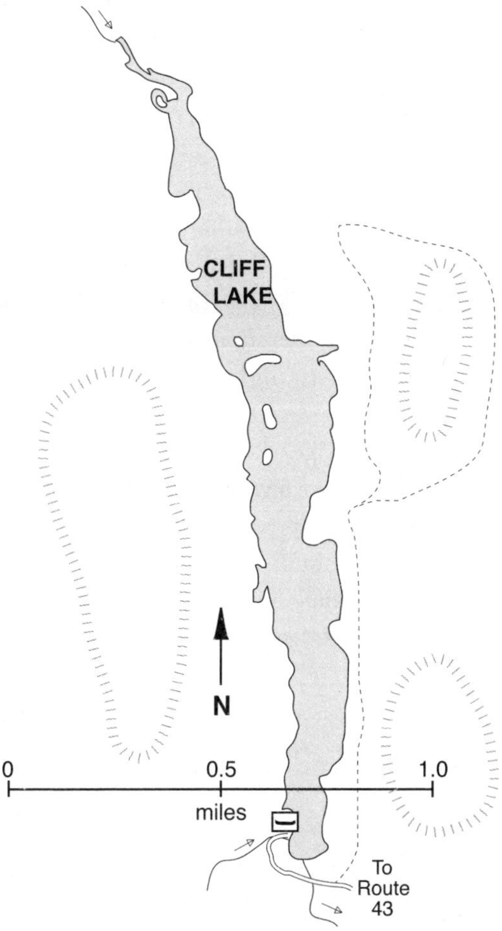

Fish: Largemouth and smallmouth bass, pickerel (see fish advisories, Appendix C)
Camping: Appendix A (118, 120)
Take Note: Gasoline motors prohibited; open May 1 to November 30

GETTING THERE

From the Mongaup Falls Reservoir access, continue 0.3 mile west on Route 43, turn right, and go 2.0 miles (2.3 miles) to the access. (41° 35.043′ N, 74° 47.701′ W)

WHAT YOU'LL SEE

Cliff Lake and the surrounding upland belong to Eagle Creek Renewable Energy, but the company allows public access from May 1 though November. We love paddling on this out-of-the-way lake, as it receives little recreational pressure.

The lake extends roughly 2 miles in a north-south orientation, with a maximum width of about a quarter-mile. When we visited in early September, the markedly low water level detracted significantly from the feel of the place. The level can be down several feet in very dry years, exposing quite a bit of shoreline. The sandy or pebbly shore suffers from erosion in some spots. The utility company usually keeps the water level higher—within 5 feet of 1,070 feet in elevation. Interestingly, Cliff Lake connects hydraulically with Swinging Bridge Reservoir through an underground aqueduct, so the two water levels remain equal. We recommend visiting before fall to improve chances of finding the reservoir full.

We saw a curious beaver lodge where the ever-industrious animals worked hard at "growing" the lodge downward, trying to keep it underwater as the lake's level dropped. Given the apparent age of some of the lodge's material, it appeared that the structure, built into a fallen tree, holds firm through the seasonal water level fluctuation—the beavers must have weighted down the sticks with stones to keep the lodge from floating away.

Beaver extended a large lodge downward as the lake level dropped.

When we hiked up to Cliff Lake and around the reservoir, the meadows—some carpeted with ferns, some filled with shade-loving grasses or sedges—struck us as particularly gorgeous. They give the woods a very open, inviting feel. Sugar maple and white pine seem to be the dominant trees here, with beech scattered throughout. We also noted a few groves of red pine.

Several islands appear just above the lake's midpoint. At the north end, we watched a number of plovers and sandpipers scurry over exposed mud flats, hunting for insects and crustaceans. Wilson's plover, looking somewhat like a killdeer but shorter and with only one neckband, was most common.

Also at the north end, we saw three bald eagles: two adults and a 3- or 4-year-old juvenile. Several eagle pairs now nest in Mongaup Valley (see trip 19).

BEAVER: WETLANDS ENGINEER

The beaver (*Castor canadensis*) is one of the most remarkable creatures found in New York's waters. Unlike most other animals, beavers actively modify their environment. The sole representative of the family Castoridae, this 30- to 100-pound rodent—the largest in North America—descends directly from a bear-sized ancestor that lived a million years ago.

Quietwater paddlers frequently see beaver dams and lodges, especially on more remote lakes and ponds. This industrious mammal uses branches pruned from streamside trees or downed timber to build these structures. In areas heavily frequented by humans, beavers work mostly under cover of darkness. In more remote, wild areas, however, many beavers build in broad daylight. We mention in our descriptions where we have seen beavers abroad during the day.

Beavers build dams to raise water levels, providing the resident colony with access to trees growing farther away. The deeper water also allows beavers to cache branches underwater for later retrieval, even when thick layers of ice cover their winter stores. They also dig small canals through marshes and meadows to transport branches. Just as humans find paddling a boat easier than carrying it, beavers prefer swimming with a branch—taking advantage

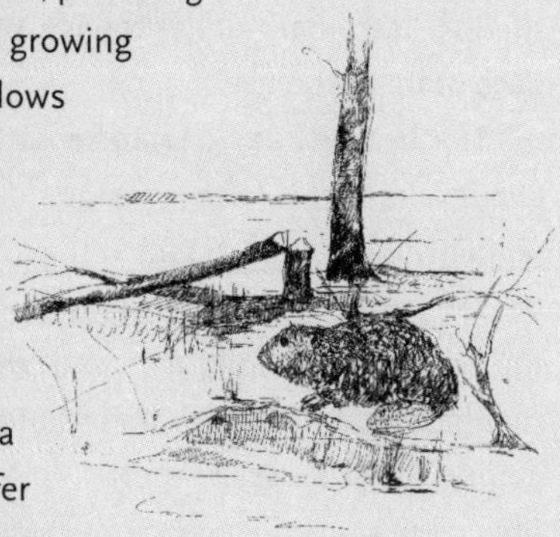

of water's buoyancy—to carrying it overland. They usually prune off leafy twigs to reduce drag.

Studies show that the sound of flowing water guides beavers in their dam building—they jam sticks into the dam where they hear the gurgle of water. In one experiment, researchers played a tape of gurgling water; beavers responded by jamming sticks into locations that emanated sound, even though no water actually flowed there. Beaver dams can be more than 10 feet high and hundreds of feet long. The largest dam ever recorded, near the present town of Berlin, New Hampshire, spanned 4,000 feet and created a lake with 40 lodges!

Beaver dams benefit many species, providing important habitat for waterfowl, fish, moose, muskrats, and other animals. Plus, the dams provide flood control, minimize erosion along stream banks, increase aquifer recharge, and improve water quality, both by allowing silt to settle out and by providing biological filtration through aquatic plants. Scientists credit beavers with creating much of America's best farmland by damming watercourses, thus allowing nutrient-rich silt to accumulate over many years. As the ponds fill in, meadows form.

The beaver lodge includes an underwater entrance and usually two platforms: a main floor about 4 inches above the water level and a sleeping shelf another 2 inches higher. Beavers may construct the lodge in a pond's center but more commonly site it on the edge. Before winter onset, they cover much of the lodge with mud, which they carry on their broad tails while swimming. The mud freezes to provide an almost impenetrable fortress. The only predator that can get in is the river otter, which can swim through the underwater entrance. Beavers leave the peak more permeable for ventilation.

Near the lodge, in deep water, beavers store up a winter's worth of branches in an underwater food cache. They jam branches butt-first into the mud to keep them under the ice and then swim out under the ice to bring back branches to eat.

The beaver has adapted remarkably well to its aquatic lifestyle. It has two layers of fur: long, silky guard hairs and a dense, woolly underfur. By regularly grooming this fur with a comblike split toenail to keep it oiled, the beaver ensures that water seldom totally wets its skin. Special valves keep the beaver's nose and ears shut underwater, and special skin folds in the mouth enable it to gnaw underwater and carry branches in its teeth without getting water down its throat. Fully webbed toes on the beaver's back feet provide propulsion, and the tail acts as a rudder, helping the beaver swim in a straight line when dragging a large branch. Its respiratory and circulatory systems have adapted to enable the beaver to stay underwater for up to 15 minutes. Finally, as with other rodents, its teeth grow constantly and remain sharp through use.

Beavers generally mate for life and maintain an extended family structure. Young stay with their parents for two years, so both yearlings and the current year's kits live with the parents in the lodge. Females usually bear two—sometimes three—kits between April and June. Born fully furred with eyes open, beavers can walk and swim almost immediately, although they rarely leave the lodge until they are at least a month old. Yearlings and both parents bring food to the kits, and yearlings help with dam and lodge construction.

The demand for beaver pelts, as much as any other factor, prompted early European exploration of North America. Trappers nearly exterminated the beaver by the late 1800s, but last-minute legislative protection in the 1890s saved it from extinction. In New York State, only one known active beaver colony—plus a few scattered individuals—remained in 1904. Then began what certainly must be one of the most successful endangered species reintroduction programs ever.

The state released six beavers in 1904 in the Old Forge area of the Adirondacks. In 1906, the state released another 25 animals imported from Yellowstone Park, and landowners released 14 more on nearby private lands. By 1915, that tiny population had expanded to an estimated 15,000 to 20,000 animals. By 1924, the state opened a limited trapping season on beavers. In 1994, the Department of Environmental Conservation estimated the New York beaver population to be 93,000 individuals in nearly 18,000 colonies.

As you paddle the shorelines of lakes or quiet rivers, keep an eye out for telltale beaver signs, including gnaw marks on trees, distinctive conical stumps of cut trees, canals leading off into the marsh, alder branches trimmed back along narrow passages, and well-worn paths coming up to the water's edge, where beavers have dragged more distant branches to the water.

We see beavers most often in late evening or early morning. Paddle quietly toward a beaver lodge around dusk. Wait patiently, and you will likely see the animals emerge for evening feeding and perhaps a bit of construction work.

21 | Toronto Reservoir

Toronto Reservoir is popular with anglers and sports a well-used beach on the east end. Because of winter drawdown, we prefer to paddle here in fall. Expect to see bald eagles, Canada geese, common mergansers, and white-tailed deer. We have spotted wild turkeys here, as well.

Location: Bethel
Maps: *New York Atlas & Gazetteer*, Map 101: D6, D7; USGS Highland Lake, White Lake
Area: 834 acres
Time: 4 hours
Habitat Type: Reservoir
Fish: Largemouth and smallmouth bass, pickerel, walleye (see fish advisories, Appendix C)
Camping: Appendix A (118, 120)
Take Note: Maximum boat size 20 feet; personal watercraft prohibited; one reservoir section off-limits

GETTING THERE

From Route 17, Exit 104, in Monticello, go 7.5 miles west on Route 17B, and turn left on Route 55. Continue 1.9 miles (9.4 miles), turn left on Moscoe Road, and go 0.8 mile (10.2 miles) to the access. (41° 38.354′ N, 74° 51.018′ W)

At times of low water, you can launch at the Toronto Reservoir dam, reached via Pine Grove Road from the hamlet of Smallwood. (41° 37.429′ N, 74° 49.711′ W)

WHAT YOU'LL SEE

Visit Toronto Reservoir early in the season. The reservoir typically gets drawn down later, exposing hundreds of feet of ugly, muddy shoreline. In winter 2010, it was drawn down an incredible 45 feet. Under provisions of recent federal relicensing of the dams now owned by Eagle Creek Renewable Energy, summer drawdown has become less extreme.

People use the reservoir primarily for fishing. The chain pickerel on New York's list of freshwater fishing records (8 pounds, 1 ounce) was caught on Toronto Reservoir in 1965 and remains one of the longest-standing entries on the list.

TRIP 21: TORONTO RESERVOIR

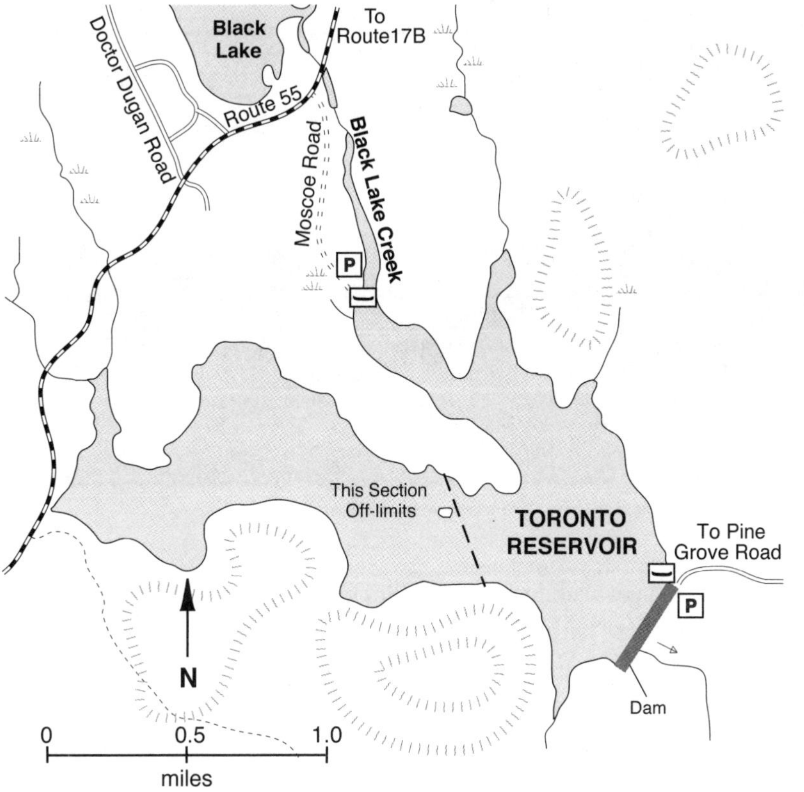

The Iroquois Hunting & Fishing Club owns roughly half of Toronto Reservoir's fairly large surface area and has posted it off-limits to the public. Large shoreline signs and several floating buoys mark this division. The club controls surface water access under an agreement with Rockland Light & Power (today, Orange & Rockland), the utility that built the dam in the late 1920s. Because the reservoir inundated land owned by the club, the utility granted the club exclusive hunting and fishing rights on that portion of the reservoir.

Toronto's rocky shoreline sports exposed outcroppings of a sedimentary, shale-like rock. Grasses and small shrubs prevail, with woodland extending away from the shore. Some tall white pines emerge above the beech-maple forest canopy. Dense groves of hemlock occur here and there, along with scattered rhododendrons in the understory.

Half a dozen deer fed on grasses along the higher banks when we visited in early morning, as mists still swirled above the reservoir. In the water, a small

A female common merganser casts a wary eye in our direction.

flock of Canada geese and several families of common mergansers hunted for food. On other trips here, we saw flocks of wild turkeys.

Near the reservoir's midpoint, we heard a distinctive raptor call and spotted a bald eagle pair sitting side by side on an oak branch. Further scanning with binoculars turned up a juvenile in a tree nearby. We observed these majestic birds for some time and witnessed a rare treat. After a while the immature eagle took off and began flying above the water in search of fish. Shortly, one of the adults joined it for what was almost certainly a fishing lesson. As we watched, the two birds made dozens of passes over the same section of water, each time dropping down and dipping feet into the water. Several times they landed on the nearby shore. Eventually, the adult caught a small fish, and the two flew off—likely to tell stories about the big one that got away.

Bald eagles, which have long wintered near the Mongaup River dams, recently resumed nesting here, as well. To protect bald eagle wintering grounds, in 1986 the state purchased 6,000 acres along the Mongaup River from Orange & Rockland Utilities and protected another 6,000 acres through easements. For more on bald eagles, see trip 19: Mongaup Falls Reservoir on page 76 and "Bald Eagle: National Bird Back from the Brink," on page 117.

22 | Lake Superior

Lake Superior harbors rafts of marshland plants, and this part of the lake is a great place to study them. But the giant stands of rhododendron—the largest we've seen in New York—would be worth a trip in late June and early July. We saw a sora rail here; expect to spot other marshland species too.

Location: Bethel
Maps: *New York Atlas & Gazetteer*, Map 101: C6, D6; USGS Lake Huntington, White Lake
Area: 188 acres
Time: 4 hours
Habitat Type: Small, shallow, weedy pond
Fish: Largemouth bass, pickerel (see fish advisories, Appendix C)
Camping: Appendix A (118, 120)
Information: Lake Superior State Park, parks.ny.gov/parks/87/details.aspx
Take Note: Gasoline motors prohibited; entrance fee

GETTING THERE

From Route 17, Exit 104, in Monticello, go 9.3 miles west on Route 17B, and turn left on Doctor Duggan Road. Go 1.5 miles (10.8 miles) south to the access at Lake Superior State Park. (41° 39.683′ N, 74° 52.192′ W)

WHAT YOU'LL SEE

The bucolic, rolling countryside of Bethel rocked to a different tune in the summer of 1969. The Woodstock Music Festival, held just a mile from Lake Superior on Max Yasgur's farm, drew several hundred thousand participants. Though the overflow crowd doubtlessly affected the site heavily, we could find only one hint there of this historic event: reference to the festival on wrappers of locally made ice-cream bars sold at a concession stand.

Lake Superior offers a very pleasant spot for a half-day paddle, mainly because of gasoline motor prohibition. Thick mats of aquatic plants populate the extensive marshy areas at the north and south ends of this highly productive pond. At the south end, a long outlet channel stretches almost a half-mile toward Black Lake. In spring, you should be able to paddle this without difficulty, but

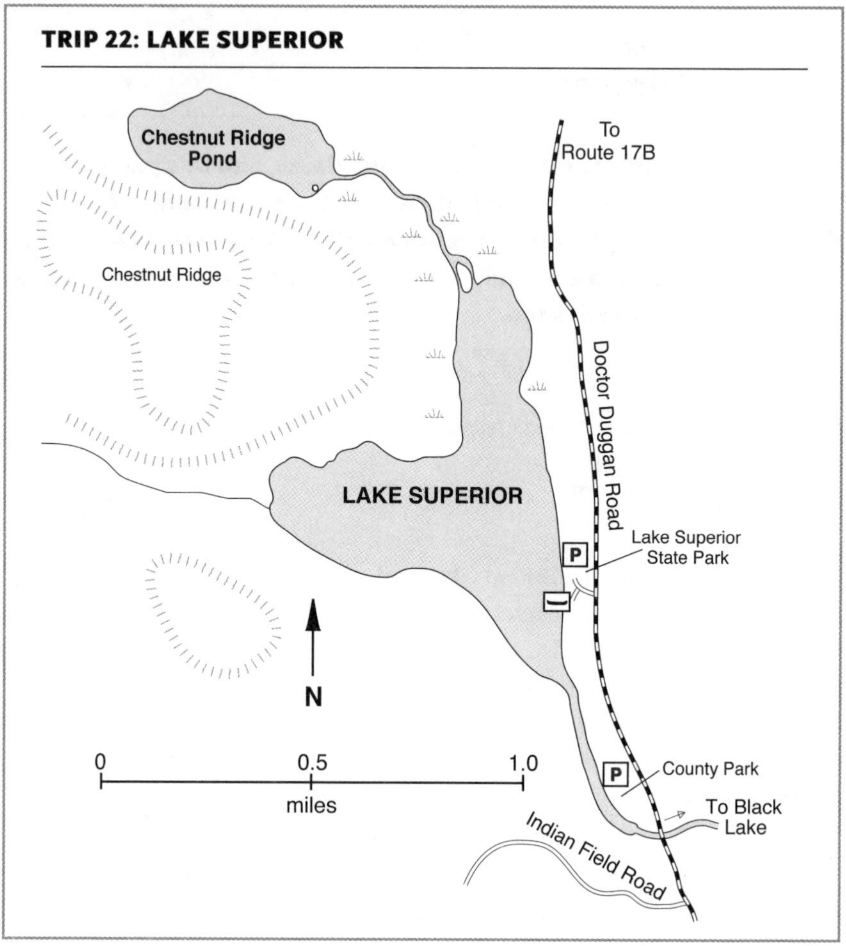

by late summer, it becomes nearly impenetrable, choked with pickerelweed, bulrush, waterlily, and sedge.

The marshy north end, very different ecologically, harbors typical swamp vegetation: red maple, buttonbush, leatherleaf, blueberry, royal fern, swamp rose, and swamp loosestrife. We had hoped to paddle up into Chestnut Ridge Pond, about a half-mile north, but try as we might, we could not penetrate the dense growth. It might be possible—although unlikely—to wend your way through in spring with a bit higher water level.

Even in late summer, however, we could explore a little way into the swamp. After a number of false starts, we managed to squeeze in 50 or 100 yards, where we sighted a sora rail, a small, elusive marsh bird, sometimes heard but rarely seen. We sat still for about half an hour as it darted in and out of view a mere 10 feet away. We recognized this brownish bird by its short bill, its triangular

Look for buttonbush, with its spherical flowers and seed heads, at Lake Superior's marshy north end.

cocked tail, and its greenish legs with striations above and very long toes below. We also saw evidence of beaver.

At the pond's northeastern tip, look for a large stand of tamarack, with delicate, feathery needles that turn yellow and drop in autumn. More common in northern New York, this species typifies the northern fen because it can become established in saturated soils—even on floating peat mats.

Waterlilies—American white waterlily, yellow pondlily, and water shield—abound. Typically, emergent plants occur along the shore, including bur-reed and pickerelweed, and then a fringe of floating waterlilies lies slightly farther out. You can pretty well judge the water depth by the plants; most aquatic plants cannot grow in more than 4 feet of water. In contrast with the mucky-bottomed marshy areas, much of the pond has a sandy bottom, providing good habitat for freshwater mussels, which occur here in abundance.

Ferns, club mosses, and wildflowers abound in the fairly open woods beneath a canopy of sugar maple, yellow birch, cherry, beech, red oak, hemlock, and white pine. Rhododendron grows in abundance, thicker here than we have seen on any other lake in the state. Visit in late June or early July, and you should be treated to rhododendron in bloom. It is thickest along the eastern shore, just north of the access, and directly across from the access along the southwestern shore. At one spot on the eastern shore, a network of tunnels through tall rhododendron groves extends away from the lake.

2 | CENTRAL NEW YORK

This region provides nine paddling opportunities, more than half on slow-flowing streams. You can visit historic places, such as Sangerfield River in Ninemile Swamp—where the outlaw Loomis Gang operated for nearly 100 years—or the original Erie Canal. We chose an 8-mile section of the canal, but one could continue for many miles beyond to the east. Three of the bodies of water are named Fish Creek: one flows into Saratoga Lake near Albany; one flows into Oneida Lake in the middle of the state; and the third, the Fish Creek West Branch, flows for many miles and then empties into the main branch that flows into Oneida Lake.

We also include the headwaters of the Susquehanna River as it flows out of Otsego Lake. The meandering channel flows through farmland, but the generally shaded banks harbor plentiful wildlife. Out in the northwest tip of this region lies the large Salmon River Reservoir at nearly 2,700 acres, the source of water for the aptly named Salmon River that supports large runs of Chinook and coho salmon coming up out of Lake Ontario.

23 | Grafton Lakes and Dunham Reservoir

We include four small ponds and Dunham Reservoir here. On Dunham, you can explore the inlet stream for about a half-mile. Undeveloped woods surrounds the water, and this is a good place for on-site camping for families. Wildlife includes ospreys, mallards, Canada geese, and beavers.

Location: Grafton
Maps: *New York Atlas & Gazetteer*, Map 67: E8; USGS Berlin, Grafton
Area: Long Pond, 113 acres; Second Pond, 29 acres; Mill Pond, 19 acres; Shaver Pond, 45 acres; Dunham Reservoir, 98 acres
Time: 6 hours
Habitat Type: Small, shallow ponds
Fish: Largemouth and smallmouth bass in Second and Mill ponds and Dunham Reservoir, brook trout in Shaver Pond, brown and rainbow trout in Long and Second ponds (see fish advisories, Appendix C; see specific advisory, health.ny.gov/environmental/outdoors/fish/health_advisories)
Camping: Grafton Lakes State Park (on-site), parks.ny.gov/parks/53/details.aspx
Take Note: No gasoline motors

GETTING THERE

Dunham Reservoir Accesses. From Troy, go east on Route 2 to the junction with Route 278, and then continue 5.4 miles on Route 2 before turning right on Dunham Road. Go 0.8 mile (6.2 miles) to a gate. Park and carry down to the reservoir's western end. To reach the eastern end, go back to Route 2, and take three right turns to the access, just before the inlet stream. (42° 44.972′ N, 73° 29.008′ W)

Long, Second, and Shaver Ponds Accesses. At the intersection with Dunham Road, continue 1.4 miles (6.8 miles) east on Route 2 to the park entrance on the right (exit road crosses back over Route 2). Follow signs to the access to Long and Second ponds. For Shaver Pond, park in the main parking area, and take the trail from the southwest end of the parking lot. (42° 46.132′ N, 73° 27.964′ W)

TRIP 23: GRAFTON LAKES AND DUNHAM RESERVOIR

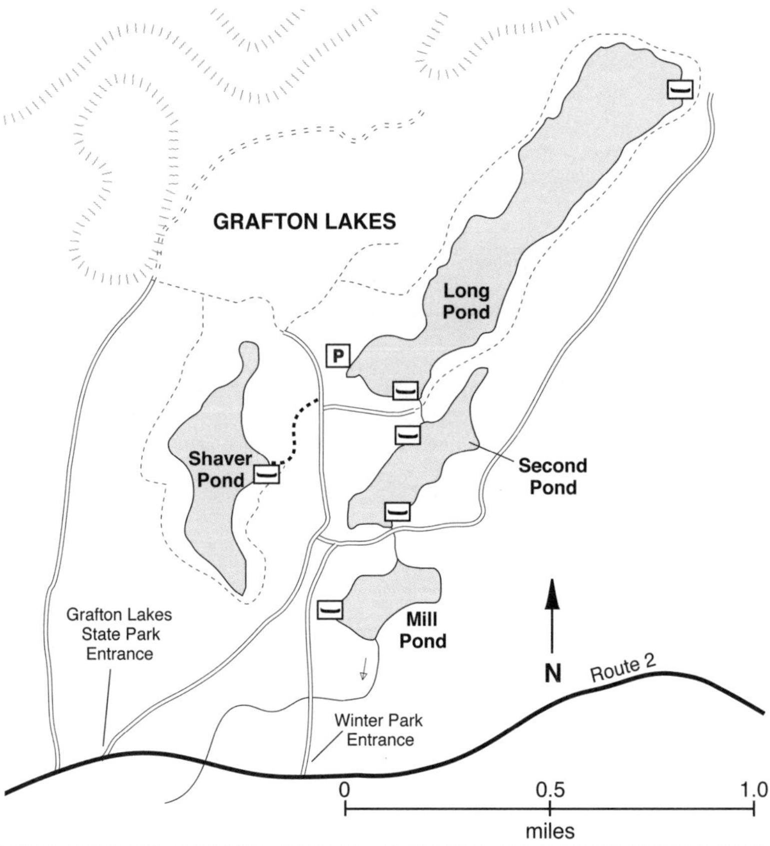

WHAT YOU'LL SEE

We like paddling here very much, and the park's close proximity to Albany and Troy draws many hikers and boaters. The large beach area on Long Pond gets crowded on sunny summer weekends, so we recommend visiting midweek or outside of the summer season.

We found the less-accessible Shaver Pond and Dunham Reservoir the most enjoyable to paddle. The easy half-mile carry into Shaver Pond follows a nature trail, suitable for a portage cart. Pick up a guide to the trees and other natural features of the Shaver Pond Trail. Dunham Reservoir, with extensive berming and a dam on the western end, supplied Troy's drinking water until the 1960s, when the reservoir area became a state park.

Explore the eastern end of Dunham Reservoir and the winding inlet stream, which you can travel for nearly a half-mile before reaching quick water and

TRIP 23: GRAFTON LAKES AND DUNHAM RESERVOIR

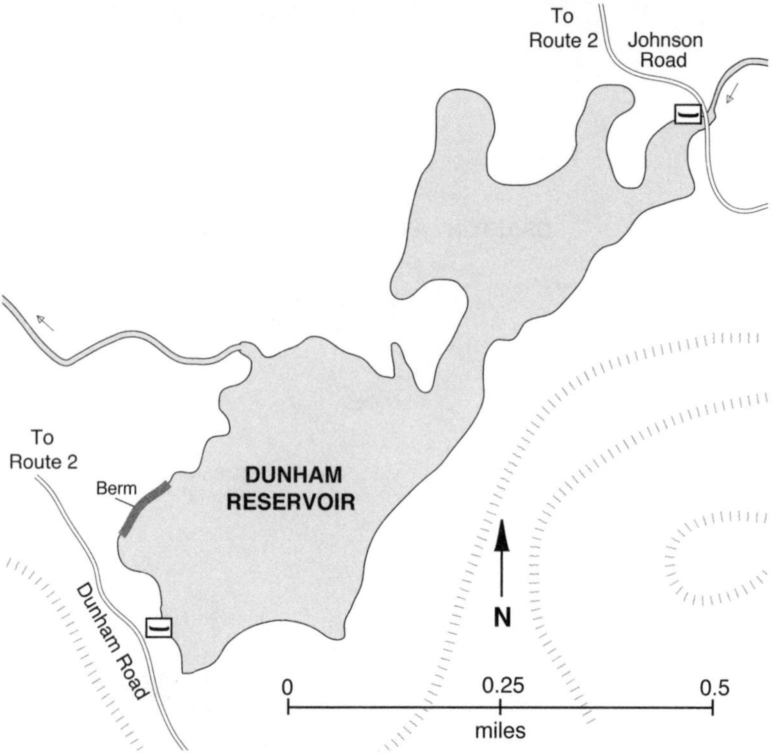

rocks. Paddling under the bridge, you enter an area thick with grasses, sedges, and other marsh plants. In late April as dusk approached, spring peepers regaled us and potential mates with their high-pitched song. Mallards glided about the shallows, Canada geese eyed us warily from a likely nesting site, kingfishers announced their presence with rattling calls as they flew ahead, and beavers swam about, harvesting the new growth of spring.

Several different species of club moss (*Lycopodium*) carpet extensive stretches of shoreline around most Grafton ponds. Among the most primitive vascular plants (those with xylem and phloem to conduct water and nutrients), several species look like tiny trees, thus the common names "ground pine" and "ground cedar." In the age of dinosaurs, club moss relatives grew as large as trees. Other species creep along the ground on long stems with short leaves extending from all sides. The soft, branching stems of staghorn club moss resemble the velvet of deer antlers in spring.

Getting ready to head out on our first paddle of the season in late April.

Deciduous woods surrounds these undeveloped ponds and includes red oak, beech, four different birches (paper, gray, black, yellow) black cherry, and red and sugar maples. Along the shore, blueberry bushes grow alongside taller shadbush, both providing edible berries in summer. We watched an osprey ply the water for its next meal, hovering, body tilted up slightly, wings flapping quickly to maintain a stationary position, peering into the water for fish.

A great place for families that enjoy both paddling and hiking, the park boasts several trails, including easy routes around Long and Shaver ponds.

24 | Fish Creek (Saratoga Lake)

We include two sections of Fish Creek here, one flowing out of Saratoga Lake, the other near the Hudson River. The section near the Hudson River is much quieter, which means you'll see a lot of birds and wildlife, potentially including great blue herons, waterfowl, kingfishers, and various songbirds. After paddling a mile or two away from Saratoga Lake, you should have the creek to yourself, except on busy summer weekends.

TRIP 23: GRAFTON LAKES AND DUNHAM RESERVOIR

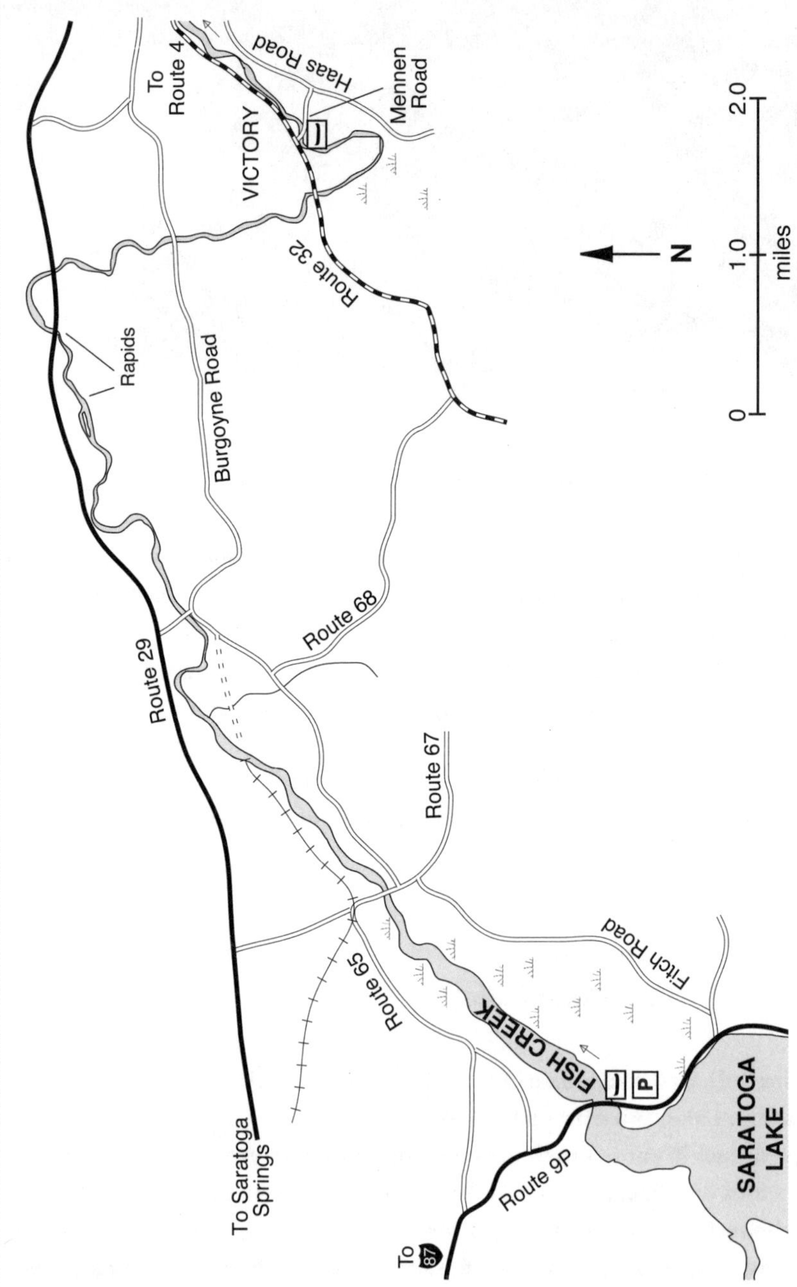

Location: Saratoga, Saratoga Springs
Maps: *New York Atlas & Gazetteer*, Map 66: A5, B5 and Map 67: A6, B6; USGS Quaker Springs, Schuylerville
Length: 11 miles one way
Time: 3 to 4 hours (each section)
Habitat Type: Slow-flowing stream
Fish: Largemouth and smallmouth bass, northern pike, walleye (see fish advisories, Appendix C)
Camping: Appendix A (41, 43, 74, 76)
Take Note: Motorboats near Saratoga Lake; access fee at Saratoga Lake

GETTING THERE

Victory Access. From Schuylerville, head south on Route 4, and turn right on Route 32. Go 1.3 miles, turn left on Mennen Road, cross the bridge, and park on the right. (43° 4.973′ N, 73° 35.906′ W)

Saratoga Lake Access. From I-87, Exit 14, go 2.0 miles east on Route 9P, and turn left into the access, just across the iron bridge. (43° 3.167′ N, 73° 43.271′ W)

WHAT YOU'LL SEE

A huge stand of willows and an RV park greet you at the northern outlet of Saratoga Lake as it forms Fish Creek. To avoid water-skiing and personal watercraft traffic, paddle Fish Creek away from Saratoga Lake, meandering toward the Hudson. Because of dams and occasional shallow rapids, you cannot paddle the whole way. We include two sections here, separated by a short section of rapids, dams, and falls. When faced with a lot of creek traffic, put in at Victory instead of at Saratoga Lake.

We have paddled here in spring and summer. Heading out from Saratoga Lake in midspring, we had to contend with a bass fishing tournament that had just begun. Dozens of 150-horsepower bass boats roared up and down the creek, rushing to the next hot spot, paradoxically putting the fish down from the commotion. Because these boats hydroplane at high speeds, displacing little water, they leave very little wake. To avoid being run over, we stayed along the edges and obviously did not see much wildlife in the heavily traveled portions of Fish Creek.

With springtime high water, however, we could paddle back into narrow creeks and coves, where we saw numerous basking turtles and surprised a male wood duck in full breeding plumage right beneath a nesting box. We also saw

Serviceberry blooms in early spring along the banks of Fish Creek.

mallards and black ducks—which sure beat the drowned tires, plastic buckets, and broken-up docks that mar Fish Creek's first few miles.

About 3.5 miles from Saratoga Lake, a pleasant little creek goes off to the right. Vines hang out over the water, and you have to thread your way through the narrow passage. We found many ducks feeding and an Eastern phoebe pair nesting under a low bridge. Cardinals called *bir-dy, bir-dy, bir-dy* from the thickets, and red-winged blackbirds sang *cong-ka-ree* from the reeds. Once we got this far from Saratoga Lake, the number of boats dwindled to zero.

The lower portion of Fish Creek, closer to the Hudson, also receives much less boat traffic. In contrast with Fish Creek's spilling over into broad marshes as it flows out of Saratoga Lake, the section near Victory flows between low banks. Dense grapevines drape streamside willows and silver maples all along the creek, closing in much of the canopy. Great blue herons, as many as three at a time, stood poised over the water on downed trees, taking flight as we passed. We threaded our way upstream through this maze, listening to cardinal, eastern phoebe, gray catbird, brown thrasher, and mockingbird songs from the undergrowth. Barn and tree swallows dipped to drink the water, a spotted sandpiper bobbed along the shore, and a belted kingfisher paced us up the waterway.

We had no trouble negotiating the midsummer current until we reached the first Route 29 bridge. Here, a small falls and rapids blocked our way upstream.

As we drifted lazily back down to Victory, listening to the haunting song of the mourning dove and the high-pitched *pee-o-wee* of the eastern wood-pewee, we reveled in the solitude so close to crowded Saratoga Lake.

25 | Susquehanna River

The Susquehanna River begins its 400-mile journey to Chesapeake Bay here, near Cooperstown and Otsego Lake. The river slowly meanders, remaining narrow compared with what it becomes far downstream. Expect to see a lot of wildlife: ospreys, harriers, ducks, great blue herons, kingfishers, swallows, and possibly beavers and white-tailed deer.

Location: Milford
Maps: *New York Atlas & Gazetteer*, Map 79: B10, C10; USGS Milford
Area and Length: Goodyear Lake, 366 acres; river length, 10 miles one way
Time: 6 hours
Habitat Type: Slow-flowing stream through farmland and woodlot
Fish: Largemouth and smallmouth bass, walleye (see fish advisories, Appendix C; see specific advisory, health.ny.gov/environmental/outdoors/fish/health_advisories)
Camping: Appendix A (4, 8, 9, 11)

GETTING THERE

Route 166 Bridge Access. From Cooperstown, at the junction of Route 28/Chestnut Street and Route 80/Glen Avenue, go 8.3 miles south on Route 28, and turn left on Route 166. Go 0.7 mile (9.0 miles) to the access on the left on either end of the bridge. (42° 35.459′ N, 74° 55.948′ W)

Crumhorn Landing Access. From the Route 166 bridge, continue 0.3 mile (9.3 miles) east on Route 166, and turn right on Route 35C. Go 0.2 mile (9.5 miles), turn right on Route 35, and go 2.7 miles (12.2 miles) to the access on the right. (42° 33.332′ N, 74° 56.275′ W)

From I-88, Exit 17, go 4.5 miles north on Route 28, and turn right on Route 35A. Go 0.3 mile (4.8 miles), turn left on Route 35, and continue north 2.5 miles (7.3 miles) to Crumhorn Landing on the left.

TRIP 25: SUSQUEHANNA RIVER

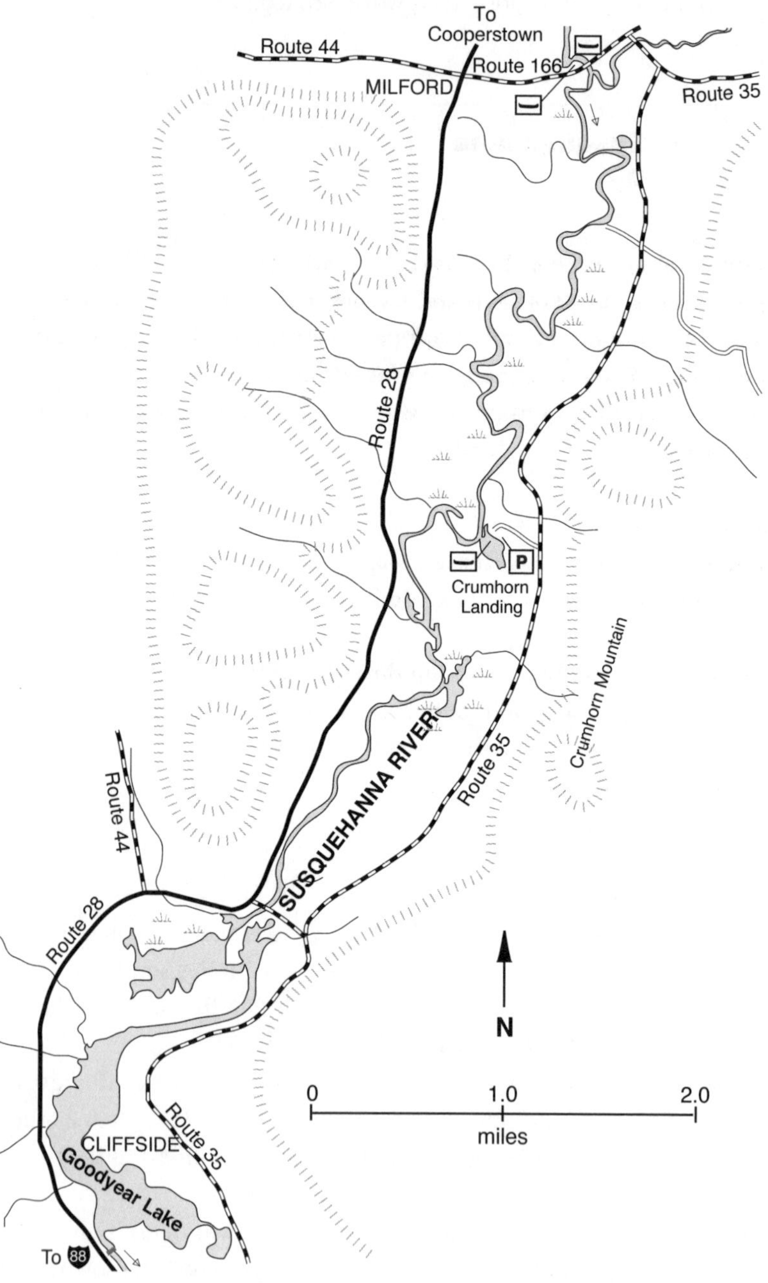

WHAT YOU'LL SEE

From modest beginnings in Otsego Lake—the famed "Glimmerglass" of James Fenimore Cooper—the Susquehanna River meanders quietly southward, gathering hundreds of feeder streams and rivers along the way. Draining much of south central New York, by the time the river exits the state about 30 miles west of Binghamton, it transforms into the major waterway that eventually forms the Chesapeake Bay estuary. The Susquehanna, more than 400 miles in length, remains second in drainage size only to the Saint Lawrence among East Coast rivers.

The General Clinton Canoe Regatta over Memorial Day weekend includes a race on the Susquehanna that begins on Otsego Lake and ends 70 miles later at Bainbridge, making it the world's longest single-day flatwater race. In August 1779, General James Clinton and his forces floated a human-made fleet of 220 boats down the Susquehanna for 170 miles to join forces with General John Sullivan at Tioga Point in Pennsylvania, in a campaign to subdue the Finger Lakes Iroquois tribes loyal to the British. Because the upper Susquehanna had little water, Clinton's troops built a 3-foot-high dam across Otsego Lake's outlet. With the newly constructed fleet loaded and ready, Clinton ordered the dam breached, and he and his troops sailed on a human-made crest down into Pennsylvania.

We chose a 10-mile section of the Susquehanna near its beginnings—just below Cooperstown—where it meanders through farmland, meadows, and woodlots so slowly that at times of low water you can hardly tell which way the river flows. We prefer to put in at Crumhorn Landing, where we can paddle upstream to the Route 166 bridge or downstream to Goodyear Lake.

A rather tame osprey greeted us with piercing cries at Crumhorn Landing, foreshadowing our close look at many more birds along the way. The river's tight turns and high banks deliver you to new sections of water with little commotion, making for good wildlife viewing. Coming out of a curve, we surprised a bittern—a reclusive, brown-streaked marsh heron that would rather hide than fly—causing it to bolt skyward with a great thrashing of wings.

We also saw mallards dabbling for underwater plants, rear ends pointing skyward; spotted sandpipers bobbing along the shoreline, aiming for a better look at rock-clinging insects; a northern harrier swooping over fields with an uptilted dihedral, searching for rodents that didn't have the good sense to stay hidden; black-capped chickadees foraging in small, loosely knit flocks, "chipping" to maintain contact; the spring's first yellow-rumped warbler, darting over the water, feeding on the first insect hatch; male ruffed grouse drumming, attracting females to begin the rites of spring; and flickers, tapping

A northern harrier hovers low over a field, searching for rodents.

out holes in dead streamside trees, providing nest cavities for themselves and wood ducks, hooded mergansers, kestrels, tree swallows, and bluebirds. We also saw or heard mourning doves, song sparrows, robins, crows, killdeers, red-winged blackbirds, white-throated sparrows, and grackles.

Beavers have cut down many streamside willows that reach out over the river, and we paddled right up to one beaver before it dove for cover. We rescued a meadow vole, thrashing in the water, returning it to dry ground. A warm southern breeze reminded us that a meandering river provides a great place to paddle when early- and late-season winds have turned large bodies of water to a foamy froth.

Although occasional traffic noise intruded as the river's course neared a road, most of the time we paddled peacefully, with great views of forested hillsides, a few with layered fields retreating into the distance. We paddled by farms with fields edging on the water and noticed occasional cottages, but most of the time we enjoyed the sounds, sights, and smells of spring in solitude.

26 | Sangerfield River (Ninemile Swamp)

Sangerfield, the home river of the nineteenth century's notorious Loomis Gang, flows south through Ninemile Swamp, and the swamp's vegetation encroaches on the relatively narrow channel. At times, you might have to portage over beaver dams or around fallen trees, but it's worth paddling here to enjoy the serenity and the wildlife. Expect to see red-tailed hawks, ducks, great blue herons, pileated woodpeckers, deer, beavers, and lots of aquatic plants.

Location: Brookfield, Hamilton
Maps: *New York Atlas & Gazetteer*, Map 62: D4, D5, E4; USGS Hubbardsville
Length: 8 miles for round trip from Wickwire Road bridge to Swamp Road bridge
Time: 3 hours
Habitat Type: Swampy stream
Fish: Largemouth bass, northern pike (see fish advisories, Appendix C)
Camping: Appendix A (5, 8, 11)
Take Note: You may have to portage over and around beaver dams and downed trees

GETTING THERE

From Utica, at the junction of Route 12 and Genesee Street, go 21.8 miles south on Route 12, and turn right on Green Road. Go 0.1 mile (21.9 miles), and turn right on Wickwire Road. Continue 0.6 mile (22.5 miles) to the access on the right. Do not block the drive down to the water. (42° 49.264′ N, 75° 26.824′ W)

WHAT YOU'LL SEE

This river's rich history includes the escapades of the infamous Loomis Gang, beginning with patriarch George Washington Loomis's arrival in 1802. Supposedly, "Wash" Loomis had run stolen horses in Vermont and fled before a posse, ending up in Sangerfield. He got married and raised a gang of outlaw children. This family of horse thieves, arsonists, highway robbers, and murderers lived on nearby Loomis Hill, overlooking the swamp from the west. Loomis Road crosses the swamp above the section described here, and the surroundings helped the gang hide themselves and their ill-gotten horses from local vigilantes. Their operation lasted until nearly 1900.

TRIP 26: SANGERFIELD RIVER (NINEMILE SWAMP)

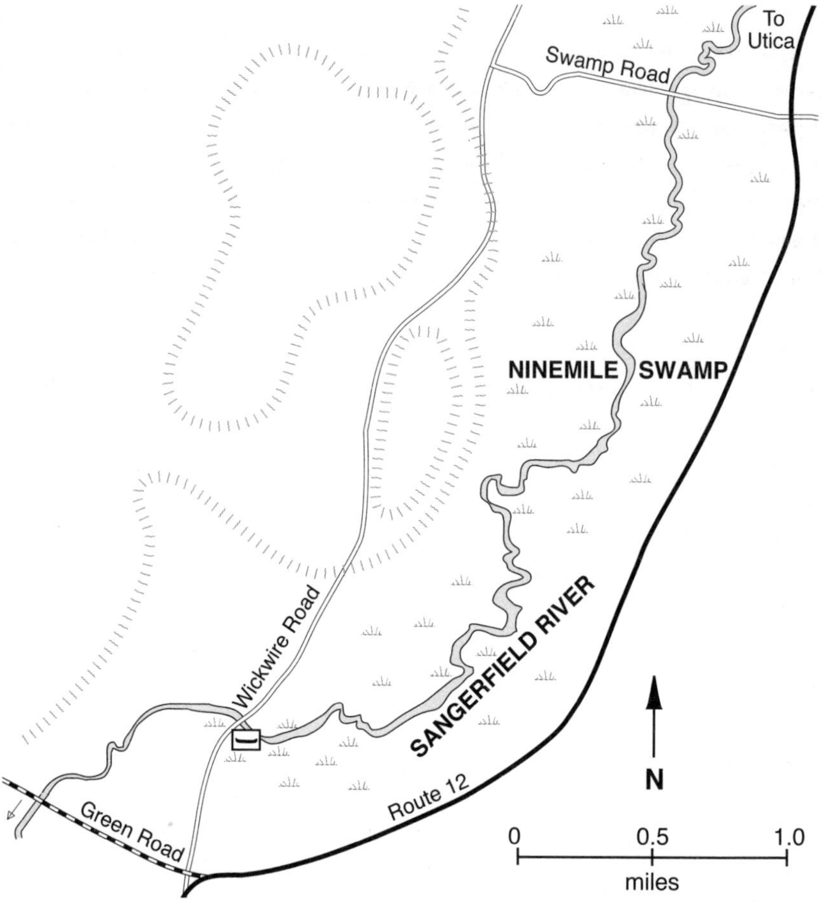

From the access, you begin an easy paddle up to Swamp Road. Even during drought years, plenty of water should carry you over the shallows and through the abundant aquatic vegetation. Snowmelt and winter rains funnel down off the surrounding hillsides, percolate through the ground around the swamp, and slowly release into the river. When other area water levels drop in midsummer, the Sangerfield usually still has plenty. Local anglers, who fish for largemouth bass and 30-inch northern pike, told us that during high water, if we did not mind getting out of our boat on occasion, we could paddle past Swamp Road, all the way to Loomis Road and beyond.

When we checked out the bridge over the creek at Loomis Road in September, the water—what there was of it—did not look at all inviting. You can still paddle up to the Swamp Road bridge, however, even though willow, alder, and other branches drape the meandering waterway.

Paddling up the beautiful valley, with layered fields on the lower hills followed by timbered mountaintops, one can easily forget time. We never tire of this wildlife paradise, with deer crossing the stream in the morning mists; crow-sized pileated woodpeckers in undulating flight, looking for a dead tree full of carpenter ants; and red-tailed hawks circling lazily above, their keen eyes watching for rodents.

Alders and huge overhanging willows dominate this wooded swamp, along with occasional box elder, sugar and red maples, oak, ash, cherry, big-tooth and quaking aspens, tall white pine, northern white cedar, and other conifers. In late September, the red maples turn brilliant scarlet, although red maple has red on it at all times: buds in winter, flowers in spring, leaf stems in summer, and leaves in fall.

Tree leaves remain green for much of the year because the dominant pigment, chlorophyll, reflects mainly green light, absorbing other colors of the visual spectrum to do photosynthetic work. When chlorophyll disappears in fall as photosynthesis ceases, brilliant reds, yellows, and oranges emerge from

The Sangerfield River alternately narrows and broadens as it meanders south through Ninemile Swamp.

the leaf's surface, reflected back by other selectively absorbing pigments. The river's fall foliage burned brightly against the brilliant blue sky of an arctic high-pressure cell when we paddled here.

Early in the year, look for turtles and frogs out sunning, and watch for swirling lily pads, a result of the movements of bass and northern pike chasing bait fish in these productive waters. In spring, mating calls of birds sound throughout the swamp.

In fall, wood ducks fatten up on acorns and aquatic vegetation and jump to the air at your approach, some blasting out from streamside branches. What a pleasure to paddle amid the glorious foliage of fall, a season free from swamp-bred biting insects! We returned in spring, however, fighting the bugs, just glad to be there again.

27 | Dryden Lake

Shallow Dryden Lake offers an opportunity for a slow paddle to explore aquatic vegetation and the animals it supports. Look for turtles and frogs, along with ospreys, Canada geese, great blue herons, and beavers. We also saw families of wood ducks. Hikers enjoy the 4.2-mile Jim Schug trail, as well.

Location: Dryden
Maps: *New York Atlas & Gazetteer*, Map 76: D4; USGS Dryden
Area: 106 acres
Time: 2 hours
Habitat Type: Small, shallow, weed-filled pond
Fish: Largemouth bass, pickerel (see fish advisories, Appendix C)
Camping and Trails: Appendix A (15, 24, 25); trails, Dryden Lake Multiple Use Area, dec.ny.gov/lands/117036.html
Take Note: No gasoline motors; Chaffee Road crosses an abandoned railroad grade, turned into a hiking/biking path

GETTING THERE

From the junction of Routes 13 and 366 east of Ithaca, go 5.9 miles east to Dryden, and turn right on South Street/Route 38. Go 2.1 miles (8.0 miles), and turn left on Chaffee Road. Go 0.3 mile (8.3 miles), turn left on West Lake

TRIP 27: DRYDEN LAKE

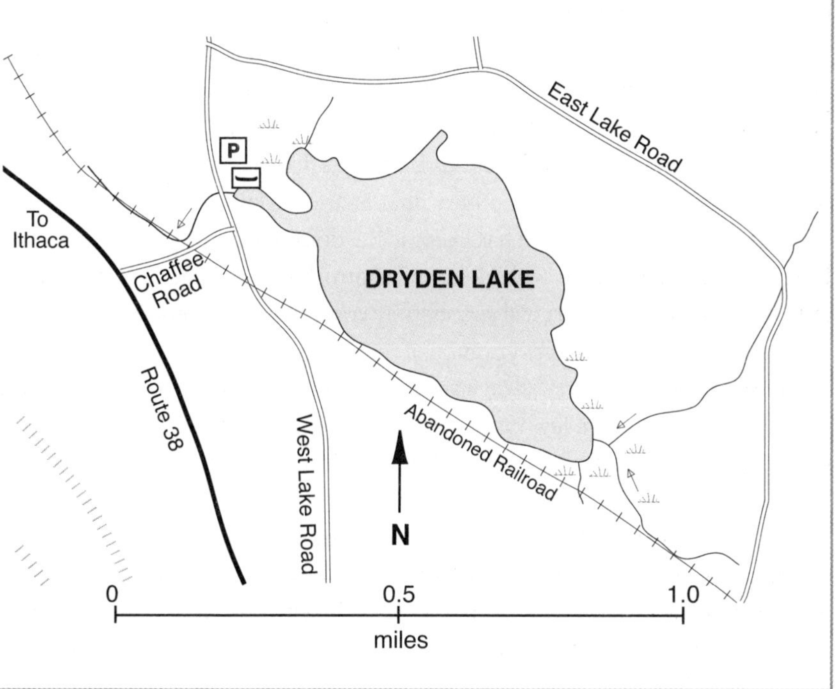

Road, and go 0.1 mile (8.4 miles) to the access on the right, just across the outlet stream bridge. (42° 27.872′ N, 76° 16.834′ W)

WHAT YOU'LL SEE

Recreational activities abound in the Ithaca region. One can enjoy spectacular Taughannock and Buttermilk falls, the Rim and Gorge trails at Taughannock Point, bike and foot trails—including an abandoned railroad grade near Dryden Park—several vineyards, state parks and forests, beaches, and cruises on Cayuga Lake. Dryden Lake presents one of the few quietwater paddling opportunities.

New York State and the Town of Dryden, through farsighted efforts, set aside Dryden Lake as a town park and a state multiple use area. A picnic site hugs the western shore, and a golf course occurs on the east. Scenic farms layer the hillsides, and fields march down to the lake's eastern shore. Cows, along with abundant Canada geese—real feces factories—fertilize these waters, ensuring abundant plant life. Neither cows nor geese move quickly, and that should serve as a metaphor for humans' approach to these waters: enjoy them slowly, study the plants, and watch the wildlife.

Usually on heavily vegetated bodies of water, frogs can use fronds as furniture. In this lake, the vegetation supports turtles. A great blue heron even stood on it, trying with some difficulty to spot passing fish. Besides the usual waterlilies, when we first paddled here, we found an aquatic member of the buttercup family in bloom, along with waterweed, a type of *Elodea*, with unusual underwater leaves one-quarter inch long by one-sixteenth inch wide, whorled in threes on slender stalks. It also bears the tiniest, barely visible purple flowers borne on tendrils; some flowers grow underwater, and others float in the surface film. In recent years, invasive Eurasian watermilfoil has become the dominant aquatic plant species in Dryden Lake. Experiments with biological control have occurred here, and we can only hope that those efforts will successfully control this noxious weed.

Narrow-leaved cattails cover much of the shore. At the marsh's south end, we spotted some basking turtles and a young red-winged blackbird that was sitting on an exposed branch a few inches above the water's surface. The male parent resented our proximity and flitted about, scolding us constantly. We hurried away, so as not to disturb the nest.

The inlet creek at the lake's southeast corner meanders through a cattail swamp, past a large beaver lodge with massive amounts of cuttings in the water. After a short distance, a beaver dam blocks the entrance to a broad meadow. As we paddled up, a green heron family bolted skyward, accompanied by loud squawking.

After things quieted, we listened to the metallic chip note of a swamp sparrow among the streamside vegetation of *Rumex*, jewelweed, bur-reed, and much more. Eventually, it appeared in the brush, with its bright rufous cap and wings, pumping its tail as it fluttered about. Melodious marsh wren song wafted by as tree swallows and cedar waxwings snatched insects in midair.

Paddling back out onto the main lake and around to the southwestern shore, we surprised a few wood duck families that scurried into the surrounding marsh. You can travel the entire circumference of this small lake and explore the inlet thoroughly in about two hours. We highly recommend a visit here for those not in a hurry who want to study plants and animals.

28 | Old Erie Canal

Part of a State Historic Park, the old Erie Canal, built in the early 1800s, is a mecca for runners, hikers, bikers, and paddlers. We include a 5.5-mile segment of the canal here, but you could travel a lot farther along this outstanding resource. With no current, paddling up and back is easy. Expect to see ospreys, ducks, cormorants, painted turtles, and muskrats.

Location: DeWitt, Manlius
Maps: *New York Atlas & Gazetteer*, Map 61: B7, B8; USGS Manlius, Syracuse East
Length: 2.5 miles, DeWitt to Manlius Center; 5.5 miles to North Kirkville Road
Time: 4 hours
Habitat Type: Shallow former canal
Fish: Largemouth bass, northern pike (see fish advisories, Appendix C)
Camping and Trails: Appendix A (10, 14)
Information: Old Erie Canal State Historic Park, parks.ny.gov/parks/17/details.aspx
Take Note: The adjacent towpath attracts many walkers, runners, and bikers, especially near Syracuse

GETTING THERE

Cedar Bay Road Access. From Syracuse, go east on Erie Boulevard/Route 5 or East Genesee Street/Route 92. From the I-481 bridge, go 0.8 mile to where Routes 5 and 92 split, and turn sharply left on Lyndon Road. Go 0.8 mile (1.6 miles) to the T intersection. Across the road is the beginning of the old Erie Canal. (43° 2.422′ N, 76° 2.671′ W)

Burdick Road Access. From the T intersection, head 1.3 miles (2.9 miles) east on Cedar Bay Road, and turn left on Burdick Road. Cross the bridge, and park on either side. (43° 2.605′ N, 76° 1.270′ W)

Manlius Center Access. After turning left on Burdick Road, go 1.1 miles (4.0 miles) north, and turn right on Route 290/Manlius Center Road. Go 1.2 miles (5.2 miles), and turn left on Minoa Road. Access is immediately on the right. (43° 3.433′ N, 76° 0.031′ W)

TRIP 28: OLD ERIE CANAL

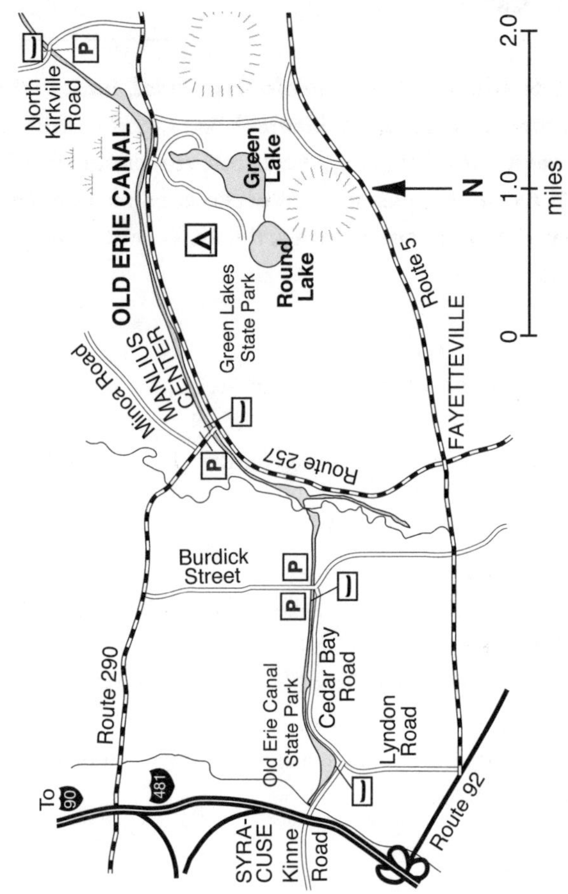

North Kirkville Road Access. From the Manlius Center access, continue 2.8 miles (8.0 miles) east on Route 290/Green Lakes Road (pass Green Lakes State Park at 1.5 miles [6.7 miles]), turn left on North Kirkville Road, and go 0.7 mile (8.7 miles) to the access on the right. (43° 4.198′ N, 75° 56.989′ W)

WHAT YOU'LL SEE

Perched on the edge of Syracuse, Old Erie Canal State Historic Park draws hundreds of visitors on warm summer days. People hike, run, and bike along the towpath, while paddlers ply the canal's shallow, still waters. Despite this activity, the canal suffers from siltation and deadfalls because of disuse and eventually will fill in.

Work began on the 363-mile Erie Canal in 1817. When the canal was completed eight years later, it stood as an engineering marvel and a tribute to human genius. Think about trying to dig a wide, deep, 363-mile-long ditch with a parallel road today . . . *with* bulldozers, draglines, and dump trucks.

In 1817, people knew little about canal construction. Fortuitously, a surveyor named Canvass White (1790–1834) perfected a waterproof hydraulic cement made from limestone that hardened underwater. Without using motorized machines, workers felled and removed trees and pulled stumps; dug through soil, rock, and swamp; and built towpaths, culverts, aqueducts, locks, gates, and bridges. When finished, they had accomplished the foremost engineering feat of their time. Western New York flourished as goods moved cheaply from New York City up to Albany and then west over the canal to Lake Erie and the hinterlands, hastening Midwest development.

A modern system of canals replaced the original Erie Canal in 1918. The new Erie, Cayuga-Seneca, Champlain, and Oswego barge canals tamed the Mohawk and Seneca rivers with dams and locks and used diesel power to cross Oneida Lake and Lakes Ontario and Erie. In many places—now crisscrossed with roads, farms, and development—no trace of the original canal remains. Thankfully, some parts of it are preserved in state parks. We wonder if the joggers, bikers, and paddlers appreciate the significance of Old Erie Canal in, appropriately, the town of DeWitt, named for DeWitt Clinton, the ten-term New York mayor (1803–1815) and two-time governor (1817–1821; 1825–1828), who sponsored building the canal.

Paddling out from the canal's beginning in DeWitt, we found a tree-covered south bank and a path-covered north bank. In between, the canal's murky water hid much of civilization's detritus—except for the elusive *Goodyearis submergicus*; although many old tires populate these waters, their bottom-dwelling habit frequently hides them from view. Tree species lining the south bank include black locust, lots of ash, black walnut, cottonwood, and box elder and other maples, including one large silver maple whose grapevine-covered branches draped way out over the water, lending a closed-in, intimate feeling.

Smaller trees and shrubs cover the north banks down to Burdick Road. When we visited in October, the wide, rounded sumac crowns had turned brilliant red. Clumps of clematis clung to streamside shrubs as the first joggers made their way down the towpath in the crisp early morning air. By midmorning, turkey vultures started to ride the thermals, painted turtles climbed out onto sun-facing logs, more people trod and biked the path, and a few other paddlers appeared, as well.

Old Erie Canal paddlers create the only ripples on leaf-strewn water in the fall.

An osprey fished a wide spot—how it could see prey in the cloudy water remains a mystery. Gray squirrels appeared frequently along the ground, harvesting seeds for winter stores. Nine wood ducks fattening up for fall migration bolted skyward as we approached. A cormorant fished for its breakfast, and black ducks and mallards dabbled along the edge of the water. Muskrats pruned the canal-side grass, as more turtles climbed out into the sun.

We saw many bird species, which surprised us, given the level of recreational use. Expect to constantly return the greetings of cheerful passersby. Past tiny Manlius Center, the crowds thin out, trees crowd in, and wildlife thrives.

We prefer to put in at the beginning of the canal and to paddle down and back on the nonexistent current. Although no longer serving as a vital transportation corridor, the Old Erie Canal still holds immense historical significance—and provides a relaxing place to paddle to boot.

29 | Fish Creek to Oneida Lake

This particular Fish Creek abounds in wildlife. During times of low water, usually in summer and into fall, you can paddle both directions in the lazy current. We saw white-tailed deer, red fox, and river otter. You might spot muskrat, mink, and beaver, as well. We also saw ducks, great blue herons, ospreys, and myriad songbirds.

Location: Vienna
Maps: *New York Atlas & Gazetteer*, Map 48: E1, E2; USGS Sylvan Beach
Length: 9 miles one way, Route 49 bridge to Sylvan
Time: 6 hours round trip
Habitat Type: Wide, shallow, slow-flowing stream
Fish: Largemouth and smallmouth bass, northern pike (see fish advisories, Appendix C)
Camping: Appendix A (7, 14)
Take Note: Can paddle both directions at low water

GETTING THERE

From the junction of Route 13 and Route 80/McClanathan Avenue, north of Sylvan Beach, go 1.2 miles north on Route 13, and turn right on Route 49. Go 5.0 miles (6.2 miles), and turn left on Herder Road. Continue 0.4 mile (6.6

TRIP 29: FISH CREEK TO ONEIDA LAKE

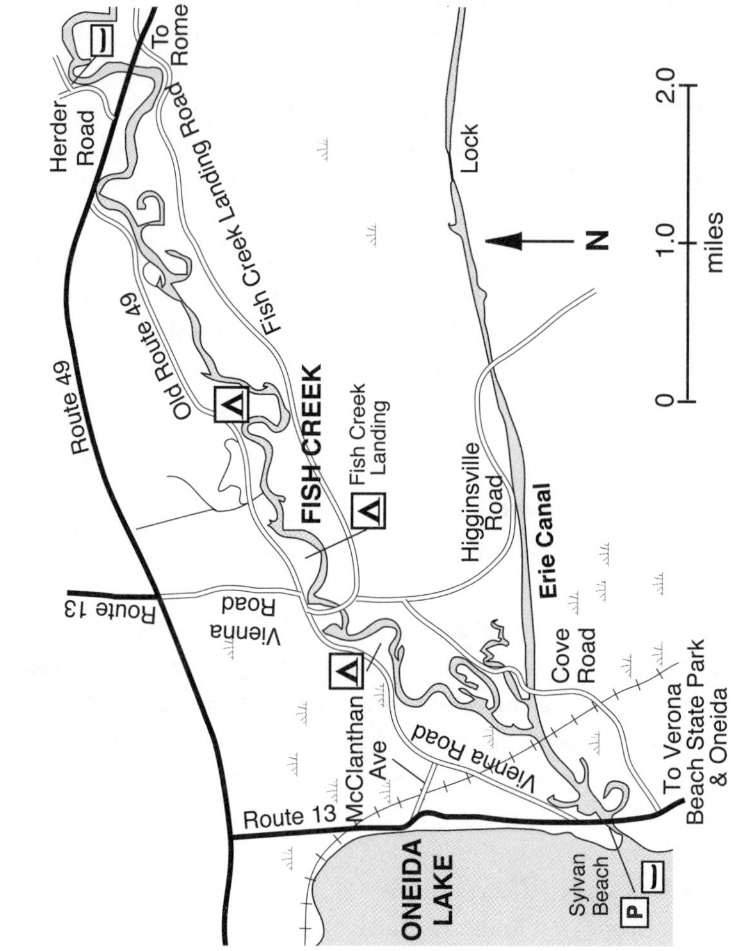

miles) to the junction with Miller Road, and park on the right (43° 14.712′ N, 75° 38.071′ W)

To paddle in one direction, leave a vehicle in Sylvan Beach at the lakefront public parking area. Take out on the right, just downstream from the Route 13 bridge. (43° 11.652′ N, 75° 43.862′ W) You can also pay to take out at one of the private campgrounds at Fish Creek Landing.

WHAT YOU'LL SEE

We did not expect much when we put into Fish Creek in early October, even though a local kayaker told us we would enjoy paddling here. Sylvan Beach and its environs serve as a summer vacation mecca, drawing visitors from far and wide to crowd Oneida Lake's shores. We found a wildlife haven on nearby Fish Creek, standing in sharp contrast with people-packed Sylvan Beach. Try to get to the water at sunrise to maximize your experience. Do not rush—paddle the shoreline quietly, looking for wildlife, trying to remain unobtrusive.

This section cuts a swath more than 100 feet wide through a broad plain. Fish Creek's shallow, clear water reveals either a sand- or dead-tree-covered bottom. Grapevine and Virginia creeper drape streamside vegetation among aspen, cottonwood, box elder, large flowing willow, sumac, and more. The layered canopy stretches for every available light ray to maximize photosynthesis; in one area, an understory of dwarf willow, a midstory of river birch, and an overstory of big-tooth aspen placed leaf surfaces in the sun from bank top to treetop. A beaver had nearly gnawed through the base of some aspen, a favorite food.

When we paddled out at dawn, the sun's first rays burned off the morning mist as white-tailed deer came down for an early drink. We listened to robins singing and blue jays squawking, and two black ducks leaped from the water at our approach. Rounding the first bend on the inside of the curve, we spied movement on the bank downstream. We quit paddling and drifted quietly in the lazy current. A red fox pounced from tuft to tuft along the bank, hunting for mice, too intent on its pursuit to see us heading toward a rendezvous. As it placed its forepaws on a log jammed against the bank, we arrived. It looked at us from 10 feet only for a moment before bounding up and over the bank in alarm.

Wood ducks blasted out of the coves as we curved to the left—in all we counted ten taking off in this short stretch. The first of three great blue herons took wing, as well. A flock of about 40 Canada geese flew over, honking noisily as they began their southward migration to water remaining open all winter. We stopped to watch a mixed foraging flock of more than 40 birds in an extensive grapevine thicket; we identified song and white-throated sparrows near the ground, yellow-rumped warblers—the last warblers to migrate south—in the midstory, and black-capped chickadees and white-breasted nuthatches overhead, all trying to glean late-season insects and berries from the foliage.

As we floated back into the current, the first of two sharp-shinned hawks drifted across the waterway, and all became still in the grapevines. How could so many birds vanish so quickly? Evolution obviously favors those that become scarce when a major bird predator such as the "sharpie" appears. Across the way in an overgrazed field, a flock of red-winged blackbirds—the males' red epaulets barely visible in their fall plumage—foraged on the ground, along with a herd of fat cows. Up in the sun-bleached branches of a dead tree, crows mobbed a red-tailed hawk as another hawk circled on gathering thermals overhead. As we paddled to the other side to get a closer look, two killdeer took to noisy flight. A greater yellowlegs, calling a descending *tew-tew-tew-tew-tew*, ran along the shore as eastern bluebirds stood on fence posts, watching for insects roused by the rising sun.

Just after passing a row of bank swallow holes in the soft, steep bank—the swallows had long ago left for warmer climes that were still abuzz with insects—we heard a noisy chomping among the branches of a deadfall. As we approached, we saw a young river otter munching away on a fish. Such manners! After a few minutes, deciding that we would not leave, it dove with its fish into the water behind the snag. A few moments later, it and its mother and two siblings tried to sneak away upstream. After swimming about 15 feet, the mother poked her head up, neck fully extended, to get a better look. With head and neck a foot above the surface and no shoulder in view, she uttered a muffled snort in our direction, clearing her nose of water. Perhaps this is not a comical sight to other otters.

While mourning doves perched on bare branches, a belted kingfisher dove headlong into the water after a fish, emerging quickly to fly off to its perch. We spent some time trying to identify a flycatcher out on a limb. After a few puzzling moments, we decided that it was one we usually identify by song: the eastern wood-pewee. We also saw the similar eastern phoebe.

As we neared Fish Creek Landing, a large flock of common mergansers rested on stumps, logs, rocks, and water in a protected cove. Using our binoculars, we counted 48 birds and turned around to avoid forcing them to fly off. Down here, closer to Oneida Lake, ring-billed gulls flew over frequently.

We paddled back at a faster pace and saw only one additional species, a rather tame green heron that let us get within 20 feet before taking flight. As we passed a rope swing suspended from a willow branch, we reflected on the prodigious amount of wildlife we had seen and wondered about the protection of this wildlife haven. The rope swing dangled from a fragile holder—willow branches shatter easily—but no more fragile than the surrounding habitat. Obviously shoreline development and tree clearing threaten this area.

Judging from the amount of downed timber, spring runoff frequently topples streamside trees. Roots of standing trees stabilize the banks, keeping the creek from broadening and getting too shallow, and also provide habitat for fish, otter, mink, muskrat, and beaver. The narrow woods bordering houses and fields provides this stream's only protection. We hope that people who enjoy nature's bounty will seek to protect the shoreline. They might ask farmers not to cut trees within 100 feet of the shore. They might encourage residents not to subdivide their land and to instead plant trees along the bank. A cooperative effort could help ensure that this fragile habitat remains for future generations to enjoy.

BALD EAGLE: NATIONAL BIRD BACK FROM THE BRINK

The bald eagle, with its unmistakable white head and tail, soars over the nation's waterways on powerful wings. In flight, this bird's large size stands out, with a wingspan up to 8 feet. From beak to tip of tail, eagles measure from 34 to 43 inches. Males weigh 8 to 9 pounds, while the larger females weigh 10 to 14 pounds. Belying the term "light as a feather," feathers alone can contribute up to 15 percent of body weight.

The bald eagle attains its distinctive plumage at 4 or 5 years of age. Until then, it resembles the dark brown golden eagle, except with some white mottling on the underside and tail. As the bald eagle matures, its head and tail become progressively whiter. At close range, the adult's large yellow beak and piercing yellow eyes convey a fierce strength. The founders of the United States evidently thought this image symbolized what the young nation stood for, selecting *Haliaeetus leucocephalus* as the national symbol. Appropriately, this is the only eagle found exclusively in North America.

Ranging throughout New York, eagles generally locate their nests in trees at the water's edge. Pairs return to the same nest for years, adding to it annually. An old eagle nest can easily measure 6 feet in diameter and 8 feet deep and weigh more than a ton. The largest nest ever found measured 9.5 feet in diameter and 20 feet deep. Because eagles often build nests in dead trees, the nest's huge mass eventually topples the tree.

Bald eagles usually lay two eggs several days apart. Incubation lasts 30 to 36 days, during which time the male and female share nesting duties. The young hatch several days apart, which improves chances of fledging at least one chick. If food is scarce, the older chick would outcompete its younger sibling for food, and the younger chick would die. Because eagles live long lives—as long as 30 years in captivity but usually much less in the wild—they really only need to fledge a few chicks to replace themselves, thus maintaining a stable population.

After ten to twelve weeks of a diet consisting mostly of fish, chicks fledge and begin to fly. For the next seven or eight weeks, they increasingly gain independence, eventually leaving the nest to migrate to coastal areas and to outfalls below dams where the water does not freeze. In years past, bald eagles congregated in great numbers off both coasts and in the Mississippi drainage each fall. They still gather by the thousands in mid-November along a 10-mile stretch of the Chilkat River in Alaska to feed on hordes of dead and dying salmon.

While bald eagles occur frequently in New York today—thanks to efforts by the Endangered Species Unit of the Department of Environmental Conservation (DEC)—just a few years ago only a handful remained. In the late 1960s and early 1970s, long-lasting chlorinated hydrocarbons—such as DDT and its breakdown product DDE, left over from mosquito control projects—reached high concentrations in osprey, eagle, peregrine falcon, and other top-of-the-food-chain bird species, causing thinned eggshells that broke during incubation. The eagle population plummeted to just one pair in western New York that doggedly nested in the same tree for more than twenty years. Only once during that time—in 1973—did they successfully hatch and raise a chick, but they served as successful foster parents for captive-born chicks over several years, starting in 1978, in the DEC's fledgling reintroduction program.

Eagle populations have rebounded to about 15,000 nesting pairs (up from 4,000 in 1993; 8,000 in 2003; 13,000 in 2013) in the United States outside Alaska. In New York, 426 pairs nested in 2017—up from 92 in 2005 and 25 in 1995—with the greatest concentration around remote lakes in the far western, far northern, and southeastern regions. In 2010, New York eagles fledged 244 young from 192 nests, up from 112 young in 2005, 30 in 1995, 15 in 1990, and 3 in 1987. In addition to the increasing number of young produced in New York, another satisfying statistic has been reported: nest success rates remain relatively high, averaging 1.2 chicks fledged per breeding pair, the same number that occurred from 1990 to 1995. This stands in contrast with less than one chick fledged per breeding pair in Maine, which hosts 300 nests. Possibly, eagles in New York suffer from less contamination by DDT, DDE, dioxins, mercury, and PCBs.

Because eagle populations rose over the 23 years after the DDT ban, aided by reintroductions in many areas of the United States, the U.S. Fish and Wildlife Service removed the bald eagle from the Endangered Species List in 1995, placing it on the Threatened List.

We feel privileged to paddle on lakes with bald eagles. Some accuse these raptors of being opportunists, and indeed we have watched a few chase smaller osprey, laboring with heavy fish, circling to gain altitude before flying off to their aeries. In one sighting, after the osprey dropped its hard-won catch, a bald eagle snatched it and flew off. This is not a case of good and evil; instead, it represents the triumph of bald eagle adaptation, ensuring its survival.

Humans still shoot eagles on occasion and build high-voltage lines that electrocute them—although designs and devices exist that reduce eagle mortality. Many eagles die when they fly into human-made structures (power lines, towers, smokestacks, and buildings). But the biggest threat to the bald eagle's continued survival comes from an expanding human population that spews toxic chemicals into the environment and continues to develop shorelines. If we wish to enjoy this majestic creature as it patrols America's waterways—and keep it from returning to the Endangered Species List—we must take steps to keep some of its habitat undeveloped and unadulterated by the harmful wastes of a consumer society. The bald eagle represents an enduring wildness that we must protect for future generations to enjoy.

30 | Gifford Lake/ West Branch Fish Creek

The little-traveled West Branch of Fish Creek offers a great opportunity to view deer, muskrat, and occasionally otter, mink, and beaver. You will see tons of marsh birds, including great blue herons, kingfishers, red-winged blackbirds, swallows, and many more.

Location: Amboy, Williamstown
Maps: *New York Atlas & Gazetteer*, Map 47: C9, C10; USGS Westdale
Length: 6 miles one way
Time: 5 hours
Habitat Type: Marshy, slow-flowing creek
Fish: Smallmouth bass, brown trout (see fish advisories, Appendix C)
Camping: Appendix A (7, 10, 14)
Take Note: Watch carefully for the partially hidden entrance to Gifford Lake

GETTING THERE

From Rome, head northwest on Route 69 to Camden, and turn right on Route 13/Main Street. Go 5.0 miles, turn right on Cemetery Road, and go 0.1 mile (5.1 miles) to the access on the right. (43° 23.355′ N, 75° 48.789′ W)

TRIP 30: GIFFORD LAKE/WEST BRANCH FISH CREEK

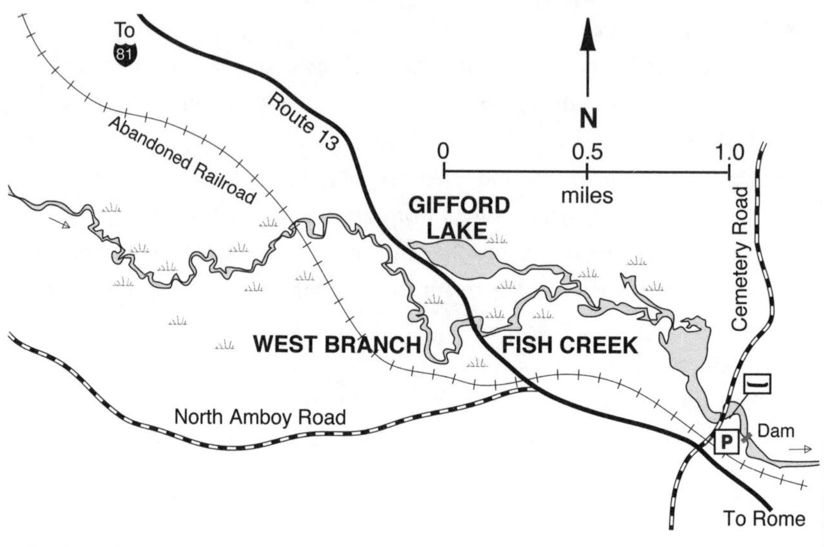

From I-81, Exit 34, go 9.5 miles east on Route 104, and turn right on Route 13. Go 7.9 miles (17.4 miles) to Cemetery Road on the left, and follow as above.

WHAT YOU'LL SEE

A popular one-way canoe route begins at the access on the downstream side of the dam on the West Branch of Fish Creek. However, except for some kayakers and local anglers, few people take advantage of the beautiful upstream paddling available here. Above the dam, the West Branch meanders through forest and marsh, passes the Gifford Lake outlet, skims unobtrusively under Route 13, and heads upstream past brushy, wooded banks. Water celery and pondweed undulate in the lazy current.

Heading upstream, we passed a cluster of houses on the right. Quite a way along, a fishing camp on the right marked the entrance to Gifford Lake. Though we could have gone farther, we turned around at an old railroad grade several miles upstream, a reminder of a time when civilization encroached more extensively on this wild little creek.

Although hemlocks and silver maples occasionally line the right-hand shore, shrubs own the banks. The first side channel on the right penetrates well back into the woods, and tons of pondweed, pickerelweed, yellow pondlily, and underwater vegetation grow in the stagnant water. Great blue herons patrol the shallows, ever watchful for the next frog or fish meal, while kingfishers hover in the air, ready to dive headlong on unwary prey.

Grasses, ferns, long-leaved *Rumex*, and shrubs dominate most of the shoreline, while extensive marshes lead off in all directions. Clumps of arrowhead grow out from the bank, while pickerelweed—growing singly—occurs in slightly deeper water. A large patch of irises among the cattails caught our attention, but in other places alders covered the banks.

The high biological productivity of this area makes it a paradise for bird-watchers and others interested in wildlife. We saw or heard great blue heron, kingfisher, robin, mourning dove, yellow-rumped warbler, yellow warbler, common yellowthroat, eastern phoebe, barn swallow, red-winged blackbird, grackle, osprey, eastern kingbird, song sparrow, rose-breasted grosbeak, and cedar waxwing. Although we did not spot beaver, we did see lodges and lots of fresh alder cuttings. A muskrat, seemingly unconcerned by our presence, harvested grasses by the shore, and we witnessed a rarity: a mink furtively fishing the shore, working stealthily along the bank, waiting to pounce on anything that moved.

The mink—like most other weasel family members—has an elongated body with large surface-area-to-volume ratio, causing high heat loss for its size, an elevated metabolic rate, and a voracious appetite. It eats just about anything: fish, rodents, frogs, crayfish, birds, and the prized hen in the henhouse. Even

Marshy areas abound at the entrance to Gifford Lake and in the many coves along the West Branch of Fish Creek.

though it usually weighs only about 2 pounds, it easily kills larger animals. Mink range widely, from Key West to arctic Alaska, from Labrador to central California. Given their huge appetite and the need to kill a lot to satisfy it, mink never appear in large numbers in any habitat. So we were fortunate to see one, especially because they usually remain nocturnal.

To reach Gifford Lake, take the right-hand fork at the fishing camp on the right, about a mile upstream from the access. Although the lake sports a beautiful hardwood stand along its shores, we prefer the scenic stream that connects the lake with the creek. A very narrow, meandering passageway leads through a wide expanse of marsh. Beaver cuttings along the way suggest that an early evening visit here would be rewarding. Arrowhead crowds the channel, and you have to weave your way through American white waterlily and yellow pondlily.

As we paddled back to the access in the waning afternoon sun, we marveled at the beauty of recently emerged iridescent green damselflies with jet-black wings that hovered over the drooping tips of streamside grasses.

31 | Salmon River Reservoir

Salmon River Reservoir's large size and east-west orientation make it susceptible to wind, though conditions are calmer in early morning. Both east and west ends offer plenty of protected paddling, with great views of waterfowl, ospreys, hawks, and deer. You might also see bald eagles, mink, otters, and beavers.

Location: Orwell, Redfield
Maps: *New York Atlas & Gazetteer*, Map 47: A8, A9, A10; USGS Orwell, Redfield
Area: 2,660 acres
Time: All day
Habitat Type: Large reservoir and marshy inlet stream
Fish: Largemouth and smallmouth bass, brown and rainbow trout (see fish advisories, Appendix C; see specific advisory, health.ny.gov/environmental/outdoors/fish/health_advisories)
Camping: On-site, campsites scattered about the lakeshore
Take Note: Main lake dangerous under windy conditions; novices should always wear personal flotation devices (PFDs)

TRIP 31: SALMON RIVER RESERVOIR

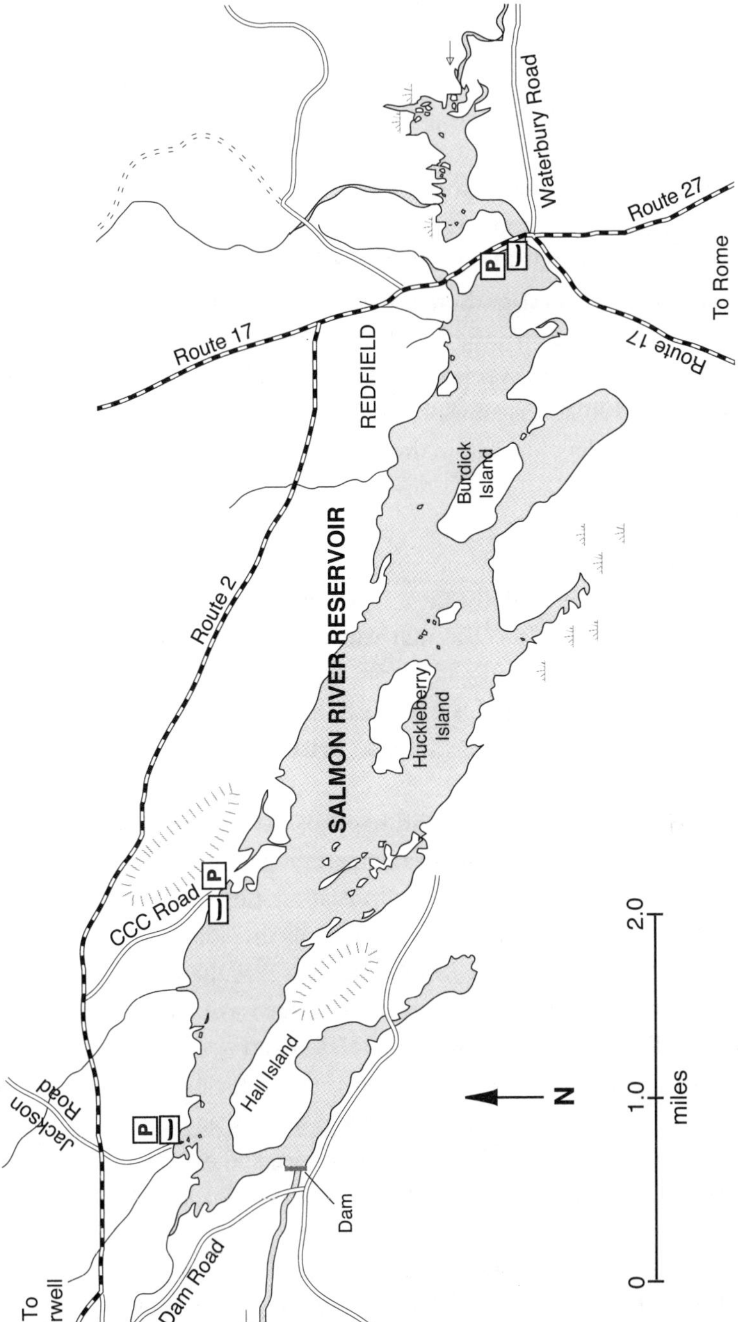

GETTING THERE

Jackson Road Access. From I-81, Exit 36, go 10.4 miles east on Route 2, and turn right on Jackson Road. Go 0.4 mile (10.8 miles) to the access. (43° 33.307′ N, 75° 55.002′ W)

CCC Road Access. From Jackson Road, continue east 0.9 mile (11.3 miles) on Route 2, and turn right on CCC Road. Go 0.9 mile (12.2 miles) to the access. (43° 33.074′ N, 75° 53.340′ W)

Redfield Bridge Access. From CCC Road, continue east 4.1 miles (15.4 miles), and turn right on Route 17. Go 1.3 miles (16.7 miles), cross the bridge, and park on the right. (43° 31.407′ N, 75° 48.963′ W)

From Rome, head west on Route 69 to Camden, and turn right on Main Street. Go 0.3 mile, and turn right on Empey Avenue. Go 0.1 mile (0.4 mile), and bear left on Route 68/River Road. Go 6.8 miles (7.2 miles), and turn left on Route 70/Redfield Road (becomes Route 27). Continue 7.3 miles (14.5 miles) to the access on the left, just before the bridge.

WHAT YOU'LL SEE

Our two favorite areas of this state-owned, little-used reservoir include the far west end—down through the cove southeast of the dam—and the far east end where Salmon River flows through extensive marshes. When paddling the west end, we use the Jackson Road access, mainly because of wind problems. When we went out at sunup in late August, the surface barely rippled, but on our return at midmorning, the wind had started to roll waves down the lake, preparing for afternoon whitecaps.

This daily cycle of calm and wind happens because the land mass heats up during the day, causing warm air to rise, drawing in cooler, denser air off nearby Lake Ontario. Due to its generally east-west orientation, the reservoir suffers from wind-driven waves from the west. By threading your way through the willow-clad islands near the Jackson Road access, then down the western shore to the southern cove, you can avoid the large waves on the main lake.

As we paddled down to the cove below Hall Island—really a peninsula—we watched gulls, loons, and crows and listened to black-capped chickadees and eastern wood-pewees in the woods. A belted kingfisher flew ahead, leading us through stump-filled shallows, under a culvert, and out into a magnificent marsh. Although we noticed a few campsites along Hall Island, we found none past the culvert. Aquatic plants—including Eurasian watermilfoil, yellow pondlily, pondweed, and water shield—choked the whole cove, dampening any swells from the freshening wind. Along the shoreline, we noticed two large, but apparently inactive, beaver lodges.

Yellow pondlily grows in the shallow waters of Salmon River Reservoir.

Three great blue herons flew off at our approach, but a kingfisher stood its ground among dead tree limbs. Paddling back up the shore through the clear water, as a common merganser brood rushed out of harm's way, we studied the shoreline trees, including red and white pines, ash, elm, sugar and red maples, box elder, eastern hemlock, birch, quaking and big-tooth aspens, cottonwood, apple, black and pin cherries, beech, yellow birch, and willow. Except for the Hall Island hump, the flat western landscape allows the water to creep up to the plateau's edge and then spill through cataracts down to Lake Ontario.

We also enjoy paddling the lake's eastern end, where the Route 17 bridge and a twisting channel through wooded shores block much of the wind. Past the bridge, the entire northern shore—honeycombed with channels through small, willow-clad islands and patches of aquatic vegetation—provides habitat for myriad fauna and flora. As we paddled the channel, a river otter paced us, periodically bobbing up with a snort to look around, head held high above the water, then diving in typical undulating otter fashion.

Feeding flocks of common mergansers, black ducks, and wood ducks scurried into the horsetails (*Equisetum*) and grasses as we approached. Two wood ducks bolted from a streamside tree as we rounded a bend, and a sharp-shinned hawk alternately flapped and glided across in front of us. This small member of the genus *Accipiter*—along with Cooper's hawk and goshawk—preys mainly on other birds, which it chases down and plucks from the sky. The "sharpie's" small size, short, rounded wings, and long tail give it agility when flying through woods that other hawks do not share.

A much larger raptor soared on wide wings overhead: an immature bald eagle, dark brown with white flecks on its tail and belly, cast a sharp eye on dead and dying suckers that littered the water. Eagles catch live fish, snaring them from the water's surface with powerful claws, but more typically eat carrion … including decaying suckers.

As we paddled by bushy basswood, through islands of grass and willow, water celery indicated current direction. Reaching a shallow riffle, we drifted back down Salmon River, following its flow, marveling at how close the pebbly bottom seemed in the crystal-clear water. Reentering the marsh, we found brilliant red cardinal flowers in bloom near a beaver impoundment on a side channel. Smartweed, a member of the buckwheat family, its leaves prostrate upon the water's surface, had sent up short bloom spikes with bright pink flowers measuring maybe an inch long. We spent hours looking at plants, animals, and birds in this huge wetland.

We paddled here alone until near the end, when a single personal watercraft flew up the river from under the bridge and then zoomed back down the reservoir. We who use this area should try to preserve the section upstream from the Route 17 bridge as motorless. Given the huge concentration of wildlife in this habitat—including bald eagle, sharp-shinned hawk, river otter, and many more species—we should attempt to protect it from noisy, disruptive incursions.

Although the lake remains popular with local anglers, Salmon River downstream attracts thousands of visitors to fish the salmon runs. To maintain stream levels for the salmon, starting in late August, the power company starts to draw down the reservoir, eventually several feet, making it a less pleasant place to paddle.

3 | ADIRONDACK PARK AND ENVIRONS

The 6 million acres of New York's Adirondack Park offer some of the finest paddling in the United States. The park lies within a half-day's drive for more than 30 million people, providing a huge opportunity for paddling these waters with their gorgeous mountain backdrops. We describe 40 locations here that range from small, readily accessible ponds to more remote chains of lakes. You can go for multiday trips on the Saint Regis lakes, the Saint Regis Canoe Area, or Fish Creek Loop, or you can spend a few hours paddling Limekiln Lake or Putnam Pond. Larger bodies of water, such as Cranberry Lake and Indian Lake, and rivers, such as the Oswegatchie River and the Beaver River Canoe Route, offer all-day or multiday paddling experiences. We include marshes along Lake Champlain in the east—Ausable Marsh and South Bay—as well as Coles Creek and Deer River Flow in the north and Canada Lake and the Sacandaga River West Branch in the south.

Several bodies of water—Eighth Lake, Raquette River, Forked Lake, and Middle and Lower Saranac lakes—are part of the 740-mile Northern Forest Canoe Trail that traces native peoples' trade routes from Old Forge to northern

Maine. Indeed, in addition to rich American Indian traditions, the writing of several descendants of European immigrants describes paddling here. Ralph Waldo Emerson wrote poems about paddling in this area in 1858. George Washington Sears, also known as Nessmuk, wrote of paddling the 10-pound Sairy Gamp canoe, built by J. Henry Rushton, throughout the park. And William Henry Harrison Murray (Adirondack Murray) in 1869 wrote a widely read book that likened the scenery to that of Switzerland.

The New York legislature included protection of public lands within the park's boundaries in the state's constitution. This protection provides wild, wonderful places to paddle. The variety could easily keep one busy for an entire summer or, indeed, for a lifetime.

32 | Canada Lake and West Lake

If you avoid Canada Lake's eastern arm, you can have a tranquil paddling experience here, especially on a trip down the outlet stream to Stewart Landing. We saw several loons, along with ospreys, waterfowl, great blue herons, and kingfishers. You will likely notice deer and muskrat and might catch sight of mink and river otter.

Location: Caroga, Stratford
Maps: *New York Atlas & Gazetteer*, Map 50: E5 and Map 80: A4, A5; USGS Canada Lake, Caroga Lake
Area: 554 acres
Time: 5 hours
Habitat Type: Deep lakes
Fish: Smallmouth bass, pickerel, lake trout (see fish advisories, Appendix C; see specific advisory, http://health.ny.gov/environmental/outdoors/fish/health_advisories)
Camping: Appendix A (108, 111)
Take Note: Main lakes dangerous under windy conditions; novices should always wear personal flotation devices (PFDs)

TRIP 32: CANADA LAKE AND WEST LAKE

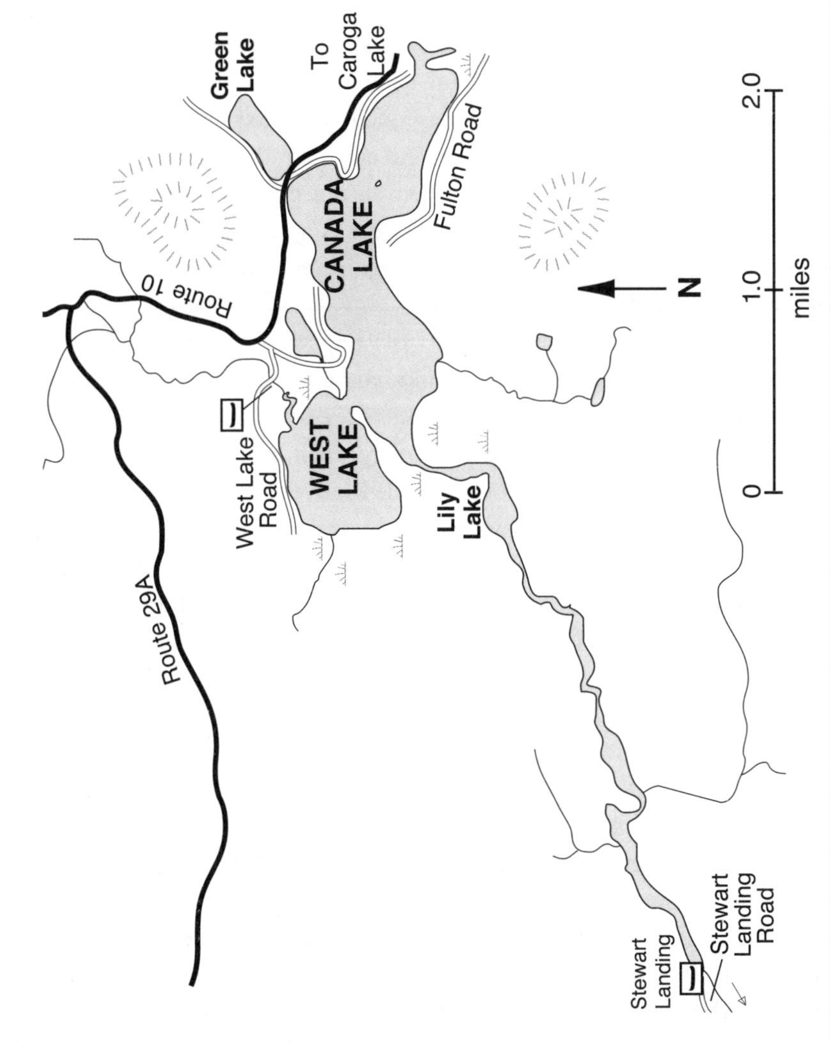

GETTING THERE

From Gloversville, at the junction of Main Street and Route 29A/Fulton Street, go 14.0 miles west on Route 29A, and turn left on Point Breeze Road. Go 0.1 mile (14.1 miles), and turn right on West Lake Road. Continue 0.2 mile (14.3 miles) to the access on the left. (43° 10.535′ N, 74° 31.860′ W)

Alternatively, from Route 119, go 3.4 miles north on Stewart Landing Road to the access on the right. (43° 8.542′ N, 74° 35.616′ W)

WHAT YOU'LL SEE

Canada and West lakes mark Adirondack Park's southern end, and although New York State owns huge tracts of forest all around these connected waterways, it does not own any significant amount of shoreline. Private inholdings abound, and with them wall-to-wall shoreline camps, bringing substantial motorboat and personal watercraft traffic. Consequently, we suggest avoiding Canada Lake's heavily developed eastern arm and concentrating on its southern shore and nearby West and Lily lakes. If you do not mind passing an occasional summer home—particularly when you near Stewart Landing—you can have a wonderful paddling experience through scenic waterways chock-full of interesting plants and wildlife.

Heading out through the winding, twisting stream leading to West Lake, with grasses and alders lining the banks, you may wonder if any large bodies of water actually exist in this area. Muskrats break from harvesting streamside grasses, song sparrows sing from the undergrowth, and red-winged blackbirds flutter from the water's edge as you paddle by. Eventually, you emerge in West Lake's northeast corner. Although some houses appear on the northwestern shore, the picturesque southern shore remains unblemished. Paddle the shoreline counterclockwise, wind permitting, to get to the pine-covered peninsula marking the entrance to Canada Lake.

Although hemlocks and white pines appear in good numbers along the shoreline, oak, sugar maple, yellow birch, cherry, and other deciduous trees dominate the surrounding hillsides. In places, a dense understory of balsam firs competes for light, stretching toward the canopy. When you round the point into Canada Lake, notice the extensive marsh along the southern shore. We saw deer taking a morning drink here as we headed for Lily Lake, and several loons plied the waters.

As we entered long, narrow Lily Lake, songbirds serenaded us with a chorus, announcing their breeding territories; white-throated sparrows called *Old Sam Peabody, Peabody, Peabody* from the undergrowth. Flickers drummed out holes for themselves and other cavity nesters, including wood duck, hooded merganser, and tree swallow, all of which we saw as we paddled down to Stewart Landing. Ducks appeared in profusion, some migrating through, others looking to nest: hooded and common mergansers, wood duck, ring-necked duck, mallard, and black duck. An osprey swooped down and snatched a fish to take back to its dead tree aerie. Other prominent birds included blue jay, kingfisher, great blue heron, and killdeer.

After a few hours of paddling down to Stewart Landing, mostly without seeing any other boats, we carefully picked our way back to West Lake. Stick to the center of these shallow waterways at times of low water to avoid rocks.

33 | Sacandaga River West Branch

We love paddling the Sacandaga River West Branch and the small ponds that feed it. Although Route 10 follows the river, forests surround the waterway, so you still feel like you're in a wilderness most of the time. Watch for bald eagle, otter, beaver, and deer here, along with lots of aquatic plants.

Location: Arietta
Maps: *New York Atlas & Gazetteer*, Map 50: D5; USGS Canada Lake, Morehouse Lake
Length: 8 miles one way
Time: All day
Habitat Type: River and connected small ponds
Fish: Brook and brown trout (see fish advisories, Appendix C)
Camping: Appendix A (108, 109, 110, 112); on-site wilderness camping
Take Note: May need to carry to pass an occasional logjam or beaver dam

GETTING THERE

Second Bridge Access. From I-90, Exit 29, head north on Route 10. From the junction of Routes 10 and 29A West, go 5.9 miles north on Route 10 to the access on the right, just past Second Bridge. (43° 15.332′ N, 74° 32.162′ W)

Northern Access. From Second Bridge, go 6.4 miles (12.3 miles) north on Route 10 to the Shaker Road access on the right. (43° 19.457′ N, 74° 32.205′ W)

WHAT YOU'LL SEE

The Sacandaga River West Branch provides spectacular paddling—our favorite place in the Adirondack Forest Preserve's southern reaches. The clear, quick-flowing river meanders generally south to north through undeveloped, wild country, although often within earshot of Route 10, which runs roughly parallel.

The river's sinewy channel passes through grassy marshland, with alders lining the banks in spots, thick masses of pickerelweed at bends, and

TRIP 33: SACANDAGA RIVER WEST BRANCH

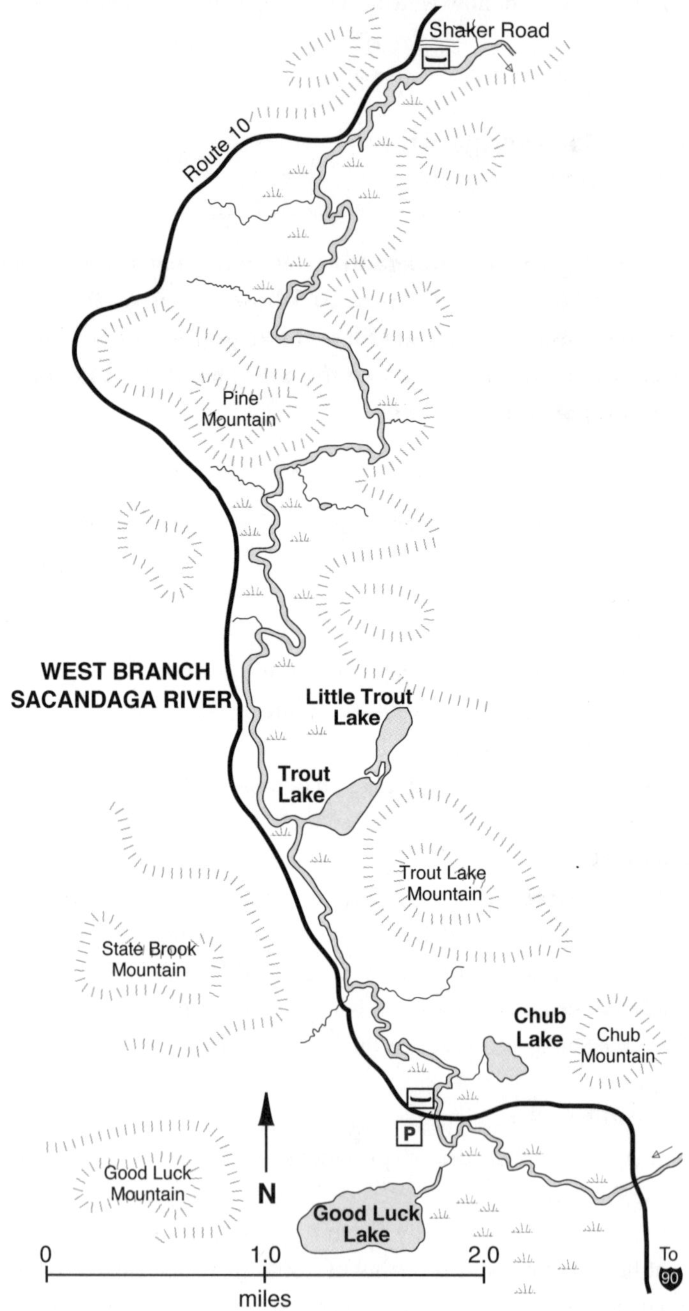

Paddling on the Sacandaga River can be enjoyable even in late November, as we were doing here. You should have the place to yourself!

underwater grasses undulating rhythmically at the river bottom. Mixed hardwoods, hemlocks, and white pines rise from the valley floor on higher ground, and steeply sloped hills gird the narrow valley. We saw some huge yellow birches here.

The river, sometimes just a dozen feet wide, can jam up with logs and beaver dams. We had to slide over a few shallow dams, and one substantial logjam required carrying across a grassy, hummocky bank—a challenging proposition with a long-haired dog that we preferred not to have shaking off water in the boat.

From the main river channel, you can make wonderful side explorations into Good Luck, Chub, Trout, and Little Trout lakes (although they are all too small to truly claim the title "lake"). The narrow outlet streams of Good Luck and Chub—in places just 5 or 6 feet across—make maneuvering a longer canoe or kayak a challenge. Also, depending on water level, gaining access to these lakes may prove difficult. To reach Good Luck from Second Bridge, paddle upstream a couple hundred yards to the small inlet stream on the right. Steeply rising hills border the roundish lake.

Look for the little inlet stream of Chub Lake on the right about a quarter-mile downstream from Second Bridge. The lake and its boggy banks abound with sphagnum, pitcher plant, tamarack, bog rosemary, and tiny-leaved cranberry.

Alex's solo canoe during a late-November paddle on the Sacandaga River.

In late summer, if you can get through the inlet, you should find large red cranberries that dwarf the plant's leaves. Entering Chub Lake, look directly across the water for a large boulder, a great place for a picnic and camping (state-designated primitive campsite).

Close by and fairly easy to find, Trout and Little Trout lakes also enter on the right a couple of miles downstream from Chub Lake. When we visited here, we had no difficulty paddling into both, but during dry years and midsummer, access might be difficult. We noticed one state campsite on Trout Lake's southern shore.

As we returned from Little Trout into Trout Lake one late afternoon, we heard some commotion and drifted quietly toward a group of four otters on a sandy island, one of which munched noisily on a bullhead. Once they spotted us, they slid from the island and, in typical otter fashion, watched us from deeper water, popping their heads up with distinctive snorts to investigate our intrusion into their solitude.

Paddling from Second Bridge down to Trout Lake and back to the put-in makes a good day trip. If planning an out-and-back trip all the way to the northern Route 10 access on Shaker Road, leave early in the morning, and remember that the current will slow your return. Of course, you could also put in at Shaker Road and paddle upstream, letting the current aid your tired arms on your return to the put-in.

---

34 | South Bay

South Bay is a great place to paddle when it's not windy. The bay's elongated shape provides miles of shoreline to explore. We prefer traveling along the western shore with its cliffs and inlets, but we also enjoy paddling the marshy inlet stream. You'll see lots of aquatic plants, along with many great blue herons, ospreys, and the occasional bald eagle and kingfisher.

Location: Dresden, Fort Ann, Whitehall
Maps: *New York Atlas & Gazetteer*, Map 53: A7, A8; USGS Whitehall
Area: 1,100 acres
Time: 4 hours
Habitat Type: Large, shallow lake with marshy bays and inlets

TRIP 34: SOUTH BAY

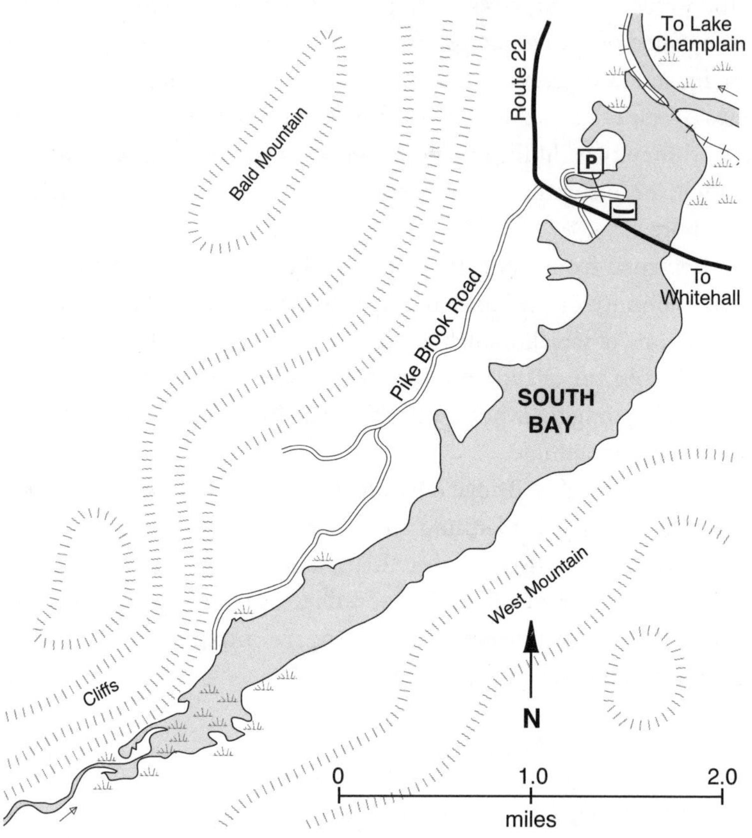

Fish: Largemouth and smallmouth bass, northern pike, walleye (see fish advisories, Appendix C)
Camping: Appendix A (73, 74, 75, 76, 77, 89)
Take Note: Avoid when windy

GETTING THERE

From the junction of Routes 22 and 4 in Whitehall, go 2.8 miles north on Route 22, cross the bridge over South Bay, and take the second right, which leads to a large parking area. (43° 34.515′ N, 73° 26.038′ W)

WHAT YOU'LL SEE

South Bay lies along Champlain Canal's western edge at the southern terminus of Lake Champlain. A pleasant surprise awaits you. Gaze down the waterway at gorgeous cliffs and hillsides receding into the distance, beckoning you to paddle south.

Note the warning at the access about picking up "hitchhikers," referring to three serious aquatic pests: Eurasian watermilfoil (*Myriophyllum spicatum*), European water chestnut (*Trapa natans*), and zebra mussel (*Dreissena polymorpha*). All three hitch rides on boat trailers, in bilges, and even on canoe and kayak hulls, to be deposited in the next waterway. Biologists worry that these alien species, introduced to the East Coast from Europe and Asia, will eventually infect most bodies of water in the East and Midwest. They arrived without natural predators and now crowd out native species.

The first time we paddled here, in the first bay on the right, we found a huge beaver lodge, a great blue heron patrolling the shallows, and a waterway choked with water chestnut. Its rosettes eventually grow so thick that they push up over other aquatic vegetation, limiting access to light, smothering it. We tried to paddle through—as we have done countless times with stands of waterlily—but it was like trying to paddle over dew-covered grass.

Another invasive, Eurasian watermilfoil, already had made its way to the south end and, indeed, all the way up the inlet creeks. This underwater plant

Steep cliffs and layered hillsides line the shores on South Bay's south end.

with its slender, lacy foliage also crowds out native vegetation. Experiments with biological control of watermilfoil seem to be working in some locations, and mechanical harvesting of both watermilfoil and European water chestnut can get rid of these scourges.

We did not see zebra mussel when we paddled here, although it has likely made it to South Bay by now. As of 2019, it was found in 32 states. This tiny mussel filters out microscopic plankton and other organisms, clarifying the water, but it may filter so effectively that the food chain gets depleted, ultimately reducing fish populations. It sticks to underwater structures in many layers and clogs intake pipes. Unless scientists can find an effective control mechanism that does not harm native species, zebra mussel will eventually infest most waterways in the United States.

However, do not let concern about alien pests spoil your paddle here, where you can enjoy stately great blue herons standing knee-deep in every bay. Near Route 22, fields march down to the water's edge; farther down the bay, they give way to layered, forested hillsides and high cliffs, a preferred nesting site of the peregrine falcon. If it nests here, it would have a spectacular view from its cliffside aerie.

A great horned owl startled us as it flew off with powerful wing beats from a bankside willow. We explored all the deep inlets that dot the western shore, paddling back into the cattails, bur-reed, pickerelweed, and waterlilies. Rufous-

Dense rosettes of European water chestnut have clogged many waterways in the Northeast.

sided towhees called from the undergrowth, and barn swallows dipped low over the water.

We traveled up the creek on the south end, with its gorgeous cliffs, in among waterlilies, pondweed, water celery, and grasses. We paddled through thick stands of pickerelweed into a swamp with alder, cattail, cardinal flower, and purple loosestrife. Two aquatic plants emerged in great mats: yellow-flowered bladderwort and a small yellow pondlily—*Nuphar rubrodisca*. Silver maple dominated the shoreline. We watched large schools of fish swim in the creek's clear water, in sharp contrast with the bay's milky consistency.

As we returned to the access, hugging the picturesque western shore, we wondered what we would find here next time. With its huge expanse of water, South Bay often suffers from strong winds, the same winds that carry nuisance aquatic plants to the waterway's far reaches.

35 | Lake George Northwest Bay

Scenic Lake George beckons many people to the eastern edge of Adirondack Park, leading to a lot of summer boat traffic. Because Northwest Bay and its inlet stream are less crowded, we have included the bay here. Besides enjoying great scenery, you will likely spot osprey, kingfisher, and waterfowl here. Surrounding hills harbor a small remnant population of timber rattlesnakes.

Location: Bolton
Maps: *New York Atlas & Gazetteer*, Map 39: E6; USGS Whitehall
Area and Length: 2 miles of brook; hundreds of acres in Northwest Bay
Time: 4 hours
Habitat Type: Shallow brook emptying into relatively small bay on huge lake
Fish: Largemouth and smallmouth bass, northern pike, landlocked salmon, lake and rainbow trout (see fish advisories, Appendix C)
Camping: Appendix A (73, 74, 75, 76, 77, 89)
Take Note: Always wear personal flotation devices (PFDs) on the main lake; avoid the main lake under windy conditions

TRIP 35: LAKE GEORGE NORTHWEST BAY

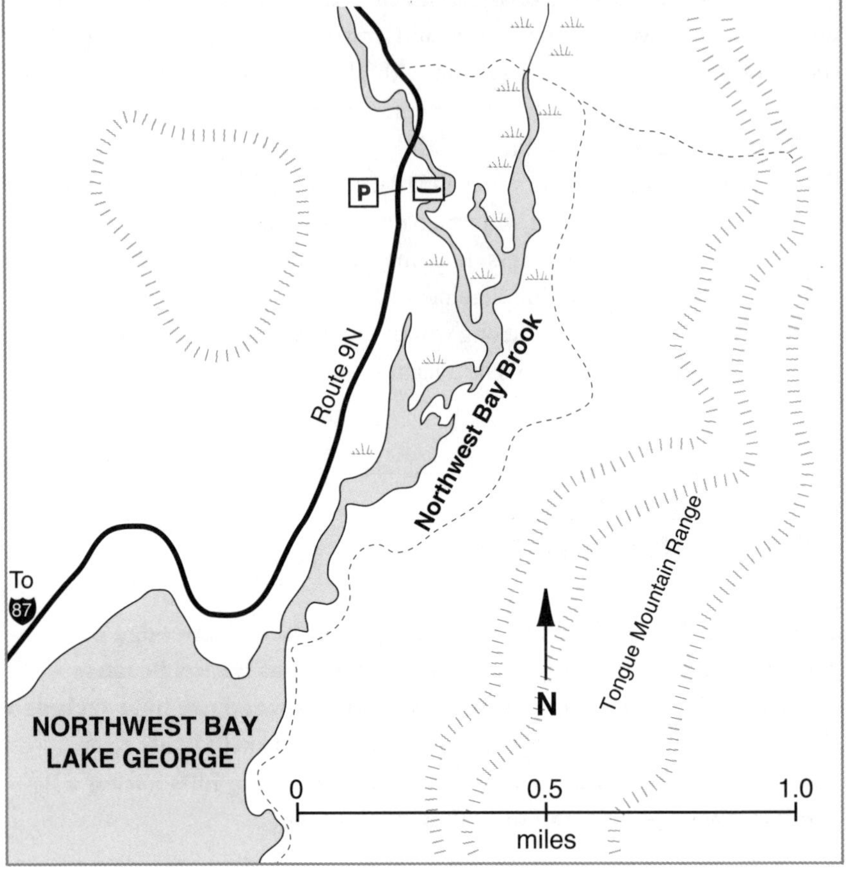

GETTING THERE

From I-87, Exit 24, go 4.7 miles east on Route 11/Bolton Landing Road, and turn left on Route 9N. Continue 4.3 miles (9.0 miles) to the access on the right. (43° 37.524′ N, 73° 36.450′ W)

WHAT YOU'LL SEE

Layered hills and forested islands—grand vistas of the North Country—contribute to Lake George's scenic setting and help attract multitudes of vacationers to its beautiful shores. The largest lake in Adirondack Park, Lake George draws many big boats to its deep, clear waters. We recommend that you stay off the main lake, with its personal watercraft, water-skiers, speedboats, and wind, which can cause huge swells to build up over miles of water, creating treacherous paddling conditions.

From the access, you can paddle to the left up a creek for about a tenth of a mile, where you will encounter lots of beaver activity, and you can paddle down Northwest Bay Brook into Northwest Bay. Take time to explore the sinuous channel of the brook's east fork. You will have to elbow your way through pondweed, water celery, bur-reed, and other aquatic vegetation, but you should find a lot more solitude here than downstream.

Yellow pondlily covers the channel in spots, and grasses and ferns carpet the banks where alders have not crowded everything out. Tall red and silver maples hang over the alders and grassy banks. Farther down the lake, after the marshes disappear, tall white pines and hemlocks grace the shores.

In several places along the creek, you will see large beaver lodges, along with downed trees and many cuttings. As we paddled here, we saw dragonflies mate on the wing along the protected, placid waters, and a large snapping turtle cruised by just below the surface. As we rounded a little island on the western shore just before the bay, we saw a sign on a dying white pine: "Caution, Rattlesnakes. Unlawful to Disturb or Take." The land belongs to The Nature Conservancy to protect a rare northern population of timber rattlesnake that dens in the rockfall on this hillside.

Species become rare on the edges of their range. Because Lake George and Champlain Valley represent the northern extension of the timber rattlesnake's range, we find very few in isolated populations. The rattlesnake probably arose in the southwestern United States and northern Mexico, where it speciated and radiated outward—as far south as southern Argentina and as far north as southern Canada. About 30 species occur in a wide variety of habitats from sea level to above 10,000 feet. In the north, its preferred habitat gets closer and closer to sea level, probably in response to colder temperatures at higher elevations.

Two species are found in New York: the timber rattler (*Crotalus horridus*) occurs in isolated populations over much of the state's southern half, while the massasauga (*Sistrurus catenatus*) occurs in two isolated populations near Lake Erie. Toward the southwest, the rattlesnake's evolutionary beginnings, more species appear: three species in Missouri, eight in Texas, and eleven in Arizona. A total of fifteen species—half of all rattlesnake species—occur in the United States.

Most people fear the rattlesnake, probably because of its famed hypodermic venom injection system, the most highly developed poison delivery system among snakes. Indeed, some rattlesnakes stand their ground when aroused and

Forested hillsides surround Northwest Bay.

vigorously defend themselves. People have eliminated them from much of their range through a combination of habitat destruction and direct extermination. However, rattlesnake venom is rarely fatal to humans. Many more people die every year from lightning strikes or allergic reactions to bee stings.

As a member of the pit viper family, the rattler has two small pits about midway between the nostrils and eyes. (If you can see these features, you have definitely gotten too close; look at them with binoculars.) These pits sense infrared energy and allow the snake to distinguish between warm organisms and the cooler environment. The rattler dines mainly on rodents but will also eat birds, frogs, and lizards.

Snakes grow throughout their lives, rapidly at first and more slowly later. As the snake grows, it sheds its stretched skin, composed of dead cells. Each time it sheds, the rattlesnake adds a segment to its rattle. Young snakes may shed twice or more per year, whereas older snakes shed once, or not at all. Also, terminal rattle segments often break off. Thus, the number usually does not reliably indicate the snake's age.

Most people shun snakes of any kind and will probably choose to ignore this hillside. But even if you love reptiles, please stick to the trails. The Nature Conservancy does not want people traipsing all over this habitat.

36 | Putnam Pond

Putnam Pond and its popular campground and hiking trails nestle among the peaks of the Pharaoh Lake Wilderness of Adirondack Park. Although the pond is small, it harbors significant bird diversity. Look for loon, red-breasted merganser, great blue heron, kingfisher, and lots more. You may see beaver or otter here in the evening or early morning.

Location: Ticonderoga
Maps: *New York Atlas & Gazetteer*, Map 39: B6, B7, C6, C7; USGS Graphite
Area: 185 acres
Time: 3 hours
Habitat Type: Shallow pond with marshy coves
Fish: Largemouth and smallmouth bass, pickerel (see fish advisories, Appendix C)
Camping: Appendix A (77, 89) (on-site)
Take Note: Watch for barely submerged boulders

GETTING THERE

From Ticonderoga, at the junction of Route 74 and Route 9N, go 4.8 miles west on Route 74, and turn left at the sign for Putnam Pond. Go 3.9 miles (8.7 miles) to the access at Putnam Pond Campground. (43° 50.286′ N, 73° 34.349′ W)

From I-87, Exit 28, go 12.5 miles east on Route 74, and turn right at the sign for Putnam Pond.

WHAT YOU'LL SEE

Nestled in the Pharaoh Lake Wilderness—with high Adirondack peaks all around—Putnam Pond sports a scenic campground and many hiking trails—some accessible only by water. Because the surrounding wilderness attracts hundreds of hikers all summer long, try to visit in spring or fall; if you must visit in summer, avoid weekends. When we paddled here mid-September, we shared the water with three other canoes.

Putnam Pond contains many beautiful features. Smooth granite boulders rise from the pond's surface and protrude from shore. About a dozen widely separated, water-accessible scenic campsites spread along the shore, seemingly wherever one of the few flat places occurs. Most include a fire grate, picnic

TRIP 36: PUTNAM POND

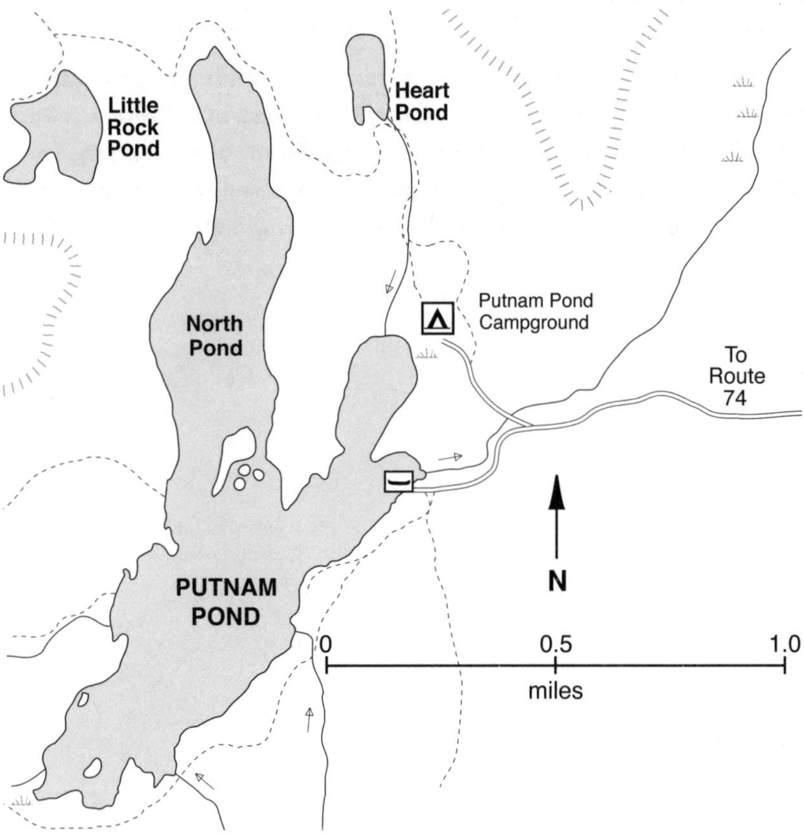

table, and outhouse. From the grassy boat launch, the point on the right boasts a wonderful picnic area. The cove to the right, filled with pickerelweed and other aquatic vegetation, leads to the main campground.

Towering hemlocks line the roadway to the water; around the pond, occasional dense hemlock stands include considerably smaller trees. Red maple, northern white cedar, and paper birch line the shore, interrupted by thick red pine stands. Large white pines grow farther back. Vast areas of aquatic vegetation accumulate in late summer—mostly water shield, along with American white waterlily, yellow pondlily, pickerelweed, and water celery. Marshy coves occur in several places, and way down on the southwest shore, a nearly pure stand of tamaracks covers a boggy island. Larger islands have more diverse tree species,

A skimmer dragonfly perches near the shore, waiting to pounce on insects that fly above it.

along with groups of flat granite boulders, perfect for picnics. Be careful when paddling near shore: the jagged surfaces of barely submerged boulders are incompatible with smooth boat hulls.

Mussel shells litter parts of the pond bottom, probably left by foraging otters or raccoons. Heavy visitation has not driven out the healthy beaver population. Along the western shore, we paddled by numbers of downed trees, floating and submerged, felled by these industrious waterway engineers. In the early evening, two beavers swimming along slapped the water's surface with their broad, flat tails to show their annoyance at our intrusion before diving for cover, only to surface a short distance away to repeat the ritual. Besides the tail-slapping beavers, several red squirrels and a kingfisher scolded us as we paddled by their pondside perches.

Two loons cruised the lower pond's center, and several flocks of ducks, including wood ducks, fed in the shallows. A red-breasted merganser family watched us warily from close range as we glided by, in stark contrast to the chaotic fluttering across the water's surface that occurs with younger broods. On a summer visit, we noted dozens of the skimmer dragonfly (*Ladona julia*) patrolling the access.

37 | Ausable Marsh

Ausable Marsh can only be described as a wildlife paradise. The marsh harbors great numbers of ducks, herons, and other marshland species. Expect to see osprey, bald eagle, waterfowl, great blue heron, several swallow species, kingfisher, kingbird, and a diversity of aquatic plants. You should see muskrat and might spot beaver, otter, mink, and deer.

Location: Ausable, Peru
Maps: *New York Atlas & Gazetteer*, Map 23: D8; USGS Graphite
Area and Length: 660 acres in the wildlife management area; 6 miles of waterways
Time: 4 hours
Habitat Type: Marshes and slow-flowing rivers
Fish: Largemouth and smallmouth bass, northern pike, walleye (see fish advisories, Appendix C)
Camping: Appendix A (78) (on-site)
Information: Ausable Marsh Wildlife Management Area, dec.ny.gov/outdoor/24400.html
Take Note: Launch from campground under windy conditions; always wear a personal flotation device (PFD) on Lake Champlain; no motors

GETTING THERE

From I-87, Exit 35, go 2.8 miles east on Bear Swamp Road/Route 442, and turn left on Route 9. Go 0.4 mile (3.2 miles) to the park entrance on the right, and continue 0.3 mile (3.5 miles) to the Lake Champlain access on the left. (44° 34.578′ N, 73° 26.182′ W)

Head 0.3 mile (3.8 miles) farther to the Dead Creek access on the right. (44° 34.368′ N, 73° 25.986′ W)

Campers may also launch from their campsites.

WHAT YOU'LL SEE

Three separate paddling areas await you at Ausable Marsh: Dead Creek, Ausable River, and the marsh between the river's mouths, all part of a broad delta formed from silt carried by the Ausable as it tumbles down out of the Adirondack High Peaks—including the state's tallest, Mount Marcy—to the Champlain Valley.

TRIP 37: AUSABLE MARSH

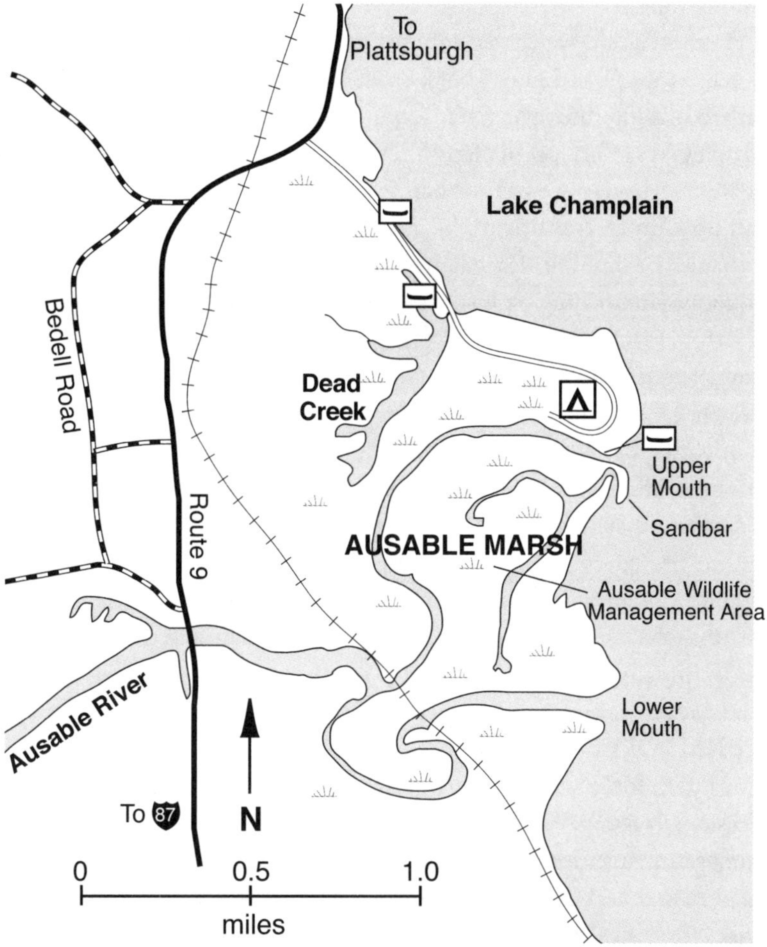

Under calm conditions, paddle south on Lake Champlain from the first access to take advantage of panoramic views of Vermont. Initially, you paddle through horsetail (*Equisetum*)—a fern relative with segmented stalk—growing near shore. Look for ducks feeding among the rushes in deeper water. We saw many, including a female mallard herding her brood. The sand bottom, easily visible in the clear water, harbors hordes of freshwater mussels. Silver maples stand shoulder to shoulder along the bank all the way down to the campground.

Belted kingfishers paced us as we paddled upriver from the sandbar at the Ausable's upper mouth. A ground-dwelling warbler, the northern waterthrush, patrolled the shore, bobbing its tail constantly. This 5-inch bird, with its streaked breast and white eye stripe, has a loud song, thought to be an adaptation for attracting mates and announcing its territory over the streamside roar of rushing water.

A sea of underwater vegetation undulated over rippled sand in the clear current as we passed gravel bars, eroded banks, and tree trunks waiting to be washed out into the lake. Even at very low water levels, paddling against the current takes effort, particularly after going under the railroad bridge. Nearing the Route 9 bridge, we worked harder than we wanted to and turned around to drift back downstream with the current, enjoying ostrich ferns towering over the banks, beautiful iridescent green damselflies mating on the wing, and a fat groundhog munching on lush streamside grass.

Before reaching the railroad bridge on your downstream paddle, look for a channel cutting back to the right (south), leading to the Ausable's lower mouth. A catch-22: at high water, strong current may preclude making this a loop trip (it might be easier going clockwise); at low water, the channel leading to the lower mouth may have insufficient water for passage.

Drifting back into the lake at the river's upper mouth, we turned right to clear the quarter-mile-long sandbar and paddle back up into the Ausable Wildlife Management Area sloughs. In retrospect, we should have carried over the 30-foot-wide sand spit rather than paddle around it, especially given that we continually ran aground trying to stay in an elusive channel.

However, taking the long way around got us a close-up sight of a very rare bird in full breeding plumage: a ruff, a Eurasian shorebird slightly larger than the killdeer with which it shared the sand spit. The ruff appears only occasionally along the East Coast and rarely this far inland. The male's breeding plumage includes long feather tufts (ruff) that stream for several inches from the head and neck down either side of the breast. The highly variable ruff color ranges from steel gray to red to white. We watched this bird—with its striking reddish-orange head, snow-white ruff, and bright orange legs—run and fly over the sand for at least ten minutes, so close we did not need binoculars. Other than seeing a bald eagle nest with young or an otter noisily chomping on fish, this provided perhaps the biggest treat of the season.

The wildlife management sloughs provided our most enjoyable paddling. Except for the occasional angler, you likely will find yourself alone in this marshy wilderness, not very far from the bustling lake. Immediately upon entering the marsh you must choose a direction—west or south—and neither channel goes far.

We paddled the whole area because of abundant wildlife—especially wood duck, eastern kingbird, flicker, and muskrat—and opportunity to study the

Abundant deadfalls occur in the clear waters of the Ausable River.

huge variety of marsh plants. According to some plant keys, more than 30 species of pondweed (genus *Potamogeton*) occur in the Northeast. We saw several species here, all with two things in common: floating leaves with parallel veins, all running the same direction as the midvein, and small, knobby flowers looking like pale raspberries, extending a few inches above the water on stout stalks. These served as aerial landing pads for the diminutive blue damselflies that darted into the air as we glided by.

We also studied bladderwort, with its yellow snapdragon-like flowers borne on short stalks above the water. Most of the plant lives underwater in dense, feathery mats, bearing hundreds of minuscule (0.02 to 0.1 inch long), bulbous traps that catch and digest microscopic animals. In most ponds, mosquito larvae form the bulk of bladderwort's diet, but the plants also ingest other insect larvae, rotifers, protozoans, small crustaceans, and even tiny tadpoles (for more on carnivorous plants, see "Carnivorous Plants: The Table is Turned," on page 361).

You can enter Dead Creek two ways: paddle in from Lake Champlain through a culvert (portage over the top during high water) or launch from the Dead Creek access. (*Note*: One of the nation's largest bodies of water not controlled by a dam, Lake Champlain's water level can vary dramatically, depending on rainfall. On occasion we have found water flowing from the lake into Dead Creek, filling the culvert to the top, with the road surface just a foot or two above the water's surface.)

We enjoyed paddling this placid water while the setting sun drew pastel colors across the western sky. Although we did not see anything new, we marveled at the sheer abundance of ducks, great blue herons, muskrats, and the insect-eating tree swallows, barn swallows, and purple martins, doing their best to keep down the ubiquitous deerflies.

We left this wildlife paradise knowing that we would return. Areas such as this have become increasingly rare as urban sprawl, strip development, and consumptive land practices gnaw away at priceless habitats. We thank the farsighted individuals who set aside this marshland for our generation and future generations to enjoy.

38 | Davis Lake and Salmon River

Because Davis Lake is not large, we generally spend most of our time on the Salmon River, really a small stream. To travel any distance, you have to portage over beaver dams. You will likely see muskrats here, and if you paddle early or late in the day, you should see beavers too.

Location: Peru, Schuyler Falls
Maps: *New York Atlas & Gazetteer*, Map 23: C6; USGS Graphite
Area and Length: 60 acres; stream length about 1 mile
Time: 3 hours
Habitat Type: Small, shallow lake; narrow, slow-flowing stream
Fish: Brown trout (see fish advisories, Appendix C)
Camping: Appendix A (64) (on-site)
Information: Macomb Reservation State Park, parks.ny.gov/parks/77/details.aspx
Take Note: No motors

GETTING THERE

From I-87, Exit 35, go 1.0 mile west on Route 442, and turn right on Route 22. Go 0.2 mile (1.2 miles), and turn left on Route 22B. Continue 2.0 miles (3.2 miles), and turn left on Brand Hollow Road. Go 1.5 miles (4.7 miles), and turn right on Clark Road for 0.4 mile (5.1 miles), then turn right on Peasleeville Road. Follow this road for 1.4 miles (6.5 miles), and veer right on Campsite

TRIP 38: DAVIS LAKE AND SALMON RIVER

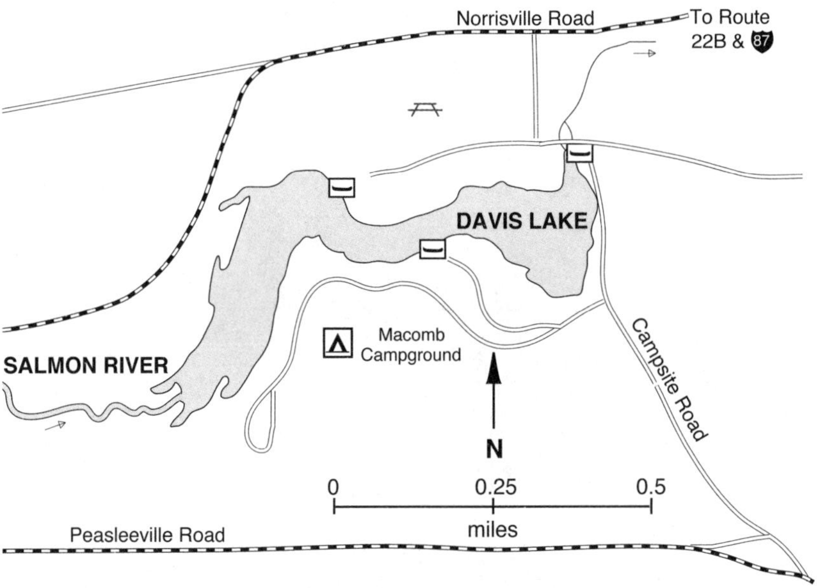

Road. Go 0.7 mile (7.2 miles) to the access on the right by the bridge. (*Note*: Other sites are available but charge fees.) (44° 37.132′ N, 73° 36.472′ W)

WHAT YOU'LL SEE

We really enjoy paddling Davis Lake and the Salmon River, which flows into its west end. Both the lake and the river are within Macomb Reservation State Park, which is surrounded by hills and wilderness and has an untamed feel to it. However, the river should be renamed "Salmon Creek," in keeping with its size and to avoid confusing it with other North Country Salmon Rivers.

Traverse small Davis Lake slowly to savor its beauty. Vegetation layers back from the water's edge, starting with ferns or cattails and various shrubs, giving way to birches and other small trees, ending with large red pines and a few scattered white pines. Near the stream entrance, narrow-leaved cattail gives way to wooded shores. Although alders have crowded almost everything else out, a fine grove of walnut trees grows here. Look for feather-like leaves resembling those of ash and deeply furrowed bark on straight trunks in older trees.

We did not get out of the boat to check to see whether the grove contained butternut or black walnut. Butternut ranges over the entire state, whereas black walnut occurs primarily in the southeast and in isolated populations in the central region. Because horticulturists have planted black walnut

A well-kept beaver dam provides a momentary impediment to paddling up the Salmon River.

widely—mainly because of their very valuable dark wood—these could be black walnut nonetheless. Black walnut has 15 to 23 leaflets per leaf, and the bark can get almost black in older trees; butternut has 11 to 17 leaflets per leaf and lighter bark.

Black walnut (and butternut to a lesser extent) has adopted an interesting strategy to limit competition for light and space from other trees. Established trees exude a chemical called juglone into the surrounding soil that inhibits germination of walnut and many other seeds, which also limits plant growth. So when we looked at the grove of even-aged walnut on Davis Lake, we suspected they were black walnut. (In retrospect, we should have checked more thoroughly to make sure they were not butternut.)

As we paddled Salmon River upstream, trout rose from their underwater haunts, deftly sucking in the evening's hatch of floating insects. However, beavers own this river. We turned around after carrying over three dams, one with a 2-foot drop and jewelweed sprouting from its bulwarks. In contrast with the muskrat that slipped quietly under the surface at our approach, three beavers on separate occasions slapped the water with their tails, splashing from bank to bank, to show their annoyance at our intrusion.

We wished the beavers had done a better job of pruning back the alders that converged on the channel, leaving only a few feet of passageway in spots. As we worked our way back down the meandering stream in the fading light, a veery called from the undergrowth. A mallard hen performed its broken wing trick, leading us away from its brood. Grapevines draped the streamside vegetation, giving sanctuary to song sparrows, yellowthroats, yellow warblers, brown thrashers, cardinals, and catbirds. The strains of the night—cicada, barred owl, frog, veery, white-throated sparrow—flooded the summer air as we paddled across Davis Lake, back to the campground in semidarkness. We strongly recommend an evening paddle into this wilderness just outside Adirondack Park's northern boundary.

39 | Taylor Pond

If it's not windy, this is a great place to paddle, and the mountainous backdrop lends the pond a wild feel. We love camping here, especially in sites accessible only by water. Expect to see loon, bald eagle, osprey, great blue heron, and a variety of woodland species. You may spy beaver in the Bear Brook area.

Location: Black Brook
Maps: *New York Atlas & Gazetteer*, Map 22: E3, E4; USGS Wilmington
Area: 803 acres
Time: 4 hours
Habitat Type: Deep oligotrophic lake
Fish: Salmon; lake, brown, and rainbow trout (see fish advisories, Appendix C)
Camping: Appendix A (94) (on-site); dec.ny.gov/outdoor/24498.html
Take Note: Nearby peaks funnel wind, making paddling treacherous in windy conditions; watch out near shore for barely submerged granite boulders.

GETTING THERE

From Saranac Lake, head north on Route 3 to Bloomingdale. Turn right on Route 3, go 11.9 miles, and turn right on Alder Brook Road. Follow this for 0.2 mile (12.1 miles), and turn left on Alder Brook Park Road. Continue 1.2 miles (13.3 miles), and bear left on Alder Brook Road/Union Falls Road. Go 5.6 miles (18.9 miles), and veer right on Silver Lake Road. After 2.8 miles (21.7 miles), turn right to Taylor Pond Campground. (44° 29.623′ N, 73° 49.504′ W)

From I-87, Exit 34, drive 9.8 miles west on Route 9N, and turn right on Palmer Street/Silver Lake Road. Go 9.4 miles (19.2 miles), and turn left to Taylor Pond Campground.

WHAT YOU'LL SEE

Surrounded by 8,000 acres of forest, Taylor Pond exudes wildness. Because of its out-of-the-way location and the campground's rustic character, the pond does not draw large numbers to its shores. We appreciate the 25 well-separated, wooded campsites but prefer those accessible only by boat. Campsites I-1 and I-2 on the tip of the peninsula separating the eastern arm from the main lake appeal to us most. Each nestles in a grove of hemlock, birch, and pine and has an outhouse, picnic table, and fire grate.

TRIP 39: TAYLOR POND

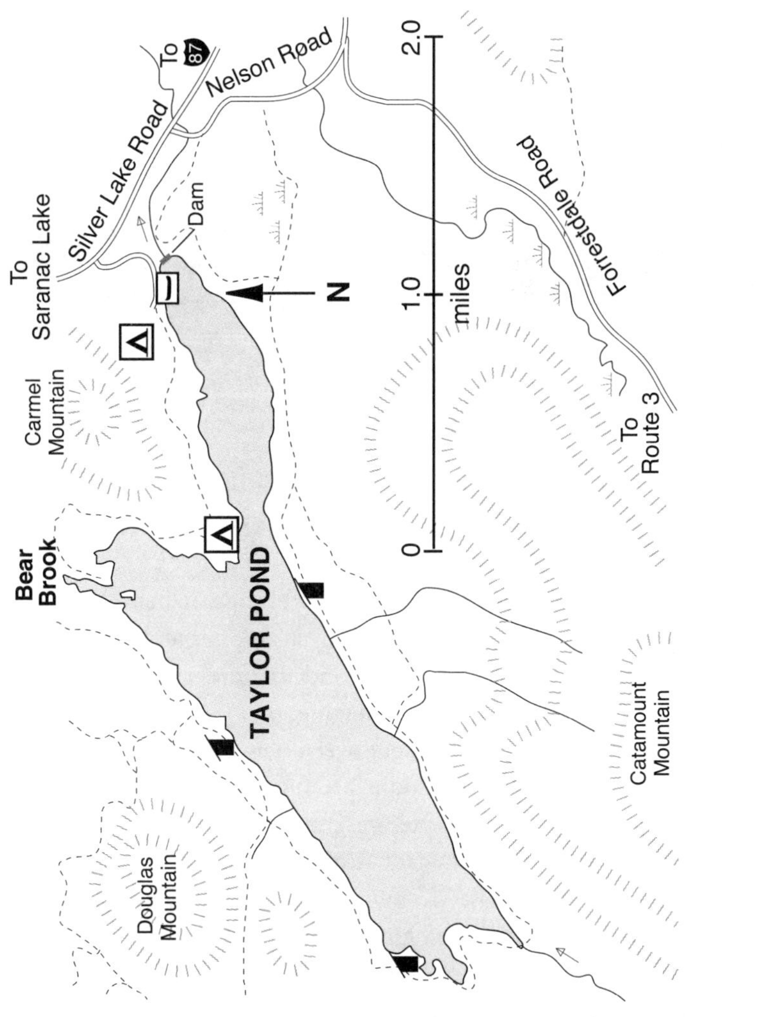

Most of the pond sports a sandy bottom, but watch out near shore for barely submerged granite boulders. Very narrow-leaved water celery floats on the surface in shallow areas, but the pond's depths do not support an abundance of aquatic vegetation. We found cranberry growing among the shoreside shrubbery, under a canopy of stunted birches and red maples. A wide array of deciduous trees dominates the hillsides, and conifers cling to the Catamount Mountain crest.

Catamount Mountain forms a backdrop for the large beaver dam at Bear Brook's mouth.

Paddling up the mouth of Bear Brook, with large, lichen-covered, pink granite boulders lining the shore, we glided by a large beaver lodge that nearly obliterated a small island. We could not find the underwater entrance; the stream bottom seemed pretty rocky for digging.

Returning to the pond, we gazed out over the water to the wooded peaks and extensive shoulders of Catamount Mountain that seem to guard the entire southern shore, providing a picturesque backdrop for a leisurely cruise. Although the mountain lion no longer patrols the shadows, we did see another species that has recently retreated from the Endangered Species List: a mature bald eagle. As we approached the peninsula, it took flight from a tall pine and soared ever higher on Catamount's thermals, becoming barely visible among the billowing white clouds. Given the midfall season, we suspect that the raptor had just started its migration to the coast or to some other body of water that does not freeze over.

We also saw wood ducks and great blue herons in quieter coves, along with the usual array of songbirds back in the woods. Hiking trails ring the pond and extend into the nearby hills, adding an extra dimension to this beautiful location.

40 | Moose Pond

This small, deep, secluded pond nestles among Adirondack peaks and the unbroken forest of the McKenzie Mountain Wilderness. Northern white cedar rings the pond, and trout swim in its depths. We are drawn to quiet camping along the shores. Expect to see many woodland bird species here.

Location: St. Armand
Maps: *New York Atlas & Gazetteer*, Map 30: A1; USGS Bloomingdale, Saranac Lake
Area: 140 acres
Time: 3 hours
Habitat Type: Small, deep oligotrophic pond
Fish: Smallmouth bass; landlocked salmon; Brook, lake, and rainbow trout (see fish advisories, Appendix C)
Camping: Appendix A (79, 86, 87, 91, 94, 95); dec.ny.gov/outdoor/89046.html
Take Note: Wind may cause treacherous paddling conditions.

GETTING THERE

From Saranac Lake, head north on Route 3 to Bloomingdale. Turn right on Route 3, go 0.2 mile, and turn right on River Road (County Highway 18). Go 1.6 miles (1.8 miles), and turn right on Moose Pond Road. Go 1.5 miles (3.3 miles) to the access. (44° 22.760′ N, 74° 3.552′ W)

WHAT YOU'LL SEE

With its 70-foot depth, Moose Pond differs from most of the area's shallow, boggy ponds, and because of that depth, it supports a coldwater trout fishery. Trout succumb readily to acidified water. Bogs, especially those with sphagnum—which secretes hydrogen ions that acidify its environment—do not support trout well. Decaying bog vegetation also gives off tannic and other acids during oxidation that add further acidity. Although trout might survive (barely) under such conditions, they certainly cannot survive the added import of acid rain from the Midwest. Acid rain is caused by sulfur dioxide—eventually converted to sulfurous and sulfuric acids in the atmosphere—along with hydrochloric and nitric acids, which emanate from unscrubbed, coal-fired power plants. Such acid rain tolls a death knell for high Adirondack lakes, and hundreds of

TRIP 40: MOOSE POND

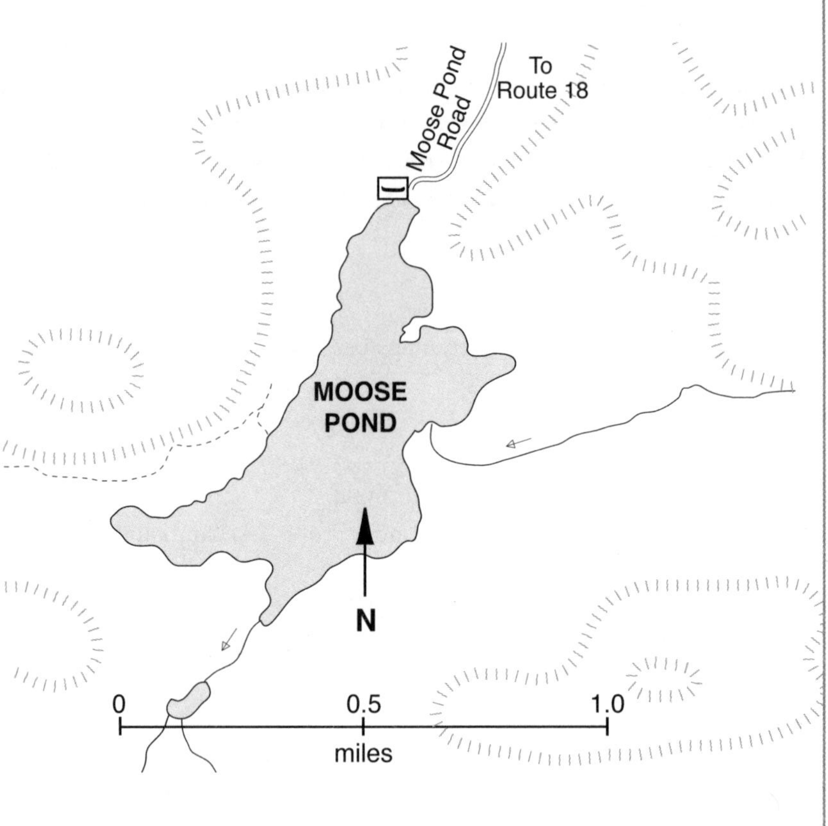

them no longer support trout. Thankfully, such environmental insults have not ruined Moose Pond.

Precambrian rock—mostly granite and gneiss (pronounced "nice")—pokes up through sedimentary rock to form the Adirondack High Peaks. Although a relatively new upthrust (evidence suggests it is ongoing), the high peak rocks date to about a billion years ago. These rocks do not react with acids and therefore do not buffer (reduce acidity of) acid rain or high-altitude bogs. Most low-elevation lakes in the Adirondacks lie over marble, a type of calcium carbonate, just like limestone. Acids readily react with calcium carbonate, liberating carbon dioxide and water, effectively neutralizing acid rain. So fish have not disappeared from low-elevation lakes as they have from higher elevations. And with the nation's reduced use of coal, many high-altitude lakes have made a comeback.

High Adirondack peaks overlook the placid waters of Moose Pond.

Surrounded by scenic, forested Adirondack peaks, Moose Pond nestles in a deep, pristine valley. These same peaks funnel north-south winds, making this small pond's waters treacherous during windy periods. Large, smooth granite boulders line the shore in places, adding to the scenery and offering easy egress for picnicking and camping at designated sites. In fall, deer hunters use the boulders for base camps as they foray off into the huge, roadless McKenzie Mountain Wilderness—home of two of the hundred tallest Adirondack peaks.

A hemlock stand grows near the access, and northern white cedars ring the pond. Thick stands of birch reflect off the clear water, standing in stark contrast to the evergreen conifers. Occasional yellow birches blend in with the hemlocks and tall white pines. Although it does not take long to paddle the complete shoreline of Moose Pond, one could camp here for days, relaxing, reading, philosophizing, and, of course, paddling in relative isolation, surrounded by clear, trout-filled waters and scenic mountains.

41 | Lake Kushaqua and Rainbow Lake

A study in contrasts, these lakes offer everything from the quietwater paddler's dream to crowds of water-skiers and personal watercraft. You could spend several days here, but if you have limited time, we suggest visiting the Saranac River North Branch. You will likely see osprey, great blue heron, waterfowl, deer, and a host of songbirds. Lots of interesting plants populate the narrows and the river.

Location: Brighton, Franklin
Maps: *New York Atlas & Gazetteer*, Map 21: D10, E9, E10; USGS Bloomingdale, Debar Mountain, Loon Lake
Area and Length: Rainbow Lake, 588 acres; Lake Kushaqua, 377 acres; river length, 3 miles one way
Time: All day
Habitat Type: Extensive interconnected lakes and river
Fish: Largemouth and smallmouth bass, northern pike, kokanee salmon, lake trout, walleye (see fish advisories, Appendix C)
Camping: Appendix A (79) (on-site); dec.ny.gov/outdoor/24457.html
Take Note: Motors allowed; trails accessed from campground

GETTING THERE

Kushaqua/Rainbow Narrows Access. From the junction of Bloomingdale Avenue/Route 3 and Church Street in Saranac Lake, go 6.4 miles north on Route 3, and continue straight on State Street/Oregon Plains Road where Route 3 goes right. After 5.8 miles (12.2 miles), turn right on Route 60/Gabriels-Onchiota Road, follow that road for 0.8 mile (13.0 miles), and continue straight on Kushaqua-Mud Pond Road where Route 60 goes right. Go 0.6 mile (13.6 miles) to the access on the left before the bridge over the narrows. (44° 30.093′ N, 74° 7.603′ W)

Lake Kushaqua Outlet Access. From the Kushaqua/Rainbow Narrows access, continue north for 0.6 mile (14.2 miles) on Kushaqua–Mud Pond Road, and bear right at the fork. Go 2.1 miles (16.3 miles) to the access on the right. (44° 31.673′ N, 74° 6.297′ W)

Buck Pond Campground Access. From the junction of Route 60 and Kushaqua–Mud Pond Road, go 0.3 mile (13.3 miles) east on Route 60 to the campground entrance on the left. (44° 29.740′ N, 74° 7.034′ W)

TRIP 41: LAKE KUSHAQUA AND RAINBOW LAKE

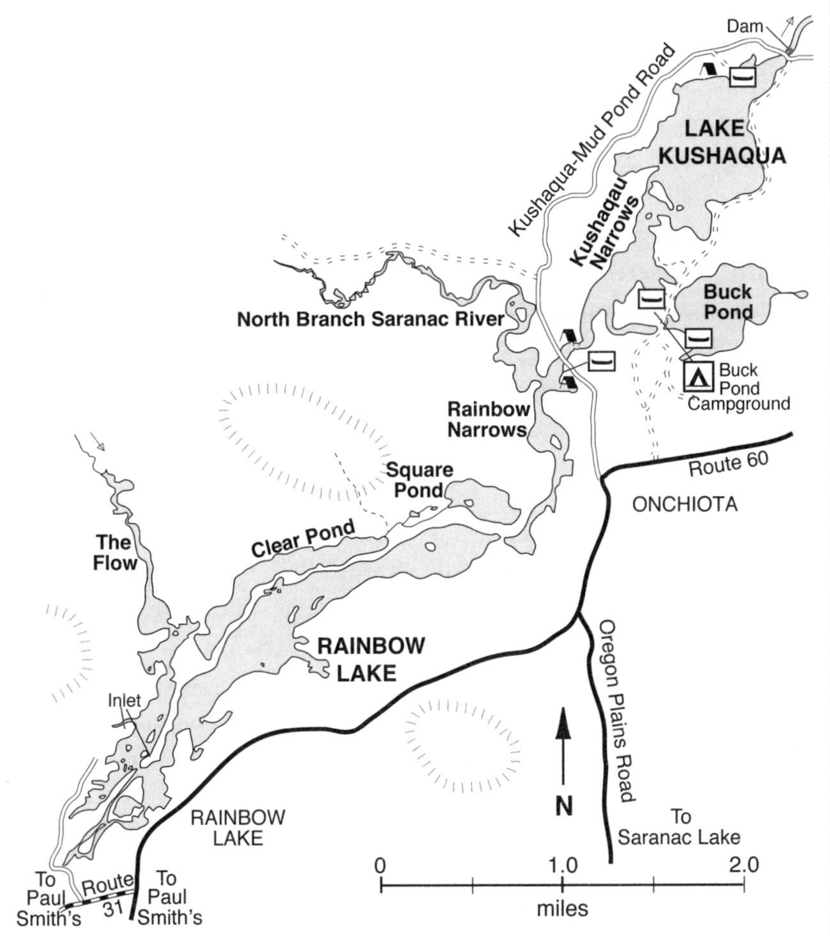

WHAT YOU'LL SEE

The Kushaqua Lake area contains several different types of water; you could spend several days exploring it all. To orient you, we start descriptions in the north and move south.

Lake Kushaqua

Kushaqua offers picturesque scenery with forested hillsides and wonderful, secluded lakeside camping, but the relatively round lake offers few inlets and marshes to explore. The delicate branches of gray birch, suspended over the water, add to the scenic beauty. In fall, the foliage—crimson and orange from many red and sugar maples, coupled with the vibrant yellow of striped maples and big-tooth aspens, viewed against a dark-green backdrop of white and red pines—makes camping a colorful experience.

Kushaqua Narrows

Explore the Narrows' interesting coves and islands. Buck Pond Campground and boat ramp do not intrude significantly. A rope swing dangled from a red pine bough, and deer nonchalantly browsed the shoreside brush and drank from the cool waters as we cruised by. A great blue heron took flight at our approach. Sweetgale and sheep laurel draped the shores, and bracken fern stretched for filtered light from the pine canopy. Mussel shells littered the bottom in the clear water.

If you paddle back through the narrow cove southeast near the base of the narrows—a quiet, idyllic spot with ducks swimming and lacy green hemlock branches draping out over the water—you can reach Buck Pond . . . eventually, by carrying up over a steep bank and road.

Saranac River North Branch

The North Branch entering the narrows from the west—beginning with a maze of drowned timber, floating vegetation, and a large, thickly forested island—provides a haven for wildlife and quietwater paddlers. We saw only one other canoe at the mouth and nary a soul in the upper reaches. If you have limited time, make this your prime destination. It avoids the lakes' congestion and noise and provides hours of solitude in pristine and varied wildlife habitats.

We felt transported back to the distant past as we paddled among the towering tamaracks, spruces, white pines, and balsam firs at the river's mouth. The primeval, forested swamp funneled down to a narrow, boulder-strewn passageway and then opened into a series of wide beaver meadows. We wondered how the aquatic plants divide the habitat as we paddled through acres of pondweed followed by acres of water shield and then acres of yellow pondlily. Water celery undulated in the light current, and alders began to appear, along with rafts of beaver cuttings, beaver dams, and lodges. Large birds showed up as well: turkey vulture, northern raven, and great blue heron.

An alder flycatcher cried a buzzy *fee-bee-o* from, appropriately enough, the alder swamp. This uncommon, inconspicuous warbler-sized bird has a very drab olive-brown back and pale yellow belly, with two white wing bars and a small white eye ring. Like the nine other similarly colored *Empidonax* species found throughout the United States and Canada, it sits upright on exposed branches, waiting to pounce on juicy insects that fly by. Listen for its song near alder stands in spring and early summer.

As we gazed into the distance, the cathedral-like spires of balsam firs provided a mesmerizing effect—we did not mind carrying up over beaver dams to penetrate farther back into the wilderness. The song of the swamp sparrow, a metallic chip followed by a musical trill, made us want to locate the furtive little bird. A painted turtle swam up to greet us in the clear water. Reluctantly, we paddled back down the river.

Rainbow Narrows

Rainbow Narrows, really just a continuation of Kushaqua Narrows, boasts much the same beauty but with slightly more boat traffic. A waterway crossroads with spires of spruces, balsam firs, and other conifers, it transports boaters between Rainbow and Kushaqua lakes and the mouth of the Saranac River North Branch. The exceedingly narrow concrete passageway keeps the bigger boats in Rainbow Lake from polluting Lake Kushaqua.

Rainbow Lake

Rainbow Lake's development started with an inn and a few rustic camps back in 1856; it now gets too much attention from personal watercraft, water-skiers, and motorboats. Cottages and houses line the banks in places. We had hoped to spend a short time on Rainbow Lake by carrying up over the mile-long esker that separates it from Clear Pond, but we decided that it was too brushy and

Conifers line the shore in many places on Lake Kushaqua, Rainbow Lake, and the Saranac River North Branch.

steep. For a fascinating discussion of eskers, see the Rainbow Lake section of *Adirondack Canoe Waters: North Flow* by Paul Jamieson and Donald Morris (Adirondack Mountain Club Books, 1988).

Clear Pond and The Flow

To reach Clear Pond and The Flow, paddle southwest on Rainbow Lake about 2.5 miles to a developed area known as Inlet. Glide through the narrow break in the esker into The Flow. Going north here, you leave the lake traffic behind and return to the peace and quiet you expect in the northern Adirondacks. About two-thirds of a mile north from the opening, a narrow channel to the right (east) leads into Clear Pond. As we paddled back through the narrows—listening to calls of white-throated sparrow, hermit thrush, ovenbird, white-breasted nuthatch, red-eyed vireo, and several species of warbler—the nesting barn swallows under the bridge exploded into the air at our passage. We knew we would be back for further explorations.

RIVER OTTER: PLAYFUL MEMBER OF THE WEASEL FAMILY

The river otter, *Lontra canadensis,* inhabits New York's remote lakes and rivers. We have seen dozens throughout the state, mostly in the Adirondacks, but also some on more southern waterways, even in the highly visited waters of Harriman State Park. Look for them in early morning and late afternoon.

Otters once inhabited virtually every U.S. watercourse, from sun-warmed southwestern rivers to icy far-northern lakes and streams. Today, because of 250 years of trapping, water pollution, and encroaching development, the otter has retreated to the far corners of its former range. Because it eats at the top of the food chain, the otter also suffers from pollution and toxic chemicals in the environment, such as heavy metals, DDT derivatives, dioxin, and PCBs.

In 1936, New York passed legislation to protect otters. Though subject to a limited trapping season, otters have returned to New York's waterways and might be seen anywhere east of I-81. In recent years, they have been sighted on Long Island and in western New York, where River Otter Project volunteers released more than 200 from 1995 to 2001.

With its long, thin body and relatively thick, sharply tapered tail, the otter can reach 4 feet in length and weigh up to 25 pounds. Long prized by trappers, its dense, dark-brown fur above gives way to lighter colors on the belly and throat.

The otter has adapted well to its aquatic environment. Nose and ears close when underwater, and webbed toes aid in swimming. Although it swims fast enough to catch trout, it usually pursues slower-moving prey: suckers, minnows, crayfish, tadpoles, and salamanders. It often thrusts its head way up above the surface, looking around and exhaling loudly.

While adapted for water, the otter does well on land, moving with a typical weasel-family undulating gait. Clocked at up to 18 MPH on the ground, it can travel 100 miles overland in search of new territory. It generally chooses dens—abandoned beaver lodges or natural cavities under tree roots—at the water's edge, with an underwater entrance.

The otter consumes smaller fish and crayfish in the water and larger prey onshore or on a protruding rock. An ingenious hunter, it sometimes herds fish into shallows or may punch a hole in a beaver dam, allowing water to escape, and then wade in and feast on flopping fish. Because they hunt so successfully, they have plenty of time to play—a famous otter trait.

Animal behaviorists believe that play among young mammals provides practice for future hunting, territorial interactions, and courtship. But otters continue to play as adults, chasing one another or repeatedly climbing a snowbank or mudbank and sliding down into the water.

Otters mate in late winter; birth occurs almost a year later. Like many weasel family members, otters delay embryo implantation, stopping development until the following winter. Usually two to four cubs are born anytime between November and April. Cubs emerge fully furred, but with eyes closed and no teeth. They venture outside the den after about three months. Although the mother provides initial care alone, the father may rejoin the family to help with rearing after about six months.

Although the otter is curious and relatively bold, keep your distance. Interference from humans may cause it to search for a more remote location.

42 | Osgood Pond, Jones Pond, and Osgood River

You won't find solitude on Osgood Pond, but Osgood River is a lot less crowded. When we paddled here, we saw many ducks, muskrats, carnivorous plants, and sphagnum bog shrubs, all surrounded by trees of the northern boreal forest. Intrepid paddlers can also work their way up the Osgood Pond inlet over to Jones Pond; expect to portage a few times along the way.

Location: Brighton
Maps: *New York Atlas & Gazetteer*, Map 21: E8, E9; USGS Bloomingdale, Saint Regis Mountain
Area and Length: Osgood Pond, 508 acres; Jones Pond, 170 acres; river lengths, 1.5 miles and 3.0 miles, each one way
Time: 5 hours
Habitat Type: Interconnected ponds and river
Fish: Largemouth and smallmouth bass, northern pike, brook trout (see fish advisories, Appendix C; see specific advisory, health.ny.gov/environmental/outdoors/fish/health_advisories)
Camping: Appendix A (79, 81, 86, 87, 90, 91)
Information: White Pine Camp, whitepinecamp.com

GETTING THERE

Osgood Pond Access. From the junction of Routes 30 and 86 at Paul Smith's College, go 0.6 mile east on Route 86, and turn left on White Pine Road. Go 0.2 mile (0.8 mile), and turn left on the access road. (44° 26.627′ N, 74° 14.260′ W)

Jones Pond Access. From Paul Smith's College, go 1.0 mile east on Route 86, and turn left on County Route 31. Go 2.6 miles (3.6 miles) to the access road on the right. (44° 27.431′ N, 74° 11.271′ W)

WHAT YOU'LL SEE

Tall white pines ring the cove at the Osgood Pond access. Occasional tamaracks and red maples and a few birches appear, as well. The shoreline surrounding the rest of the pond also contains large numbers of pines. Despite the forested shores, noise from Route 30 and nearby summer cabins intrudes on the pond's solitude. Fortunately, solitude begins about a mile from the access, as you paddle north down the Osgood River outlet.

TRIP 42: OSGOOD POND, JONES POND, AND OSGOOD RIVER

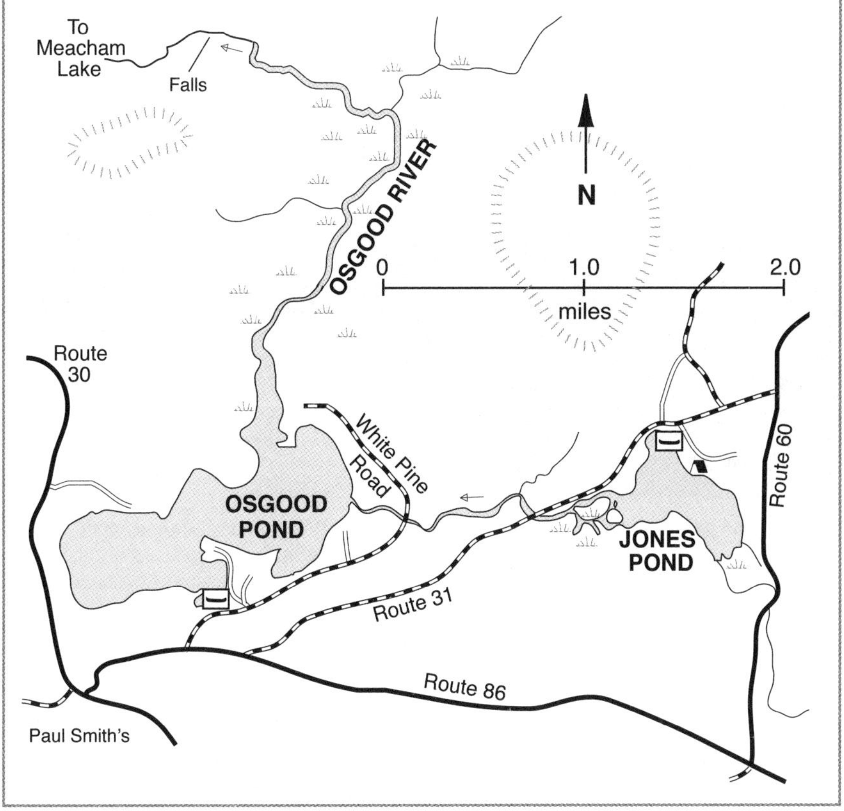

Trees of the northern boreal forest—tamarack, spruce, northern white cedar, and balsam fir—dominate the river's western bank, and pines cover the eastern side's higher ground. Among these trees—many actually red pines—lies White Pine Camp, the site of Calvin Coolidge's 1926 summer White House. With its twenty buildings and walkways surrounded by rhododendron, the restored camp is open to the public as an inn. One of the great rustic estates of the Adirondacks, the camp boasts 3,900 feet of shoreline and 35 acres and was featured on the cover of this book's second edition.

As the camp gives way to state-owned land along the river, note the stunted, spire-like black spruces of the sphagnum bog, the only spruce species that tolerates partially submerged roots. We paddled downriver about 3 miles, until we reached a series of waterfalls. If you want to continue at this point for an adventure, refer to Paul Jamieson and Donald Morris's *Adirondack Canoe Waters: North Flow* (Adirondack Mountain Club Books, 1988). In places, the

Tamarack and balsam fir line the shores of Osgood River as it flows out of Osgood Pond.

river disappears under marsh vegetation, making the trek down to Meacham Lake a real challenge.

Conifers completely dominate the boggy northern boreal forest here; we saw only a handful of deciduous trees along the river. A wide variety of shrubs perch on the sphagnum hummocks, including sweetgale, leatherleaf, sheep laurel, bog laurel, and bog rosemary. Large clumps of pitcher plants line the shore in spots, and diminutive sundew rosettes glisten in the sun, awaiting insects drawn to their traps' sticky "dew." Yellow pondlily, American white waterlily, pondweed, and water celery crowd the channel, while bur-reed and pickerelweed compete for space along the shore.

As we rounded each bend, through early morning autumn mists drifting slowly across the water, small flocks of black ducks sprang into the air, beating their wings furiously. Many groups of three to twelve wood ducks, some all males in bright plumage, erupted from the water while sounding out their mournful, un-duck-like cries. They circled around behind us, only to be disturbed once again on our return trip. This attractive duck, driven to the verge of extinction around the turn of the century by unregulated hunting and clearing of forests, has rebounded nicely. Prompted by the then newly formed National Audubon Society, the government passed legislation in the early 1900s that protected the wood duck and other migratory species. Bird-watchers and wildlife management officials began erecting wood duck nesting boxes in the 1940s, leading to greatly increased populations of this beautiful bird, one of North America's few cavity-nesting ducks.

A logjam followed by a series of falls indicated the end of the line. Lichens festooning some spruces provided a primeval look as the bog gave way to forest. Reluctantly, we turned around to retrace our way back to the pond.

Reaching the pond, we paddled southeast to the Jones Pond outlet and traveled this small creek all the way up to Jones Pond, carrying over a few beaver dams and one road. Water had breached some abandoned dams, and we eased our way through the narrow channels. Most alders that formerly lined the banks had disappeared, leaving only stumps and conifers, which beaver rarely eat. Apparently, the beavers had eaten themselves out of house and home, leaving only grasses to feed the muskrats that we saw occasionally.

On Jones Pond, a pleasant, informal camping area extends along a dirt road from the access. Ovenbirds call from the midstory in an extensive red pine grove. Camping here on several occasions, we never tired of the nighttime sounds of whip-poor-will, barred owl, and great horned owl.

43 | Deer River Flow and Horseshoe Pond

The northern boreal forest that surrounds Deer River Flow in the northern Adirondacks harbors lots of wildlife. Expect to see bald eagle, loon, northern harrier, kingfisher, great blue heron, deer, beaver, and muskrat. You could also spot mink and otter. You will definitely see rafts of a variety of marshland plants in these shallow waters.

Location: Duane
Maps: *New York Atlas & Gazetteer*, Map 21: B8, C8; USGS Large Titus
Area: 500 acres
Time: 5 hours
Habitat Type: Shallow, marshy pond surrounded by northern boreal forest
Fish: Largemouth and smallmouth bass, northern pike (see fish advisories, Appendix C)
Camping: Appendix A (79, 86, 94)
Take Note: Some road noise from Route 30 near the access; some development on Horseshoe Pond

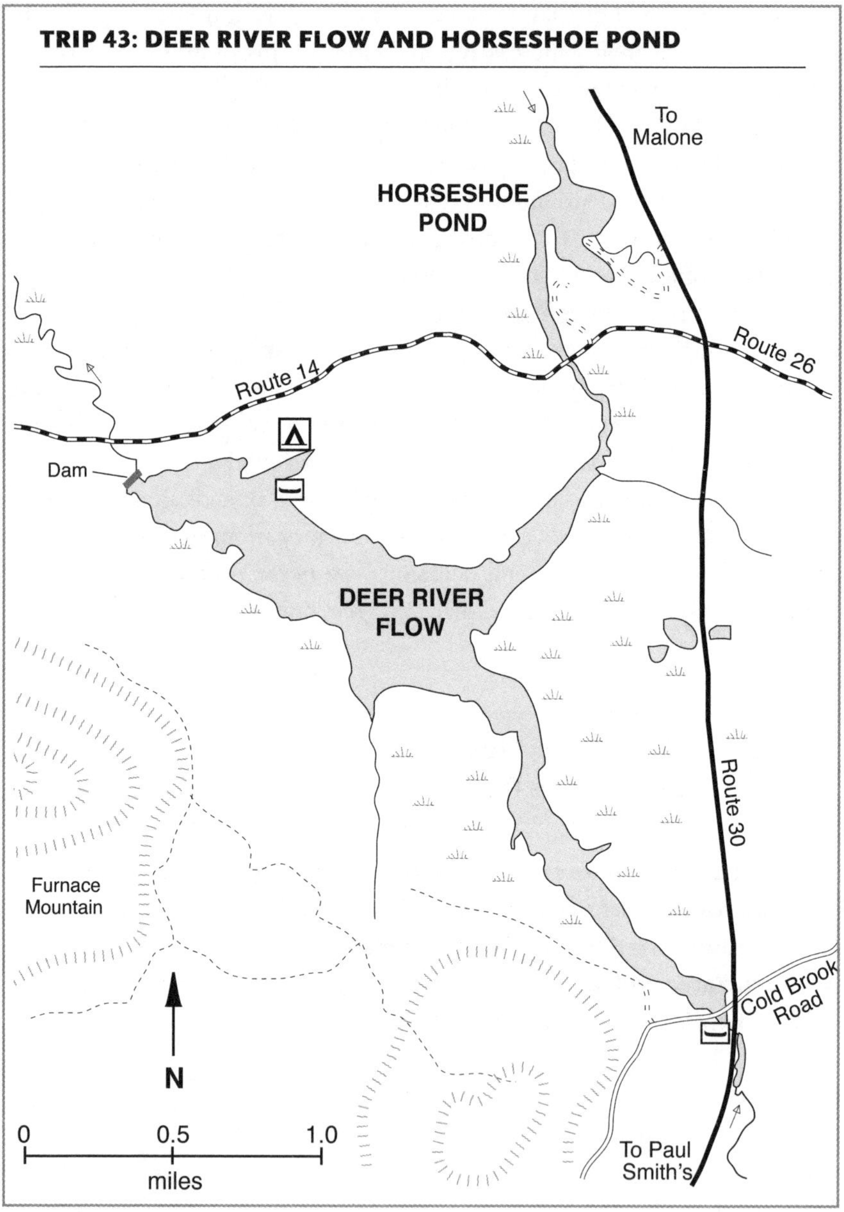

GETTING THERE

From Paul Smith's College, go 15.1 miles north on Route 30, and turn left on Cold Brook Road. Go 0.2 mile (15.3 miles) to the access road on the right. (44° 37.959′ N, 74° 16.909′ W)

From Malone, go 16.6 miles south on Route 30, turn right on Cold Brook Road, and follow the directions above.

WHAT YOU'LL SEE

Paddling in the shallow, tea-colored water, we felt transported to the time of nineteenth-century Adirondack guides. Ringed by spire-like conifers—tall tamaracks, balsam firs, black and red spruces, northern white cedars, white pines—with gorgeous mountain views to the south and west, Deer River Flow retains a magical aura, even though Route 30 intrudes a little on its southern arm.

The magic increased dramatically when we spotted a bald eagle nest with two nearly grown fledglings perched on side branches. Seeing four eagles at once made our paddle here superbly enjoyable. Bald eagles nested widely in the Adirondacks until they were nearly done in by DDT poisoning and habitat destruction. Beginning in the late 1980s, they resumed nesting—the result of a massive reintroduction program that began in 1976. Although we have seen many bald eagles in our intensive exploration of the state's quiet waters, we still marvel at the grace and strength of this remarkable raptor. Awe-inspiring is the only way to describe seeing one swoop down to the water's surface on powerful wing beats to snatch a fish in its talons. For more on the bald eagle, see "Bald Eagle: National Bird Back from the Brink," on page 117.

As we scanned the skies for more birds, a northern harrier glided low over the marsh, on the watch for rodents. But the shoreline habitat along both Deer

A pine seeks light over open water.

River Flow and Horseshoe Pond belongs to the red-winged blackbird. The territories must be worth defending, because the males sing from cattails every few feet along the marsh. The shrubby shoreline, lined with sweetgale, bog rosemary—with its long, narrow leaves, green on top, white underneath—sheep laurel, and more, also provides excellent habitat for the common yellowthroat, a diminutive yellow warbler with a black mask across its eyes, looking rather like a robber ready to pounce on unwary insects.

Out on the flow, mussel shells litter the bottom near the boggy shore. Although tamaracks have started to invade the peat bog and will eventually fill it in, it still supports plenty of bog specialists, including sundews and pitcher plants. Because pitcher plants and sundews live in nutrient-poor soils, they supplement the meager nitrogen available by capturing and digesting insects. Pitchers fill with rainwater, into which the plant secretes digestive enzymes. When unlucky insects fall in, downward-pointing hairs keep them from crawling back out. Eventually they drown and give up their precious nutrient stores to the plant.

The sundew operates in a similar manner. Glistening dew-like secretions on stalks emanating from the sundew pad attract insects, which become trapped on the sticky substance. The plant rolls the insect inward slightly to come in contact with shorter stalks that contain digestive enzymes. The degraded insect material provides needed nitrogen to the plant (for more on carnivorous plants, see "Carnivorous Plants: The Table is Turned," on page 361).

The shallow water harbors acres of yellow pondlily, American white waterlily, and water celery, with its long, narrow leaves floating on the surface, especially on the connecting stream into Horseshoe Pond. As you enter Horseshoe Pond, an occasional house intrudes on the right-hand shore, while sphagnum, black spruce, tamarack, and carnivorous plants cover the left.

We loved paddling here and found it hard to leave. We spent quite a bit of time trying to photograph iridescent green damselflies. In addition to observing the eagles and harrier, we watched deer come down to the water's edge for a drink and numerous muskrats harvesting aquatic vegetation. We spied one beaver and evidence of many more. We highly recommend paddling here, especially in early morning or late afternoon, to see wildlife and to study myriad bog and aquatic plants. But please keep your distance, especially around eagle nests.

44 | Osgood River and Meacham Lake

Meacham Lake attracts a lot of water-skiers and personal watercraft in summer, which is why we stick to the quiet, marshy, ever-meandering Osgood River, which is really a small creek. Look for muskrat, beaver, a diminutive yellow waterlily species, sundew, pitcher plant, and other marshland species.

Location: Brighton, Duane
Maps: *New York Atlas & Gazetteer*, Map 21: D8; USGS Meacham Lake
Area and Length: 1,203 acres; river length 6 miles one way
Time: 3 hours to all day on Osgood River
Habitat Type: Large lake, marshy stream, northern boreal forest
Fish: Smallmouth bass, northern pike, landlocked salmon, splake, brown trout (see fish advisories, Appendix C; see specific advisory, health.ny.gov/environmental/outdoors/fish/health_advisories)
Camping: Appendix A (86) (on-site); dec.ny.gov/outdoor/24481.html
Take Note: Wind can cause huge waves on Meacham Lake; when windy, use the Route 30 access to reach Osgood River.

GETTING THERE

Dam access. From Paul Smith's College, go 9.1 miles north on Route 30, and turn right to arrive at the dam, just past the bridge. (44° 33.228′ N, 74° 18.515′ W)

Upper access. From the dam, continue 2.6 miles (11.7 miles) north on Route 30, and turn right on State Camp Road, which leads to the access and campground. (44° 35.159′ N, 74° 17.502′ W)

WHAT YOU'LL SEE

Although the state owns the land surrounding Meacham Lake, it allows motorboats and personal watercraft. On summer weekends, the lake's surface fills with noise and wakes, which is not surprising given that the campground has 222 sites. We vastly prefer paddling up Osgood River on the south end, easily reached by putting in at the dam on the outflow and heading east along the shoreline. Even when the wind blows from the north, abundant aquatic vegetation on the south end dampens the swells. On a very windy day, we had little difficulty traversing over to the river and back, even though we had to paddle in wave troughs.

TRIP 43: DEER RIVER FLOW AND HORSESHOE POND

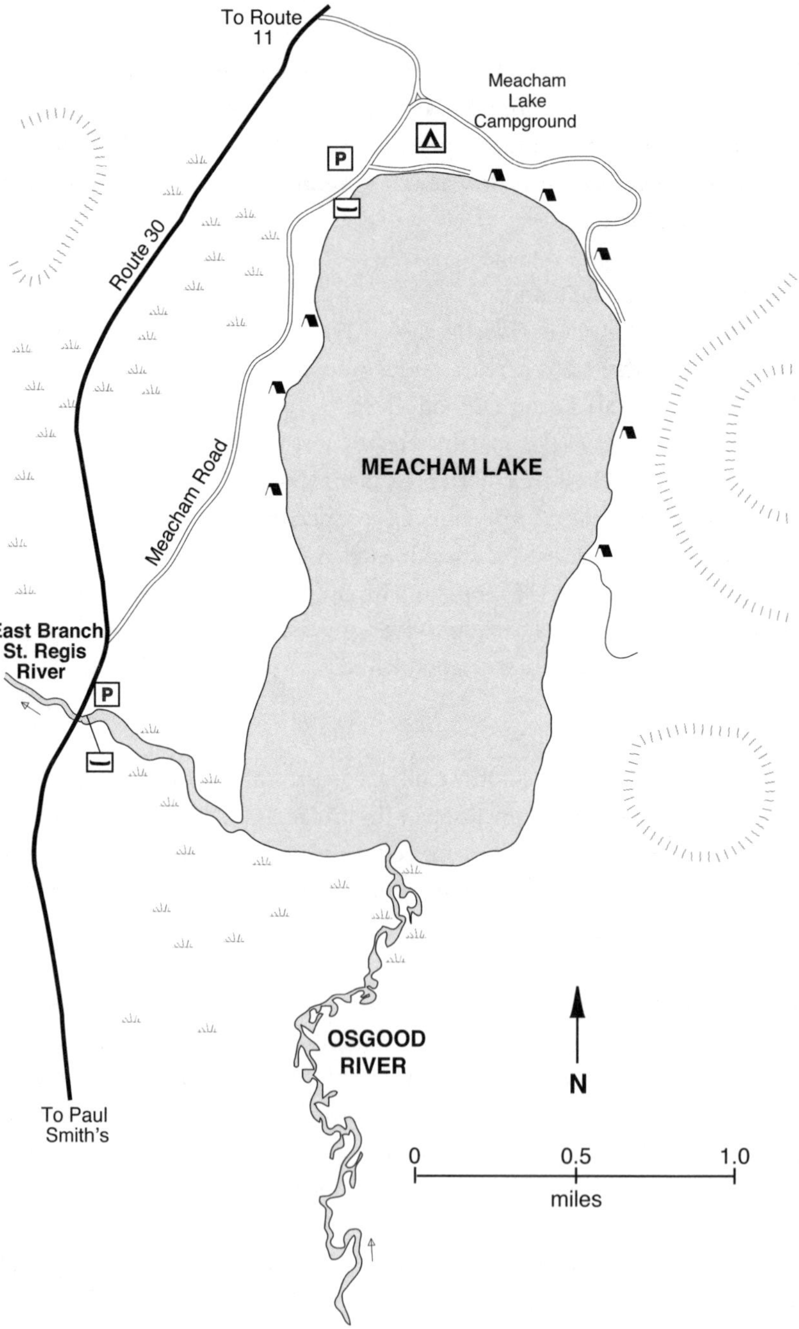

We paddled up Osgood River, and the same scene unfolded before us that we experienced when we paddled the upper reaches flowing out of Osgood Pond (see trip 42). Few deciduous trees appear among the abundant conifers along the marshy shores. This northern boreal forest supports an unusual array of bird species rarely seen farther south in New York, including gray jay—the so-called whiskey jack or camp robber—which exhibits little fear of humans; boreal chickadee, with its gray-brown cap and nasal call; spruce grouse, a quite tame, chunkier relative of the ruffed grouse; and crossbills, both red and white-winged, with beaks that cross instead of meeting together when closed, an adaptation they use to good advantage in prying seeds loose from pinecones.

Tamaracks and black spruces, both of which withstand partially submerged roots, grow on sphagnum substrate. Balsam firs and white pines grow on the banks and on islands, with red and white spruces on drier ground. Paddling here in fall provides a rare and beautiful treat: the golden-needled tamarack against a backdrop of dark-green conifers. Tamarack drops all of its needles in fall, the only conifer to do so. Other conifers drop only two- or three-year-old needles, leaving a healthy crop of new green needles growing at twig ends.

Another interesting plant occurs in Osgood River: the smallest of the yellow pondlilies (*Nuphar microphyllum*), which, as its scientific name suggests, has very small leaves—less than 5 inches long—compared with larger waterlilies. Its diminutive flower measures less than an inch across when fully open.

The smallest yellow pondlily—*Nuphar microphyllum*—grows amid pondweed leaves on Osgood River.

You can paddle up Osgood for many miles before it becomes impassable, disappearing under swamp vegetation. To paddle from Osgood Pond to Meacham Lake would be quite an adventure. Reluctantly, after a few miles of slow progress on this endlessly meandering stream, carrying over downed logs and half-hearted beaver dams, we contemplated paddling back to the access. The dams, beaver lodges, and abundant cuttings—all alder wood—reminded us that beavers generally do not forage on conifers' resinous bark, thereby limiting numbers on Osgood River. As beavers hack down streamside alders, they literally eat themselves out of house and home. As the fast-growing alders return, so do beavers to start the cycle once again.

Trappers extirpated the beaver in New York in the late 1800s. In 1904, conservation officials released six beavers near Old Forge; in 1906, they released 25 more from Yellowstone Park. From this nucleus, the prolific rodents reached a population of nearly 20,000 by 1915. Amazingly, beavers now cover the state, numbering about 100,000 individuals. You will see them on Osgood River in early evening . . . unless they have decimated the alders again (for more on the beaver, see "Beaver: Wetlands Engineer," on page 81).

Paddling back to the river's mouth on calm water, we had almost forgotten the north wind–driven swells on Meacham Lake, but after a short sprint to the outlet channel, we again met calm waters. The outlet channel leading to and from the dam differs significantly from Osgood River. Rounded boulders poke up above the water's surface, and the boggy areas contain sundews and pitcher plants in profusion. Deciduous trees—a rare commodity in the boreal forest—grow along the bank. And instead of the exotic bird species of the coniferous forest, here red-winged blackbirds, black-throated green warblers, and white-throated sparrows serenade from streamside perches. Dwarf gray birches grace the shores, along with alders, sheep laurel, and other shrubs; horsetail, floating heart, pickerelweed, and pondweed cover patches of water.

45 | Saint Regis Lakes and Spitfire Lake

These lakes, gateway to the Saint Regis Canoe Area, are worth paddling on their own. You will see loon, osprey, deer, and lots more as you explore boggy areas and admire spectacular Adirondack architecture along the shorelines.

Location: Brighton, Harrietstown
Maps: *New York Atlas & Gazetteer*, Map 21: E8, E9 and Map 29: A8; USGS Bloomingdale, Saint Regis Mountain
Area: Lower Saint Regis Lake, 365 acres; Spitfire Lake, 254 acres; Upper Saint Regis Lake, 711 acres
Time: All day or multiday
Habitat Type: Lakes with many islands and coves
Fish: Largemouth and smallmouth bass, northern pike, landlocked salmon, splake, lake trout (see fish advisories, Appendix C)
Camping: On-site wilderness camping
Information: St. Regis Canoe Outfitters, canoeoutfitters.com
Take Note: Provides access to Saint Regis Canoe Area

GETTING THERE

Lower Saint Regis Lake Access. At the junction of Routes 86 and 30, enter the campus of Paul Smith's College directly across from Route 86, and bear right to two parking areas behind Franklin and Essex residence halls. If leaving your vehicle overnight, check with campus security. (44° 26.071′ N, 74° 15.241′ W)

Upper Saint Regis Lake Access. From the junction of Routes 86 and 30, go 3.9 miles south on Route 30, turn right on Saint Regis Carry Road, and go 0.4 mile (4.3 miles) to the access. (44° 23.701′ N, 74° 16.187′ W)

From Lake Clear Junction, go 2.9 miles north on Route 30, and turn left on Saint Regis Carry Road.

WHAT YOU'LL SEE

Lower Saint Regis Lake

Lower Saint Regis, the northernmost of these lakes, suffers much less from development and therefore sports a more varied habitat, including extensive marshy areas. Several lean-tos are available for camping. While Paul Smith's College dominates its environs, most of the shoreline remains undeveloped.

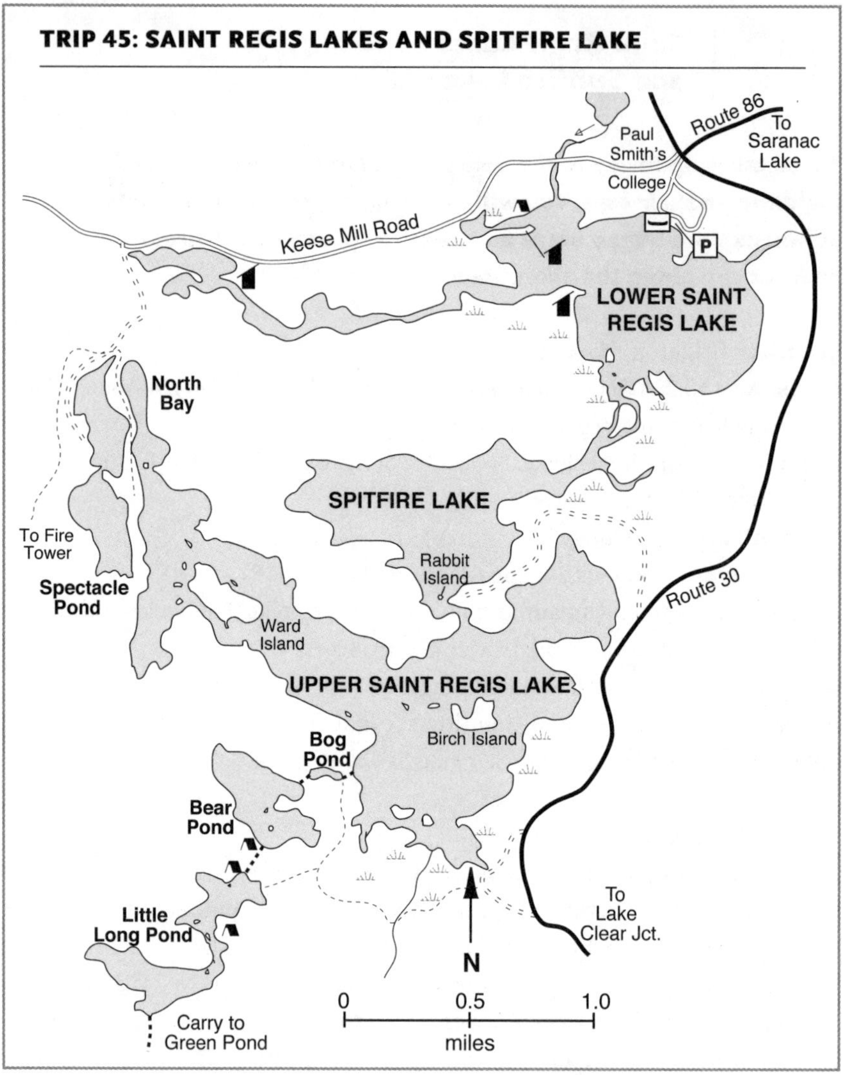

Botanists will find the small inlet west of the college particularly interesting. Its boggy perimeter harbors a classic northern fen ecosystem, thick with leatherleaf, sheep laurel, bog rosemary, cranberry, sweetgale, sphagnum, pitcher plant, rose pogonia, and tamarack.

The college gets its name from Paul Smith, who owned thousands of acres in this area. In 1859, Smith opened the Saint Regis House on Lower Saint Regis, and it quickly became a playground for the rich and famous, including three U.S. presidents and P. T. Barnum. The original Saint Regis House—commonly known as Paul Smith's—had a modest seventeen rooms, but the building mushroomed to a sprawling 225-unit complex by the early 1900s, with gardens, casino, bowling alley, and—for visiting financiers—even a direct line to the New York Stock Exchange.

Much more important than being the site of luxury accommodations of ages past, this area played a role in awakening interest in the environment. In *An Adirondack Passage: The Cruise of the Canoe Sairy Gamp* (Breakaway Books, 2013), the author, Christine Jerome, describes how the region cemented a young Theodore Roosevelt's interest in natural history into a lifelong commitment that helped usher in this nation's conservation movement. Drawing on several visits here as a boy and a June 1877 visit as a Harvard student, Roosevelt published twelve pages describing his observations of the area's bird life in what became his first natural history contribution: *The Summer Birds of the Adirondacks in Franklin County, N.Y.*

Not far from here, 24 years later, then vice president of the United States, Teddy Roosevelt climbed the state's highest peak, Mount Marcy. On the hike back down, he learned that President McKinley had been shot and gravely wounded. By the time Roosevelt reached North Creek town by horse, McKinley had died, and Roosevelt became president. Appreciation of the outdoors gained in the Adirondacks no doubt played an important role in his determination to protect the nation's natural treasures—which he did with the creation of the National Park Service and the National Forest System.

A beautiful lean-to perches on Peters Rock, across from the college; several others, all built by students, occur along the wide, 2-mile-long outlet toward Keese Mill. The marshy south end of Lower Saint Regis Lake and the channel into Spitfire Lake abound with thick floating vegetation by early summer. Depending on water level, you can explore several navigable channels and islands in the marsh.

Spitfire and Upper Saint Regis Lakes

Rabbit Island at Spitfire's south end played a role in important medical research; in 1886, Dr. Edward Livingston Trudeau studied how the environment influenced the spread of tuberculosis within a rabbit colony. The island kept the rabbits—and presumably the disease—isolated.

Normally, we would not include lakes such as Upper Saint Regis and Spitfire because of development, but here you will find classic old Adirondack vacation homes, many dating from the late 1800s. The area became a wilderness retreat for New York's aristocracy, who traveled here by train from Albany and New York City. Architecturally spectacular homes adorn the shores, many with large three- or four-bay boathouses that store wooden motorboats from the early

Looking across Upper Saint Regis Lake from the carry into Bog Pond and the Saint Regis Canoe Area.

1900s. One could spend a day paddling the 11-mile shoreline of these two lakes, gazing at the buildings, whose rustic architecture became known as the Adirondack style.

Summering New York Yacht Club members founded a sailing club on Upper Saint Regis in 1897 and designed their own sailboat—the Idem class. With all boats identical, races tested participants' skills, not differences in their boats.

Camp Topridge, most grandiose of the estates on Upper Saint Regis, sits on the western arm extending to the north. Marjorie Merriweather Post, heiress of the cereal company that later became General Foods, built the scattered 60 or so buildings in the early 1900s. At one time, the "camp" employed 85 staff members. When Post died in 1973, the heirs gave the property to the state, which then sold it in 1985 for less than $1 million to Roger Jakubowski of New Jersey, who went bankrupt in 1993. It has since sold to another private owner.

From the end of North Bay, a trail extends around Spectacle Pond, up to the top of Saint Regis Mountain at 2,874 feet. The peak's fire lookout tower undoubtedly provides tremendous views out over the Saint Regis Canoe Wilderness Area.

Despite the development, loons nest successfully, as evidenced by the parent with two chicks we watched on our paddle through. To fully enjoy your time on these lakes, paddle early in the morning, midweek, or before or after the main vacation season.

Gateway to the Saint Regis Canoe Area

Near the south end of Upper Saint Regis Lake, a carry into Bog Pond and the Saint Regis Canoe Area begins (see trip 46). Even when not doing a backcountry trip, we carry into Bear Pond and Little Long Pond to get a sense of the wild, remote country in this spectacular region.

The carries into Bog Pond and Bear Pond—only 50 to 60 yards each—provide a taste of canoe carrying, but not enough to wear you out. Tiny, aptly named Bog Pond, with its mucky bottom and shores thick with sheep laurel and other shrubs, also harbors pitcher plants and other bog vegetation.

In contrast, deeper Bear Pond sparkles with clear water and sections of sandy shore. Huge white pines grow here, along with hemlock, spruce, and balsam fir. We saw a loon and several great blue herons.

---

46 | Saint Regis Canoe Area

The Saint Regis Canoe Area in the northern boreal forest offers the finest backcountry paddling in New York. Fifty-eight lakes and ponds—most of them accessible by water or short carries—dot the landscape throughout this 18,000-acre wilderness. Although it's a popular destination, you can often find seclusion here and will certainly see lots of wildlife.

Location: Santa Clara
Maps: *New York Atlas & Gazetteer*, Map 29: A6, A7, A8; USGS Saint Regis Mountain, Upper Saranac Lake
Area: Saint Regis Pond, 383 acres; Hoel Pond, 455 acres; Rollins Pond, 445 acres; Polliwog Pond, 185 acres; Ledge Pond, 43 acres
Time: All day or multiday
Habitat Type: Small- to medium-sized ponds connected by short carries, surrounded by northern boreal forest
Fish: Largemouth and smallmouth bass; northern pike; kokanee salmon; splake; brook, brown, and lake trout (see fish advisories, Appendix C; see specific advisory, health.ny.gov/environmental/outdoors/fish/health_advisories)
Camping: On-site wilderness camping
Information: St. Regis Canoe Outfitters, canoeoutfitters.com

TRIP 46: SAINT REGIS CANOE AREA

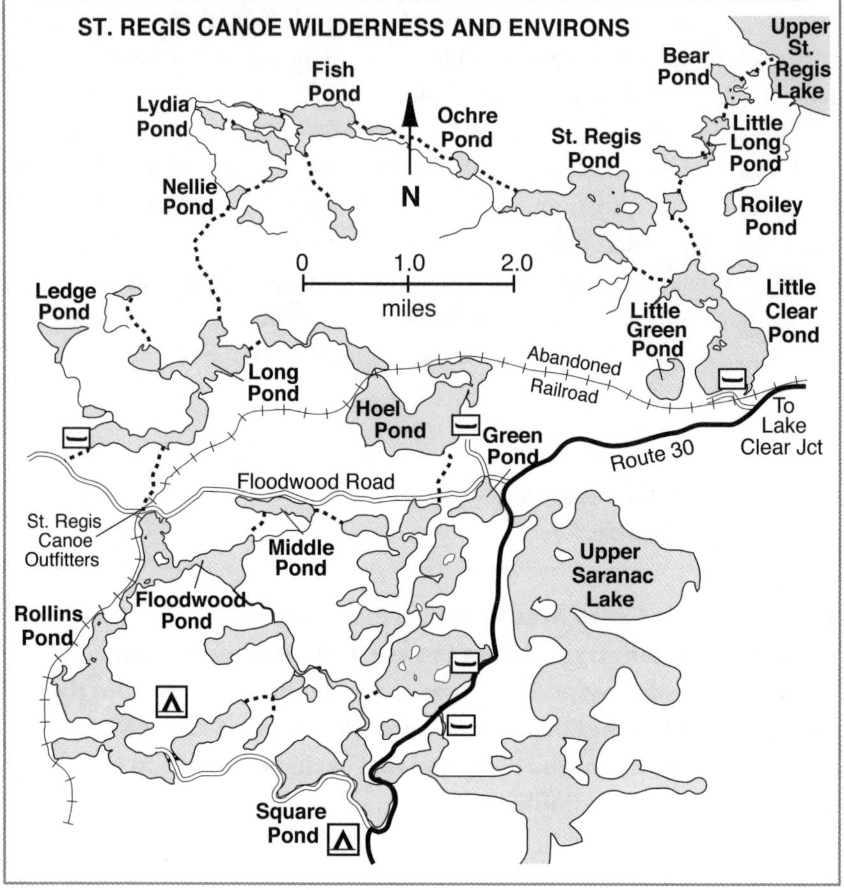

Take Note: Dozens of ponds in 18,000-acre Saint Regis Canoe Area covered here; portages required; no motors

GETTING THERE

Five primary access locations:

Lower Saint Regis Lake at Paul Smith's College Access. See trip 45.

Upper Saint Regis Lake Access. See trip 45.

Little Clear Pond Access. From Lake Clear Junction, go 2.7 miles west on Route 30, and turn right on Fish Hatchery Road. Follow signs to access. (44° 21.242′ N, 74° 16.912′ W)

TRIP 46: SAINT REGIS CANOE AREA

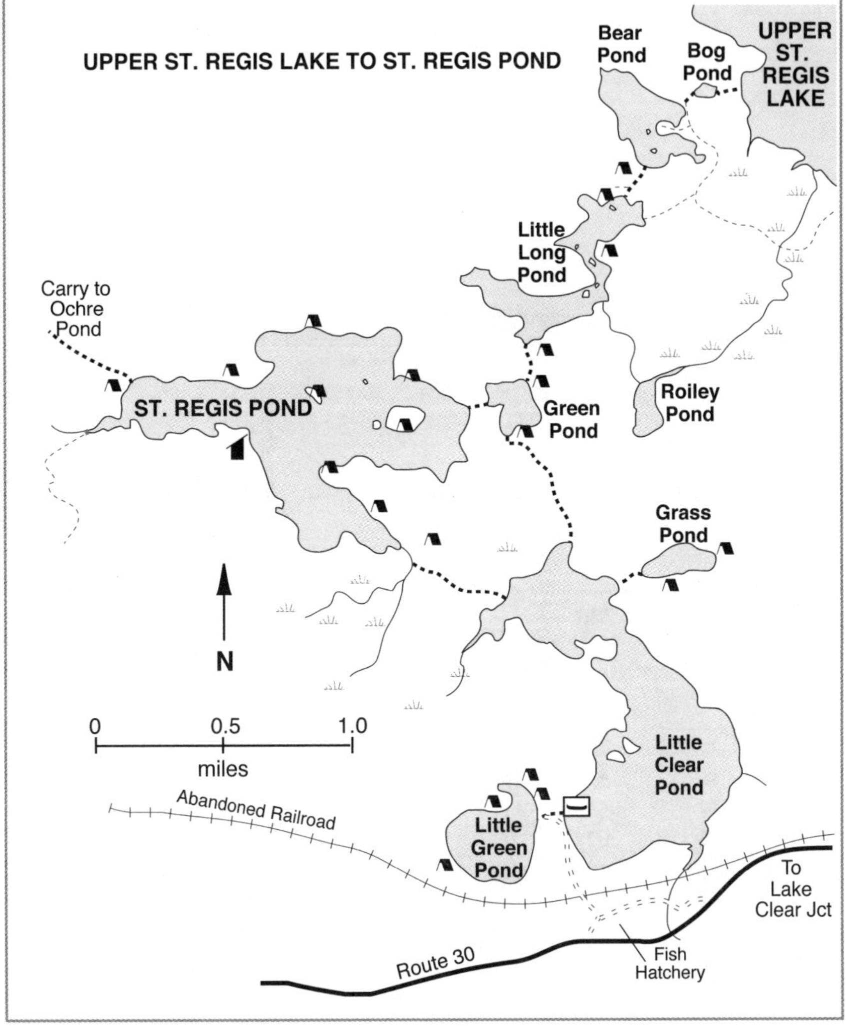

Hoel Pond Access. From Lake Clear Junction, go 5.4 miles west on Route 30, and turn right on Floodwood Road. Go 0.3 mile (5.7 miles), and bear right on Hoel Pond Road. Go 0.3 mile (6.0 miles), and turn left on the access road at the golf course's northern edge. (44° 20.797′ N, 74° 20.338′ W)

Long Pond Access. From Route 30, go 5.1 miles west on Floodwood Road (pass St. Regis Canoe Outfitters on left), and turn right to access. (44° 20.775′ N, 74° 25.304′ W) (Carry trail to Long Pond suitable for portage cart; most other carries not suitable.)

TRIP 46: SAINT REGIS CANOE AREA

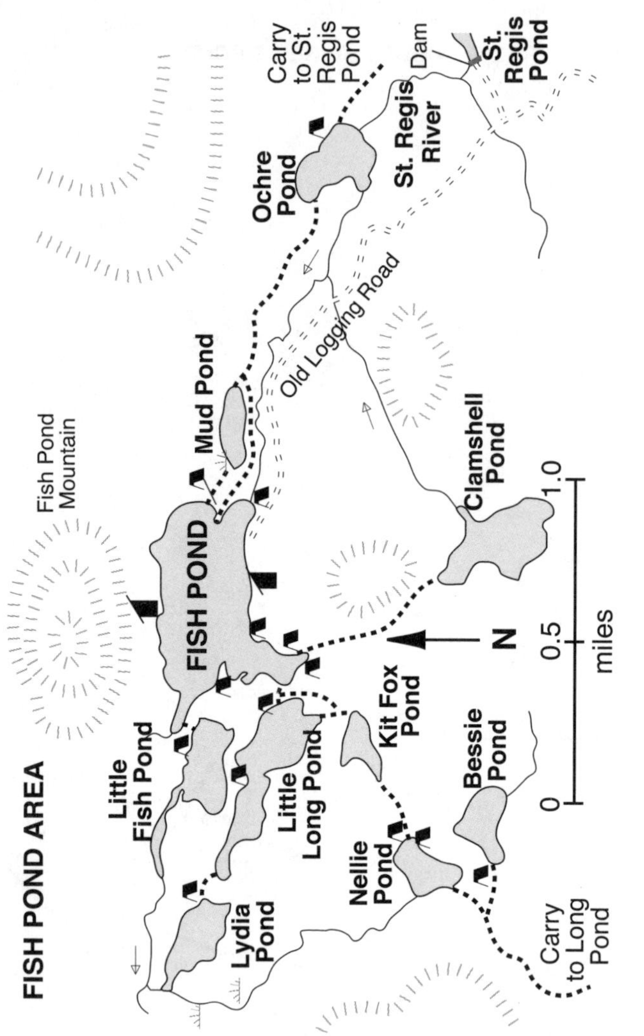

WHAT YOU'LL SEE

Wild. Remote. Gorgeous. Pristine. The Saint Regis Canoe Area offers the finest backcountry paddling in New York. Fifty-eight lakes and ponds—most of them accessible by water or short carries—dot the landscape throughout this 18,000-acre wilderness. In the 1970s, New York State set aside this part of Adirondack Park for nonmotorized use and temporary (rather than seasonal) camping. The state banned all motorboats, motorized vehicles, airplanes, and snowmobiles from the Canoe Area.

TRIP 46: SAINT REGIS CANOE AREA

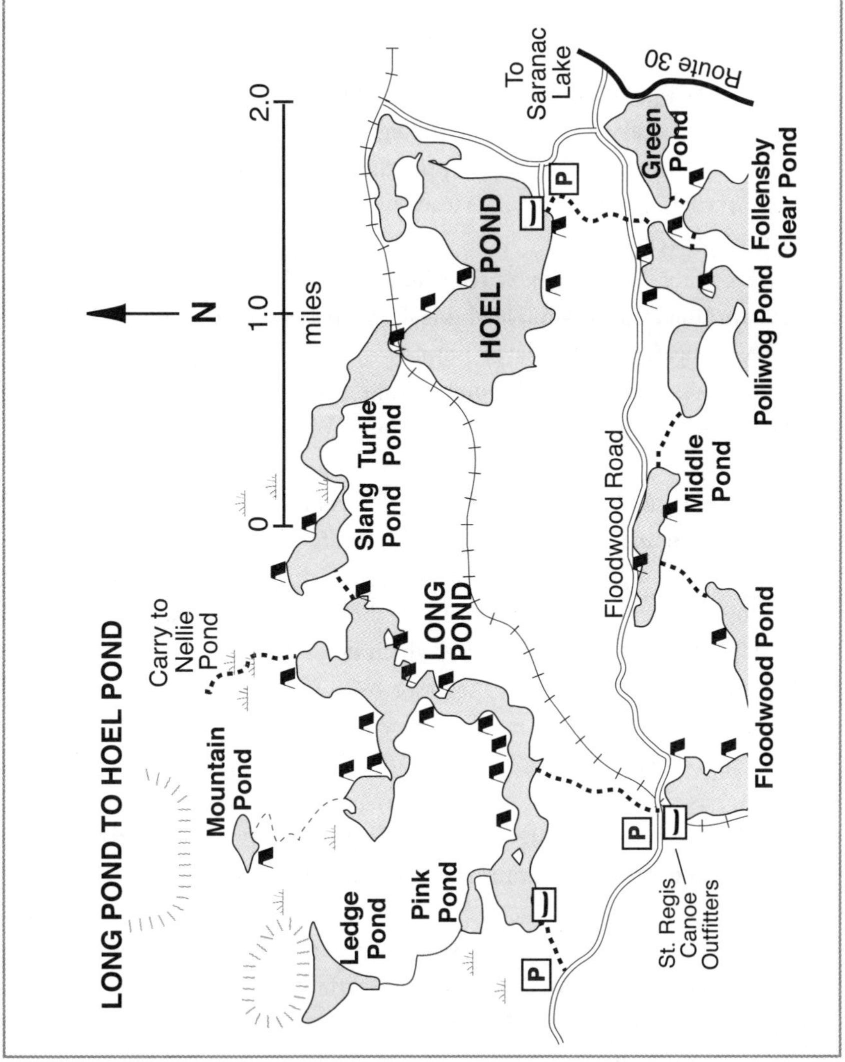

For the paddler, several excellent trips wend their way through the Canoe Area. You can opt for a multiday loop or in-and-out trip, but we prefer a through-trip—put in at one location and take out at another. Use two vehicles or hire an outfitter to shuttle you and your gear.

The most common loop trip winds through Hoel, Turtle, Slang, and Long ponds in the Canoe Area and then through Floodwood, Middle, and Polliwog ponds just to the south. For a through-trip, put in or take out on Lower or Upper Saint Regis lakes or on Little Clear, Hoel, or Long ponds. For an extended trip, put in on Rainbow Lake to the northeast or on a number of southern bodies of water, such as Rollins Pond, Fish Creek Pond, or the Saranac lakes. We describe several routes here.

Upper Saint Regis Lake to Saint Regis Pond

Although a fairly easy trip, Upper Saint Regis Lake to Saint Regis Pond involves five relatively short carries. Near Upper Saint Regis's southern end (see trip 45), a short carry of about 50 yards leads to Bog Pond, which marks the Canoe Area's northeastern end.

Entering tiny Bog Pond, just a few hundred yards long, you initially paddle along a winding channel amid leatherleaf, sheep laurel, pitcher plant, and other typical bog vegetation. The large number of frogs here—and on most of the area's ponds—surprised us. A quick paddle (longer if you study the plants) brings you to the pond's western end; look for the rectangular white sign marking the carry into Bear Pond.

After a short carry, you arrive at a very different pond, with deep, clear water and sandy shoreline sections. Tall, ancient white pines rise from Bear Pond's picturesque shores. We watched loons dive for fish and great blue herons stalk the shallows. Even if you paddle the entire shoreline and around all the islands, you will quickly reach the next carry, which takes you into Little Long Pond.

Although a little longer than the first two—with a bit of up and down—the carry into Little Long Pond remains very manageable (warming you up for more strenuous carries to come). S-shaped Little Long Pond, about a mile in length, has the highest elevation of any pond in this section. Little Long, Bear, and Bog ponds drain into the Saint Regis River Middle Branch, whereas other ponds covered here drain into the Saint Regis River West Branch or Saranac River.

Conifers, including hemlock, spruce, fir, tamarack, and some towering, wind-sculpted white pine, dominate the Little Long Pond shoreline. Most paddlers choose to push on into Saint Regis Pond to camp, but there are several great campsites here. Watch for the carry to Green Pond at the pond's southernmost tip. Abundant wildflowers border the carry—we saw pink lady's slipper, trillium, and Indian cucumber root nestled among the thick club moss and hobblebush. The 125-yard trail winds through deep woods of yellow birch, sugar maple, and beech. On tiny Green Pond—as with quite a few others—you can see the carry sign around to the right before getting in your boat (the trail at the southern tip leads to Little Clear Pond in about 0.6 mile).

One of the finest Adirondack camping spots, Saint Regis Pond looks a bit like a flying duck, with the bill at the far west end by a dam. From bill tip to tail,

Small creeks flow between many of the lakes in the Saint Regis Canoe Area.

the pond stretches about 1.5 miles. A well-kept shelter perches on the south shore where the pond narrows to the west. The superb campsite across from the shelter features a massive slab of granite that extends down into the water, perfect for swimming. To the north, you can see Saint Regis Mountain, which rises to 2,874 feet, with a fire lookout tower on top.

Many people know that Saint Regis Pond—although a true wilderness pond—provides a wonderful place to camp, with most of the dozen or so campsites frequently in use. For more solitude here, visit after Labor Day when most summer vacationers (and mosquitoes) have fled.

From Saint Regis Pond's southern arm, you can paddle for several hundred yards up the winding inlet creek, an area rich with aquatic vegetation, including pickerelweed, yellow bladderwort, sundew, pitcher plant, wild calla or water arum—with heart-shaped leaves somewhat rounder than those of pickerelweed—and yellow pondlily. Sweetgale lines the banks, and feathery spires of tamarack rise from the ground farther back. Paddling up this creek a few hundred yards, you reach a boardwalk extending across the boggy shore from the left—the carry to Little Clear Pond.

Little Clear Pond

Some paddlers reach Saint Regis Pond from the access on Little Clear Pond; for others, Little Clear Pond makes a great day trip from Saint Regis Pond. The nearly 0.7-mile carry starts out somewhat steeply, with lots of exposed tree roots, and then levels out for most of the distance.

From the end of the carry, you can paddle to the right (southwest) into a shallow cattail marsh leading to a small inlet creek. By midsummer, dense mats of water shield and other floating vegetation cover the cove's surface. We saw wood ducks here, watched great blue herons hunt methodically, spooked a few painted turtles, and noticed a sizable beaver lodge. Although it's impossible to paddle up the inlet creek in summer, it might be possible in spring.

Because a nearby state fish hatchery uses water from Little Clear Pond, the state prohibits camping and fishing to ensure water quality and to prevent introduction of unwanted fish species, which suits the resident osprey just fine, assuring them plenty of meals. Along with osprey, we saw as many as six loons here, including one adult with two chicks near the small islands. We were troubled, though, to see one loon with a deformed bill—possible evidence of dioxin or PCB poisoning.

At the north end of Little Clear Pond, a short carry leads to Grass Pond. When we visited, low water levels had exposed a rather unappealing muddy shoreline. If you get a chance, visit the state fish hatchery, which is at the southern end. The southeastern end remains off-limits, so you have to enter from Route 30. You will see mammoth landlocked salmon and brook trout breeding stock, some about 2 feet long. Some of the tanks had pails of food that visitors could use to feed the fish. The hatchery's visitor center is a great place to take kids.

Fish Pond Loop

Getting to Fish Pond requires effort, which helps make it such a wonderful spot. You can carry to Fish Pond from Hoel, Long, or Saint Regis ponds, each including a somewhat rugged stretch of a mile or more. You could use a portage cart along much smoother abandoned logging roads from the dam at Saint Regis Pond to Fish Pond—a distance of about 2 miles— but carts are useless elsewhere in the Canoe Area. In spring it may be possible to paddle or pole a canoe from the dam on Saint Regis Pond down the Saint Regis West Branch to Ochre Pond, but this is not possible at times of low water.

The half-mile carry from Saint Regis Pond begins near the pond's western end, northeast of the dam, and involves some up and down, with lots of exposed rocks and roots. Upon arriving at small Ochre Pond, you can see the next carry sign on the other side. The pond gets its name from its ochre color. Rust-colored deposits form in some mountain lakes when conditions are just right to provide a food source for iron-loving bacteria. Acidic bog water dissolves iron out of rocks and soils, putting it in solution as ferrous ion (Fe++). Iron-rich—but oxygen-poor—spring water welling up into oxygen-rich surface water creates the perfect environment to support a type of "iron bacterium" that obtains energy by converting ferrous ion and oxygen to ferric oxide (Fe+++). This bacterium uses the energy to fix carbon dioxide into organic matter, just as plants convert carbon dioxide and water into organic matter, driven by the sun's energy through photosynthesis. The bacterium-catalyzed reactions precipitate ferric oxide in flocculent orange masses in some areas—including Ochre Pond. Over time, the ferric oxide gradually changes into less hydrated forms, with earthy colors ranging from yellow to red and brown.

Going from Ochre Pond to Fish Pond entails traversing a carry of 1.25 miles, but over a gorgeous trail, passing along a ridge studded with mammoth old-growth white pines and hemlocks. You can carry to Fish Pond or turn off to the right after about 0.7 mile and visit tiny Mud Pond. We carried our gear to Fish Pond but paddled Mud Pond anyway—and were glad we did.

Surrounded by cathedral-like white pines, the shallow pond's rich bog life includes floating logs festooned with fascinating plants: delicate rose pogonia orchids; carnivorous pitcher plants with nodding bloom spikes and long, cuplike leaves; terrestrial horned bladderworts, with small yellow flowers that have long, drooping spurs (most bladderworts are aquatic); and a low, reddish carpet of sundews, which use sticky droplets to entrap tiny insects. This floating-log ecosystem really showcases plant adaptation to nutrient-poor environments. (For more on carnivorous plants, see "Carnivorous Plants: The Table is Turned," on page 361.)

From Mud Pond's western end, a short carry leads to Fish Pond, a spectacular place, less than a mile across, nestled beneath Fish Pond Mountain. Because you must work hard to get here, plan to spend a few days—if you can find an available campsite. We counted two lean-tos and another eight campsites. Enjoy the excellent fishing for brook trout and lake trout, as well.

The northwestern cove—by the outlet into Little Fish Pond—offers a great spot to observe beaver. Paddle up here in the evening, and you'll likely see (and hear) this industrious rodent hard at work. One day, we watched two large snapping turtles soak up the late-afternoon sun on some large boulders extending out of the water. Rarely have we seen snappers sunning—although painted turtles do so all the time—yet references in the journal at the Blagden Lean-to led us to believe that the turtles in this particular location sun themselves frequently. They may be trying to rid themselves of leeches that attach to their fleshy underparts.

From Fish Pond, you can take wonderful day trips into nearby ponds, including Little Fish, Little Long (a different Little Long Pond from the one referred to in earlier sections), Lydia, Kit Fox, Nellie, Bessie, and Clamshell ponds. Reach tranquil and pristine Little Fish Pond from near the end of Fish Pond's northwestern outlet cove. Leatherleaf, sheep laurel, and bracken and royal ferns line the shrubby shoreline. During an evening paddle on Little Fish Pond, the still air scarcely rippled the water's surface.

Along the southern shore, we saw several freshwater sponge colonies. Though sponges (phylum *Porifera*, loosely aggregated colonies of primitive animals) occur far more commonly in the ocean, a few freshwater species exist in very pure water. We probably saw *Spongilla lacustris*, which looks more like a plant than an animal. These bright green, branching sponges attach to submerged sticks and rocks. The green color comes from single-celled algae, *Zoochlorellae*, that live symbiotically with the sponge colony. We have seen colonies more than a foot in height.

In a few spots along Little Fish Pond's southern shore, you can walk up and over the steep ridge into Little Long Pond. You can get your boat into Little Long Pond from Fish Pond's southern arm—watch your footing on this short up-and-down carry. Little Long Pond, deep and oligotrophic, had an odd milky-blue color when we visited—quite different from the color of other area ponds. We saw one campsite, roughly centered on the northern shore. A retreating glacier left a deposit of sand and rock on that shore, an esker that now separates Little Long and Little Fish ponds.

The sand suits the snapping turtle very well, as it uses the steep exposed sand banks for building nests. When we visited in mid-July, we saw hundreds of curled pieces of leathery eggshell, likely the remains of nests dug up by raccoons, foxes, otters, or some other predators. Very few snapping turtle offspring make it to the water, but the species survives because once in the water, it may live for 30 or more years, reproducing many times.

Lydia Pond, accessible by carrying from Little Long Pond's western end, lies along the same esker. The single campsite on Lydia lies at the end of the carry from Little Long Pond. As on Little Long, we saw evidence of snapping turtle nests on sandy northern shores. Although whitened drift logs blocked further exploration of the marshy outlet at Lydia's west end, we did see rose pogonia orchids, pitcher plants, sundews, and muskrats—plus a lone loon.

A trek into Clamshell Pond makes another pleasant day trip from Fish Pond—with or without a canoe. The carry travels south from near the tip of Fish Pond's southern arm (across from the carry into Little Long Pond). The 0.6-mile hike has significant ups and downs but winds through beautiful old-growth hemlocks and yellow birches—some the largest we have seen.

Occasional boulders dot Clamshell Pond's shoreline and generally sandy bottom, and a mixed hardwood-conifer forest surrounds the pond with white pine, hemlock, northern white cedar, spruce, sugar maple, and yellow birch. Through-paddlers can carry from here down to Turtle and Hoel ponds, although the path from Clamshell to Turtle is quite long and steep.

The third route out of (or into) Fish Pond, via Kit Fox, Nellie, and Long ponds, proceeds from Fish Pond's southern arm. Carry to Little Long Pond, as described earlier, and then paddle to Little Long's southern tip to the carry to Kit Fox Pond. Alternatively, from Fish Pond, you can carry all the way to Kit Fox, avoiding a steep trail down into Little Long. The alternate trail to Kit Fox branches off from the trail between Fish and Little Long ponds.

Tiny Kit Fox Pond, an easy carry from Little Long Pond, is well worth exploring. As we slowly skirted the perimeter, we happened on a bullfrog bedded down in a soft (sticky) mat of sundews beneath a healthy clump of pitcher plants atop a floating log. Many ancient logs extended from shore or floated in the shallow water and muck. The significantly longer carry to Nellie Pond can be quite wet in spring but should be dry in summer. A couple of campsites greet you as you reach Nellie Pond.

The conifer canopy and heath-family understory on Little Long Pond is typical of the Saint Regis Canoe Area.

The carry you have built up for traverses from Nellie to Long Pond. Only 1.5 miles long, beavers have flooded parts of it. About 0.1 mile from Nellie, a trail bears sharply left to Bessie Pond, which has a gorgeous campsite on a thick pine-needle carpet. A huge floating log extends 60 or 70 feet into the water from shore, providing a prime swimming or fishing platform. If you make two trips at the Long Pond carry, Bessie Pond offers a great midpoint break. One trail section passes through a beautiful pitch pine forest, a very unusual sight in this part of New York. The trail section that passed through a beaver-flooded swamp near the south end provided the greatest surprise, however. You can easily paddle this well-signed 100-yard section of trail.

Long Pond to Hoel Pond

Reaching 2-mile-long Long Pond by carrying 0.25 mile from Floodwood Road requires just enough effort to give one a feeling of accomplishment—but nothing like the achievement of reaching Long Pond from Fish Pond! The dozen or so campsites that dot the shoreline spread out enough that you can find solitude here.

From Long Pond, take a pleasant evening or early morning paddle up to Pink Pond, where you should see beaver and other wildlife. Near Long Pond's western end, paddle up the entering creek's narrow channel. When we visited, we carried over a beaver dam almost immediately, and then quietly wended our way up into small Pink Pond. The channel banks grow thick with leatherleaf, sheep laurel, sweetgale, royal fern, pickerelweed, wild calla, and grasses and sedges on the many sphagnum hummocks. In the late afternoon, sunlight filters through feathery tamarack branches. The water harbors yellow pondlily, American white waterlily, water shield, and long, floating leaves of bur-reed.

We had the good fortune to watch a beaver family lazily munching on yellow pondlily stems. Although the adult disappeared as our canoe drifted close, we got to study the young, who seemed oblivious to our presence. As evening settled in, we spotted a deer drinking from shore and listened to a white-throated sparrow's melodious *Old Sam Peabody, Peabody, Peabody* song.

From Long Pond's eastern end, you can make a short carry into Slang Pond, where you will find a few campsites. From Slang, you can usually paddle through to Turtle Pond, but at low water, you may have to wade through the shallow passage. The one campsite on Turtle Pond sits east of the carry to Hoel Pond.

At Turtle Pond's eastern end, you have to carry up over abandoned railroad tracks to get to Hoel Pond. About 1 mile long and 0.5 mile across, Hoel offers an alternate put-in point for a Canoe Area trip. Because it lies outside the wilderness area, however, you will encounter development and powerboats. Avoid Hoel Pond under windy conditions, as waves build up very quickly across its broad expanse, and the shoreline affords little protection on most of the pond.

47 | Fish Creek Loops

Fish Creek Loops cover several ponds and Fish Creek. You could plan day or multiday trips from any of the access points.

Location: Santa Clara
Maps: *New York Atlas & Gazetteer*, Map 29: A7, B6, B7; USGS Upper Saranac Lake
Area: Follensby Clear Pond, 491 acres; Rollins Pond, 445 acres; Polliwog Pond, 185 acres; Ledge Pond, 43 acres; Whey Pond, 108 acres
Time: All day or multiday
Habitat Type: Ponds, some connected by streams, surrounded by forest
Fish: Largemouth and smallmouth bass; northern pike; kokanee and landlocked salmon; brook, brown, and rainbow trout (see fish advisories, Appendix C)
Camping: Appendix A (81, 90); on-site wilderness camping
Information: St. Regis Canoe Outfitters, canoeoutfitters.com
Take Note: Some short portages required to reach some ponds

GETTING THERE

Floodwood Pond Access. From Lake Clear Junction, go 5.4 miles west on Route 30, and turn right on Floodwood Road. Go 4.1 miles (9.5 miles) to the access on the left, just short of the canoe outfitter. (44° 20.354′ N, 74° 24.322′ W)

Follensby Clear Pond Accesses. From the junction of Route 30 and Floodwood Road, go 1.7 miles (7.1 miles) south on Route 30 to the access across from Moss Rock Road (44° 19.188′ N, 74° 20.118′ W) or 2.7 miles (8.1 miles) south to the access on the right, just past Beaverwood Road. (44° 18.617′ N, 74° 20.795′ W)

TRIP 47: FISH CREEK LOOPS

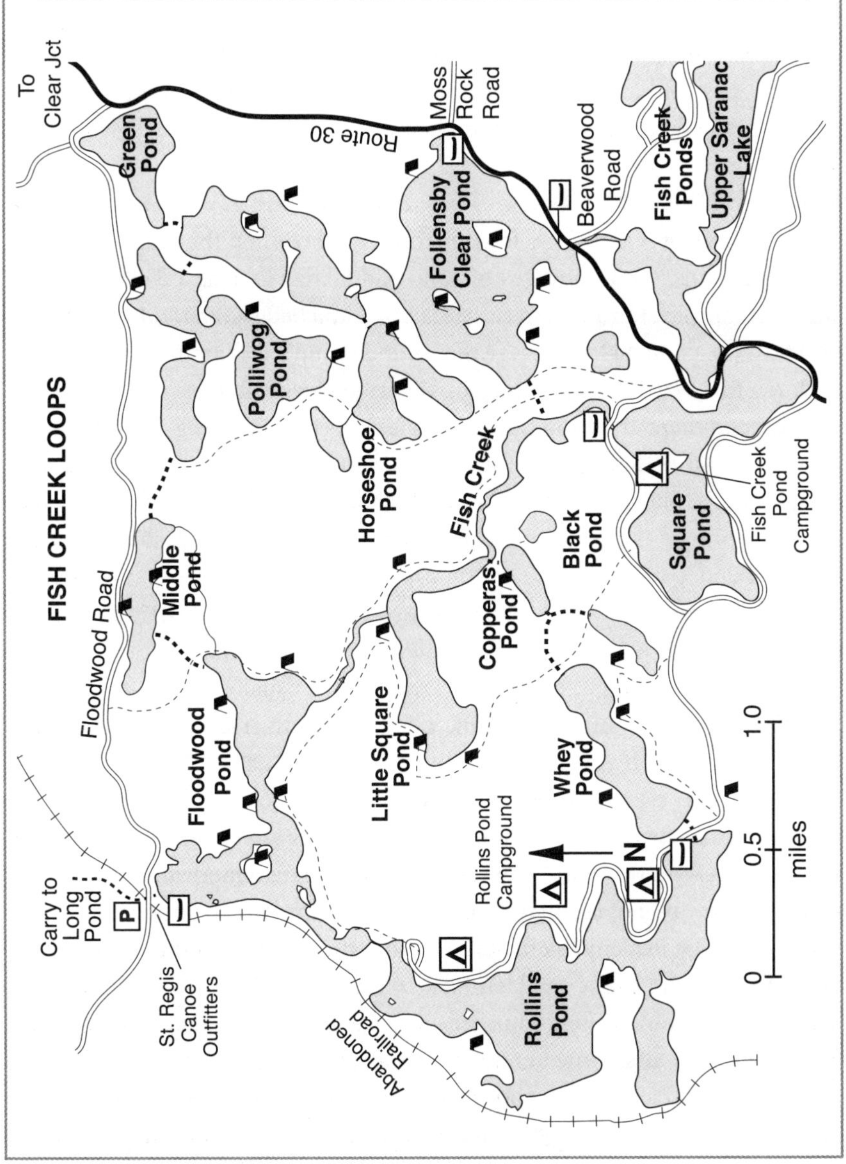

Rollins Pond Campground Access. From the junction of Route 30 and Floodwood Road, go 4.3 miles (9.7 miles) south on Route 30 to the campground entrance on the right. (44° 17.677′ N, 74° 21.540′ W)

WHAT YOU'LL SEE

Fish Creek Loops allow you to paddle a string of ponds with minimal carrying, ending at the starting point. The compact scale of these loops, with just a few short carries, makes them ideal first trips for young paddlers. Our 5- and 8-year-old girls executed a half-dozen carries superbly and explored nine different ponds during three days and two nights here.

Floodwood Pond–Fish Creek–Whey Pond–Rollins Pond Loop

Several points provide access for this route, as shown on the map. One could camp at Rollins Pond Campground and paddle this loop as a day trip from a lakeside campsite. On a visit in early May, we launched from Floodwood Pond's northern tip, paddled to the large island, and set up base camp, from which we explored this loop, as well as the loop described below.

We recommend traveling clockwise, which permits paddling downstream on Fish Creek rather than against the light current between Floodwood and Little Square ponds. Starting on Rollins Pond, paddle north from the campground (or from one of the primitive campsites along the western shore). At the northern end, paddle to the east (right). The pond narrows to a small stream that connects to Floodwood. In May, the stream floated our boat, although we had to lie down to maneuver under a fallen birch tree and had to drag our canoe over a small beaver dam. Later in the season, you usually need to carry along a small portage trail on the left bank. Look for a path leading off to the left as the pond narrows. If you paddle through, watch for rocks.

Floodwood's narrow western end, with an abandoned railway bed on the north side, also has a few vacation houses along the shore—the only ones you will encounter on this trip. As with most ponds here, Floodwood has a fairly sandy bottom and not too many rocks. The shoreline's thick understory makes landing a canoe just anywhere out of the question, although the woods opens up as it rises from the water. Hemlock, white pine, yellow birch, white birch, beech, and sugar maple predominate. Because the area has not been logged for more than 100 years, some hemlocks have grown to huge size.

Red pine and hemlock—both providing an open, accessible forest floor—dominate Floodwood's large island, with campsites and outhouses scattered about. When we camped here, merlins nested in one of the island's tall pines. Their cries advertised their presence many times during our two-night stay. This relatively rare falcon looks very much like a peregrine, but about half the size—slightly larger than a kestrel, a more common falcon. We observed with binoculars as one devoured a small rodent 50 feet up on a dead snag.

Floodwood resembles a butterfly, with Fish Creek flowing out the eastern wing's bottom lobe toward Little Square, Copperas, and Fish Creek ponds. Fish Creek's first section—between Floodwood and Little Square ponds—flows shallow and quick, although without rapids. Rocks and many logs create an obstacle course of sorts. In times of low water, passage may be difficult. Shortly after leaving Floodwood, pass under a wooden hiking/snowmobile bridge. In several places, kind souls have notched out large submerged logs to provide passage. We had to squeeze over a couple of tiny beaver dams when we visited.

Be sure not to rush through. Beautiful Fish Creek features quite varied vegetation. In some sections, the streambed meanders through shaded woodland, with trees overhanging the channel. In other places, it winds through marsh thick with grasses, sedges, and cattails, where you might startle a great blue heron from its patient fishing. Everywhere in the gently flowing stream you will see yellow pondlilies and various other floating and emergent aquatic plants. Leatherleaf—with its small, leathery leaves and drooping clusters of inconspicuous bell-like white flowers—dominates most of the shoreline.

About a half-mile below Floodwood, Fish Creek flows into Little Square Pond's eastern end. If west winds do not blow too strongly, you may want to explore this pond, but each time we visited, the waves coming off Little Square Pond discouraged us from more thorough exploration.

A portage cart makes light work on a carry, as Lillian and Frances demonstrate.

Below Little Square Pond, Fish Creek widens, and the vegetation becomes more fen-like, with feathery tamaracks, particularly along the western shore. On the sphagnum tussocks, watch for carnivorous pitcher plants. As the channel begins to narrow again, keep an eye out for the small stream heading off right to Copperas Pond. You can easily miss this turn in summer when thick pond vegetation covers the surface. Paddle southwest through Copperas to the carry into Whey Pond. Conspicuous rectangular white signs and yellow trail markers point the way to and down the carries. The trail to Whey Pond heads due west from the take-out; another trail from the same point leads south into Black Pond.

Like most carries on park lands, the Whey Pond carry traverses gentle terrain, through thick beds of wildflowers, ferns, and club mosses. Although paddling your boat is distinctly easier than carrying it, the carries provide a chance to stretch your legs, to exercise your sore buns, to enjoy the woods from a distinctly different perspective, and to study wildflowers—particularly when bugs do not patrol. During an early spring visit, we noticed huge, velvety buds of hobblebush just beginning to unfurl, while the bell-like yellow flowers of trout lily bloomed fully.

Whey Pond, a little less than 1 mile long, runs in a northeast-southwest orientation. At the southwestern end, look for the carry sign to Rollins Pond. Of the two carries there, the southern one is shorter and ends at a boat launch on Rollins, whereas the northern one ends at the campground road.

Rollins Pond, much larger than the other ponds on this loop, can become quite choppy on a windy day, so use caution. Do not expect solitude, as 288 campsites line the eastern shore. The campground offers an attractive setting, with ample room between sites. To get the most out of a paddle on Rollins Pond, though, stick to the western shore, where you can escape into several deep coves—or visit early in the season before the campground opens.

Floodwood Pond–Fish Creek–Follensby Clear Pond–Polliwog Pond Loop

This trip covers six ponds connected by Fish Creek and by four relatively short carries. The carries, although somewhat longer and a bit steeper than those in the preceding section, still allow you to complete the loop as a day trip. Camping opportunities abound on Follensby Clear Pond, and several campsites nestle along the shores of most other ponds. You can also camp at Fish Creek Pond Campground and paddle north into Follensby Clear Pond via the Spider Creek Passage.

Starting at Floodwood, paddle southeast into Fish Creek. Pass through Little Square Pond's eastern end, and continue in a generally southeastern direction, keeping an eye out for the carry to Follensby Clear Pond on the left. It begins with a wooden boardwalk that extends into the water, but vegetation may hide it by early summer. Ferns, club mosses, and wildflowers line the 0.25-mile trail to perhaps the prettiest pond in this area, Follensby Clear Pond, which remains our favorite.

Seven islands, most with campsites, dot the 2-mile-long pond's surface. Several sites sport sandy beaches, topping off the wilderness splendor. Hemlock, its shade providing an open, inviting woodland and its needles leaving a soft, footstep-quieting carpet, dominates the forest. We paddled alone here, sharing the water only with loons and mergansers.

After paddling north through the pond's narrowest part, you can get to Horseshoe Pond by heading into the cove on the left. A well-marked and very short carry over a slight rise brings you to true-to-its-name Horseshoe Pond. Several campsites cluster near the portage trail, and one lies directly across from it.

Near Follensby Clear Pond's northwestern end, look for a somewhat hidden carry to Polliwog Pond. The trail passes through a beautiful old-growth hemlock forest. Although timber companies clear-cut much of the Adirondacks in the mid-1800s, about 60,000 acres remain as virgin forest, some right here. Since 1892, no logging has occurred on public lands in the park, thus returning much more of the forest to old-growth. The carry into Polliwog Pond gives you a sense of what virgin forest looks and feels like. Note the standing dead trees, the moss-covered logs slowly rotting into the ground, the tremendous variation in tree age, and the high diversity of plant species.

Polliwog Pond has a sandy bottom, and several campsites offer attractive sand beaches. Depending on water level, the point of land to the left after you enter the pond will either be a peninsula or an island. Another peninsula comes in from the west across the pond. To get to Middle Pond, pass through a narrow section of Polliwog into the pond's western extension. At the western end, a sign marks the carry to Middle Pond. The exception that proves the rule about gentle carries, this trail goes up and down somewhat steeply for 0.3 mile—again, among gorgeous, deep woods.

A westerly breeze can generate surprisingly large waves on Middle Pond, with its long, narrow, east-west orientation. One campsite perches along Floodwood Road, with another on the pond's southern side. On our spring visit, tree swallows patrolled the air, swooping for flying insects, then returning to dead trees that no doubt provide nesting sites. A solitary loon, clearly oblivious to the cold wind and choppy waves, dove for fish near the pond's center. Watch for the carry to Floodwood Pond along the south shore about three-quarters of the way up this pond. This final carry in the loop starts out steeply but then becomes an easy walk.

48 | Middle Saranac Lake

Middle Saranac is the least traveled of the three Saranac lakes, and you can usually find some seclusion here, especially in the Weller ponds and South Creek. Look for osprey, great blue heron, waterfowl, deer, and beaver. Paddling can be treacherous under windy conditions.

Location: Harrietstown, Santa Clara
Maps: *New York Atlas & Gazetteer*, Map 29: B8, B9; USGS Saranac Lake, Tupper Lake, Upper Saranac Lake
Area: 1,193 acres
Time: 5 hours
Habitat Type: Large lake with marshy coves and outlet stream
Fish: Largemouth and smallmouth bass; northern pike (see fish advisories, Appendix C)
Camping: Appendix A (91); on-site wilderness camping
Take Note: Treacherous paddling when windy

GETTING THERE

From the junction of Route 3/River Street and Church Street in Saranac Lake, go 9.9 miles west on Route 3 to the South Creek access on the left. (44° 14.691′ N, 74° 16.083′ W)

From Tupper Lake, go east on Routes 3 and 30; when the roads divide, continue 5.4 miles east on Route 3 to the South Creek access on the right.

WHAT YOU'LL SEE

The middle of three Saranac lakes remains the least heavily traveled because of its more difficult access. You can launch from the South Creek hand-carry access on Route 3, or traverse the half-mile through Bartlett Carry from Upper Saranac Lake, or pass through the lock that connects Middle and Lower Saranac lakes.

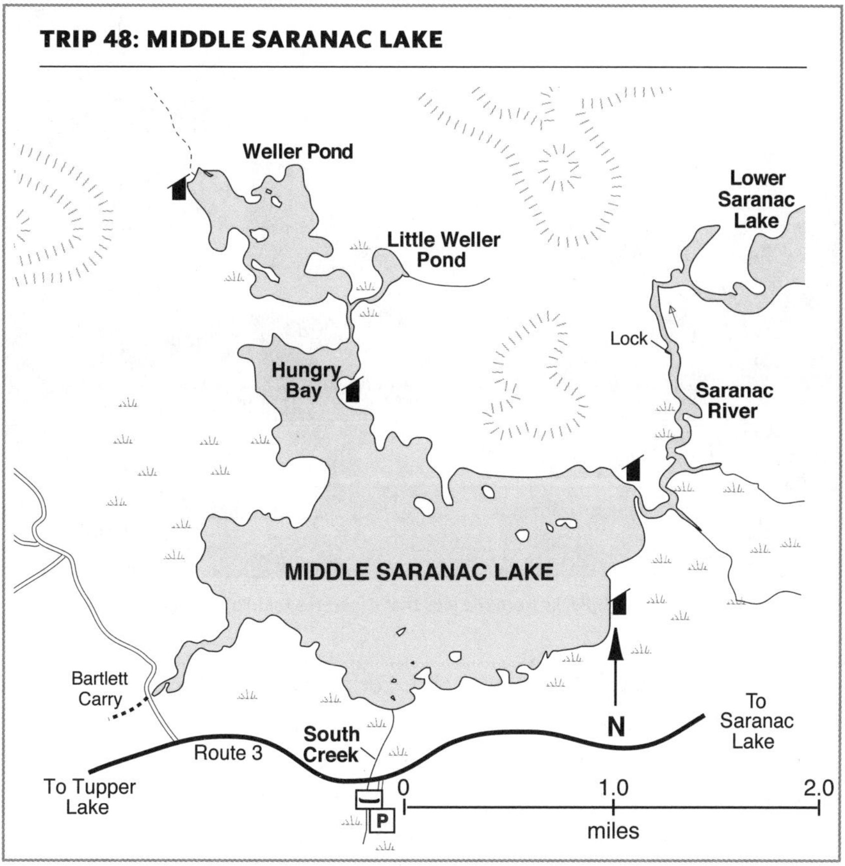

Middle Saranac lies along two popular long-distance canoe routes. One comes down from the hamlet of Saranac Inn, traversing the length of Upper Saranac to Bartlett Carry, east to Middle Saranac, through the outlet stream into Lower Saranac, and then either directly to or through Ossetah Lake to the town of Saranac Lake. The second route, which is also part of the Northern Forest Canoe Trail, travels the length of Long Lake to Axton Landing, up through Stony Creek Ponds, with a 0.75-mile carry to Upper Saranac, followed by a 2-mile paddle to Bartlett Carry, finishing as previously.

Launching from the South Creek access, we could not resist paddling upstream on South Creek through a cedar-lined beaver swamp. We carried over a few beaver dams but decided not to clamber over the downed timber that clogs the waterway.

Resist the temptation to bolt downstream onto the lake. Take time to study the South Creek channel. We found huge pitcher plant clumps perched precariously on sphagnum hummocks, trying to elbow the ubiquitous leatherleaf out of the

View of the Adirondack High Peaks from the lock that separates Middle and Lower Saranac lakes.

way. In all of our travels throughout New York, this may be the easiest place to view pitcher plants from a boat.

Tamarack, northern white cedar, and black spruce have invaded the sphagnum bog as it makes the gradual transition from wetland to upland. Eventually, trees will crowd out the sheep laurel, leatherleaf, bog rosemary, sweetgale, winterberry, and pitcher plant, and decaying vegetation will build up an overlying soil.

Even though traversing the lock from Lower Saranac into Middle Saranac remains a popular pastime for motorboaters, Middle Saranac retains a wilderness character, mostly because of lack of development along the shore. The state owns about three-quarters of the shoreline, starting at the southwestern corner of Hungry Bay, moving clockwise up through Weller and Little Weller ponds, down along the northern shore through the lock into Lower Saranac, down the eastern shore of Middle Saranac, and around the southern shore, stopping just short of the South Creek entrance.

Paddling clockwise around the lake, we noted the many conifer species lining the shore, as well as the few small birches fast disappearing as beavers cut them down to drag to their lakeside lodges for winter food. We wondered whether the preponderance of white pine, northern white cedar, tamarack, hemlock, and spruce here resulted from selective cutting by beavers. We also noticed the conspicuous browse line on the shoreline cedars, where deer sliding along the ice in winter gnawed on low-hanging branches.

As you paddle the lake's western end—most of its cedar-lined shore owned by the Bartlett Carry Company—look back east and savor the view of saw-toothed peaks in the McKenzie Mountain Wilderness. The protected coves contain patches of pickerelweed, pondweed, and water celery, as well as waterfowl. Paddling here in fall, we found many loons in twos and threes; hundreds of ducks ate ravenously, trying to gain a few last ounces of fat to fuel their migratory flight.

Weller and Little Weller ponds—the most interesting, secluded, and scenic portions of the lake—harbor a sea of aquatic vegetation among the many side channels, coves, and islands. Tamarack, a conifer with golden needles that drop in fall, has invaded the marsh, and leatherleaf lines the waterways. Cedar and scrub birch along shore give way to conifer-clad hillsides. Wildlife abounds—frogs, great blue herons, red-winged blackbirds, beavers, yellow-rumped warblers, belted kingfishers—and one can enjoy it in quiet seclusion. As you paddle back to the main lake, Stony Creek and Ampersand mountains dominate the skyline, but several other peaks are also visible, including a few in the distant High Peaks Wilderness.

A marshy area also exists along the narrow connecting river between Middle and Lower Saranac lakes. The channel rules include a 5-mile-per-hour speed limit, so keep your speed down when passing motorboats. You can explore side channels during high water, carrying up over beaver dams, where you will see lots of wildlife, including a variety of ducks—wood, black, mallard, teal, and ring-necked—and possibly yellowlegs and spotted sandpipers. We listened to the strange call of the American bittern (*woooom-pah-pah*) as we paddled back in.

When you get to the lock, you have four choices: turn around, go through the lock, carry around, or run the river to the right at medium to high water. If you choose the river, scout first because of boulders and a sharp left turn at the bottom of the run. The lock intrigued us because of its counterweighted wood construction and hand operation. In the off-season, you can operate it yourself, following posted instructions.

49 | Lower Saranac Lake

Lower Saranac's numerous islands and deep coves provide many miles of shoreline to explore. When paddling here in spring, we saw myriad songbirds and many marshland plant and animal species. Surrounding Adirondack peaks lend a scenic backdrop. Wind can sometimes be a problem, but the islands make it somewhat less treacherous than other large lakes in the region.

Location: Harrietstown
Maps: *New York Atlas & Gazetteer*, Map 29: B9, B10; USGS Saranac Lake
Area: 2,214 acres
Time: All day
Habitat Type: Large lake with many islands, deep coves, and two adjacent ponds
Fish: Largemouth and smallmouth bass; northern pike (see fish advisories, Appendix C; see specific advisory, health.ny.gov/environmental/outdoors/fish/health_advisories)
Camping: Appendix A (91); on-site wilderness camping
Take Note: Treacherous paddling when windy

GETTING THERE

From the junction of Route 3/River Street and Church Street in Saranac Lake, go 4.3 miles west on Route 3 to the Second Pond access on the left. (44° 17.301′ N, 74° 11.110′ W) Paddle under the Route 3 bridge to the left.

From Tupper Lake, go east on Routes 3 and 30; when the roads divide, head 12.1 miles east on Route 3 to the Second Pond access on the right.

WHAT YOU'LL SEE

You will encounter more boat traffic here than on Middle Saranac. Trailers often jam the large Second Pond fishing access parking lot. You can also launch at the much-less-used South Creek access on Middle Saranac Lake and then paddle into the lower lake. Despite the motorboat traffic, Lower Saranac presents a wonderful, historical place to paddle, especially because the state owns the vast majority of shoreline around it and First and Second ponds.

Much of the early guide lore and its literature took place on Saranac lakes, which served as a gateway to all northern Adirondack drainages. This should

TRIP 49: LOWER SARANAC LAKE

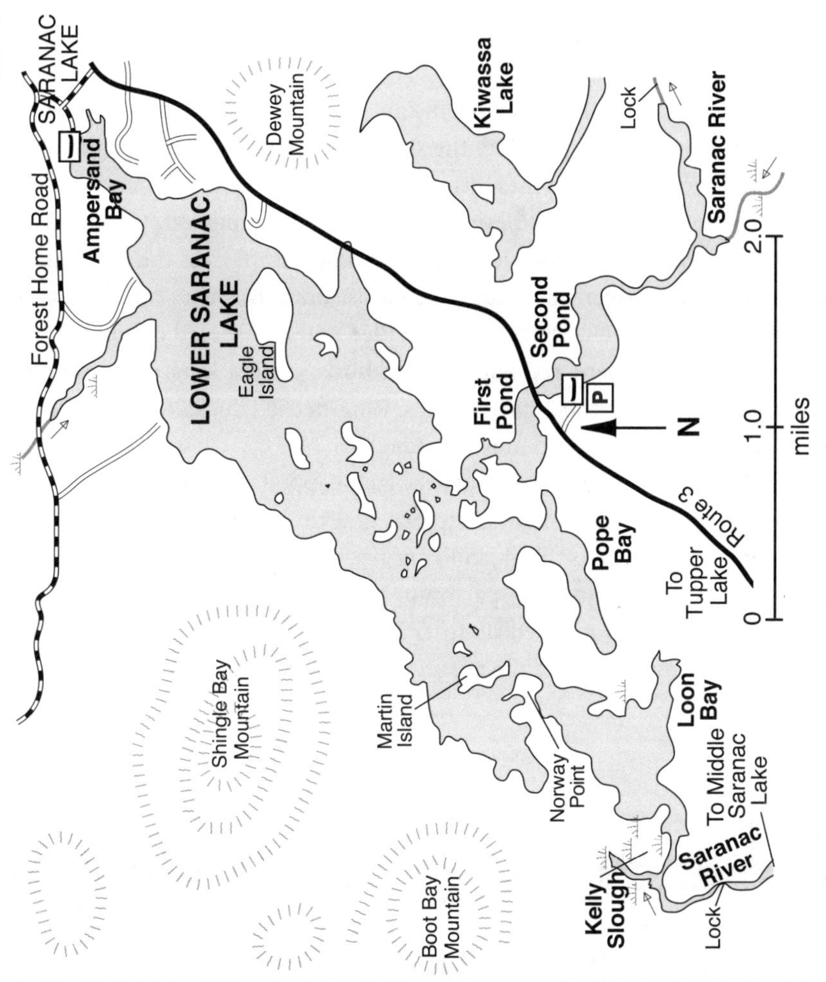

not be surprising, given the area's central location, its linkages to other river and lake systems, and its beauty. The surrounding Adirondack peaks form a dramatic backdrop, providing many hiking trails for those seeking a wilderness experience.

Many islands dot Lower Saranac's surface, breaking up the view, making the lake seem much smaller than its large area would indicate. These same islands provide many attractive campsites and block the wind—indeed, wind can pose more of a problem on smaller, but less protected, Middle Saranac.

Because development on Lower Saranac concentrates at the northeast end, we focused on the southern half and the winding coves and bays to the southwest. It takes quite a while to explore fully the lake's 17 miles of shoreline and many islands—making this a great location for a several-day vacation, especially off-season.

At the Second Pond access, note the many towering hemlocks; on the pond, northern white cedars dominate the shoreline, joined by an occasional birch and a few very tall white pines. From here, paddle northwest onto First Pond and work your way out onto Lower Saranac. Continuing left, you eventually reach the Saranac River lock leading to Middle Saranac. As the lake narrows into the Saranac River inlet, quite a contrast unfolds: sheer, cedar-clad cliffs stand guard on the left, while flat, bird-filled marshes spread out on the right. When we paddled here, red-winged blackbirds, eastern kingbirds, and ducks filled the marsh with their spring songs. Ring-necked ducks scattered into the emerging marsh vegetation in Kelly Slough.

We heard or saw eastern phoebe, black-capped chickadee, crow, winter wren, hermit thrush, spotted sandpiper, grackle, yellow-rumped and black-throated green warblers, black and ring-necked ducks, robin, red-eyed vireo, and white-throated and song sparrows.

Negligible winds allowed us to cruise around the islands, enjoying the emerging spring plants and the gorgeous mountainside scenery.

Views of the Adirondack tall peaks lend scenic character to Lower Saranac Lake.

50 | Raquette River

This section of the Raquette River slowly winds back and forth, making it easy to paddle in both directions. If you have time, explore the quiet, marshy outlet of Follensby Pond. You will probably see osprey, bald eagle, waterfowl, great blue heron, beaver, and deer along this historic Adirondack waterway.

Location: Harrietstown
Maps: *New York Atlas & Gazetteer*, Map 29: C7, C8; USGS Tupper Lake
Length: 10 miles one way
Time: All day
Habitat Type: Slow-flowing, marshy river
Fish: Smallmouth bass, northern pike, walleye (see fish advisories, Appendix C)
Camping: On-site wilderness camping
Information: Canoe/kayak rental, shuttle service, Raquette River Outfitters, raquetteriveroutfitters.com
Take Note: Paddle near shore to avoid the occasional motorboat

GETTING THERE

Route 3 Access. From the junction of Routes 3 and 30 and Mill Street in Tupper Lake, go 3.9 miles east on Route 3 to the access on the right. (44° 14.384′ N, 74° 23.311′ W)

Axton Landing Access. From the junction of Routes 3 and 30 east of Tupper Lake, go 2.6 miles east on Route 3, and turn right on Coreys Road. Go 1.9 miles (4.5 miles) on a rough road to the access on the right. (44° 12.330′ N, 74° 19.502′ W)

WHAT YOU'LL SEE

The Raquette (pronounced "rocket"), the second-longest river in New York, features prominently in early Adirondack lore, from Ralph Waldo Emerson's poem "The Adirondacs," about his explorations in 1858, to the voyages of Nessmuk (George Washington Sears) in J. Henry Rushton's 10-pound *Sairy Gamp* canoe in the late nineteenth century, to the guide-boat race from Old Forge to Saranac Lake in this century. Still very popular today, the Raquette accommodates many paddlers in July and August. Long-distance travelers

TRIP 50: RAQUETTE RIVER

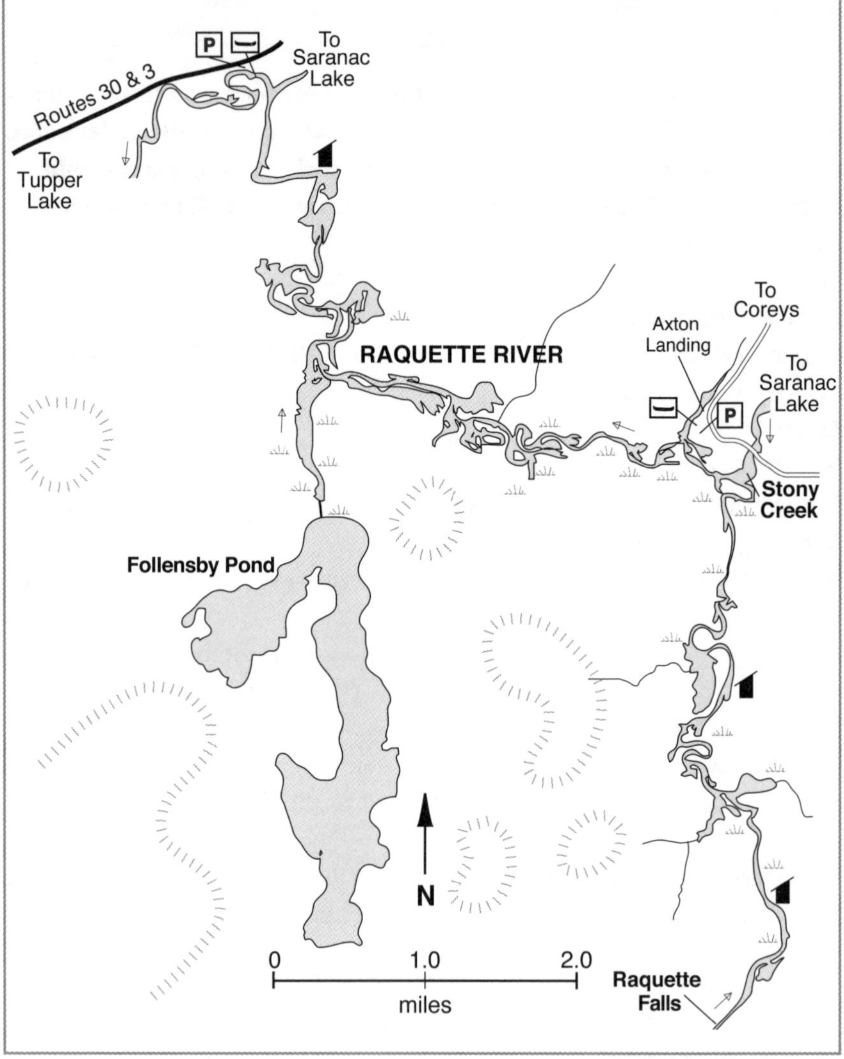

paddle from Long Lake, carrying around Raquette Falls and continuing through Stony Creek Ponds to Upper Saranac Lake.

We chose the section between Raquette Falls and the Route 3 access east of Tupper Lake because of its slow meandering and wilderness character, which makes one sometimes question current direction. In *Adirondack Canoe Waters: North Flow*, authors Paul Jamieson and Donald Morris say that a dam only 10 feet high constructed in Piercefield in 1870 flooded the valley for nearly 30 miles, all the way back to Raquette Falls near Long Lake. Fifteen years later, after many protests, officials lowered the dam to where it stands today. During times of high water, much of the formerly flooded marshland becomes accessible by boat again for a short time.

The state owns both sides of the river between Route 3 and a mile or so upstream of Follensby Pond outlet. After that, up to Raquette Rapids, the state owns only the eastern shore. The High Peaks Wilderness Area borders the river's eastern shore upstream from Axton Landing.

One could spend days here, exploring the oxbows and inlets, the braided channels and side streams, watching the professorial great blue heron preside over the marsh, stealthily hunting fish, frogs—indeed, anything that moves. The channel turns back on itself over and over, occasionally doubling or even tripling the water distance between two points. Ducks erupt from the water's surface as you round the bends, startling you as much as you startle them.

Flooding more than a century ago killed the large trees that lined the banks, although some tall white pines and relatively large northern white cedars have grown back. Today, streamside silver maples provide forage for many beavers. Watch for the large number of beaver dams on inflows and side channels. Carry up over the dams and explore in quiet seclusion, away from motorboats that occasionally roar around the bends. We found anglers to be quite courteous toward paddlers . . . if they see you!

A not-so-quiet section of the Raquette River that one can walk to from the quieter sections of the river.

We particularly enjoyed paddling up the expansive marshy connector to Follensby Pond, as did Emerson nearly 150 years ago in a guide boat. He camped there for a few weeks in August 1858, under some huge pines and maples, as he wrote about in his poem "The Adirondacs."

> Next morn, we swept with oars the Saranac,
> With skies of benediction, to Round Lake [Middle Saranac],
> Where all the sacred mountains drew around us,
> Tahawus, Seward, MacIntyre, Baldhead,
> And other Titans without muse or name.
> Pleased with these grand companions, we glide on,
> Instead of flowers, crowned with a wreath of hills,
> And made our distance wider, boat from boat,
> As each would hear the oracle alone.
> By the bright morn the gay flotilla slid
> Through files of flags that gleamed like bayonets,
> Through gold-moth-haunted beds of pickerel-flower,
> Through scented banks of lilies white and gold,
> Where the deer feeds at night, the teal by day,
> On through Upper Saranac, and up
> Pere Raquette stream, to a small tortuous pass
> Winding through grassy shallows in and out,
> Two creeping miles of rushes, pads, and sponge,
> To Follansbee Water and the Lake of Loons.
>
> —Ralph Waldo Emerson, *Poems* (Houghton Mifflin, 1904)

Although Follensby Pond remains off-limits after its purchase by The Nature Conservancy in 2008, one can explore the outflow creek. You will need a map and compass to find it; if you succeed, you will not regret the effort. Paddling upstream, look for a broad, marshy expanse to the right as the river curves left. As you enter, paddle over barely submerged posts from a long-abandoned bridge, back into a broad expanse of pickerelweed and other aquatic vegetation. Grasses line the banks, and many ducks raise their broods, fattening them up for fall migration. Paddling here in fall, we saw many black ducks (smaller wood ducks and teal migrated earlier). The biggest flock numbered about 30.

Two shelters perch on the bank, as indicated on this book's map. Several other obvious camping spots—flat, grassy, needle-carpeted—beckon from under hemlocks and pines. We saw little other evidence of human activity, save two rope swings hanging from birches.

51 | Lows Lake (Bog River Flow)

Long, narrow, marshy Lows Lake offers an outstanding wilderness paddling and camping experience. Because of its popularity, we prefer to visit in spring and fall. You will see lots of wildlife: osprey, loon, waterfowl, spruce grouse, raven, beaver, deer, bear, and bald eagle.

Location: Clifton, Colton, Long Lake, Piercefield
Maps: *New York Atlas & Gazetteer*, Map 28: D2, D3, D4, E2; USGS Little Tupper Lake, Wolf Mountain
Area: 2,845 acres
Time: All day or multiday
Habitat Type: Long, narrow, shallow, marshy lake
Fish: Largemouth bass, brook trout (see fish advisories, Appendix C)
Camping: On-site wilderness camping; map of campsite locations, dec.ny.gov/lands/75295.html
Take Note: West winds can make paddling hazardous

GETTING THERE

From Route 30 north of Long Lake or south of Tupper Lake, go 5.8 miles west on Route 421, and turn left on Lows Lower Dam access road. Go 0.7 mile (6.5 miles) to the access. (44° 6.958′ N, 74° 37.592′ W)

WHAT YOU'LL SEE

Bog River Flow and its lakes and ponds, islands and shores, floating bogs and surrounding forests represent an extraordinary paddling resource. Two dams built by A. A. Low in 1903 and 1907 provide sufficient water to allow a 14.5-mile paddle from the lower dam to Lows Lake's west end. A hiking trail of more than 3 miles through the woods connects the far western end with the upper reaches of the Oswegatchie River East Branch (see trip 68).

Thirty-nine numbered campsites, available on a first-come, first-served basis, provide wonderful camping opportunities. Check the bulletin board at the access for campsite locations. If necessary, you may camp at nondesignated sites, but only on state land, which increased by 1,000 acres in 2006. The state restricts parties to nine but encourages six or fewer to reduce impact on fragile bog habitat. This popular recreation destination suffers from too

TRIP 51: LOWS LAKE (BOG RIVER FLOW)

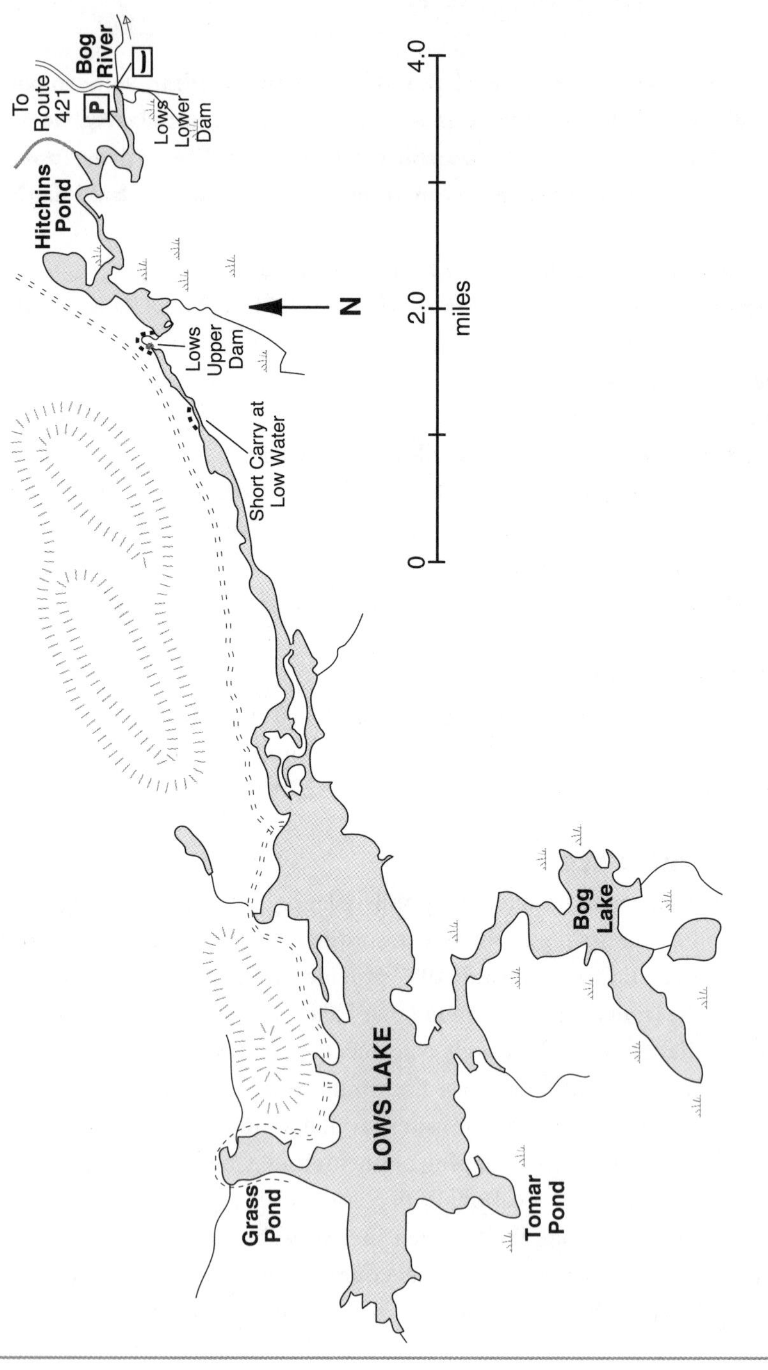

many paddlers in summer. We recommend paddling here in spring or fall or on weekdays during summer.

Tall spruces and pines perch precariously on huge granite boulders that line the narrow passageway leading out from Lows Lower Dam at the flow's eastern end. Mosses, lichens, and ferns cling to rock faces, and pine needles carpet the forest floor.

Bears patrol the shores and islands, looking to destroy food bags and coolers left carelessly lying about. Spruce grouse, the ruffed grouse's increasingly rare northern cousin, might turn up in the dense conifer stands. These birds often stand in plain view, allowing humans to approach closely, which probably explains their reduced numbers. Ravens appear in pairs, croaking out their hoarse cries. When we paddled here, we saw lots of deer, as well. In the not-too-distant past, one might have seen a rare golden eagle soaring overhead, along with much more common osprey.

Perhaps most impressive, however, is the loon population—the state's largest—that inhabits the far reaches of the flowage's ponds. Loons suffer from human disturbance: boat wakes drown their nests, lead sinkers poison them, and repeated encounters with humans drive them away. Fortunately, the Department of Environmental Conservation excludes motors between Lows Lower and Upper dams. The upper section of the lake borders the Five

A tall beaver dam holds back the water on a Bog River Flow tributary just upstream from the access.

Ponds Wilderness Area, and we hope the state would officially designate it a wilderness someday, which would eliminate all motors.

We saw many other species in our all-too-brief stay in this wildlife paradise. We noted a large number of beaver lodges, along with mounds of fresh cuttings set aside as winter food. One enterprising beaver had just downed a large paper birch. Given that these rodents prefer deciduous trees—probably because of the resins in conifers—one wonders why they eat so much resinous paper birch. Firewood users know that unsplit paper birch logs rot from the inside out in short order because the resinous bark does not allow moisture to escape.

After a short carry around Lows Upper Dam and about a mile paddle, we reached a floating bog blocking the narrow channel leading to the main lake. In high water, you can probably paddle over or around the bog, but we had to carry on the north to get past it, taking care not to harm the fragile sphagnum mat with its few dwarf tamaracks, along with sundew, pitcher plant, leatherleaf, sweetgale, and other bog specialists.

Spire-like spruce and balsam fir ring Lows Lake's shore, providing habitat for spruce grouse and many other species. Appropriately, an extensive sphagnum bog guards the entrance to Bog Lake. Scattered tamaracks and a carpet of leatherleaf cover the bog; sweetgale and grasses adorn the edges. A great blue heron watched warily as we passed, and an osprey wheeled overhead. This

A marshy area in one of the coves of Lows Lake.

extraordinarily rich and varied habitat, filled with myriad plants and wildlife, offers one of the finest paddling experiences in the Adirondacks.

In January 1974, the St. Lawrence County Historical Association chronicled the enterprises of A. A. Low, who built the two dams on the lake, one in 1903 and one in 1907. The dams generated electricity for the small enclave at the lake and for Low's residence on nearby Lake Marian and provided water for log drives. Low owned 40,000 acres, which he used to produce timber and maple syrup. He tapped more than 10,000 maple trees and produced 20,000 gallons of maple syrup in the peak year of 1907. An innovator, Low used tubs, pipes, and troughs to bring sap to railcars to transport to his huge evaporator. He held more than 200 patents, including several on sap-boiling devices and one on a square bottle used to package virgin Adirondack forest spring water that he sent to New York City. His company, the Horseshoe Forestry Company, met its demise in a devastating fire in 1908. Low died in 1912.

The historical association's account of this amazingly accomplished man ends with these words: "In life his aim had been to develop, improve, and utilize the fruits of his mountain empire without despoiling it. His spirit roams the Bog River Valley. Today it must be pleased that two monuments to his enterprise [the dams] still stand tall and proud after more than 60 [now 100] years."

ADIRONDACK PARK

Sweeping mountain vistas, sparkling waterfalls, the loon's haunting cry, the river otter's playful antics, clear mountain lakes in steep glaciated terrain, broad expanses of untrammeled wilderness—all these identify the remarkable Adirondack Park. Located less than a half-day's drive for more than 30 million people and covering an area larger than either Massachusetts or New Hampshire, Adirondack Park has a fascinating history.

History

Before the Industrial Age and the resource consumption that fueled it, European colonists knew little about what is now the Adirondack Park region. American Indians traversed the mountains and traveled the region's rivers, linking with lands as far away as Maine. High northerly elevations, where winter lingered long and cold, relegated indigenous populations and European immigrants to a transient existence. Early colonial adventurers explored the Pacific Northwest and Rockies long before mapping the Adirondacks.

During the 1800s, the area fell victim to greed and waste. Loggers penetrated nearly every corner of the park, mainly to remove tall white pine—some towering 150 feet or more, standing well above other forest trees. Logs floated down the Hudson and every other river of consequence. Hemlock, cut and stripped of its bark, provided tannic acid for the tanning industry. When the logging boom ended in the late 1800s, only 1 percent of the original 6 million acres remained untouched. Hunters killed the last moose in the 1860s; extirpated the cougar, wolf, lynx, and wolverine by 1900; and relentlessly trapped beaver until only a handful remained in 1904.

Ironically, though, wealthy industrialists—whose mills and factories depleted the region's forests and despoiled its air and water—finally led the charge to protect the Adirondacks. The wealthy literally fled to the mountains for its clean air and water. Recreational visitation mushroomed in 1869 when Boston preacher William H. H. "Adirondack" Murray wrote the widely read book *Adventures in the Wilderness; or, Camp-Life in the Adirondacks*. He likened the "magnificent scenery" to that of Switzerland. In the 1880s, George Washington Sears, under the pen name Nessmuk, wrote in *Forest and Stream* exciting accounts of his adventures paddling the Sairy Gamp, a 10-pound canoe built by J. Henry Rushton, through the Adirondack wildlands.

People came in droves for the pure mountain air that might cure tuberculosis or offer relief from New York or Boston's polluted air. Intellectuals, including Ralph Waldo Emerson, James Russell Lowell, and Louis Agassiz, came to "rough it" at the "Philosophers' Camp" on Follensby Pond. They used waterway corridors to explore the remote wilderness in famed Adirondack guide boats. Entrepreneurs catered to the wealthy with dozens of grand hotels—the Prospect House on Blue Mountain Lake was the first hotel in the world to have electric lighting in every room—and luxurious fishing and hunting camps. The guide industry flourished, and many of today's carry trails were in use long before roads. While enjoying the outdoors, these industrialists also witnessed the destruction of the Adirondacks around them, including their own rampant overfishing and overhunting.

They heard the message from Vermont lawyer George Perkins Marsh in his groundbreaking 1864 book *Man and Nature*. Marsh convinced many powerful New Yorkers that denuded slopes would hold neither soil nor water, that floods and droughts would increase, that the prized artery of commerce, the Erie Canal, might go dry.

A young, well-to-do Albany lawyer, Verplanck Colvin, reinforced Marsh's message. Colvin gave up lawyering to survey the Adirondacks for more than twenty years, climbing its peaks and mapping its valleys, taking every opportunity to write and speak about the threats to this glorious land. Colvin and his powerful allies convinced the state legislature in 1872 to set up a commission to study the Adirondacks, eventually leading to the Forest Preserve Law of 1885: the Adirondacks and Catskills would be "forever kept as wild forest lands."

But because of continuing abuses, Governor David Hill asked the Forest Commission to draw a line around those lands most worthy of protection, resulting in 1892 in the first "blue line" around 2 million acres of the Adirondack Forest Preserve. A state constitutional convention in 1894 gave protection to these lands with the passage of Article 14:

> The lands of the State, now owned or hereafter acquired, constituting the forest preserve, as now fixed by law, shall be forever kept as wild forest lands. They shall not be leased, sold, or exchanged or taken by any corporation, public or private, nor shall the timber thereon be sold, removed, or destroyed.

The publicly owned lands within the Adirondack Park blue line are among the most fully protected lands in the nation. To open these lands for logging or development would require not just the passage of a new law but amending the state constitution. Over the years, the blue line has expanded to the park's present boundaries, encompassing approximately 6 million acres.

Adirondack Park includes a mix of public and private land. The Forest Preserve founders hoped to acquire all of the land within the blue line eventually, but that will not occur. The state has acquired about 45 percent of the land within the park, and that fraction is expected to creep upward gradually as the state purchases additional lands.

Unprecedented massive land ownership changes all across the Northern Forest, from New York to Maine, have occurred since the first edition of this book in 1996. Timber companies have sold vast parcels of land to other timber companies, investment companies, private developers, states, and The Nature Conservancy. Sales started in Maine, where 5.5 million acres—nearly 30 percent of northern Maine—changed hands between 1998 and 2003; to put this into perspective, the 8,600 square miles sold is 2.5 times the size of Yellowstone National Park and twice as large as the public holdings in Adirondack Park.

Public and private land protection efforts in the park in recent decades have been significant. The dramatic 2007 sale of 161,000 acres of Finch, Pruyn & Company timberland to The Nature Conservancy was the largest transaction in recent decades. The Finch Pruyn tract includes 415 miles of rivers and streams, 300 lakes and ponds, 90 mountain peaks, and 16,000 acres of wetlands. Of this land, 95,000 acres remains in timber production, but with stringent conservation easements on the land; 65,000 acres have been transferred to the State of New York to be part of the Adirondack Forest Preserve; and the remaining 1,100 acres have been set aside for community purposes in three towns. The land transferred to the state includes the Essex Chain Lakes, which has been added to the third edition of this guide (see trip 56).

Geology

The Adirondacks' unique character stems in large part from its geological history. The Canadian Shield inexplicably pushed up through overlying sedimentary rock, exposing ancient Precambrian metamorphic rock. A distinct dome, extending generally northeast to southwest, covers an area of roughly 120 miles by 80 miles. Although much of the rock formed a billion years ago, the mountains themselves formed much more recently—only about 15 million years ago—making them far younger than the weathered, 350-million-year-old Appalachian Mountains of neighboring Vermont. Some geologists believe that the Adirondacks continue to rise. Because no active tectonic plates collide beneath the Adirondacks, the usual mountain-building mechanism does not explain the mountains' recent, and possibly continuing, uplift.

The Adirondacks' high-mountain granite, quartz, and gneiss (pronounced "nice") do not react with acid. Thus, airborne acids from coal-fired power plants in the Ohio River Valley—deposited on the peaks as acid rain, dew, frost, and snow—acidify high-elevation waterways. Native brook trout and other game fish cannot reproduce under moderately acidic conditions, so many Adirondack lakes and ponds have become depleted of fish. In contrast, lower elevations' underlying marble—made up of calcium carbonate, just like limestone—neutralizes acidity. Consequently, lower-elevation lakes have not suffered the drastic declines in fish populations that have occurred at higher elevations.

Looking Toward the Future

Adirondack Park contains the largest wilderness area and the vast majority of remaining virgin old-growth forest in the eastern United States. The region offers a tremendous resource for learning about forest ecosystems and wildlife habitat, and it could serve as the site for reintroduction of species long extirpated from the Northeast, such as the timber wolf and mountain lion. The Adirondacks, part of 26 million acres of the Northern Forest, stretching from

northern New York to northern Maine, should serve as a model for preserving these magnificent forests for future generations. But major conflicts have arisen over management—as one might expect when 10 million visitors per year descend on an area that just 130,000 residents call home. Most residents depend on visitors for their livelihoods, but many resent regulatory controls from "downstate."

Ultimately, the goals of residents and visitors coincide. Both want scenic vistas, deep forests, and pristine waterways that support hiking, canoeing, camping, hunting, and fishing. But keeping privately owned portions of the park attractive to visitors, upon whom the residents depend, means some controls on development. No one wants to see cheek-to-jowl vacation homes, such as those dotting the Fulton lakeshores, expand to the rest of the park, a very real risk for much of the 55 percent of the land in private ownership.

The state and conservation organizations seem to have arrived at a workable solution by purchasing available paper lands—while continuing to pay taxes on those lands—and by purchasing conservation easements on other lands. This effort's ultimate success hinges on state residents' willingness to continue to support setting aside the necessary funds for these purchases. So far, that willingness remains intact.

Among the highest priorities for Adirondack Park, in our estimation, are the following:

1. Control shoreline development. Current zoning requires that single-family homes sit on parcels of at least several acres, except along shorelines with a minimum lot size of only 1.2 acres. This carving up of private land around our waterways introduces pollutants from high population densities. We should place a moratorium on shoreline development until we can agree on a master plan that adequately protects river and lake shores.
2. Purchase all 400,000 acres of the Bob Marshall Great Wilderness in the park's core. Link the Oswegatchie wildlands into one wilderness corridor. When the New York legislature agreed to the original blue line that enclosed the most significant natural features on the Adirondacks, it intended to purchase all lands inside. Many of those lands still remain in private hands more than a hundred years later.
3. Use voluntary check-offs on tax returns, the sale of vanity license plates, funds from nonprofit organizations such as The Nature Conservancy, designated surcharges on recreational equipment (including binoculars, canoes, and fishing gear), and renewed emphasis on bond issues to fund land acquisition within the park's core. Pay year-round residents for conservation easements, which provide a way for residents to receive money for their land, yet keep the land intact—as most would choose to do.

4. Support sustainable, nonpolluting businesses that strengthen the local Adirondack economy. Look for products labeled as "Made in the Adirondacks," for example. If residents have a dependable source of year-round income, the pressure to develop or sell land would decrease.

Those of us who love the Adirondacks—residents and visitors, loggers and birders, anglers and paddlers—must work together to guarantee its continued splendor for future generations to know and enjoy. Get to know this most remarkable of parks. Paddle its lakes and rivers, climb its mountains, hike its trails, explore its history, study its wildlife and geology.

52 | Lake Lila

Lake Lila, entirely within the William C. Whitney Wilderness Area, offers yet another wilderness experience with on-site camping in the Tupper Lake/Long Lake area. Look for osprey, loon, marshland bird species, and the occasional bald eagle. Expect to see beaver in the evening.

Location: Long Lake
Maps: *New York Atlas & Gazetteer*, Map 28: E2, E3 and Map 36: A2, A3; USGS Beaver River, Forked Lake, Little Tupper Lake, Wolf Mountain
Area: 1,490 acres
Time: All day or multiday
Habitat Type: Shallow wilderness lake
Fish: Smallmouth bass, landlocked salmon, brook and lake trout (see fish advisories, Appendix C)
Camping: 24 on-site wilderness campsites
Take Note: Suffers from overuse in midsummer; no motors

GETTING THERE

From the junction of Routes 3 and 30 in Tupper Lake, go 11.2 miles south on Route 30, and turn right on Sabbatis Circle Road. Go 3.0 miles (14.2 miles), and bear right on Sabbatis Road. Continue 4.5 miles (18.7 miles), turn left, and go 5.7 miles (24.4 miles) to the access. (44° 1.123′ N, 74° 43.788′ W)

TRIP 52: LAKE LILA

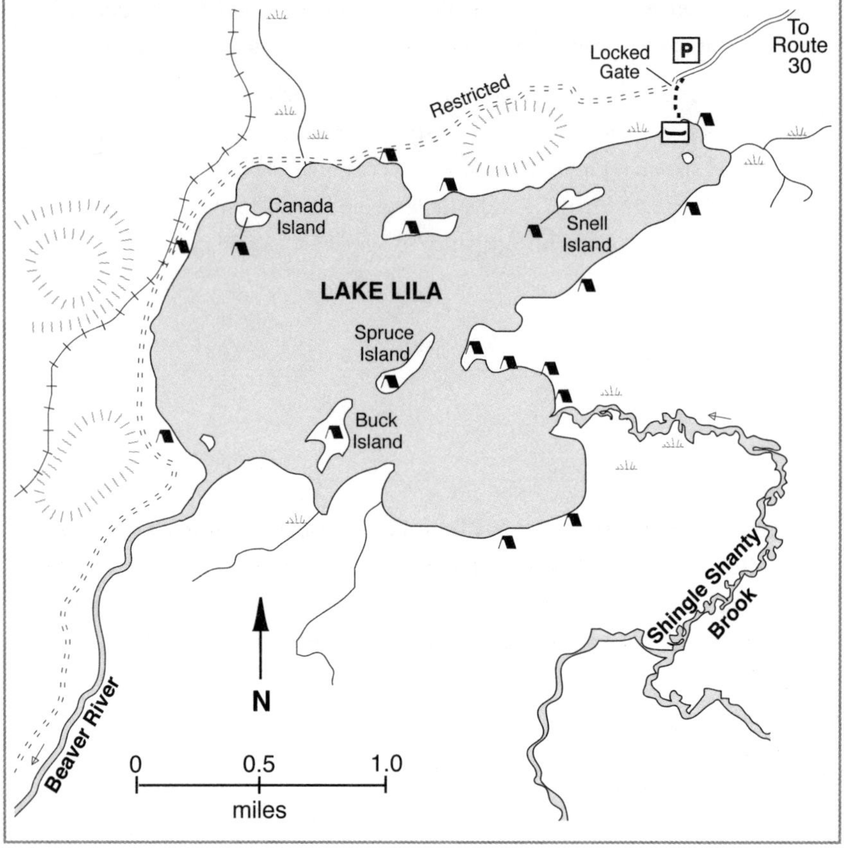

From Long Lake at the junction of Routes 30 and 28N, go 7.1 miles north on Route 30, and turn left on Circle Road. Go 3.0 miles (10.1 miles), bear left on Sabbatis Road, and follow as above.

WHAT YOU'LL SEE

As we paddled out early one October morning, fall-hued foliage of beeches, sugar and red maples, and paper and yellow birches reflected off the glass-like surface of Lake Lila. Wisps of mist, burned off the lake's surface by the rising sun, rose gently into a cloudless sky. We paddled alone—not surprising so late in the season.

The state owns the entire shoreline of this wonderful place and prohibits motors in the William C. Whitney Wilderness Area, which encompasses the entire lake. Great campsites exist all around the lake's perimeter and on some of its islands. Shingle Shanty Brook offers hours of pleasant diversion, and paddlers can travel Beaver River down to the falls, roughly halfway to Nehasane Lake, which lies about 2 miles to the southwest. Intrepid explorers can paddle through Nehasane all the way to Stillwater Reservoir, at least during high water. Clear water makes it possible to avoid barely submerged boulders that rush up to greet your hull.

Rocks, shrubs, and tall white pines dominate Lake Lila's shoreline, along with occasional stands of red pine, spruce, northern white cedar, red maple, and a few mountain maples. Pines and paper birches cover the islands. In contrast to the lakeshore, deciduous trees rule the hillsides, along with some dense conifer patches.

On our October visit, an osprey hovered over Lake Lila's placid waters, waiting to crash-dive onto unsuspecting fish. Yellow-rumped warblers searched for insects, still fattening up for their fall migration. Of the 52 nesting U.S. warbler species, 31 nest in New York, and two more pass through during migration. The yellow-rumped arrives first in spring, leaves last in fall, and winters farther north than any other warbler—as far as coastal Massachusetts. Given that most warblers feed nearly exclusively on insects, the yellow-rumped has had to adapt to insectless conditions in fall and winter by eating berries. Even though insects remain its preferred food, it commonly eats poison ivy berries, bayberries, and others during cold weather. This adaptation has served these birds well, as they remain one of our most abundant warblers.

Early morning mist on Lake Lila.

Shingle Shanty Brook, Beaver River, and the lake all showed evidence of extensive beaver activity. We saw these rodents foraging in the middle of the day. Beavers naturally forage during daylight hours, but in the presence of human disturbance, they become crepuscular (out in twilight), if not completely nocturnal.

We very much enjoyed our three-hour paddle on Shingle Shanty Brook, one of the most meandering bodies of water we have ever paddled. Grasses, clematis, sweetgale, alder, swamp rose, and other shrubs line the banks, with the pointed spires of golden-needled tamarack, spruce, and balsam fir providing contrasting habitat. Bur-reed and water celery, our constant companions, had little trouble in the light current. With a combination of paddling and portaging, intrepid explorers can now travel from Round Lake through Little Tupper Lake to Rock Pond (see trip 53) to Hardigan Pond to Lily Pad Lake to Shingle Shanty Brook to Lake Lila and on beyond to Lows Lake (see trip 51) or to Stillwater Reservoir (see trip 65).

Beaver River, flowing out of Lake Lila, cuts a broad, shallow, scenic swath through coniferous forest, connecting Lake Lila with Nehasane Lake and eventually Stillwater Reservoir. About halfway to Nehasane Lake, a short falls bars the way. To avoid walking your boat through miles of shallows, attempt the trek down to Stillwater only during high water.

53 | Little Tupper Lake, Round Lake, and Rock Pond

Little Tupper Lake and its connected waterways are among the premier paddling destinations in the Northeast. In addition to providing beautiful scenery, the coves and marshlands harbor large wildlife populations. Expect to see bald eagle, osprey, loon, merlin, otter, beaver, and lots more.

Location: Long Lake
Maps: *New York Atlas & Gazetteer*, Map 28: E4, E5; USGS Forked Lake, Little Tupper Lake
Area: Little Tupper Lake, 2,300 acres; Round Lake, 800 acres; Rock Pond, 282 acres
Time: All day or multiday
Habitat Type: Interconnected lakes with marshy inlets and coves

TRIP 53: LITTLE TUPPER LAKE, ROUND LAKE, AND ROCK POND

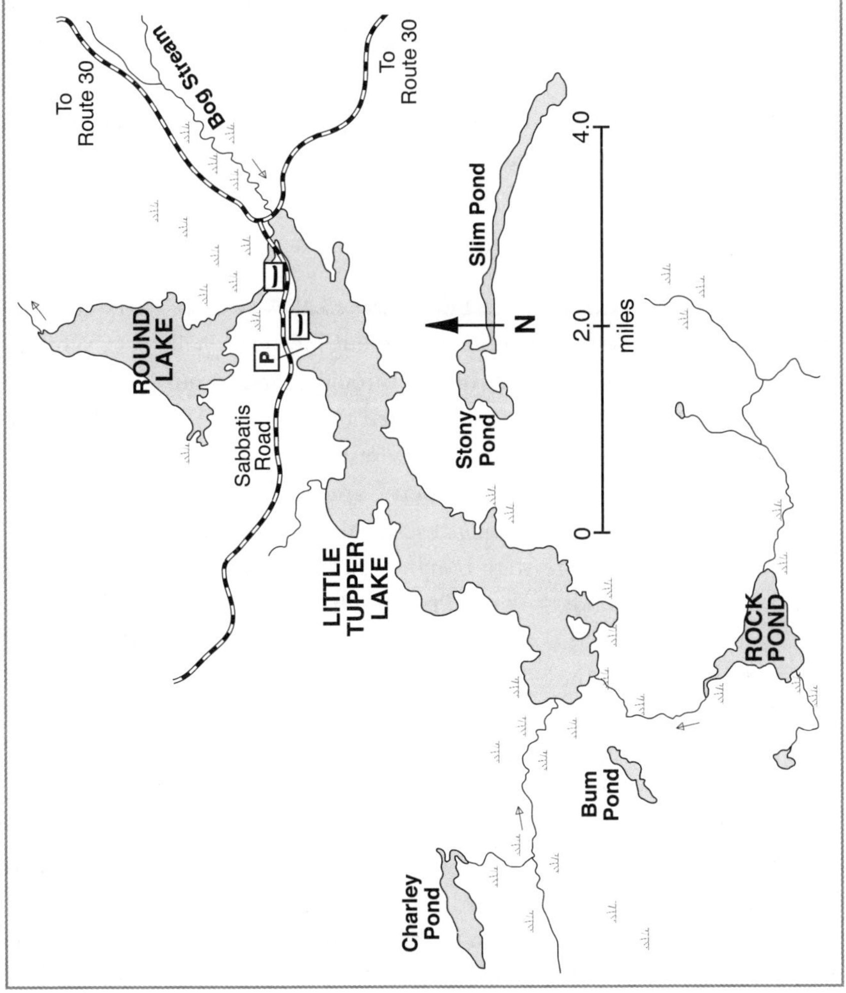

Fish: Brook trout—a strain unique to these lakes (see fish advisories, Appendix C)
Camping: On-site wilderness camping; campsite and trails map, dec.ny.gov/lands/9165.html
Take Note: Hazardous paddling during windy conditions

GETTING THERE

Little Tupper Lake Access. From the junction of Routes 3 and 30 in Tupper Lake, go 11.2 miles south on Route 30, and turn right on Sabbatis Circle Road.

Go 3.0 miles (14.2 miles), and bear right on Sabbatis Road. Continue 1.3 miles (15.5 miles) to the access on the left. (44° 3.020′ N, 74° 35.033′ W)

From Long Lake at the junction of Routes 30 and 28N, go 7.1 miles north on Route 30, turn left on Sabbatis Road, go 3.0 miles (10.1 miles), bear left on Sabbatis Road, and follow as above.

Round Lake Access. Access from Little Tupper Lake or park at the junction of Sabbatis and Circle roads and carry to the right as you walk southwest toward the overpass over the Little Tupper outlet. (44° 3.317′ N, 74° 33.714′ W)

WHAT YOU'LL SEE

Since being purchased by the state, Little Tupper Lake and associated waterways have joined New York's best quietwater paddling locations. William C. Whitney and a partner bought 68,000 acres of land through several acquisitions between 1896 and 1898. Whitney eventually named the property Whitney Park. An ardent conservationist, Whitney hired forester Henry Graves, a protégé of Gifford Pinchot, to manage the property, and early forest operations here became one of the first applications of scientifically based forest management.

In December 1997, the state bought 15,000 acres of Whitney Park for inclusion in the Adirondack Forest Preserve. In March 2000, the Adirondack Park Agency combined this purchase with a portion of the Lake Lila Primitive Area and designated it the William C. Whitney Wilderness Area.

In January 2001, The Nature Conservancy purchased 26,500 acres of land from International Paper, including three parcels of great interest to paddlers: the 9,926-acre Round Lake tract at Little Tupper Lake's northeast end; the 15,536-acre Shingle Shanty Pond tract that links Little Tupper with Lake Lila; and the 1,100-acre Bog Lake–Clear Pond tract that links Lows Lake and Bog River Flow (see trip 51) with Lake Lila (see trip 52). The Conservancy subsequently transferred a portion to the state to provide a publicly accessible waterway corridor from Round Lake through Little Tupper, into Lake Lila, and then to Lows Lake.

Little Tupper Lake

We have paddled Little Tupper Lake three times since the 1997 purchase. In 1999, we saw much evidence of the intense microburst of July 15, 1995 (we had camped in two different locations not far away during that storm). Winds in excess of 100 miles per hour felled thousands of trees around Little Tupper, including more than half the trees in some western sections. By August 2006, we saw far fewer signs of the 1995 disaster.

As called for by the wilderness management plan for Adirondack Forest Preserve, the state established well-separated campsites—24 in all. More heavily used sites have pit privies, and all have fire circles (the only allowable fire locations), but no grills or picnic tables. From Short Island campsite 14, we watched three otters fishing on an early mid-September morning. From campsite 18, we saw a merlin (a small falcon) and a bald eagle. On another trip, we watched a bald eagle swoop low over the lake. Loons seem ever-present.

Development intrudes on the shoreline in only two places: at the access, where the former Whitney Industries headquarters now serves as Little Tupper Lake headquarters, and at two private dwellings retained by the Whitney family: Camp Francis and Camp on the Point. Hemlock, some giant yellow birch, balsam fir, beech, red maple, red spruce, and scattered white pine—including a few huge vestiges of the ancient forest that once stood here—occur along the shore.

Typical northern shrubs, including sweetgale, blueberry, huckleberry, and a variety of ferns, grow along Little Tupper's 20 miles of rocky shoreline. At the half-dozen inlets, shallow waters grow thick with floating and emergent wetland plants: American white and yellow waterlilies, water shield, pickerelweed, water celery, and bulrush, with thick mats of bladderwort beneath the surface.

At the lake's far western tip, we paddled up the Charley Pond outlet in an early August evening's waning light—after winds had died down. The gently meandering stream leaves an open channel in an otherwise vegetation-covered

Exploring the many inlets and coves on Little Tupper Lake.

surface. Dozens of beaver lodges occur along here. In about a mile, we went under a steel I-beam bridge, and in another mile, we passed the remains of an old crib dam or bridge. Beyond that, the stream narrowed, with progress eventually blocked—first by beaver dams, then by fallen trees.

Rock Pond

At Little Tupper's southwestern tip, about two-thirds of a mile west of Short Island, you can make a great day trip up the easy 2-mile outlet from 282-acre Rock Pond. Floating vegetation, pickerelweed, wetland shrubs, royal fern, alder, and tamarack line the wide, meandering stream. We saw a few dozen clumps of pitcher plants, along with tiny sundews on exposed logs. Expect to see beavers—or at least evidence of their work. On our most recent visit, we watched two otters frolic.

In 2006, we carried over two beaver dams and over another portage (150 yards, crossing an old logging road). Along the carry trail, note the huge white pine, measuring more than 4 feet in diameter at breast height. In mid-August in wet years, raspberries grow in abundance here.

Some sizable granite outcroppings in Rock Pond make excellent picnic stops. The five campsites along the shoreline, plus one on the island and two along the outlet stream, see much less use than those on Little Tupper. On an August weekend in 2006, with most of the Little Tupper campsites occupied, only one party camped on Rock Pond. One site even had seedlings growing in the fire pit.

At the pond's southwestern tip, we explored some marshy sphagnum islands but could not paddle far up the inlet creek. Near here, the carry trail leading to Hardigan Pond and Lake Lila takes off to the west. At the eastern tip, we traveled quite a distance up the inlet creek, winding through alders, where we watched a young beaver in a hidden recess as its mother paced back and forth just upstream, until she finally slapped her tail in warning. Beaver dams eventually blocked our upstream progress. We also saw a merlin here.

Round Lake

To reach Round Lake, paddle under Sabbatis Road to the left, 300 yards short of Little Tupper's east end. The inlet stream immediately opens up and remains a wide, shallow, slow-flowing, serpentine channel, thick with waterlilies and other floating vegetation, for the 1.5-mile downstream trip to Round Lake.

From a far northern campsite, close to the outlet, we watched three young otters in first light and then saw them again farther down the western shore. On a mid-August twilight paddle, we watched several duck families skitter into thick shoreline vegetation, and we surprised several beavers beginning their nocturnal forays. We also saw deer, great blue herons, and kingfishers. The inlet stream gradually opens up into roughly triangular Round Lake.

Cliffs extend down into the water along the spectacular western shore, with huge lichen-encrusted boulders capped with polypody fern, clumps of interrupted and royal ferns, wild sarsaparilla, steeplebush, bottle gentian, and a variety of shrubs. You will see the same trees here as on Little Tupper Lake: yellow birch, hemlock, balsam fir, red maple, red spruce, and white pine. Watch for occasional striped maple and mountain ash—the ash's berries turn bright red in fall. Inland from the western shoreline, the land rises steeply, with large outcroppings and cliffs.

At the lake's southwestern tip, you can examine the mucky shallows to some extent, although by early summer, floating vegetation restricts paddling. Note the feathery tamaracks set back from the water's edge. Coves and a handful of islands along the deeply folded southern shoreline beg to be explored.

54 | Long Lake

We paddle Long Lake primarily for its scenic vistas of the High Peaks Wilderness, and you also can get a lot of exercise here if you paddle to the end and back. Look for loons, bald eagles, ospreys, and beavers. We also saw a Cooper's hawk. Because Long Lake funnels wind, avoid it under windy conditions.

Location: Long Lake
Maps: *New York Atlas & Gazetteer*, Map 29: D8, E7, E8 and Map 37: A6, A7; USGS Deerland, Kempshall Mountain
Area: 3,904 acres
Time: All day or multiday
Habitat Type: Long, wide lake with coves, islands, and inlet streams
Fish: Largemouth and smallmouth bass, northern pike, brook trout (see fish advisories, Appendix C; see specific advisory, health.ny.gov/environmental/outdoors/fish/health_advisories)
Camping: On-site wilderness camping
Take Note: Hazardous paddling during windy conditions

TRIP 53: LITTLE TUPPER LAKE, ROUND LAKE, AND ROCK POND

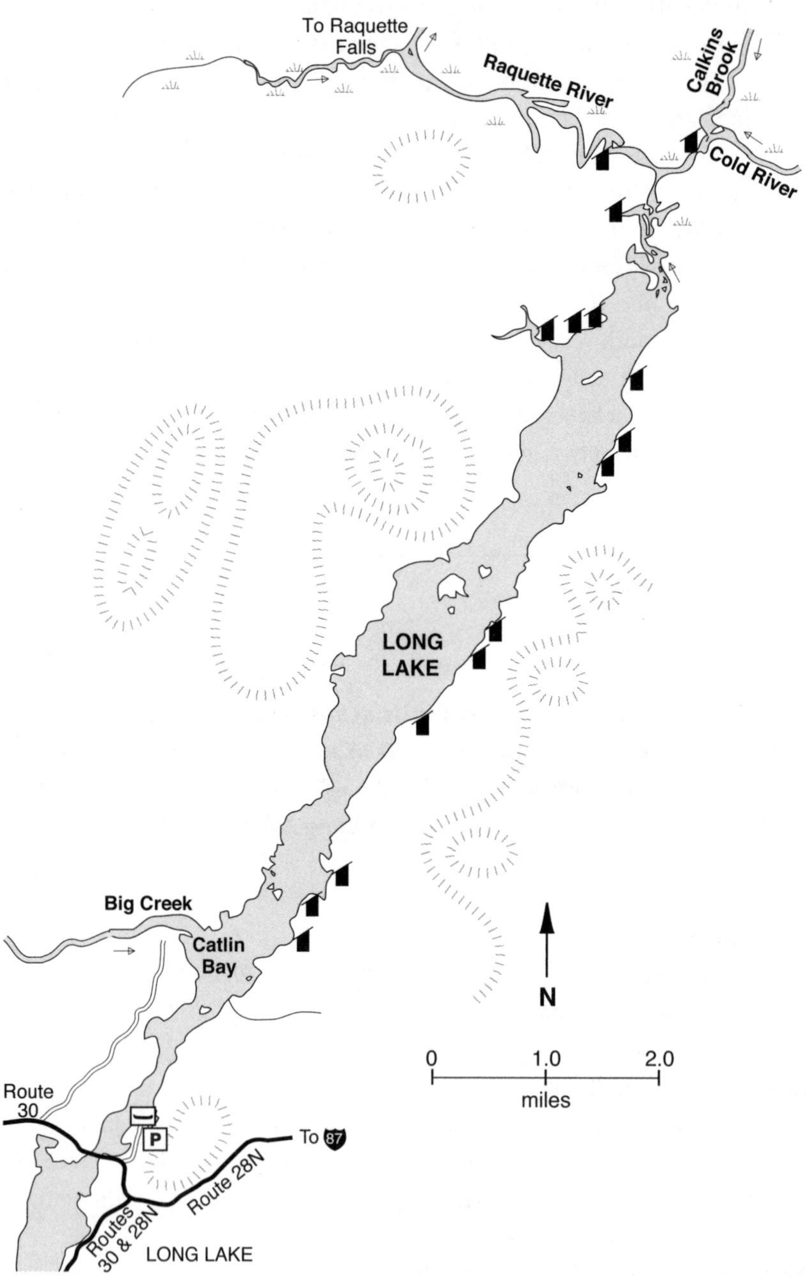

GETTING THERE

From the junction of Routes 30 and 28N in Long Lake, go 0.4 mile north on Route 30, and turn right on Dock Road. Go 0.4 mile (0.8 mile) to the access. (43° 58.714′ N, 74° 24.991′ W)

WHAT YOU'LL SEE

The 4,000-foot mountains of the High Peaks Wilderness dominate the view to the northeast from Long Lake, which lies in the glaciated Raquette River valley. The view alone makes the northern stretch of Long Lake worth paddling. Long-distance paddlers, including those on the 740-mile Northern Forest Canoe Trail, traverse Long Lake on their way to Tupper Lake or to the Saranac lakes via Stony Creek Ponds.

Long Lake's 14-mile southwest-to-northeast length funnels winds. We have paddled here with 2-foot waves crashing over the bow and under dead-calm conditions. We advise that you choose smaller, more protected bodies of water during strong winds.

Do not let the personal watercraft, floatplanes, and motorboats hovering about the village of Long Lake intimidate you. The lake stretches for many miles and includes several small streams where you can escape the noise and congestion. At the lake's northern end, where it narrows, and continuing on

Beautiful views await paddlers on Long Lake.

the 6 miles to the Raquette Falls carry, the Raquette River has earned a federal scenic river designation, which keeps out motorboats and personal watercraft.

The lake's high elevation (1,627 feet) and considerable depth keep the water quite cool until midsummer, making early season swimming a brisk experience. Twenty shelters dot the shoreline, providing wonderful camping spots, especially those with a view down the scenic valley toward the High Peaks Wilderness. The state owns much of the eastern shore but not the western until far down the lake. A grove of large red pines helps conceal the eastern shore's first shelter, announcing the beginning of state-owned land.

Hikers along the 133-mile Northville-Placid Trail that follows the right side of the lake compete for shelter use on the southern shore. Near the lake's northeastern end, several shelters sit on the opposite shore, away from the trail. However, we suggest taking a tent along in July and August, as the shelters may be in use.

Northern white cedar, paper birch, and hemlock line the shore, along with a wide assortment of pines and deciduous trees. We saw few ducks when we paddled here, but loons appeared in good numbers. We watched several crows chase a Cooper's hawk. Like the other accipiters—the larger goshawk and smaller sharp-shinned hawk—the Cooper's hawk preys on other birds. We delighted in seeing this increasingly rare bird's agile flight on short, rounded wings, using its long tail as a rudder. Although we have not witnessed a Cooper's hawk kill, we have observed several kills by the similar, but smaller, sharp-shinned hawk. Agility allows it to take songbirds on the wing, leaving nothing but a puff of feathers drifting slowly to the ground.

Take time to explore two waterways that flow into Long Lake: Big Creek and Cold River. Big Creek flows into Catlin Bay on the northern shore. Pickerelweed, bulrush, and grasses greet you at the outlet, along with lots of beaver activity. We paddled through two breached beaver dams and carried up over a third. About a half-mile upstream, we passed under an unusual bridge with four 8-inch-wide-by-3-feet-deep laminated wooden support beams.

About a quarter-mile after the bridge, a rock fall blocked the way, the rounded boulders forming a sizable rapids flanked by a large stand of tall, pointed balsam firs. Yellow birches dominate the southern shore, with some alders along the bank. Occasional red maples and paper birches occur, as well, in this beautiful and peaceful setting. We noted lots of open mussel shells in the clear water and many species of aquatic plants, including American white waterlily, yellow pondlily, and pondweed.

Cold River flows into the Raquette about a mile downstream from Long Lake's northern end. You can paddle back up its marshy wilderness for nearly 2 miles during high water. Other coves and inlets on Long Lake harbor marshes and their assorted plants and animals. And the river's myriad channels at the northern end down to Raquette Falls provide many more exploration opportunities against the magnificent High Peaks Wilderness backdrop. One has to paddle here for a few days to investigate it all.

55 | Harris Lake and Rich Lake

Marsh vegetation jams the coves and creeks here, providing lots of varied wildlife habitat. Expect to see osprey, loon, wood and ring-necked ducks, deer, otter, beaver, and possibly bald eagle. We also saw a black bear here with two cubs.

Location: Newcomb
Maps: *New York Atlas & Gazetteer*, Map 37: A9, A10; USGS Deerland
Area: Harris Lake, 310 acres; Rich Lake, 342 acres
Time: 5 hours; all day if you paddle the creeks
Habitat Type: Small lakes with extensive marshes and access to the upper Hudson River
Fish: Smallmouth bass, northern pike (see fish advisories, Appendix C)
Camping: Appendix A (83, 84)
Take Note: Avoid Hudson River Class III rapids downstream

GETTING THERE

Harris Lake Access. From Long Lake, at the junction of Routes 28N and 30, go 14.6 miles east on Route 28N, and turn left at the sign for Newcomb Town Beach. (43° 58.271′ N, 74° 08.797′ W)

From I-87, Exit 29, go about 18.8 miles west on Route 84/Blue Ridge Road, and turn right on Route 28N. Go 4.3 miles (23.1 miles) to the access on the right, 0.9 mile after crossing the Hudson River.

Rich Lake Access. From Long Lake, at the junction of Routes 28N and 30, go 11.9 miles east on Route 28N, and turn left on Rich Lake Lane (SUNY Syracuse research center). Park in the lot on the left. Carry 120 yards to the water. Access is 2.7 miles west of Harris Lake. (43° 58.330′ N, 74° 12.006′ W)

TRIP 55: HARRIS LAKE AND RICH LAKE

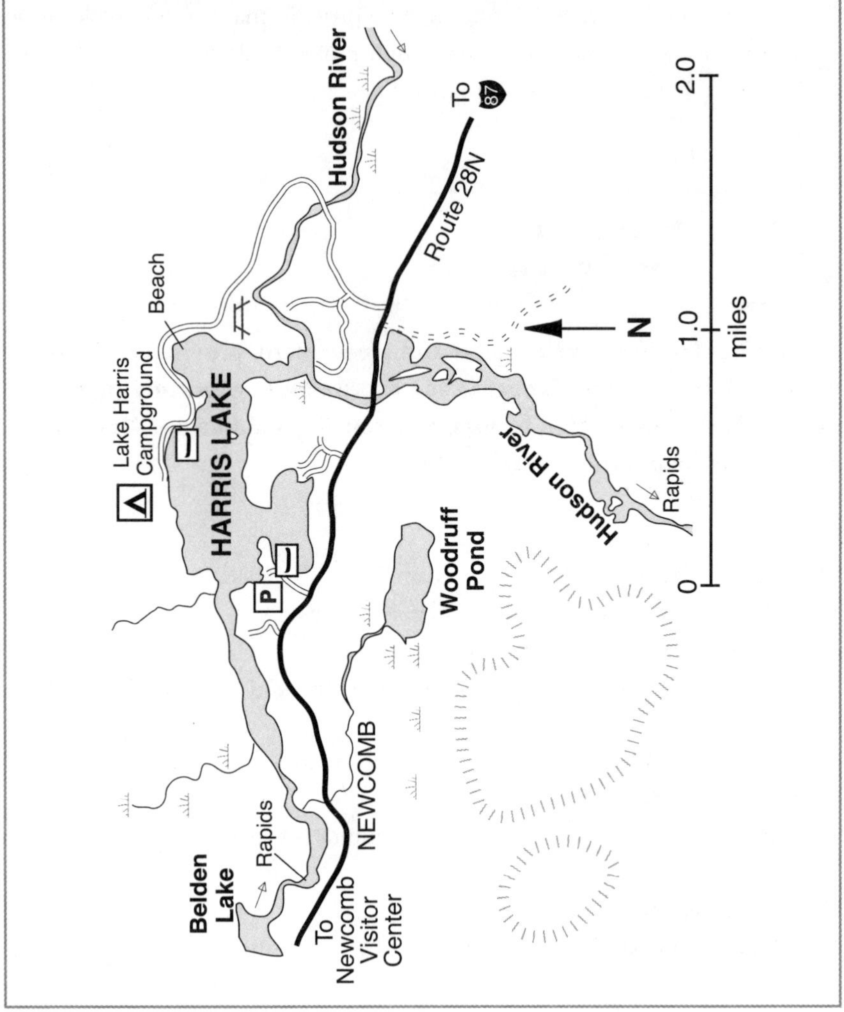

WHAT YOU'LL SEE

Harris Lake

Although Harris Lake lies adjacent to Route 28N, we enjoy paddling here for the gorgeous scenery on the nearby Hudson—and because three cavorting river otters thought it remote enough for them. The otter, a weasel family member with a 30-inch body length and 25-pound weight, ranges from northern Alaska to the Labrador region in Canada, south to Florida's tip, and west to Yuma, Arizona. Despite this huge range, people rarely encounter this magnificent creature, which has grown increasingly rare as development and commotion

TRIP 55: HARRIS LAKE AND RICH LAKE

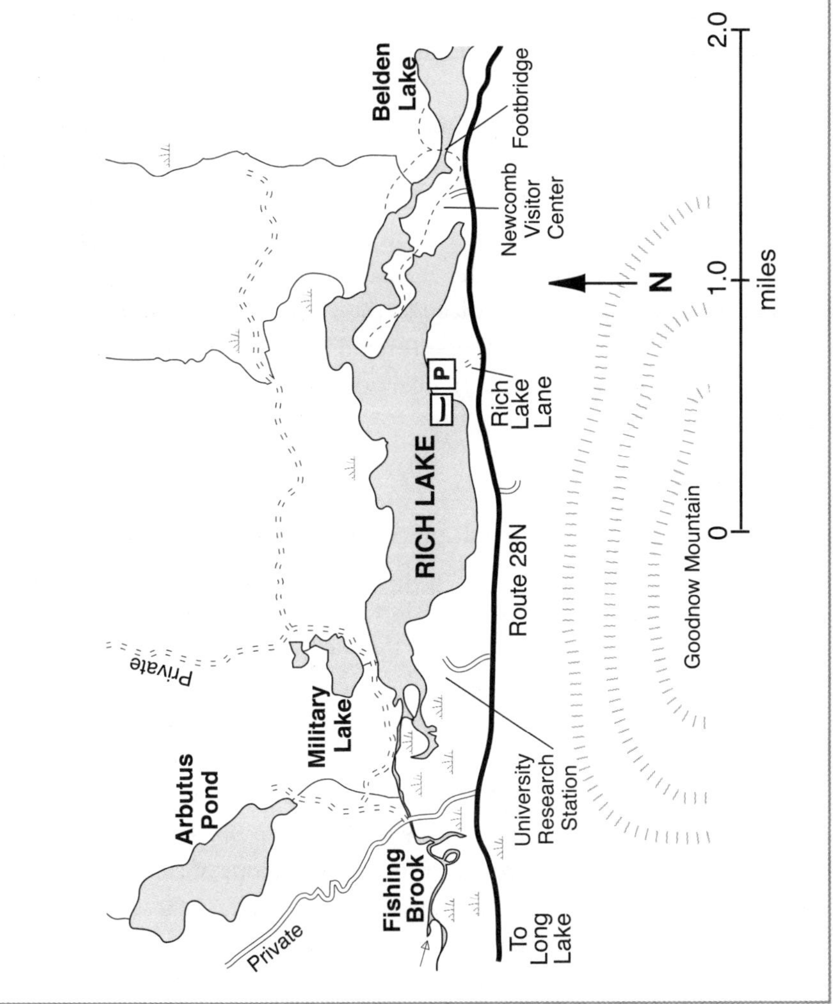

drive it away. (For more on the otter, see "River Otter: Playful Member of the Weasel Family," on page 164.)

Scattered development along the southern and western shores of Harris Lake did not seem to bother the resident loons or other birds, either. Crows searched for washed-up food, and a kingfisher eyed the water for those last few fish to eat before migrating on to warmer climes. Northern white cedars lined the bank, along with patches of tall, pointed firs, occasional white pines, and sugar and red maples. White-tailed deer had carved a noticeable browse line by munching on leaves while standing on the winter ice.

Rushes inhabit the shallows here, along with pondweed, pickerelweed, water celery, and waterlilies. Bur-reed also occurs in places, and royal fern graces the banks. Water shield, a member of the waterlily family, with stems entering the center of a floating oval leaf, occurs in large patches. The stems have a slimy, gelatinous coating.

Paddling east, you enter the mighty Hudson, New York's longest river, near the beginning of its almost 300-mile sojourn from Lake Tear of the Clouds on Mount Marcy to the Verrazano-Narrows Bridge and the Atlantic Ocean. You can paddle upstream a short distance before meeting quick water or go a mile downstream, passing under the Route 28N bridge. Note the warning signs for impending rapids that lead to the Hudson River Gorge. (*Caution*: Avoid getting swept into these Class III rapids, not usually run in open boats. Only really serious whitewater paddlers traverse the gorge's Class V water farther downstream.)

Rich Lake

As we paddled out one early fall morning, mist swirled slowly down this shallow, sandy-bottomed lake. Mussel shells lay in piles near the shore, where raccoons and otters feasted on nightly forays. Looking from the sand beach at the access, we could see a marsh across the way . . . and no development. This wild place offers hours of exploration.

Rich Lake allegedly got its name when early settlers discovered graphite flakes in the surrounding rocks and thought it silver ore. Miners later extracted graphite, a form of carbon, from the deposits near Ticonderoga for the "lead" in lead pencils.

Paddling to the right, you reach the lake's eastern tip, which narrows to a rocky stream with definite current. A footbridge on one of three nature trails crosses overhead; after this, a short rapids leads to Belden Lake and eventually Harris Lake. At low water, you would have to walk your boat down these rapids.

On the main lake, we saw loon, kingfisher, and osprey, all three fishing in different ways: the loon gliding underwater, snaring fish in its bill; the kingfisher in the air, folding its wings at the last moment, diving headlong into the water, catching a fish in its beak; and the osprey hovering overhead, swooping down, crashing into the water, grabbing a fish with its talons.

Fishing Brook enters on the lake's northwestern end, but you can also paddle through an extensive beaver swamp on the south that extends back quite a way through encroaching pickerelweed to a marsh of a few hundred acres. At various places, if you carry up over a few well-kept beaver dams, some surprisingly high, you enter Fishing Brook. Many more dams occur on the brook's myriad channels.

The rocky shoreline of Rich Lake.

A universally-accessible boardwalk and observation platform make the beauty of Rich Lake accessible to all.

Grasses grow on banks, along with thick stands of sweetgale, leatherleaf, swamp milkweed, sheep laurel, bur-reed, and many more swamp specialists. Northern white cedars, with a few towering white pines, occasional hemlocks and balsam firs, some paper and yellow birches, and lots of red, sugar, and silver maples occur on higher ground.

We paddled back up the alder-lined brook, with occasional dogwood and viburnum interspersed, for about three-quarters of a mile, until we reached a large area flooded by a beaver dam. Having carried over many beaver dams already, we turned around and paddled back to the lake.

On our travels through the marsh, several small flocks of wood ducks and ring-necked ducks sprang to air as we interrupted their fattening up for fall migration. But the wildlife highlight came as we left the lake. Right in front of us, a female black bear with two young cubs bounded across the road, with mom woofing copious instructions. Black bear populations have increased significantly in Adirondack Park in recent years. In dry summers, bears seem to move around often, undoubtedly because of less plentiful traditional food sources. If you spend time in wild areas, you stand a good chance of seeing them.

56 | Essex Chain Lakes

Recently acquired by New York State, this area remains wild and remote. A portage is required. You will see a wide variety of native vegetation and lots of wildlife, such as osprey, loon, great blue heron, wood duck, beaver, otter, and white-tailed deer.

Location: Long Lake, Minerva, Newcomb
Maps: *New York Atlas & Gazetteer*, Map 37: B8, B9; USGS Bad Luck Mountain, Dun Brook Mountain, Newcomb, Rock Lake
Area: Twelve lakes, largest 262 acres
Time: All day or multiday
Habitat Type: Connected small lakes with extensive marshes, wooded shorelines
Fish: Landlocked salmon, brook and rainbow trout (see fish advisories, Appendix C)
Camping: On-site wilderness camping
Take Note: Portage required to reach access; motors prohibited

TRIP 56: ESSEX CHAIN LAKES

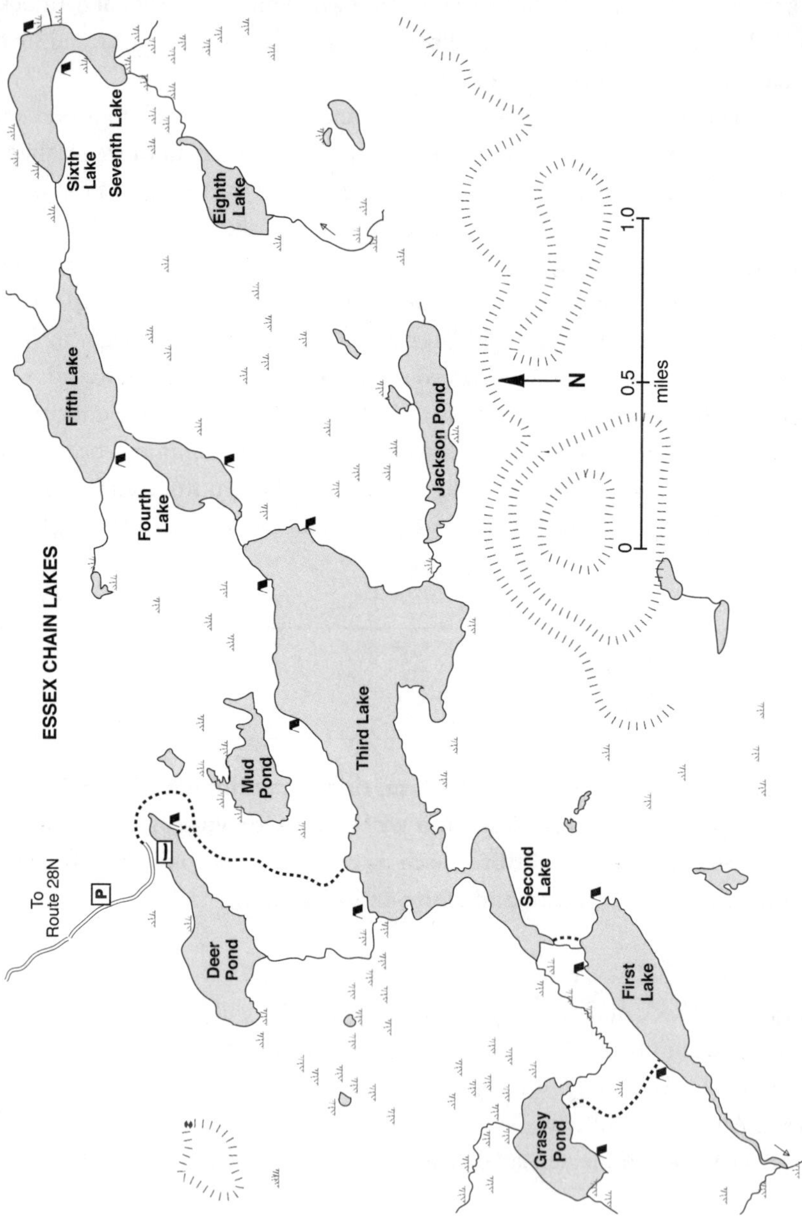

GETTING THERE

From Route 28N in Newcomb, go south on Pine Tree Road at the sign for Essex Chain Lakes. Turn right immediately on Goodnow Flow Road, go 4.5 miles, and turn right on Woody's Road. Go 6.1 miles (10.6 miles) to Deer Pond access (follow signs to Deer Pond access at turns).

Carry 0.25 mile to Deer Pond, paddle directly across, and carry 0.5 mile to Third Lake. Or carry 1.0 mile around Deer Pond directly to Third Lake. Most of the carry is along packed gravel roads; portage wheels work well. (43° 53.293′ N, 74° 15.871′ W)

WHAT YOU'LL SEE

The 19,600-acre Essex Chain Lakes Complex came into public ownership in 2014; until then, the area lacked public access. What a privilege to have this spectacular resource now available to all!

While getting to these waters takes some work—either two modest carries via Deer Pond or a longer carry with some up-and-down—they're worth the effort. Few places in the Adirondacks are as remote and wild as this chain of lakes.

Eight lakes compose the Essex Chain, with Second through Seventh lakes connected by channels that can be paddled. Fairly easy carries take you to First Lake and Grassy Lake. The Deer Pond carry brings you to the western end of the largest lake, Third Lake. The last private camp here was removed in 2018, leaving the area totally without development, except for ten scattered primitive campsites, plus two floatplane-accessible sites on First Lake.

Remarkably, we didn't see a single non-native plant, even along the carries. The pristine vegetation boasts a diverse mix of yellow birch, hemlock, striped maple, sugar maple, northern white cedar, red spruce, and a smattering of tall white pines, left from years of timber harvests under the previous owner.

Typical submerged and emergent wetland plants—sweetgale, leatherleaf, sheep laurel, bog rosemary, yellow pondlily, American white waterlily, royal and cinnamon fern, water shield, pickerelweed, and mats of bladderwort—populate the shallow coves and inlets. Swamp loosestrife (a relative of the non-native purple loosestrife), which can become invasive even though it is native, dominates one cove on Third Lake.

On higher ground, look for a variety of wildflowers, including bunchberry, sarsaparilla, Canada mayflower, hobblebush, and lowbush blueberry. Areas with an overstory of white pine have far different wildflowers than areas dominated by other trees.

A view of Fourth Lake from the sandy road between Fourth and Fifth lakes. You can paddle through the culvert connecting these lakes.

In the narrow channels connecting the lakes, particularly the channel between Fifth and Sixth lakes, you will find spectacular numbers of rose pogonia (*Pogonia ophioglossoides*). The delicate pink orchids grow interspersed with northern pitcher plants. Pitcher plants, with their tall, reddish flowers and cuplike leaves, represent one of several insectivorous plants found here. Tiny rosettes of sundew appear on floating logs and the tussocks of vegetation. A sizable patch of horned bladderwort sports bright yellow flowers and no visible leaves (for more on carnivorous plants, see "Carnivorous Plants: The Table is Turned," on page 361).

The marshy channels provide prime habitat for beavers, which made their presence known with occasional tail slaps as we paddled along, particularly toward dusk. We must have seen more than a dozen lodges. A huge, well-made dam at the Second Lake outlet—probably more than 100 feet long and 4 feet high—helped to maintain the water level in this series of lakes.

Near the Second Lake beaver dam, we happened on four young river otters; both otters and mink are relatively common throughout these lakes. When we paddled along the southern shore of Third Lake, we spied young osprey in a nest high in a tree on a spit of land jutting out into the lake—and its parent, not too happy with our presence.

To pass from Fourth into Fifth Lake, you have to pull through a culvert; we sat on the canoe's floor to avoid ducking. The culvert is too small to use a paddle, but a convenient fixed rope is available. A handicapped-accessible campsite exists on Fifth Lake, just north of the culvert.

On the sandy road crossing the culvert, look for telltale signs of snapping turtle nests. You may see bits of curled, dried, leathery shells left by hatchlings or dug up by raccoons or skunks. During three days here, we saw several snapping turtles. At our campsite on Fourth Lake, we spotted the distinctive triangular snout of a modest-sized snapping turtle 10 feet from shore, and along the edge of Sixth Lake we saw a snapper basking in the sun on a log. In the late afternoon on Sixth Lake, we saw a lone painted turtle on a mat of uprooted pondlilies.

Right in our campsite, we discovered the hidden ground nest of a white-throated sparrow, evidence that these sites get little to modest use. Other birds we saw during our explorations include great blue heron, wood duck, common merganser, belted kingfisher, and eastern kingbird. We also heard barred owls.

We came across a loon nest along the shore on one of the lakes, with two greenish, oblong eggs. We quickly paddled away, fearing that we would keep the adult from returning.

A paddler squeezing through the culvert connecting Fourth and Fifth lakes.

Throughout the lakes, lots of freshwater mussels indicate pure water. In some shallow coves you'll find shell middens, left perhaps by raccoons or otters enjoying this important food source. A raccoon, probably in search of mussels, happened along the shoreline at our campsite and quickly climbed a tall hemlock when it saw us.

Among larger wildlife, we saw a few white-tailed deer along the shores, including two that were chest deep in the water, grazing on pond vegetation. This remote habitat should draw moose as they repopulate the state's northern reaches, and you could easily spot a black bear here.

You could spend a lot of time camping here and exploring these spectacular lakes, but you could also paddle most of the lakes in one long day.

57 | Forked Lake

Elongated Forked Lake offers miles of shoreline to explore; you could spend a full day here, especially if you paddled the connecting streams. Although you won't be alone, there's plenty of room to give a sense of seclusion. You will likely see osprey, loon, and deer; an otter sighting is possible.

Location: Arietta, Long Lake
Maps: *New York Atlas & Gazetteer*, Map 36: A4, A5, B4, B5; USGS Forked Lake
Area: 1,248 acres
Time: 6 hours; all day if paddling the connecting streams
Habitat Type: Long, large lake
Fish: Largemouth and smallmouth bass, landlocked salmon, brook and lake trout (see fish advisories, Appendix C; see specific advisory, health.ny.gov/environmental/outdoors/fish/health_advisories)
Camping: Appendix A (101) (on-site, including some island campsites accessible only by boat)
Take Note: Treacherous paddling under windy conditions

GETTING THERE

From the junction of Routes 28N and 30 in Long Lake, go 3.0 miles south on Routes 28N and 30, and turn right on North Point Road. Go 2.9 miles (5.9

TRIP 57: FORKED LAKE

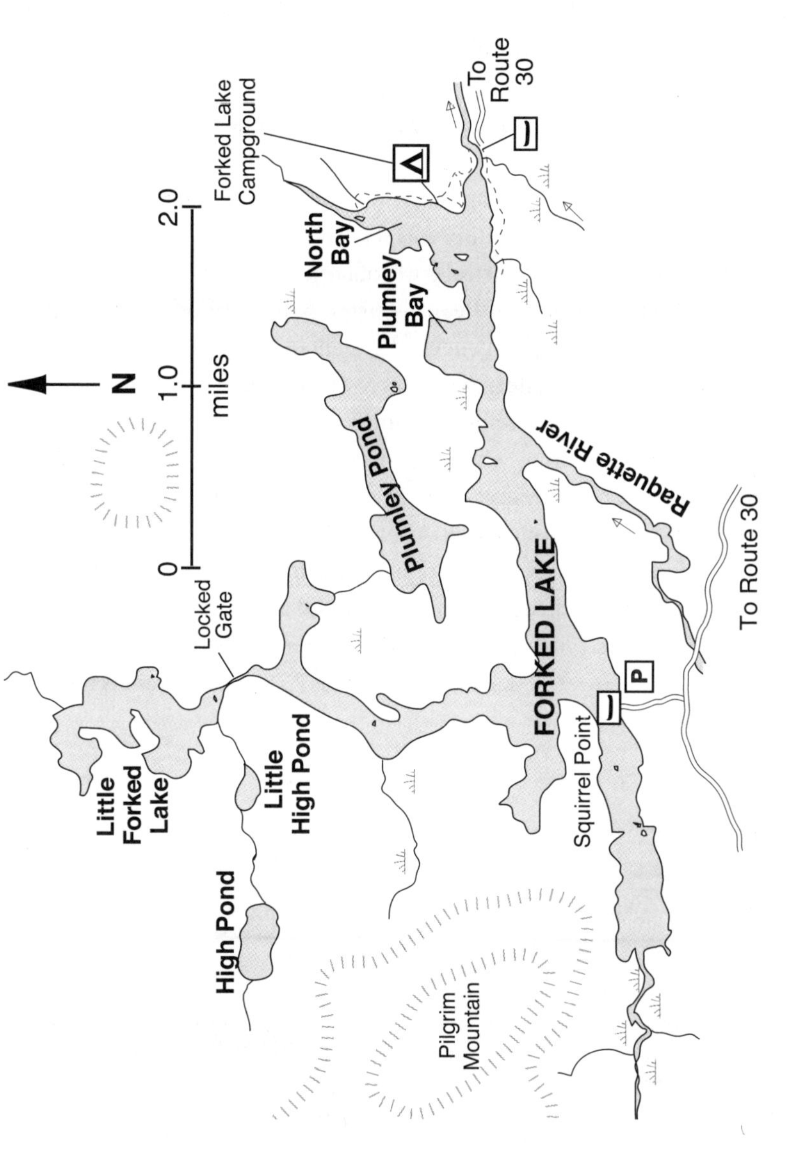

miles), and bear right on Forked Lake Road. Continue 1.8 miles (7.7 miles) to Forked Lake Campground access (fee). (43° 54.313′ N, 74° 31.545′ W) Alternatively, go 8.6 miles (11.6 miles) on North Point Road to Canoe Carry Road on the right (free). (43° 53.546′ N, 74° 35.577′ W)

WHAT YOU'LL SEE

On a calm day, Forked Lake (pronounced with two syllables: "fork-ed") offers miles of wonderful shoreline paddling and exploration. The lake stretches 5 miles east to west, with a 2-mile section extending to the north.

Northern white cedar occupies much of Forked Lake's shore. White-tailed deer love cedar twigs, resulting in a visible browse line marking the height deer can reach while standing on the ice in winter. White pine, red spruce, balsam fir, hemlock, red and sugar maples, yellow and paper birches, and beech round out the diverse hardwood-conifer forest surrounding the lake. Dense stands of hobblebush, with its symmetrical pairs of large, heart-shaped leaves, dominate the understory. A variety of heaths—principally leatherleaf, blueberry, and sheep laurel—create a thick, generally impenetrable shoreline.

Where the lake's western end narrows to a meandering inlet channel from Brandreth Lake, the shore becomes much boggier. Tamarack grows on sphagnum hillocks, along with bog rosemary, pitcher plant, leatherleaf, and broad expanses of marsh grass. Thick vegetation clogs the shallow inlet, but you can work west for quite a way. After a mile or so, the channel narrows, hills gradually close in, a sandy bottom replaces the muck, and the current increases. We carried above one beaver dam and stopped at quick water.

Towering white pines on the creek's northern hillsides—some growing to 150 feet—rise up toward Pilgrim Mountain (at 2,785 feet, the area's tallest peak).

Hobblebush (*Viburnum alnifolium*) flowers in late spring.

The bog and steep slopes probably protected this stand from logging in the 1800s, leaving an old-growth forest remnant for future generations to enjoy.

A fence and locked gate block access to Little Forked Lake, part of private Whitney Park. The state acquired other Whitney lands to the north that now comprise the William C. Whitney Wilderness Area, which contains Little Tupper Lake (see trip 53).

We saw quite a few loons on Forked Lake—including one pair with a chick—along with great blue herons, common mergansers, kingfishers, and a great horned owl. On the lake's southern side, you can paddle up the Raquette River toward Raquette Lake, but you will reach quick water and rapids in less than a mile.

58 | Blue Mountain, Eagle, and Utowana Lakes and Marion River

This 20-mile round-trip scenic paddle exudes wildness, except for possible boat traffic on Blue Mountain Lake. You will see lots of wildlife here, especially early and late in the day: loon, osprey, bald eagle, waterfowl, deer, and possibly otter.

Location: Indian Lake
Maps: *New York Atlas & Gazetteer*, Map 36: B4, B5, C4, C5 and Map 37: B6; USGS Blue Mountain Lake, Raquette Lake
Area and Length: Blue Mountain Lake, 1,220 acres; Blue Mountain Lake to Raquette Lake, 10 miles one way
Time: All day or multiday
Habitat Type: Large lake; long, narrow, connecting lakes; slow-flowing river
Fish: Largemouth and smallmouth bass, northern pike, landlocked salmon, lake trout (see fish advisories, Appendix C; see specific advisory, health.ny.gov/environmental/outdoors/fish/health_advisories)
Camping: Appendix A (101, 104); on-site wilderness camping
Take Note: Blue Mountain Lake can be treacherous under windy conditions

GETTING THERE

From the junction of Routes 28, 28N, and 30 in Blue Mountain Lake, go 0.3 mile west on Route 28 to the access on the right. Park along the fence. (43° 51.279′ N, 74° 26.062′ W)

TRIP 57: BLUE MOUNTAIN, EAGLE, AND UTOWANA LAKES AND MARION RIVER

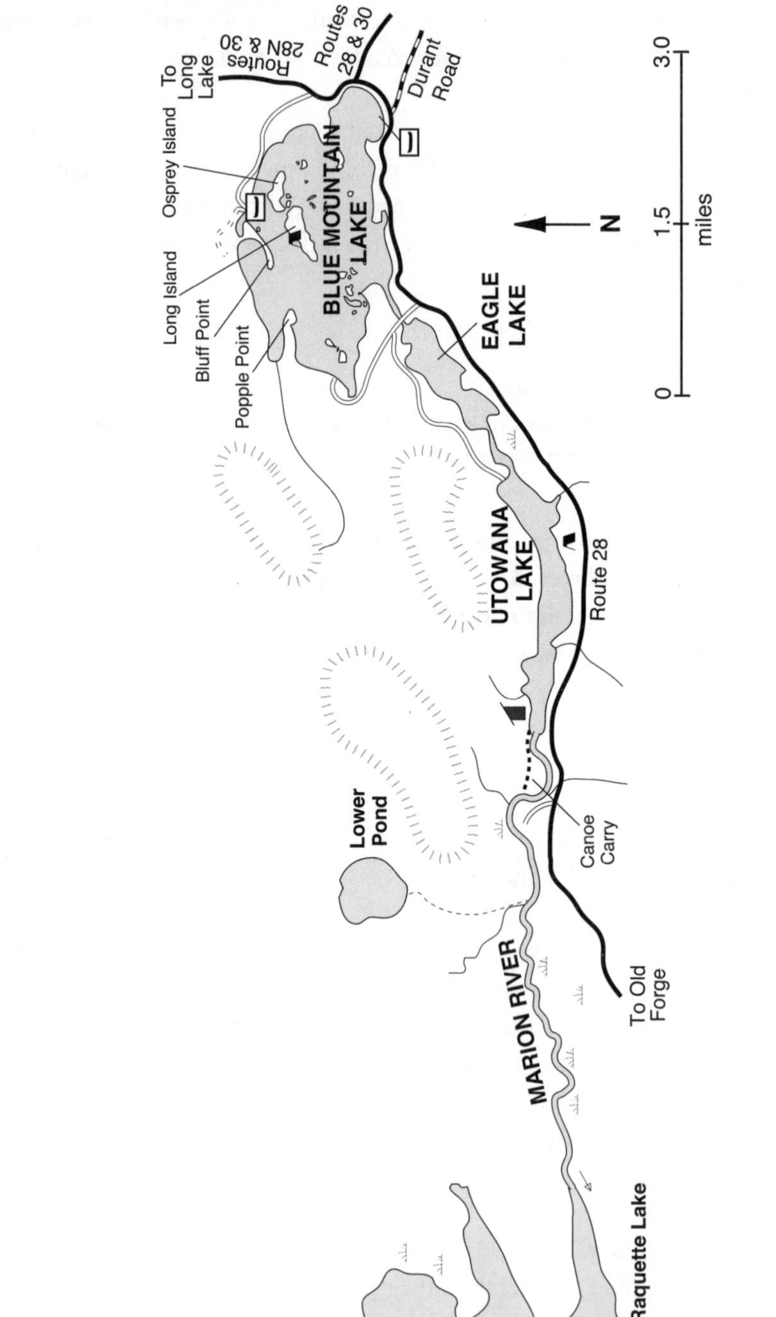

WHAT YOU'LL SEE

Blue Mountain Lake

A sign at the Blue Mountain Lake public access area says "Boat Speed Limit 45 MPH"... not very encouraging and probably a good reason to avoid this lake on busy summer weekends. When we visited in September, few high-speed boats plied these waters, and we enjoyed the beauty of one of the most scenic locations in the central Adirondacks.

Blue Mountain Lake, at an elevation of 1,790 feet, nestles among the Adirondack High Peaks, with Blue Mountain on the east rising to more than 3,600 feet. Looking back from the lake's western end, you can see how the mountain got its name: ringed with high-altitude conifers, the peak's upper reaches look dark blue.

Scenic granite boulders and islands dot the lake. One cannot help but notice, especially on the lake's western end, a browse line on the northern white cedars that hang out over the water. Deer often yard up in cedar stands; here, they nibble the shoreline cedars up to head height as they walk along the ice in winter.

Holding a special place in history, Blue Mountain Lake's environs served as the heart of the Adirondacks during its first wave of popularity. Luxury hotels and a full range of amenities greeted the rich and famous in the 1880s as they completed railroad and stagecoach excursions from cities east and south.

Prospect House here became the first hotel in the world to have electric lighting in every room! At this hotel in August 1883, Verplanck Colvin outlined his vision of protecting the Adirondacks as a state park. Beginning in 1872, Colvin, a lawyer by training, spent three decades mapping and describing the Adirondack region. Thanks largely to his efforts, the legislature created a state Forest Preserve in 1885. In 1892, Adirondack Park came into being. Then, in 1894, voters approved Article 14 of the state constitution, which mandated that the park would remain forever wild. (Sadly, however, all of the grand hotels burned to the ground over the years.)

Except near the village of Blue Mountain Lake and on the northeast side of the lake, little development intrudes on the shoreline. But despite the gorgeous setting and a huge expanse of boat-free water, we prefer to paddle on Eagle and Utowana lakes—the rest of what some refer to as the Eckford Chain—and the Marion River. These locations feature more habitat diversity, including a small waterfall on Utowana Lake, extensive marshes, more aquatic plants, and a lot more wildlife. And they do not suffer nearly as much from wind and summer boat traffic.

Eagle Lake

As you paddle into Eagle Lake, stay to the right, passing under the north bridge. The stone bulwarks date to 1891, when William West Durant built the Pioneer Bridge in memory of his father, Dr. Thomas Clark Durant, conceiver, builder, vice president, and general manager of the first transcontinental railroad, the Union Pacific. The elder Mr. Durant also served as president and builder of the Adirondack Railroad.

Little development mars Eagle Lake. Eagle Nest Park owns the surrounding lands and most of Utowana Lake, preserving them from development. The north shore houses a summer artist colony. On one morning excursion, we paddled along with someone heading from Blue Mountain Lake to the colony. A kingfisher accompanied us down the connecting waterway, as black ducks dabbled for aquatic plants and crows called in the distance. Common mergansers fled before us as we glided through a canopy of cedars, hemlocks, balsam firs, spruces, and very tall white pines, along with occasional sugar and red maples, and paper and yellow birches. As we neared the end of Eagle Lake, towering hemlocks appeared.

Utowana Lake

Resist the temptation to hurry to get into Utowana Lake. The long connector contains an extensive swamp with many side channels to explore. Along with bog rosemary, sweetgale, alder, and other typical bog vegetation, tall white pines and many large spruces cover the islands. Red and sugar maples and yellow birches grow here as well. Ferns line the banks, and pickerelweed, water celery—with its long, narrow leaves floating on the water's surface—and American white waterlilies grow in profusion in the shallows.

Once on Utowana Lake, stick to the southern shore. Watch for a small creek flowing into the lake, the entrance guarded by large patches of pickerelweed and a grove of tamarack that give way to balsam fir, yellow birch, striped and red maples, and alder. Paddle up this creek to a small waterfall that tumbles down over moss-covered granite boulders. Hemlocks drape out over the water to shade the falls, and ferns grow in clumps under the canopy. Look for pitcher plants in the marshy areas.

Eagle Nest Park maintains a campsite on Utowana's southern shore, just down from the creek. Mussel shells litter the area near the campsite, probably the work of foraging raccoons. Farther down the lake on the northern shore, near the outlet, the state maintains a lean-to shelter. The marshy area in front of the shelter provides habitat for an extensive patch of small pitcher plants.

The Thomas Clark Durant Bridge at the entrance to Eagle Lake.

Conifers dominate the shore and surrounding hills. Large, feathery tamaracks mix with red maples at the west end, along with tall hemlocks, a few white pines, spruces, yellow birches, and lots of balsam firs. A few mountain ashes—not technically an ash at all but actually a member of the rose family—drip with large clusters of bright red berries in fall. The marshes contain acres of American white waterlilies, along with cattails and some pickerelweed.

These lakes provide excellent views of ring-billed gull, loon, kingfisher, black duck, common merganser, and crow, and the marshes treat visitors to the sounds and sights of wood duck, common yellowthroat, white-throated sparrow, yellow-rumped warbler, and great blue heron.

Marion River

A carry around the first few hundred feet of the Marion River begins at the end of Utowana Lake, and it took us through a dense stand of balsam fir, interspersed with a few tall white pines and hemlocks. A group of flickers called raucously, contrasting with the white-breasted nuthatches that called softly, while we fought off the few remaining but determined mosquitoes.

At its beginnings at the small dam on Utowana, the clear, shallow Marion River carves out a narrow, meandering channel, lined with alders, ferns, cattails, and grasses, affording a relatively unobstructed view of surrounding hillsides.

Aquatic vegetation, including bur-reed, pickerelweed, water celery, yellow pondlily, and American white waterlily, chokes the marshy stream. Milkweed, sweetgale, swamp rose, and viburnum—with large clusters of dark purple berries—appear in bunches. We paddled over a couple of beaver dams, marked with fresh cuttings.

Extensive marshes keep the conifers at bay as they sink their roots into higher ground back from the water's edge. The pointed spires of tamarack and balsam fir, along with tall white pine and northern white cedar, mark the inexorable advance of higher ground as the marsh slowly fills in.

Many side channels lead off through the marsh, a wonderland filled with plants and wildlife, including many beautifully hued wood ducks, red-breasted mergansers, and several great blue herons. We watched a northern harrier as it hunted, tilting back and forth on motionless wings, ready to pounce on hapless rodents.

"Civilization" intruded on our wilderness experience as we passed out of the river's mouth into Raquette Lake, with its noisy personal watercraft and shoreline development. Disappointed by the proximity of such threats to the marsh, we immediately turned around to retrace our steps. The river's negligible current did not impede our progress, and the entire round trip of 20 miles took one day—but it was a very long day. You might want to arrange a pickup to make this a one-way trip or plan to camp en route.

The hardest part of the journey awaited us back at Blue Mountain Lake, where the late-afternoon wind had whipped the surface to a froth, providing a wet ride through ever-deepening troughs of whitecaps. With our cameras, binoculars, and field guides safely tucked away in watertight bags and with the knowledge that our life jackets would keep us afloat if we tipped, we plunged on beneath darkening skies that only enhanced the eerie beauty of the surrounding deep blue peaks. A long—but absolutely extraordinary—day, to be sure.

59 | Lake Durant and Rock Pond

These two bodies of water lie in a scenic valley just east of Blue Mountain Lake. Aquatic vegetation covers the abundant shallows, providing habitat for fish and other wildlife—wood, ring-necked, and black ducks, Canada geese, ospreys, deer, and lots more.

Location: Indian Lake
Maps: *New York Atlas & Gazetteer*, Map 37: B6, B7; USGS Blue Mountain Lake
Area: 330 acres
Time: 4 hours
Habitat Type: Long, shallow, marshy lake and pond
Fish: Largemouth bass, tiger muskellunge (see fish advisories, Appendix C; see specific advisory, health.ny.gov/environmental/outdoors/fish/health_advisories)
Camping: Appendix A (104) (on-site)
Take Note: East-west winds can cause treacherous conditions

GETTING THERE

Durant Road Access. From Blue Mountain Lake, go 0.8 mile east on Routes 28 and 30, and turn sharply right on Durant Road. Go 0.2 mile (1.0 mile), turn left at the Cascade Pond Trailhead sign, and continue 0.2 mile (1.2 miles) to the access. (43° 50.824′ N, 74° 25.343′ W)

Campground Access. From the Durant Road junction, go another 2.1 miles (2.9 miles) on Routes 28 and 30, and turn right to enter Lake Durant Campground. (43° 50.376′ N, 74° 22.829′ W)

WHAT YOU'LL SEE

Although the highway parallels the shore for about a mile, we include Lake Durant and connected Rock Pond because of their scenic beauty, productivity, and lowered susceptibility to windy conditions—at least compared with nearby Blue Mountain Lake. To get an appreciation of Durant's beauty, stop at the roadside rest area and gaze out over the water at the distant hills. Hemlock at the water's edge gives way to mixed hardwoods that cover the slopes, with patches of darker conifers adding to the multihued beauty. When we paddled

TRIP 59: LAKE DURANT AND ROCK POND

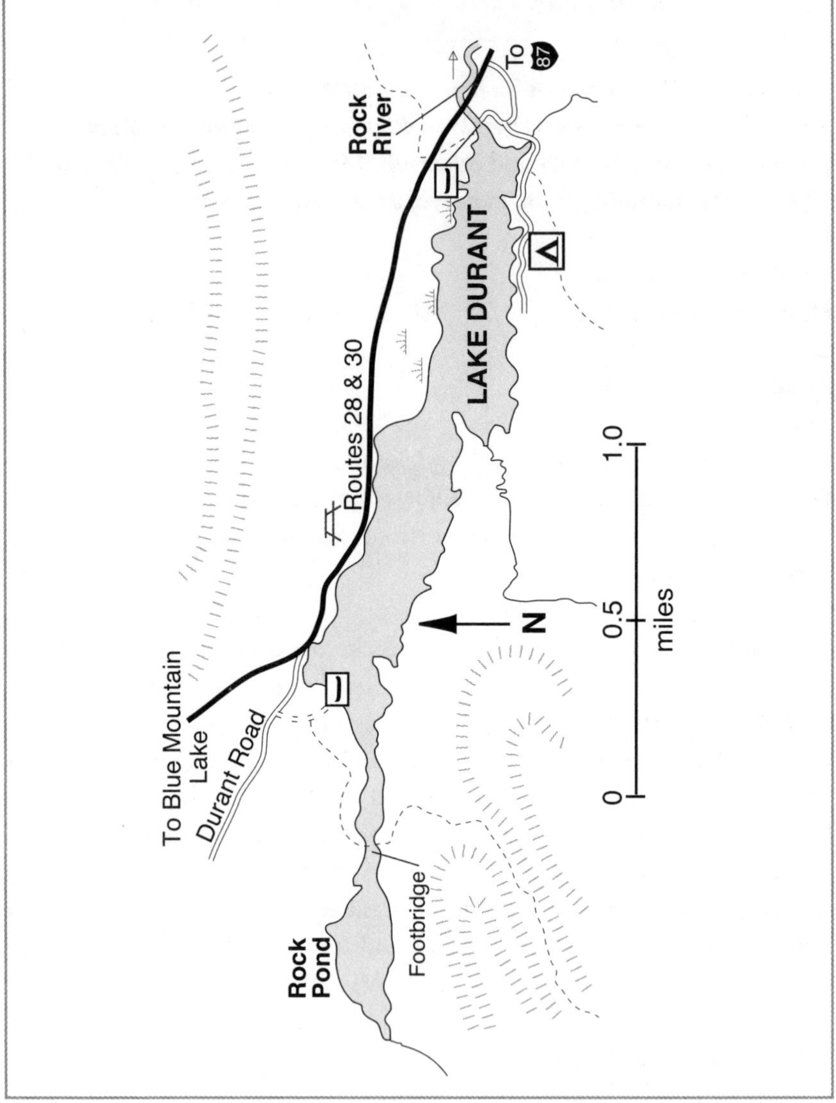

here in early fall, it looked like a deep-green canvas splashed with red, yellow, and orange.

The lake's productivity draws people to its waters. Anglers come to catch trophy tiger muskellunge (muskies) and smallmouth bass, their success attested to by the many photographs on the campground bulletin board. This stands in stark contrast to events that occur in many other area lakes. The airborne

Many types of aquatic vegetation crowd the surface of the shallows in Lake Durant. In fall, surrounding hillsides glow with red, yellow, and orange leaves

pollutants that cause acid rain spew from tall smokestacks in the Ohio River Valley and rain down on Adirondack lakes. Sulfuric and nitric acids acidify the water, lowering pH to the point where aquatic organisms no longer reproduce, resulting in barren, lifeless lakes. We should enjoy the primordial productivity of Lake Durant and do what we can to protect it from the continued airborne assault of midwestern pollution.

Carpets of aquatic vegetation cover the coves and shallows of Lake Durant and Rock Pond. American white waterlily, pickerelweed, floating heart, water celery, smartweed, water shield, cattails, and yellow pondlily seemingly compete for every inch of surface space in the shallows. In many areas around the lakes, hobblebush dominates the understory.

Paddling west by a stand of beautiful balsam fir—majestic spires and upright purple cones pointing skyward—into the connector between Lake Durant and Rock Pond, many flat-topped granite boulders greet you, clearly identifying how Rock Pond got its name. A low footbridge separates the two bodies of water. Part of the Blue Ridge Wilderness Area, Rock Pond enjoys a prohibition on motors. Two large islands add character and varied habitat to the pond, a superb place to view wildlife early or late in the day among the rafts of aquatic vegetation.

We listened to the whistling wings of wood ducks as they sprang into the air upon our approach. Black ducks bobbed for aquatic plants, and several great blue herons stalked fish and frogs in the shallows, while kingfishers dove for minnows. White-throated sparrows called from the underbrush as we paddled in solitude.

60 | Cedar River Flow

Cedar River Flow, one of the best places to paddle in New York, offers a wonderful wilderness experience. Enjoy the open water, surrounding marshes, and two inlet streams. You're guaranteed to see osprey, loon, ruffed grouse, deer, and beaver, and you may also see bald eagle, mink, and otter.

Location: Lake Pleasant
Maps: *New York Atlas & Gazetteer*, Map 37: D6; USGS Indian Lake
Area and Length: 710 acres; many miles of inlet streams
Time: 4 hours to multiday
Habitat Type: Shallow, weed-filled lake and slow-flowing river
Fish: Brook trout (see fish advisories, Appendix C)
Camping: On-site wilderness camping
Take Note: Lots of barely submerged boulders

GETTING THERE

From the junction of Routes 28 and 30 in the village of Indian Lake, head 2.1 miles north on Routes 28 and 30, and turn left on Cedar River Road. Go 12.0 miles (14.1 miles) to the access on the left. (43° 43.579′ N, 74° 28.397′ W)

WHAT YOU'LL SEE

Cedar River Flow remains one of the south-central Adirondacks' little-known treasures. Fed by cool, clear mountain water flowing out of Cedar Lakes in the West Canada Lake Wilderness Area, the flow provides wilderness camping, paddling, and hiking opportunities, all of them above 2,100 feet elevation. The flow will impress you with its wild, spectacular character. Although it extends only 3 miles south-southwest from Wakely Dam, many more miles of meandering streams and beaver meadows offer hours, or even days, of paddling pleasure.

TRIP 60: CEDAR RIVER FLOW

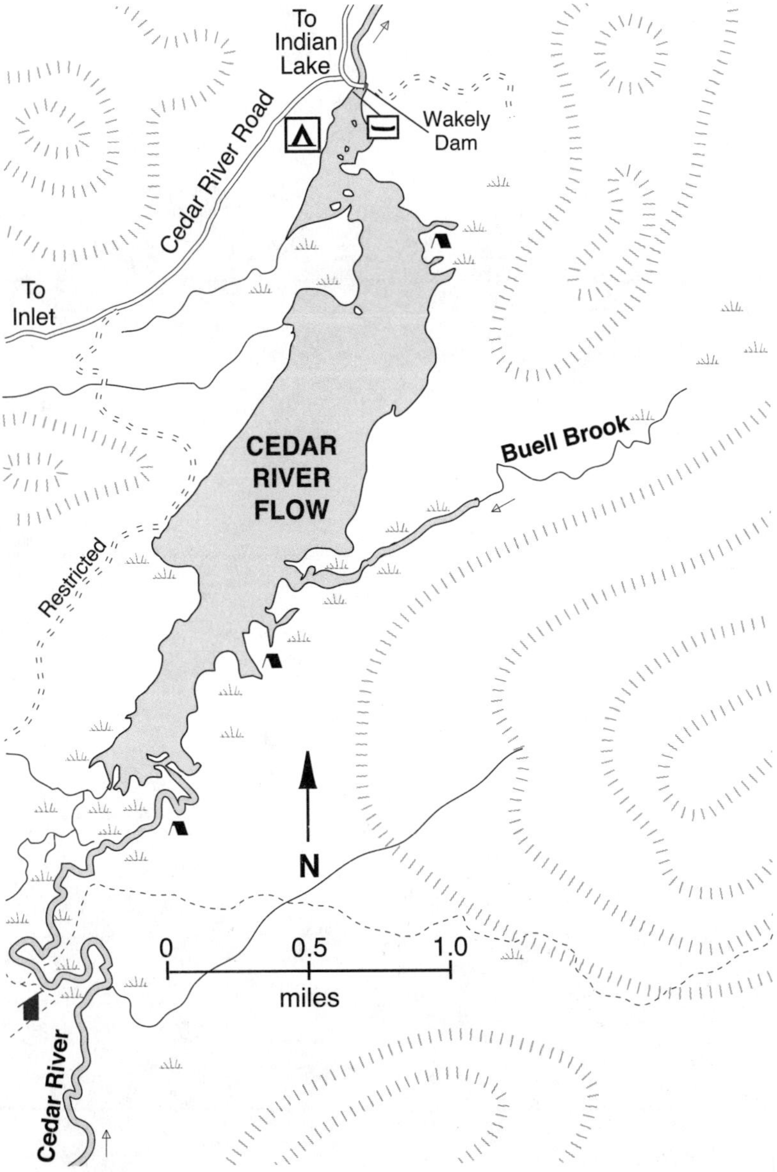

Dew covers a spiderweb.

An aspen grove guards the entrance to the first cove on the right; farther back, spire-like balsam fir rings the shore. The shallow water harbors, in addition to submerged rocks, tons of water shield and water celery, plus a beaver lodge with its stash of cuttings stored for the coming winter.

On the main lake, we encountered piles of mussel shells; lots of paper birch, balsam fir, and sugar maple; masses of water shield, pondweed, and bulrush; and submerged rocks. Difficult to see in the dark water, the rocks made frequent contact with our hulls—a small price to pay for the privilege of paddling such pristine waters.

Buell Brook enters from the opposite (eastern) shore, about two-thirds of the way up the flow, its mouth hidden amid a sea of bulrushes. We paddled up the shallow, sinewy, sandy-bottomed brook for about a mile, its depth varying from more than 8 feet to just a few inches where sand and gravel deposits collect. Initially, the brook passes through a grassy marsh with Christmas tree–perfect balsam fir spires here and there. We expected to see tamarack and black spruce, given the marshy conditions. Fallen red maple leaves swirled in the undulating, crystal-clear current during an early October visit. Huge mats collected in the eddies, reminding us, sadly, that we neared the end of paddling season.

Back out on the flow at the southern tip, we paddled up over several beaver dams to explore the marsh. Alders abound, along with other typical marsh shrubbery, including sweetgale, leatherleaf, bur-reed, and much more. Occasional stands of tamarack foreshadow the filling in of the marsh. This area does not connect with Cedar River, which enters the flow at the southeastern corner. Shortcuts will not get you to the river, as we found out after several attempts. Look for a thick line of alders and some trees, and head for where they end out in the lake. Follow the deep, broad channel, guarded by bulrushes, with downward-pointing underwater vegetation indicating the current's direction.

The meandering Cedar River flows clear, the sun illuminating its sandy bottom. But after we had gone a few hundred yards past a lean-to on the right shore, the formerly barely noticeable current started to pick up. We turned around reluctantly, and as we paddled back under darkening skies, a beaver swam before us. When it finally realized that we had paddled mere feet from its tail, it got even for the intrusion by splashing us with that flat, broad appendage as it dove for cover.

We recommend visiting in early spring or in late summer or fall because of mosquito hatches from the swamps and blackflies from the river.

61 | Indian Lake

People visit here mostly for secluded island camping. Scenic forests cover the hillsides, but those same hillsides also funnel wind; paddling here is treacherous when windy. Expect to see osprey, loon, barred owl, waterfowl, and deer. Look for peregrine falcons that may nest on exposed cliffs.

Location: Indian Lake, Lake Pleasant
Maps: *New York Atlas & Gazetteer*, Map 37: D7, D8, E7; USGS Indian Lake, Page Mountain
Area: 4,255 acres
Time: All day to multiday
Habitat Type: Huge, deep lake
Fish: Smallmouth bass, northern pike, landlocked salmon, brown and lake trout (see fish advisories, Appendix C; see specific advisory, health.ny.gov/environmental/outdoors/fish/health_advisories)
Camping: On-site, wilderness camping; dec.ny.gov/outdoor/24471.html
Take Note: Strong winds, funneled by nearby mountains, can cause treacherous conditions; novice paddlers should avoid this lake

GETTING THERE

From the junction of Routes 28 and 30 in the village of Indian Lake, go 11.7 miles south on Route 30, and turn left into Indian Lake Islands Campground and access. (43° 39.118′ N, 74° 23.270′ W)

WHAT YOU'LL SEE

Tired of camping cheek-to-jowl in noisy, crowded campgrounds? Indian Lake offers a peaceful alternative with 55 widely separated campsites where you can listen to loons, barred owls, and whip-poor-wills calling at night, instead of noisy neighbors.

At 14 miles long, narrow and scenic Indian Lake nestles among the sculpted cliffs and forested hillsides of the Adirondack peaks. Many people come here for weeklong camping. Consequently, we avoid the lake on the busiest holiday weekends, even though it can accommodate a lot of boat traffic. Under calm or modest wind conditions, Indian Lake offers wonderful paddling opportunities, with many bays, inlets, protected coves, and islands

TRIP 61: INDIAN LAKE

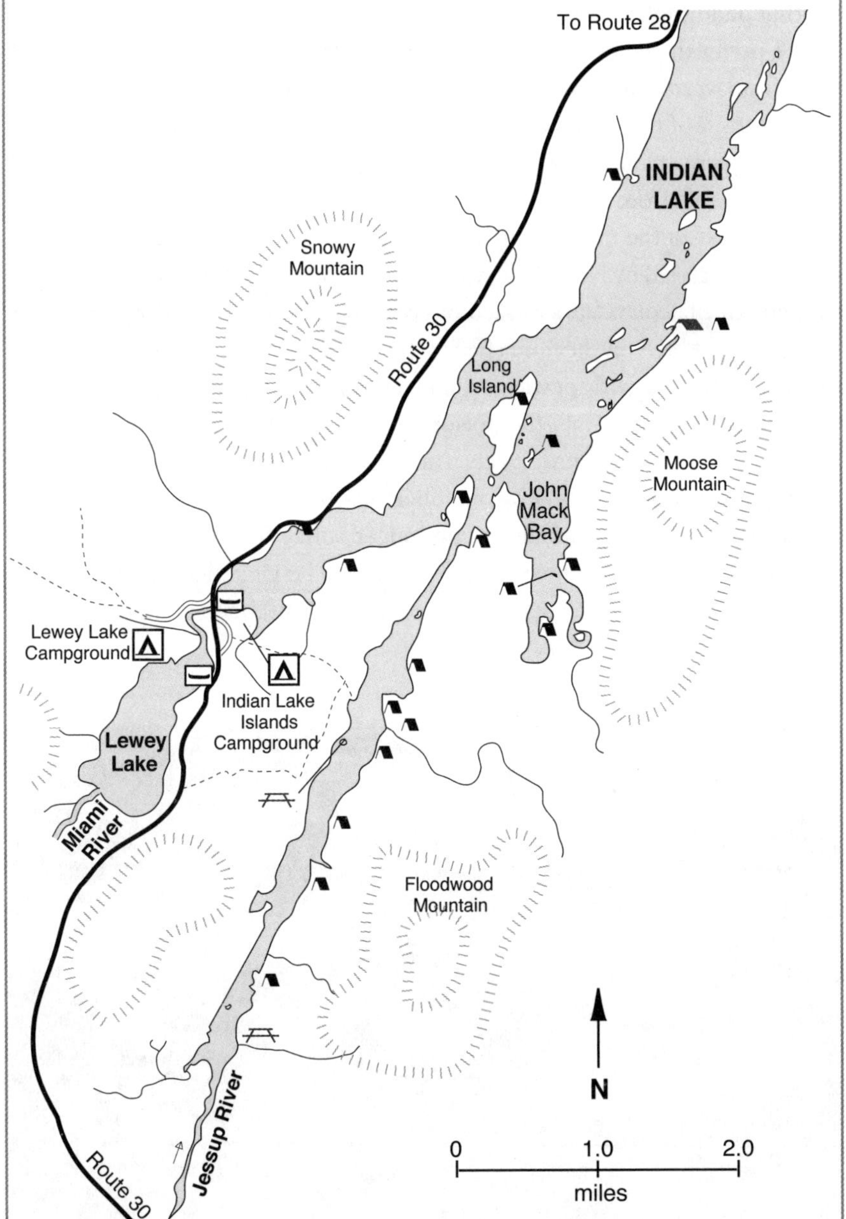

to explore. However, when the wind blows strongly from any direction, the surrounding hillsides funnel it, raising whitecaps and 2- to 4-foot swells, making paddling extremely hazardous.

We prefer the lake's southern half because the northern half suffers much more from weather, development, and motorboat traffic. The southern half also harbors most of the area's campsites, almost all accessible only by water. Each site has a picnic table and a fire grate.

Paddling out from the access on the western arm, note the bare cliffs of Snowy Mountain off to the north, which provides a good spot for nesting peregrine falcons. Efforts led by New York's Cornell Ornithology Laboratory have helped the peregrine falcon make a miraculous comeback from the brink of extinction. Peregrines eat high on the food chain, where biocides get concentrated. Insects eat leaves sprayed with pesticides, concentrating the poisons. Insectivorous birds, in turn, concentrate the poisons even more. When the peregrine eats bird after poison-laden bird, it gets a much higher dose than that intended for the original insects. Now that we no longer use the most deleterious pesticides in this country, peregrine falcons no longer suffer from disastrous eggshell thinning, which nearly wiped them out. (*Note*: The United States still exports these lethal poisons to the rest of the world to poison their avifauna.)

A northern water snake suns on a dense patch of aquatic vegetation. It swims underwater to catch small fish.

We saw one of these incredible birds over the entrance to the lake's southwestern arm. The peregrine soars high in the sky, swooping down on ducks and other birds at speeds as great as an incredible 180 miles per hour. As it careens by its target, its talons rip open the bird, leaving a puff of feathers to drift slowly to the ground. We have seen this bird take waterfowl on the wing (its name in the time of Audubon was "duck hawk"), but its preferred prey in cities is the ubiquitous pigeon.

Peregrines now nest on all large bridges leading to Manhattan and the other islands, on all Hudson River bridges north to Albany, and on skyscrapers; at least 20 pairs nest on cliffs in upstate New York. In 1994, 22 pairs fledged 35 young, and in 1998, 36 pairs fledged 69 young. By 2003, there were nearly 50 mated pairs, showing that the peregrine in New York continues on its recovery path.

As you paddle up the western arm, note the size of the deciduous trees along the way. Mature yellow and paper birches, sugar and red maples, beeches, and aspens, along with hemlocks, balsam firs (particularly in wetter areas), spruces, and white and red pines cover the shoreline. Look for tall, conical balsam firs and hefty hemlocks lining the narrow channel at the southern arm entrance. The usually quite-clear water in this lake (maximum depth 85 feet) indicates low biological productivity.

In selecting a campsite, particularly in the early season, choose an exposed one, trading some tent flapping at night for an insect-reducing breeze during the day. The following campsites fill this need: 39, at the point separating the western and southwestern arms; 32, on the northern point of the small island on the eastern side of Long Island (lots of large boulders sloping to the water for lounging around; nice view up the lake, as well); 34, on the northern tip of Long Island; 28, on an island in John Mack Bay; and 45, on a peninsula jutting out from the eastern shore about 1.5 miles down the southern arm.

A nice picnic site perches on an island along the southern arm's western shore, about 2 miles down. A larger one at the very end of the arm has three picnic tables, a grate, and an outhouse. Although it nestles back into a protected area that can suffer from mosquitoes, it boasts a beautiful series of cascading waterfalls flowing down a brook into a pleasant pool for swimming. This picturesque spot makes traveling all the way down the arm well worthwhile.

At the end of the long southern arm, Jessup River flows into the lake. In spring, if you are willing to get out of your boat occasionally in shallow riffles and at beaver dams, you can paddle upstream all the way to the Route 30 bridge. This great wildlife-viewing area remains totally free of motorboat traffic.

62 | Eighth Lake (Fulton Chain)

We include Eighth Lake because of its significance in guide boat lore and for its access to Raquette Lake. Expect to see loon, black duck, merganser, kingfisher, and deer in this scenic valley. We saw a black bear here, and you might see bald eagles.

Location: Inlet
Maps: *New York Atlas & Gazetteer*, Map 36: C3; USGS Raquette Lake
Area: 320 acres
Time: 2 hours; all day with portage and paddle to Raquette Lake
Habitat Type: Small lake in a valley
Fish: Smallmouth bass, lake and rainbow trout (see fish advisories, Appendix C)
Camping: On-site camping; dec.ny.gov/outdoor/24465.html
Take Note: Part of a historic guide-boat water trail

GETTING THERE

From the junction of Routes 28 and 30 in Blue Mountain Lake, go 17.8 miles west on Route 28 to Eighth Lake Campground on the right. (43° 45.971′ N, 74° 42.272′ W)

From the junction of Route 28 and South Shore Road in Inlet, go 5.9 miles east on Route 28 to the campground on the left.

WHAT YOU'LL SEE

The Fulton Chain of eight lakes (named First Lake, Second Lake, and so on) figures prominently in early Adirondack guide lore and, indeed, in American Indian lore before that. Early Indians hunted in the heart of the Adirondacks but did not live there. They originally settled in the Champlain and Hudson River valleys, the Lake George region, and around Oneida Lake. Some bands retreated to the rugged Adirondacks in the late 1700s after major conflicts with European immigrants.

One hundred years later, intrepid mid-nineteenth-century explorers plied these waters in elegant, lightweight wooden guide boats, taking visitors from downstate out into the wilds to fish and hunt. Guiding became a major North Country industry that offered transportation, shelter, and food along with access to game and fish for the well-to-do. Clients expected guides to provide everything needed for a relatively comfortable wilderness foray that sometimes lasted a few weeks. The builders of the best 60-pound boats, which could carry

TRIP 62: EIGHTH LAKE (FULTON CHAIN)

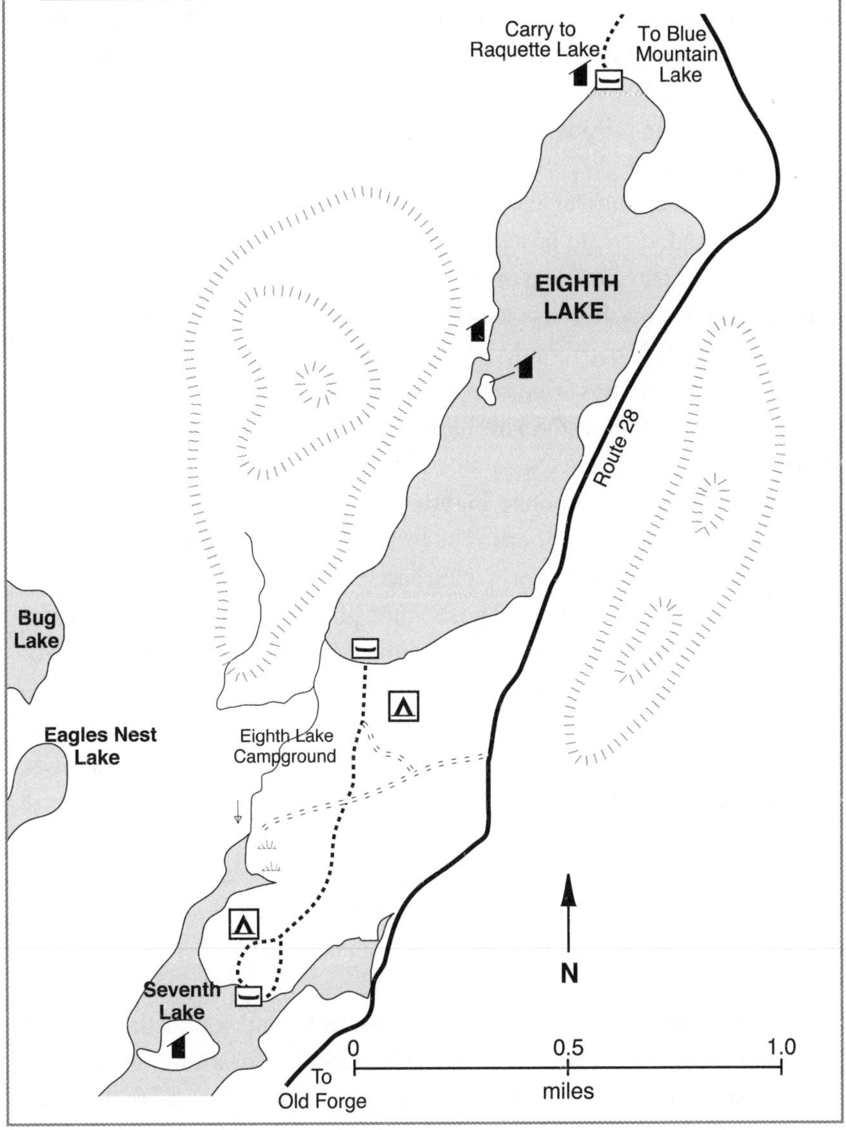

an astounding amount—three clients, all their gear and food, and any game they shot—charged $50 to $70 for a new boat. Those boats, now more than 100 years old, often sell for $20,000.

Today, the 90-mile guide-boat race from Old Forge to Saranac Lake draws overflow crowds as paddlers and rowers work their way up Fulton Chain into Browns Tract Inlet, which joins the Raquette River drainage.

Some modern explorers prefer floatplanes, high-speed boats, and personal watercraft (PWC), all of which dominate the chain's first seven lakes. Only on Eighth Lake, with its state-owned shoreline, can paddlers escape the development and powerboating that characterize the rest of the chain. The invasion of PWC is more insidious than the invasion of Eurasian watermilfoil. PWC exist for one purpose: thrill seeking. Many operators jump wakes, drive 45 MPH or faster, tow children on tubes at high speed, run over swimmers, crash into each other and into boats, intrude on the peace and calm, and pollute the atmosphere and water. In proportion to their numbers, PWC cause accidents and complaints far more than other watercraft. When will people wake up and ban these cursed machines, at least from small lakes, ponds, and rivers?

Nestled in a valley surrounded by hills and lying in a north-south orientation, Eighth Lake suffers less from prevailing westerly winds than the rest of the chain. The relative calm stood in sharp contrast to the wind-driven swells and whitecaps that dominated the surface of Seventh Lake when we paddled here.

Tame black ducks populate Eighth Lake, along with belted kingfishers, common mergansers, and loons. The forested shores include northern white cedar, hemlock, red and striped maples, beech, and yellow birch, with white pine towering over all. The sole island hosts white pine, paper birch, northern white cedar, and nice rock outcroppings for swimming and sunning. Hobblebush fills much of the understory. Three shelters, independent of the campground, are available on a first-come, first-served basis: one on the island, one on the nearby shore, and one on the northwestern corner of the lake next to the canoe carry.

The clear water indicates low biological productivity, and without marshy areas, you may run out of places to explore and vistas to enjoy. Because you cannot paddle the outlet of Eighth Lake, you have to carry about 0.8 mile through the campground to Seventh Lake if you're on a long-distance paddle or wish to observe PWC action and seaplane takeoffs.

But if you crave wilderness adventure, paddle up Eighth Lake to the northwestern corner and carry from there the 1.3 miles into Browns Tract Inlet, a beautiful marshy stream that meanders east for a little more than 2 miles, making its way to South Bay on Raquette Lake. From there, we would suggest that you paddle northeast, skirting the left side of Big Island, and head up the Marion River toward Utowana, Eagle, and Blue Mountain lakes (see trip 58). Alternatively, you could paddle around to the right upon entering South Bay and on the east end paddle under Route 28 into the 2-mile-long South Inlet. This is another marshy stream, reputedly one of the most gorgeous in the Adirondacks. We assure you that you will see a lot more than tame black ducks while paddling through this marshland.

A black bear peers at us from its resting place in the woods near Eighth Lake.

When we paddled Eighth Lake in the drought summer of 1995, low water conditions and lack of rain reduced food availability somewhat, causing wildlife to move about more than usual. While here, we saw a fairly large black bear whiling away the afternoon, back to a large tree, pretty much unconcerned by the presence of our cameras about 50 feet away.

Although we did not see the abundant wildlife that we would likely see on the Marion River or the North Branch of the Moose River, for example, we did enjoy our only paddle in the Fulton Chain valley along the historic Old Forge to Saranac Lake guide route. We felt part of history as we hiked the extremely well-worn path to Browns Tract Inlet.

LOON: VOICE OF THE NORTHERN WILDERNESS

Perhaps no animal better symbolizes wilderness than the loon, whose haunting cry resonates through the night air on many northern New York ponds. The bird seems almost mystical, with its distinctive black-and-white plumage, daggerlike bill, and piercing red eyes. But like the remaining wilderness itself, the loon is threatened over much of its range. As recreational pressures increase, the loon gets pushed farther away. We who share its waters bear responsibility for protecting this wonderful bird.

The common loon (*Gavia immer*), a large diving bird, lives almost its entire life in water, visiting land only to mate and to incubate eggs. Although adapted remarkably well to water, the loon has difficulty on land because its rearward leg position—a swimming aid—prevents it from walking easily. Unlike most birds, the loon has solid bones, allowing it to dive to great depths. An internal air sac controls how high it floats; by compressing this sac, it can submerge gradually, with barely a ripple, or swim with just its head above water.

The loon's heavy body and rearward legs make takeoff difficult, however. For example, a loon may require a quarter-mile to build up enough speed to lift off, and it may need to circle a small lake several times to gain enough altitude to clear nearby hills. When migrating, a loon flies rapidly—up to 90 MPH—but cannot soar.

Loons generally mate for life and can live for 30 years. The female lays two moss-green eggs in early May, and both male and female incubate them. Loons most often nest on islands to hide the eggs from predators. They build nests close to shore, however, where a passing paddler can inadvertently scare birds away or a motorboat wake can flood a nest with cold water.

Loon chicks hatch covered in black down and usually enter the water a day after hatching. Young chicks often ride on a parent's back, which allows them to conserve heat and to avoid predators. Chicks grow quickly on a diet of small fish and crustaceans; within two weeks of birth, they reach half the adult size and can dive to relatively deep lake bottoms. Loon chicks remain dependent on their parents for about eight weeks. At ten to twelve weeks, they can fly. After leaving the nest, loons return to land in three or four years, when they reach breeding age. Juveniles mature at sea, having followed adult loons to saltwater wintering areas.

Although New York lists the species as one of "special concern," the loon remains fairly plentiful in parts of the Adirondacks. A statewide survey in 1984–1985 found more than 700 loons on 518 surveyed lakes, including 157 breeding pairs with 197 chicks. Of those lakes with breeding loons, 95 percent had only one pair, although a few lakes had more—notably Stillwater Reservoir with 15 pairs and Lows Lake with six. By extrapolating the results to unsurveyed lakes, the state estimated a total population of as many as 1,000 adults and 270 breeding pairs. Since then, the loon population has slowly increased. Indeed, many biologists believe that the Adirondack lakes are nearing their loon carrying capacity.

Breeding pairs are territorial, which limits the ultimate population size within the state. It remains unclear whether populations are also dampened by lead shot and fishing weights remaining on lake bottoms, along with continued mercury emanations from coal-fired power plants. According to Tufts University Wildlife Veterinary Clinic, chicks die primarily from collisions with personal watercraft and motorboats, and adults die primarily from ingestion of lead sinkers and jigs. As is the case with other diving waterfowl, ingestion of lead sinkers and shotgun pellets causes loon mortality. Although anglers no longer use small lead fishing weights, and hunters no longer use lead shot for waterfowl, the large amounts of lead deposited on lake bottoms over the last 100 years still linger throughout New York's loon habitat.

Besides lead poisoning, encroachment by humans, and nest predation by raccoons and skunks, loons suffer mortality in many other ways. Anglers must avoid leaving spent monofilament line behind, as it causes deaths via entanglement. Because paddlers can easily disturb loons, watch for warning displays during nesting season, early May through mid-July. If a nest fails, loons may try up to two more times, although the later a chick hatches, the lower its chance of survival.

The loon has lived in the Northeast longer than any other bird—an estimated 60 million years. Let's make sure this wonderful species remains protected so future generations may listen to its enchanting music on a still, moonlit night. For more information, visit the website of the Adirondack Center for Loon Conservation, http://adkloon.org.

63 | Limekiln Lake

Scenic Limekiln Lake sees a little less traffic than nearby lakes. Make sure you paddle the marshy inlet stream on the southeast corner. You should see yellow warbler, loon, merganser, and black duck.

Location: Inlet, Ohio
Maps: *New York Atlas & Gazetteer*, Map 36: D2; USGS Old Forge
Area: 457 acres
Time: 4 hours
Habitat Type: Oligotrophic lake with marshy inlet stream
Fish: Splake (state-record 13 pounds, 8 ounces caught here in 2004) (see fish advisories, Appendix C; see specific advisory, health.ny.gov/environmental/outdoors/fish/health_advisories)
Camping: On-site camping; dec.ny.gov/outdoor/24476.html
Take Note: Surrounded by scenic hillsides

GETTING THERE

From the village of Inlet, go 1.8 miles south on Limekiln Road, and turn right to enter the campground. Continue 0.6 mile (2.4 miles) to the access. (43° 43.029′ N, 74° 48.047′ W)

WHAT YOU'LL SEE

Our first exploration began more than 50 years ago, when one of us paddled here as a boy. The lakeshore has changed some, but we were happy to see upon our return that state-owned lands surround most of Limekiln Lake, making it a rare jewel in the western Adirondack high country. Limited private lands on the northeastern corner suffer from a fair amount of development, so you will see a number of motorboats during summer—far more than we recall from the 1960s. Even so, Limekiln Lake has much less traffic than most of the Fulton Chain vacation region. Nick's Lake Campground just outside of Old Forge fills up each night of summer, whereas Limekiln Lake Campground often does not.

Despite the motorboats, Limekiln Lake provides a quality quietwater experience. Its high elevation (1,885 feet) and considerable depth make the lake oligotrophic, meaning it has very low biological productivity. The crystal-clear water allows you to peer into its depths and shows almost no evidence of tannic acid, which results from plant decay and turns water yellowish brown.

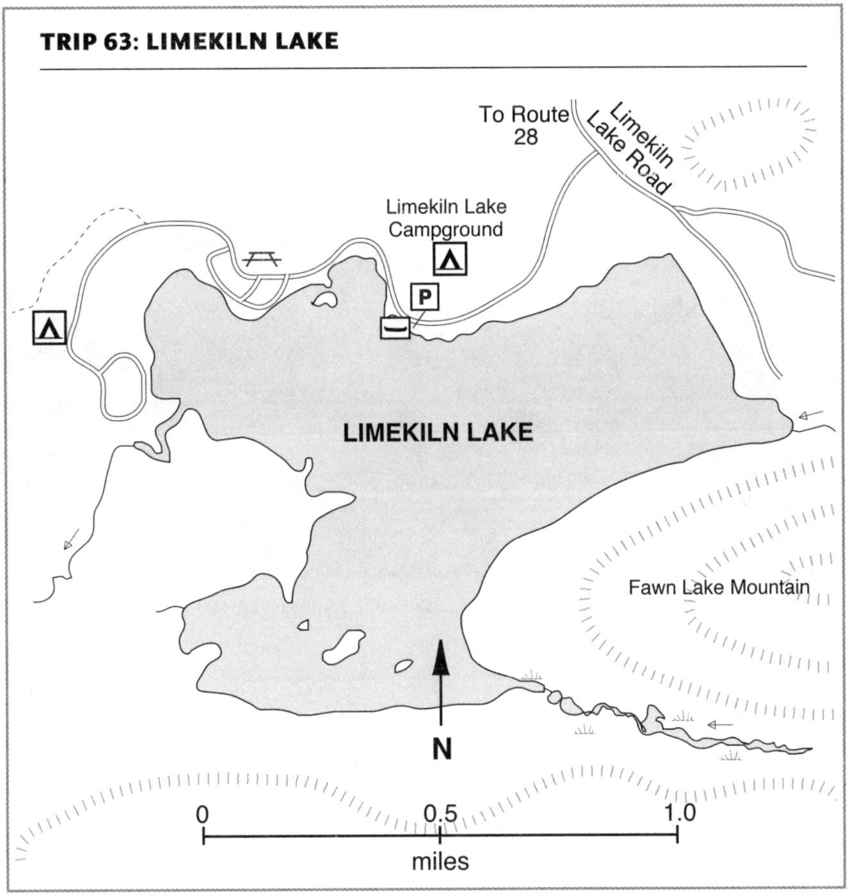

Coves, inlets, islands, and bays characterize this small lake, and we enjoyed exploring each of them, studying the fauna and flora. Forested hillsides surround Limekiln with some modest vertical relief. Studying the high diversity of tree species around the shore provides a diversion from wildlife-watching; red and sugar maples, tamarack, balsam fir, black and red spruces, hemlock, and white pine grow in profusion. Thick shrubbery dominates the understory.

In shallower sections of the lake, we found water shield, yellow pondlily, and other aquatic vegetation, but the dwarf American white waterlilies provided a real surprise. Distinguishing characteristics of the two dominant subspecies of this waterlily include the following: *tuberosa* has green leaf undersides, green sepals, and leaves that can grow to a foot across, while *odorata* has purple leaf undersides, purple sepals, and smaller leaves. The diminutive deep purple leaves—measuring no more than 2 or so inches long—of the waterlilies in Limekiln Lake matched the minuscule flowers in size. We wondered whether

A marshy stream flows through beaver meadows into the southeastern corner of Limekiln Lake.

the cold water of this high-altitude lake kept them from growing larger or whether this population of *odorata* has a genetic disposition to dwarfism.

Out on the main lake, loons dove for fish, and a common merganser family rested on a log, casting wary eyes at us as we paddled by. We suspect that the numerous black ducks hanging around the campground were looking for illegal handouts.

The small creek that flows into the southeastern corner remains our favorite spot on the lake. As you paddle through the sinuous channel, note the large tamaracks starting to fill in the marsh. We paddled by sphagnum islands loaded with carnivorous pitcher plants and sundews, trying to eke out a little extra nitrogen from passing insects. You would have to travel widely to find a higher density of pitcher plants.

Balsam fir, black spruce, and yellow birch grow here, along with sheep laurel and other shrubs. Crush a leaf of one of the sweetgale plants that grow in profusion, and note its sweet aroma. We lingered here for a long while, observing the bright colors of a male yellow warbler with red streaking on its breast. We listened to hoarse *chick-a-dee-dee* calls of foraging boreal chickadees. We studied bankside flowers and watched the sun dip behind the western hills. Mesmerized by the reflected glow from still waters, we hated to leave this tranquil spot.

64 | Moss Lake

Ospreys nest on an island in Moss Lake, and loons also nest on this small, marshy body of water. A flat hiking trail circles the lake, which has nine primitive campsites. For more seclusion and a chance to see additional wildlife, paddle the marshy outlet stream; you will have to portage over beaver dams.

Location: Webb
Maps: *New York Atlas & Gazetteer*, Map 36: C1; USGS Eagle Bay
Area: 115 acres
Time: 2 hours; more if paddling down the outlet stream
Habitat Type: Small, shallow, marshy lake and outlet stream
Fish: Brook trout (see fish advisories, Appendix C)
Camping: On-site wilderness camping
Take Note: Hiking trail around lake

GETTING THERE

From the junction of Routes 1 and 28 at Eagle Bay on Fourth Lake, go 2.1 miles north on Big Moose Road/Route 1 to the access on the left. Carry down to the water. (43° 47.327′ N, 74° 50.671′ W)

WHAT YOU'LL SEE

Simply gorgeous Moss Lake nestles beneath the rolling, forested peaks that typify this part of the Adirondacks. Its lack of development stands in stark contrast with the heavily developed and overused Fulton Chain just to the south. Although very small, Moss Lake can provide an exceptionally pleasant few hours of paddling, hiking, and enjoying fauna and flora.

Surprisingly for the time of year, we saw a loon pair with chick during an early October visit. Although nearly grown, the chick must have hatched from a second nesting, after the first failed. Otherwise, the adults would have already migrated to the coast. The loon nests very early, giving it an opportunity to lay a second pair of eggs if the first clutch fails. The loons we saw probably nest on the lake's sole island, where osprey also have nested in recent years on a dead pine tree.

The Moss Lake Camp for Girls occupied the lake and 600 surrounding acres from 1923 until 1972, spreading along the northern and eastern

TRIP 64: MOSS LAKE

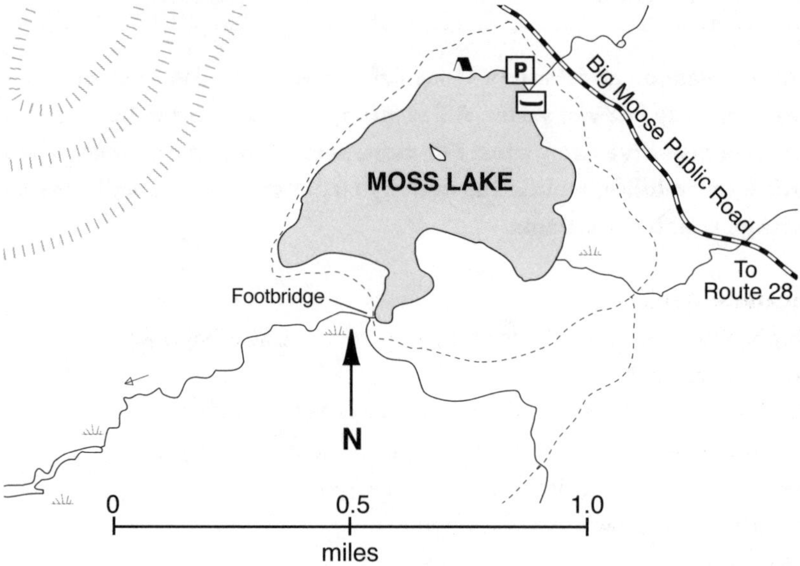

shores and providing horseback riding, hiking, and canoeing. In 1973, Dr. George Longstaff, who developed the camp, sold the property to The Nature Conservancy, which subsequently deeded the land to the state to become part of the Adirondack Forest Preserve. From 1974 to 1978, a group of Ganienkeh Mohawks claimed title to and occupied the land but eventually moved their settlement north to the Canadian border. In 1979, the Department of Environmental Conservation razed the remaining buildings in an attempt to return the lake to its primeval condition.

A 3-mile trail—formerly the camp's bridle path, built in 1924—extends around the lake. Cross-country skiers use the trail in winter, and hikers enjoy it in summer. The trail wanders through mostly deciduous forest, dominated by sugar maple. We saw massive yellow birches and one enormous cherry tree, its roots folding over a large rock. A few large hemlock, spruce, and white pine added variety to the tree canopy. The understory was thick with hobblebush (*Viburnum alnifolium*), ferns, and club mosses.

Alex paddles back up the brushy outlet of Moss Lake.

The trees form a backdrop to the water-loving shrubs at the lake's edge: leatherleaf, sweetgale, alder, and winterberry (a member of the holly family with bright red-orange fall-ripening berries attached directly to the branches without stalks). During our fall visit, a few scattered mountain ashes added an extra spot of brilliance to the foliage.

At the south end, a footbridge crosses the outlet stream. To explore below the bridge, you have to lift your boat over. The sandy-bottomed channel flows gently to the southwest through marshy vegetation, but beaver dams block progress fairly quickly. We carried across a couple of small dams but did not explore far. With a little effort, one might be able to go as much as a mile down this creek before running into quick water.

65 | Stillwater Reservoir

Enormous Stillwater Reservoir on Beaver River abounds in wildlife. In summer, there may be as many as 40 loons here. Expect to see waterfowl, great blue heron, deer, shore birds, and osprey; you may also see wild turkey, bald eagle, otter, mink, beaver, and muskrat. Stillwater's great length allows wind to build up over miles of water, making it unsafe for novice paddlers.

Location: Webb
Maps: *New York Atlas & Gazetteer*, Map 35: A10, B9, B10 and Map 36: A1, B1; USGS Beaver River, Eagle Bay, Number Four, Stillwater
Area: 6,195 acres
Time: All day or multiday
Habitat Type: Very large, shallow reservoir
Fish: Smallmouth bass, splake (see fish advisories, Appendix C; see specific advisory, health.ny.gov/environmental/outdoors/fish/health_advisories)
Camping: On-site wilderness camping; dec.ny.gov/outdoor/34382.html
Take Note: Unsafe for novice paddlers

GETTING THERE

From the junction of River and State streets in Lowville, go 4.3 miles east on River Street/Number 4 Road, and turn left on Number 4 Road. Go 13.5 miles (17.8 miles), and turn right on Stillwater Road. Continue 8.2 miles (26.0 miles) to the access. (43° 53.419′ N, 75° 2.149′ W)

From Eagle Bay on Fourth Lake at the junction of Routes 1 and 28, go 17.6 miles north on Big Moose Road/Route 1, turn right on Stillwater Road, and go 0.4 mile (18.0 miles) to the access.

WHAT YOU'LL SEE

Beaver River flows west out of Lake Lila (see trip 52) into privately owned Nehasane Lake, down to Stillwater Reservoir, out into Moshier Lake, and into the lakes that compose the Beaver River Canoe Route (Beaver Lake, Soft Maple Reservoir, Effley Falls Pond, Elmer Falls Pond, and Taylorville Pond; see trip 66). From there, Beaver River courses another dozen miles to its confluence with Black River, which eventually flows into Lake Ontario at Black River Bay.

TRIP 65: STILLWATER RESERVOIR

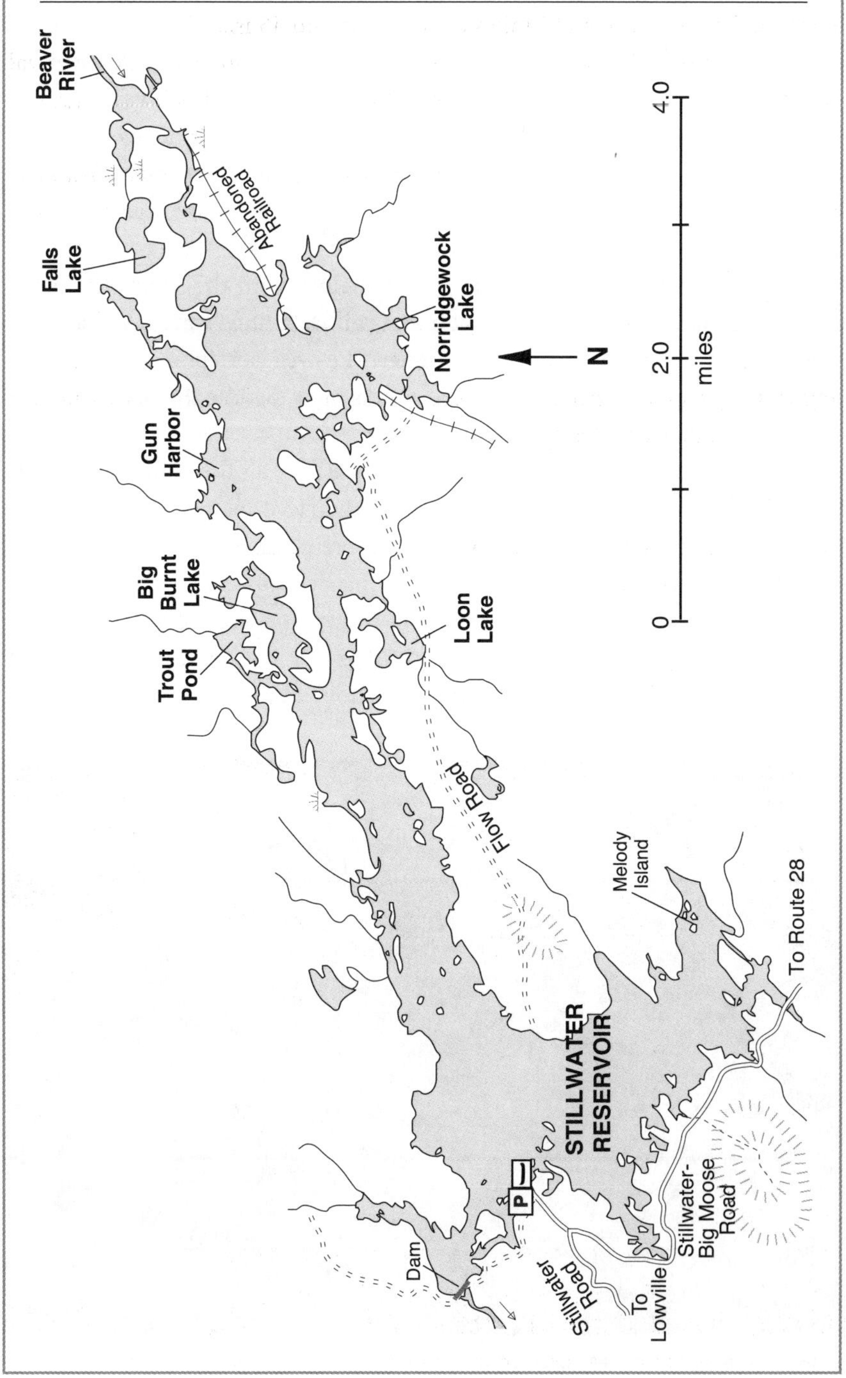

Beaver River's heavily impounded route provides many opportunities for paddling, including at Stillwater Reservoir, by far the largest body of water on the river. The reservoir's 117 miles of shoreline and 45 islands beckon boaters in large numbers. During our trips to Stillwater, we observed about equal numbers of paddlers and motorboaters. Based on a rough survey, paddlers occupied more than half of the 46 campsites sprinkled around the reservoir. Many motorboaters visit this body of water during the day to take advantage of the smallmouth bass fishing. Fortunately, the personal watercraft crowd has not appeared in great numbers . . . yet.

Even with 45 islands providing some shelter from the wind that blows off Lake Ontario, Stillwater Reservoir can roll with huge waves. We strongly suggest that you paddle here only when the weather forecast includes a stagnant high-pressure cell. When the winds blow, paddle the nearby Beaver River Canoe Route instead.

The first time we paddled here, a modest easterly air flow kicked up 2-foot swells, but the second time, the reservoir lived up to its name, with the surface barely rippling as arctic high pressure kept the breezes at bay. The winds off Lake Ontario also carry a lot of moisture, and as the air cools during its Adirondack Plateau ascent, it cannot hold as much moisture. Consequently, a lot of water wrings out along the western slopes, including at Stillwater Reservoir. Indeed, Stillwater also receives a huge amount of snow, carried aloft by winds over

A lesser yellowlegs, a large sandpiper often seen in migration, runs along the shore.

Lake Ontario; the record from the winter of 1971–1972 is 375 inches—more than 31 feet!

You can get away from most other boaters on Stillwater by staying on its connected lakes and bays. We paddled most of the shoreline, including a stretch of Beaver River leading to Nehasane Lake. While on the lake's eastern end, we met a solo paddler who had gone to Lake Lila and back. He spent four hours of this trek walking his boat through shallows during a low-water year. We recommend that the adventuresome paddle this in only one direction, from Lake Lila down to Stillwater.

Our favorite locations on Stillwater include the southwest cove's Melody Island area; the sheltered coves of Trout Pond along the northern shore; the deep, narrow, unnamed cove on the northeastern shore; and Loon Lake along the southern shore, with its beautiful island for camping. We had to carry into Loon Lake on a short, rocky stream that keeps out the motorized crowd.

The fishing must be good on Stillwater, as evidenced by the huge loon population. On one trip, we counted 34, including four young, as we paddled the southern shore from the access to the mouth of Beaver River; of course, we surely missed some along the northern shore. The small number of young did not surprise us. The large loon population may lead to loss of young. Growing evidence shows that unmated adult loons kill young loons. And even with 117 miles of shoreline, the lake does not provide a lot of good nesting sites. First, nest sites must be free from human and predator disturbance; second, fluctuating water levels drown nests or, more often, strand them; third, loons nest on mounds of grass or other vegetation. Due to a dry summer that year, exposed rocky shorelines appeared, providing anything but ideal loon nesting habitat.

We observed a lot of wildlife here, including black duck, herring gull, raven, crow, great blue heron, lesser yellowlegs, spotted sandpiper, and dozens more bird species. We watched deer wander along the shore, but the biggest treat was to see a wild turkey flock approach the shore either to get a drink or to pick up gravel to help grind food—you would need gravel, too, if you ate acorns whole.

Back in the protected coves we studied yellow-flowered bladderwort—an aquatic carnivorous plant—and several species of waterlily. Because marsh and swamp specialists do not appear in high numbers here because of lack of habitat, Stillwater stands in marked contrast to our usual destinations: swamps, marshes, bogs, and meandering, slow-flowing streams. The higher productivity of these latter habitats means more wildlife to view and plants to study. But in Stillwater you can stretch your paddling muscles on a multiday trip that provides many nooks and crannies to explore—just keep your eye on that weather!

66 | Beaver River Canoe Route

We prefer to paddle this 10-mile section in spring and fall when fewer people take to the water on these popular reservoirs. Although you can travel both directions, we recommend that you paddle only downstream. You will see loon, deer, beaver, and lots of songbirds.

Location: Croghan, Watson, Webb
Maps: *New York Atlas & Gazetteer*, Map 35: A6, A7, B6. B7, B8; USGS Belfort, Number Four, Stillwater
Area and Length: Soft Maple Reservoir, 271 acres; Effley Falls Pond, 294 acres; Beaver Lake, 238 acres; 10 miles one way
Time: All day or multiday
Habitat Type: Interconnected small lakes with portages
Fish: Smallmouth bass, brook trout (see fish advisories, Appendix C; see specific advisory, health.ny.gov/environmental/outdoors/fish/health_advisories)
Camping: Soft Maple Reservoir campground
Take Note: Reservoirs sometimes get crowded with motors

GETTING THERE

Beaver Lake Access. From the junction of River and State streets in Lowville, go 4.3 miles east on River Street/Number 4 Road, and turn left on Number 4 Road. Go 13.5 miles (17.8 miles), and turn right on Stillwater Road. Follow it for 2.0 miles (19.8 miles), and turn left on Moshier Road. Go 0.6 mile (20.4 miles), and park on the right. Carry 0.3 mile to the water. (43° 52.238′ N, 75° 8.257′ W)

From Eagle Bay on Fourth Lake at the junction of Routes 1 and 28, go 17.6 miles north on Big Moose Road/Route 1, and turn left on Stillwater Road. Go 5.8 miles (23.4 miles), and turn right on Moshier Road.

Taylorville Pond Access. From the junction of Stillwater, Number 4, and Buck Point roads, go 8.5 miles west on Number 4 Road, and turn right on Erie Canal Road. Go 7.4 miles (15.9 miles), and turn right on Belfort Road. Follow it for 0.3 mile (16.2 miles), and turn right on Long Pond Road. Go 0.1 mile (16.3 miles), turn right on Taylorville Road, and continue 1.0 mile (17.3 miles) to the access. (43° 55.682′ N, 75° 18.710′ W)

TRIP 66: BEAVER RIVER CANOE ROUTE

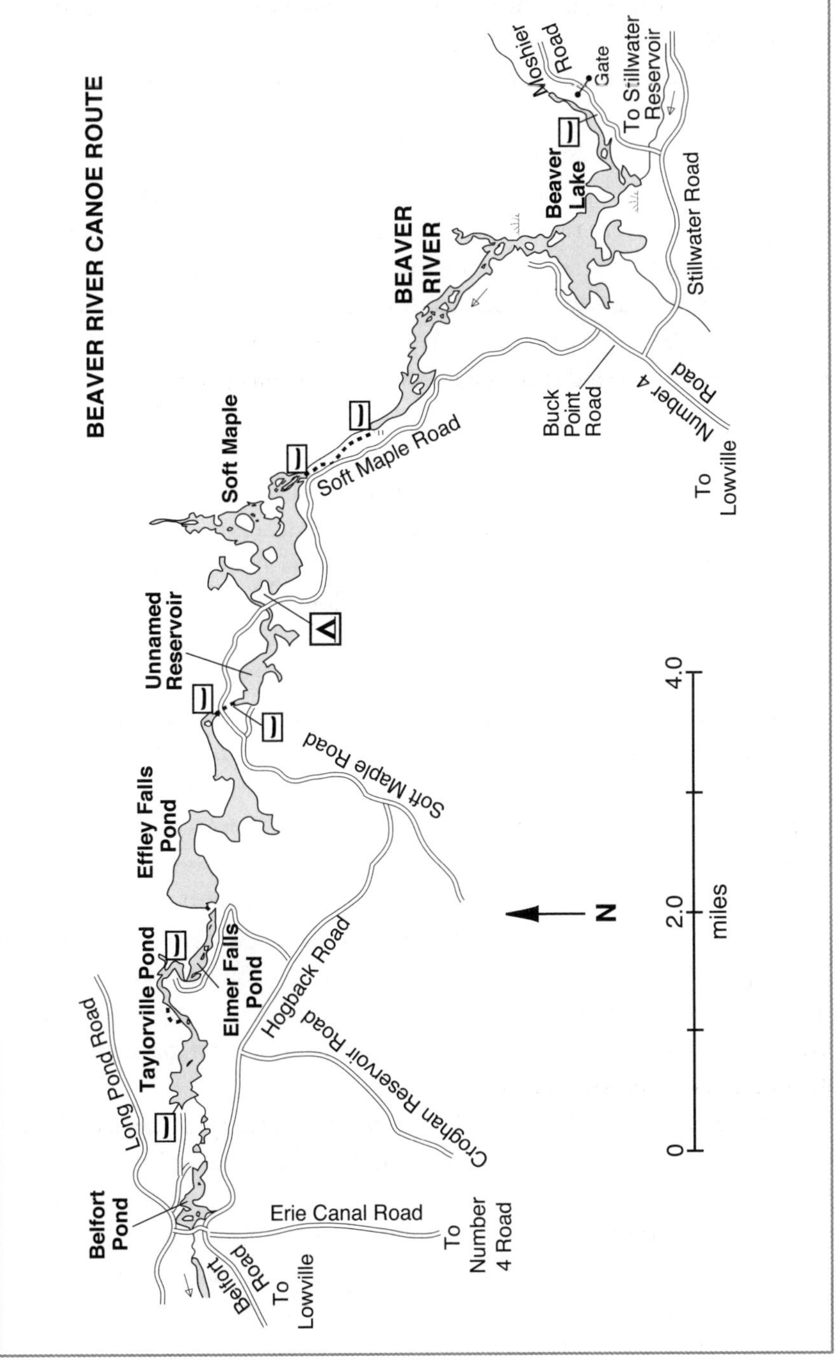

WHAT YOU'LL SEE

A series of connected reservoirs forms the popular Beaver River Canoe Route. To travel this route, start at Moshier Falls and paddle east to west downstream through Beaver Lake, Soft Maple Reservoir, an unnamed reservoir, Effley Falls Pond, Elmer Falls Pond, and Taylorville Pond. Should you decide to paddle the route both ways, the current impedes upstream progress in only a few spots because of dams. During high-water conditions, fighting the current between Beaver Lake and Soft Maple Reservoir may prove difficult. Near the access at the beginning of every reservoir, water rushes out of turbines in proportion to power generated. At peak generation times, paddling against the current back to the put-in spot may be dangerous. Another consideration: on your return, all of the carries go straight uphill. We paddled this route in both directions and heartily recommend it as a one-way trip . . . downstream.

Beaver Lake

A study in contrasts, Beaver Lake begins at the Moshier Falls power plant, travels through an ever-widening marsh, necks down as it enters the main lake—which has a fair amount of development—and then enters a long, beautiful stretch of Beaver River, which in places has significant flow.

Just past the access, we observed two adult loons, along with a nearly grown offspring, in the marsh, which is ringed with pickerelweed and cattails. If you have time, linger among the yellow pondlily, American white waterlily, and other aquatic plants that dot the huge swamp on the unpopulated southeast end. The extensive marshy areas that head off in all directions not only harbor a great deal of wildlife but also represent the only examples of this habitat on the Canoe Route.

As you approach the main lake, stay to the right to avoid the houses and to enter Beaver River as it flows north out of the lake. Paddling around Beaver Lake represents profitless enterprise—that is, unless you want to see who can spot the most different kinds of watercraft. We saw canoe, kayak, pontoon boat, sailboat, outboard, inboard, stern drive, personal watercraft, bass boat, water-ski boat, floatplane, rowboat, and inner tube.

Fortunately, the next 3.5 miles take you down a relatively unpopulated broad channel, past occasional islands, with scenic wooded hillsides all around. Watch for eastern kingbird—a black-and-white flycatcher with a white-tipped tail—perched on streamside branches, waiting to pounce on passing insects. The narrow leaves of water celery point the way downstream as a belted kingfisher flies before you. Flocks of cedar waxwings, with their conspicuous crests, alternately catch flies and search for ripened berries.

Of the entire route, this passage remains our favorite. If you have limited time, we recommend that you stick to Beaver Lake and Beaver River.

Soft Maple Reservoir

We paddled alone for an hour and then completed the long 0.8-mile carry into Soft Maple Reservoir, where a pack of five personal watercraft (PWC) greeted us. Soft Maple Reservoir, arguably once the most scenic lake on this route, suffers greatly from summer home development and has become overrun with powerboats and PWC. We paddled across quickly. Unfortunately, Soft Maple harbors the Canoe Route's only legal campsites—on the western shore near the dam and the lake's outlet.

We slowed down after clearing the peninsula to enjoy the yellow birch lining the shore at the outlet, which passes under an iron bridge into an unnamed reservoir. On our return trip, paddling back in the late afternoon, we had our only beaver sighting on Beaver River. This lone rodent stayed close to the power plant, undoubtedly the area with the least human activity. It probably wandered here in spring when parents drove away last year's brood to make way for new kits. And it probably recognized its poor choice 'long about Memorial Day.

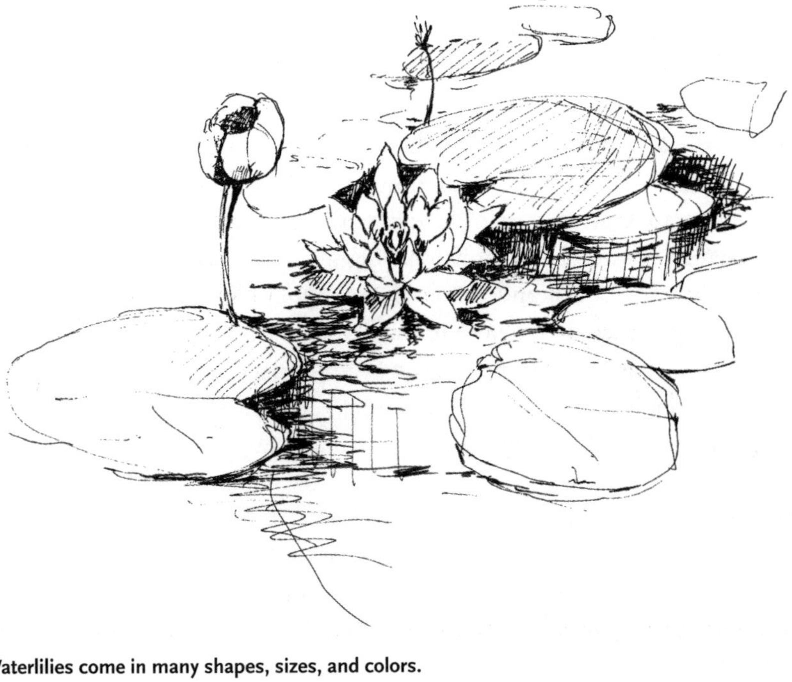

Waterlilies come in many shapes, sizes, and colors.

Unnamed Reservoir

A few well-kept, year-round houses greeted us as we paddled out onto this unnamed reservoir, peaceful and calm in comparison with our recent experience. Because no dam separates this body of water from Soft Maple, people might count this as a continuation of the previous reservoir. We hope this book starts a movement to secede. The two bodies of water bear no resemblance.

The generally wooded shore, with branches hanging out over the water, reminded us to slow down, that we intended to study plants and wildlife rather than boat wakes and paddle whirlpools and that—as Gandhi said—"There is more to life than simply increasing its speed." Although no marsh exists here to draw in wildlife, we lingered, enjoying the peaceful surroundings, as two people on a Sunfish searched in vain for a breeze. On our late-afternoon return trip, the glasslike surface reflected the sun's inexorable march down through the trees to the horizon.

At the western end of the reservoir, on the left side of a narrow channel, the carry heads off briefly but steeply uphill, followed by a half-mile downhill to Effley Falls Pond.

Effley Falls Pond

Effley Falls Pond has some development but not nearly the traffic of Soft Maple. We stopped to talk to other paddlers and to some swimmers. And we saw nary a motorboat, much to the liking of the four loons swimming about.

We observed late-summer monarch butterflies sucking nectar from clumps of purple aster to provide fuel for flight. The monarch, *Danaus plexippus*—one of a very few long-distance migratory insects—summers from southeast Alaska to Newfoundland and south throughout the United States and Canada. It also ranges to Argentina, Hawaii, and many other locations throughout the world. Remarkably, each fall monarchs migrate by the millions to Michoacán in central Mexico, Southern California, and South Florida. They overwinter as adults, mate in late winter and immediately begin their sometimes many-thousand-mile northward migration, an extraordinary undertaking, given that most butterfly adults live for only a few weeks. The amazing monarch hatches during summer, grows through several caterpillar stages, pupates into an adult, flies from New York to central Mexico, hibernates among millions of other monarchs, mates, flies north to New York, lays its eggs, and dies!

Tracing individual flight paths among millions of migrating monarchs has not proved easy. After marking thousands of individuals in the Mexican highlands with wing tags, researchers then searched the northern United States and Canada, hoping to recapture a few marked individuals. They found one in New York and later found one in Mexico that had been marked in Toronto. Those overwintering in Southern California migrate to the Great Basin and the Pacific Northwest.

What allows such a seemingly fragile species to survive the rigors of two such journeys? Part of the answer lies in its larval diet of milkweed leaves. Plants with milky sap often indicate the presence of toxins. Milkweed contains chemicals called cardiac glycosides—heart poisons such as calactin, calotropin, and calotoxin. Of the monarchs examined in the Northeast, 90 percent had sequestered cardiac glycosides. Birds that eat larvae or adults with these poisons generally vomit and then avoid eating any more. Monarchs rely on this food aversion to avoid predation on their long, slow flights. Flying at 12 MPH, they would be easy prey during the 250- to 300-hour trip from New York to Mexico. When we see late-season monarchs fueling up on flower nectar, we look at them in awe, knowing the long perilous journey that awaits them.

Elmer Falls Pond

We regret that Elmer Falls Pond, with no development whatsoever, extends for just less than a mile. A slow cruise in the early morning or late afternoon should provide glimpses of wildlife. We paddled quietly up to a doe with two spotted fawns that had come down for a late-afternoon drink under spreading hemlock boughs. A common merganser herded her flock of nine nearly mature young before us. The carry at the end goes over the right bank and then steeply downhill into Taylorville Pond.

Taylorville Pond

Perhaps the nicest of the reservoirs—with tree-lined grassy banks, fields of ferns under large, lacy green hemlocks, red maples hanging out over water, and majestic white pines—Taylorville marks the end of this section of the Canoe Route. The narrow upper channel necks down as it spills out onto the main lake, revealing a gorgeous forested island. Past the island, a power line looms in the distance, reminding visitors that these reservoirs serve people's insatiable need for electricity. Paddling the final lake in a hand-powered craft, listening to the haunting call of the loon, the epitome of northern wilderness, we should reflect on energy usage in our lives. Do we drive fuel-efficient cars? Carpool? Take mass transit? What can we do to reduce our consumption of natural resources?

The character of the short drop into the main lake changes with water level; when we paddled here, we dropped less than a foot. But, coupled with narrow banks, the water moved swiftly, forming whirlpools below. On our return to

Beaver Lake, after a futile effort trying to paddle back up over the drop, we carried left (north), hopped out onto a gigantic pink granite boulder, hiked back a few hundred feet through a hemlock grove, and relaunched in the widened channel's slackened current.

We hated to leave this idyllic spot with loon echoes bouncing off forested hills, nuthatches chattering softly from streamside, brilliant red cardinal flowers beckoning from the bank, and the sweet smell of balsam fir wafting in from the woods.

---

67 | Long Pond, Round Pond, and Oswegatchie River West Branch

---

Long and Round ponds offer a few hours of quiet paddling, where you can listen to loons call and study the abundant aquatic vegetation. But if you want solitude, travel up the marshy Oswegatchie River West Branch, portaging over beaver dams. Expect to see wood duck, raven, ruffed grouse, muskrat, and possibly beaver.

Location: Croghan
Maps: *New York Atlas & Gazetteer*, Map 35: A7, A8; USGS Stillwater
Area and Length: Long Pond, 146 acres; West Branch, 1.5 miles one way
Time: 5 hours
Habitat Type: Small ponds and slow-flowing, marshy river
Fish: Splake, brook and brown trout (see fish advisories, Appendix C)
Take Note: Ponds sometimes heavily used by nearby camp

GETTING THERE

Long and Round Ponds Access. From the junction of Route 812 and Bostwick Street in Lowville, go 9.7 miles north on Route 812, and bear right on Belfort Road. Continue 3.6 miles (13.3 miles), and turn right on Long Pond Road. Go 4.3 miles (17.6 miles), and veer right on Prentice Road. Go 4.4 miles (22.0 miles), stay straight as Prentice Road veers right, and go an additional 0.1 mile (22.1 miles) to the access on the left. (43° 58.539′ N, 75° 11.769′ W)

Oswegatchie River West Branch Access. From the junction with Prentice Road, continue 5.8 miles (23.4 miles) on Long Pond Road to the access on the right. Hike 0.3 mile along Jakes Pond Trail, taking the left fork to the first footbridge. Put in on the far left side. (43° 59.672′ N, 75° 10.759′ W)

TRIP 67: LONG POND, ROUND POND, AND OSWEGATCHIE RIVER WEST BRANCH

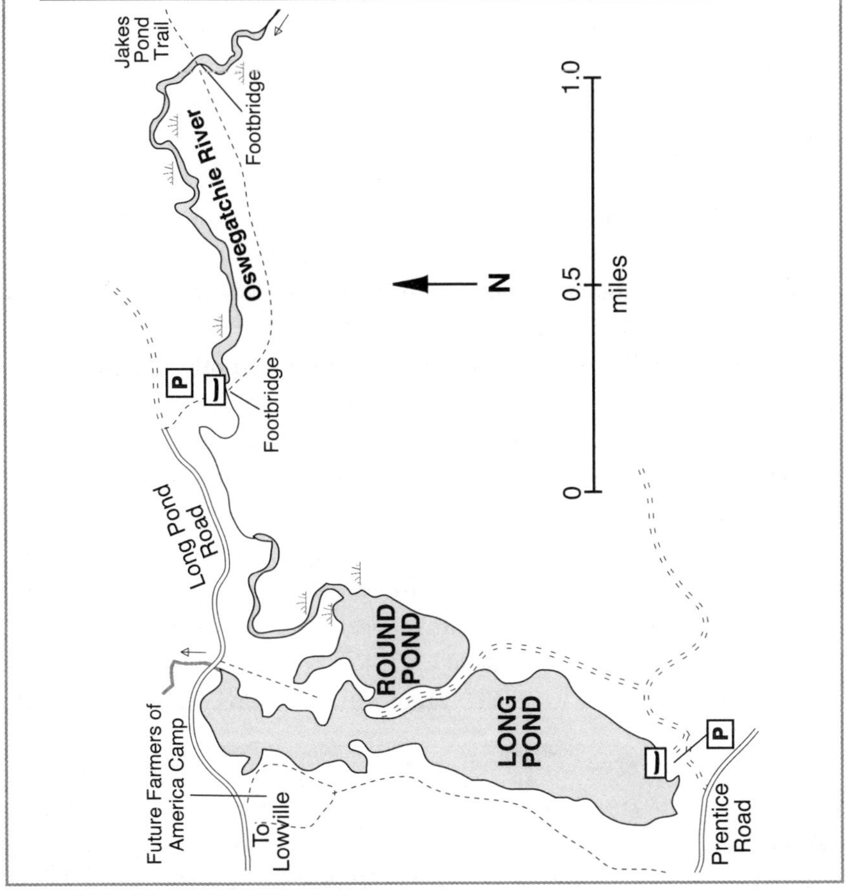

WHAT YOU'LL SEE

Long and Round ponds, in holes left by retreating glaciers, form two wide spots in the Oswegatchie River West Branch. We include these two ponds, along with an upstream portion of the Oswegatchie. (*Note*: You cannot paddle the river between the two ponds and the upstream section of river because of current and shallow water.)

Long and Round Ponds

The Future Farmers of America (FFA) maintains a camp on the northern shore of Long and Round ponds and owns the land surrounding these ponds. Fortunately, the organization allows the public to paddle here, in a cooperative agreement with the Department of Environmental Conservation.

Arriving the night before our paddle, we camped nearby, dropping our sleeping bags on the ground and listening to the loon's haunting call echoing off the hillsides. A barred owl asked *who-cooks-for-you, who-cooks-for-you* from the woods, and small mammals scurried through the dense brush. Still, we had no problem drifting to sleep, soothed by the sounds of the night.

We started paddling at first light, as mist drifted slowly across the water, and noticed a conspicuous browse line on the bankside hemlocks that dominate Long Pond's south end. Deer nibble the branch ends from the ice in winter. As we watched, a deer ambled down for an early morning drink. The loon began to call again as we made our way north on still water.

Although many tree species occur along the shore, nearly pure stands grow in spots: hemlock along the east side of Long Pond and red pine, punctuated by an occasional tall white pine, along the peninsula separating the two ponds. The generally shrubby shoreline gives way to a carpet of needles under the pines. Out in the water, American white waterlily blankets the protected coves, along with minor amounts of pickerelweed, some pondweed, and a few large patches of water shield.

A ruffed grouse drummed on a log in the woods, and two ravens practiced their aerial acrobatics. A flock of yellow-rumped warblers cast about for insects, and barn swallows skimmed the pond's surface. Two common mergansers tried to hide from us among the reeds of a shallow cove, and a belted kingfisher announced our presence to the FFA camp with its rattling cry. We felt slightly

American white waterlilies reflect early morning light from the rippled surface of Round Pond.

guilty about causing such a ruckus but later retracted those feelings: Tuesday is mechanized day at camp!

While some campers took turns spinning around the lake on water skis, others took fifteen-minute floatplane rides—over and over, all morning long. Surprisingly, this did not affect the resident loons as much as it did us. We paddled up the inlet for its navigable half-mile and watched the dew dry off streamside spiderwebs. We listened to a white-throated sparrow and a catbird call from the undergrowth, searched the water for the beavers that owned a nearby lodge, admired purple elderberries, and then paddled back through tea-colored water to the access, under the floatplane's pontoons and across the ski-boat wake.

Along the way, we investigated the outflow under the bridge on Long Pond's north end. The current here tumbles down over a rock-strewn streambed. We turned around because paddling back up would be difficult at best.

Oswegatchie River West Branch

The contrast between the two ponds and the Oswegatchie River's upstream section stands out in our memory. Because you have to hike in, few people paddle here among the tall tamaracks and pines that dot the river's extensive marshland. From the widened upstream section described here downstream to the entrance to Round Pond, the river passes under the first Jakes Pond Trail footbridge and cascades over beautiful waterfalls. But upstream from these cascades, the river barely flows through a sphagnum bog that covers a flat plateau. Because the huge surrounding marsh accumulates copious quantities of snow over the winter, water releases slowly, maintaining levels that allow paddling, even during dry summers.

Brushy banks covered with alder, leatherleaf, sweetgale, and other streamside vegetation lead to mats of floating aquatic plants. We carried up over a beaver dam and paddled through another. You can paddle back in for about a mile and a half, eventually ending in an enormous beaver meadow and sphagnum bog that stretches off into the distance. At the second Jakes Pond Trail footbridge, paddlers have to walk their boats through the shallows during times of low water. We had to negotiate around a bald-faced hornet nest attached to the downstream side of the bridge.

Because we did not paddle here in early June, we missed the azalea bloom, which is mentioned in the guidebook *Adirondack Canoe Waters: North Flow*. These showy flowers—members of the heath family, along with rhododendron, mountain laurel, sheep laurel, blueberry, cranberry, and many other bog specialists—should enrich any paddling excursion.

Besides the beaver activity, expect to see beautiful wood ducks feeding on abundant aquatic vegetation that laces the tea-colored water. Muskrats harvest grasses, deer come to the water's edge to drink, and birds flit about in profusion. (Perhaps moose will one day tramp the area again. In recent years, this largest member of the deer family has returned to New York after more than a hundred years' absence.) A feeling of remoteness and peacefulness surrounds this extraordinary place. If you want wilderness, this is a good place to find it.

68 | Oswegatchie River

The Oswegatchie offers arguably the finest river paddling in New York. The surrounding northern boreal forest harbors lots of wildlife. Expect to see osprey, wood duck, boreal chickadee, spruce grouse, gray jay, beaver, and otter; you might also see mink.

Location: Fine
Maps: *New York Atlas & Gazetteer*, Map 27: D10, E10 and Map 28: E1; USGS Five Ponds, Newton Falls
Length: 13 miles one way
Time: All day or multiday
Habitat Type: Twisting wilderness stream through northern boreal forest
Fish: Brook trout (see fish advisories, Appendix C)
Camping: On-site wilderness camping
Take Note: No motors; during high water, paddling upstream is slow

GETTING THERE

From the junction of Route 3 and Mill Street in the village of Cranberry Lake, go 10.7 miles west on Route 3, and turn left on Sunny Lake Road (Inlet Road). Turn sharply left, and go 3.0 miles (13.7 miles) to the road's end at Inlet. (44° 7.476′ N, 74° 57.595′ W)

WHAT YOU'LL SEE

The remarkable Oswegatchie River upstream (right) from Inlet, an extraordinary canoe wilderness, drains the high country of the Five Ponds Wilderness Area. This is one of the few places in the Adirondacks that does not allow motors, so paddlers treasure it. Don't expect to paddle alone.

This trip travels upstream (south) to High Falls and returns. You can paddle several miles beyond the falls, penetrating ever deeper into wilderness, but that

TRIP 68: OSWEGATCHIE RIVER

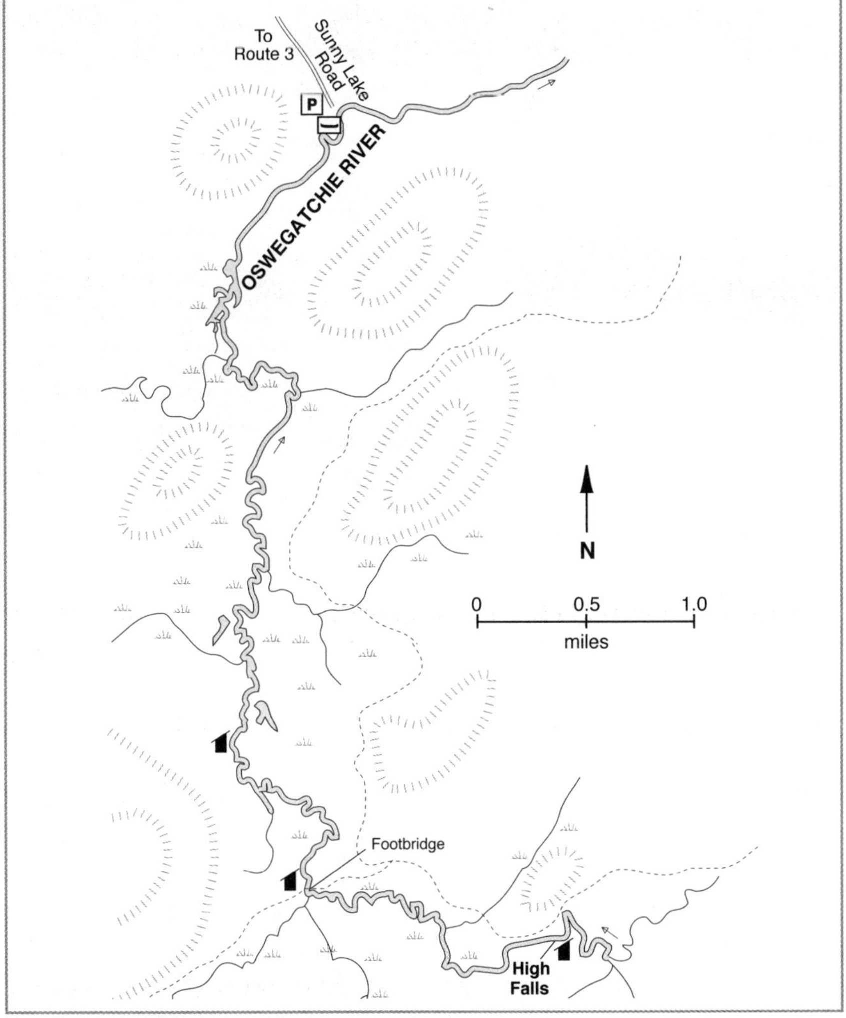

has become a little more difficult since a violent windstorm ripped through this section of the Adirondacks in mid-July 1995.

We camped near Inlet on the night of July 14, 1995, and planned to paddle the Oswegatchie the next morning. As first light neared on the 15th, we awoke to hear and feel the wind trying to shred our tent. Desperately, we held onto the tent's fragile fabric. After a few minutes, the wind subsided, and we emerged to find the landscape littered with fallen trees. With nearly all roads blocked by downed trees and power lines, we retreated outside the park to the north, the only direction with open roads.

Early morning mists rise from the surface of the Oswegatchie River in the Five Ponds Wilderness Area.

When we returned to paddle the Oswegatchie three weeks later, we witnessed indescribable devastation. The Five Ponds Wilderness had been the epicenter of a storm that destroyed about a million acres of timber. A little more than 100,000 acres suffered greater than 60 percent tree loss, while the rest sustained about half that loss.

Blown-over and snapped-off trees—all facing west to east—dominated much of the river's course. We skirted countless treetops, ducked under many leaners, and carried over several logjams. Many sections remained untouched, but then hundreds of acres of twisted wreckage confronted us as we rounded the next bend.

Hardly a tree remained standing on the right side of High Falls. One large cherry tree had crashed down on the lean-to on the right side; the lean-to had occupants—as it always did. Fortunately, the log structure held, protecting the campers. Amazingly, none of the more than 30 paddlers and hikers in that wilderness died, although falling trees killed a camper at Eighth Lake Campground and another at Lake Lila.

Signs at the access warning "Caution, Wind Damage, Unsafe Conditions" did not deter us or the several other paddlers we encountered. As we paddled out in the early morning mists through spire-like balsam firs, a beaver swam by, totally unconcerned by our presence, answering our question about what had happened to the wildlife during the storm.

As we penetrated farther into the wilderness, beaver meadows appeared on side channels. If you have time, carry up over the banks through joe-pye weed into these meadows, as they provide excellent wildlife habitat. A bittern that had stationed itself upright to blend in with the streamside grass bolted skyward when we got too close. A snowshoe hare, wearing its summer browns, munched on grass, while flocks of cedar waxwings ate everything in sight, except the ripening winterberries. These bright red fruits persist well into winter because of low nutritional value. Birds and mammals prefer more nutritious fruit and insects. However, after depleting other food sources, the waxwing and other animals do eat these berries, eventually scattering the plant's seeds to new locations in their droppings.

As we neared the first of five obstructions across the stream, an otter that sat feeding on a fish slid gracefully into the tea-colored water. Tannic and other organic acids liberated from decaying vegetation in the surrounding swamp had turned the water a rich yellow-brown. Animal droppings on nearly every exposed rock told us that the otter and the beaver we had seen earlier had much company. The ubiquitous beavers had also done a good job of pruning back the streamside alders.

The surrounding boreal forest of tamarack, black spruce, white pine, and balsam fir provides habitat for rare northern species, including spruce grouse, gray jay, and boreal chickadee. We encountered only the boreal chickadee, with its gray cap and hoarse *chick-a-dee-dee* call. This habitat will eventually again include moose. Their wide cloven hooves and very long legs—the largest moose stand 7.5 feet at the shoulder—adapt them to life in beaver meadows.

A little way upstream, you reach a footbridge at the top of a riffle. At high-water levels, you have to carry over or pole through the riffle. Just after the footbridge, at campsite 22, a sign says "Spring" with an arrow pointing the way. Depending on water level, it can take all day—or longer—to reach High Falls. You may have to carry around an occasional logjam or beaver dam. The downstream trip with the current and with lighter food packs should take much less than a full day. It takes more than three days to fully explore the wilderness.

As we drifted back lazily with the current, we remarked at the abundant wildlife. In addition to the species noted earlier, we saw crow, catbird, northern harrier, yellow-rumped warbler, downy woodpecker, wood duck, common yellowthroat, American redstart, and black-and-white, magnolia, yellow, and yellow-rumped warblers. A garter snake swam in S-shaped arcs across the river before us, and an osprey and red-tailed hawks circled above. We wondered if their nest trees had been blown down—at least the adults had survived to build new nests next year. We would be back to check on their progress.

69 | Cranberry Lake

Shallow Cranberry Lake, although quite large, has many protected coves and marshlands that block the wind. You can almost always find quiet places to paddle in this wildlife paradise, where you will see osprey, loon, waterfowl, great blue heron, beaver, otter, and lots more.

Location: Clifton, Colton, Fine
Maps: *New York Atlas & Gazetteer*, Map 28: C1, C2, D1, D2; USGS Cranberry Lake, Five Ponds, Newton Falls
Area: 6,995 acres
Time: All day or multiday
Habitat Type: Large, shallow lake
Fish: Smallmouth bass, brook trout (see fish advisories, Appendix C; see specific advisory, health.ny.gov/environmental/outdoors/fish/health_advisories)
Camping: Appendix A (98) (on-site); dec.ny.gov/outdoor/24460.html; an additional 46 free campsites scattered along shore and islands (map of sites: dec.ny.gov/lands/34715.html)
Take Note: Wind can make paddling treacherous

GETTING THERE

Northern Access. From the junction of Route 3 and Mill Street in the village of Cranberry Lake, go 1.1 miles west on Route 3, and turn at the access on South Columbian Road. (44° 13.203′ N, 74° 50.845′ W)

Wanakena Access. From the village of Cranberry Lake, go 7.8 miles west on Route 3, and turn left on Route 61. Go 0.9 mile (8.7 miles), turn left on Ranger School Road, and continue 0.4 mile (9.1 miles) to the access on the right. (44° 8.302′ N, 74° 54.938′ W)

WHAT YOU'LL SEE

Cranberry Lake's size (third-largest lake in the Adirondacks) might intimidate those familiar with Lake George and Great Sacandaga Lake and their well-defined north-south channels that funnel even modest breezes into threatening swells. Although wind-driven waves on Cranberry's main body might swamp an open boat, you can safely access much of the lake. It harbors 55 miles of shoreline with jagged fingers extending back into many quiet coves, resembling a Rorschach

TRIP 69: CRANBERRY LAKE

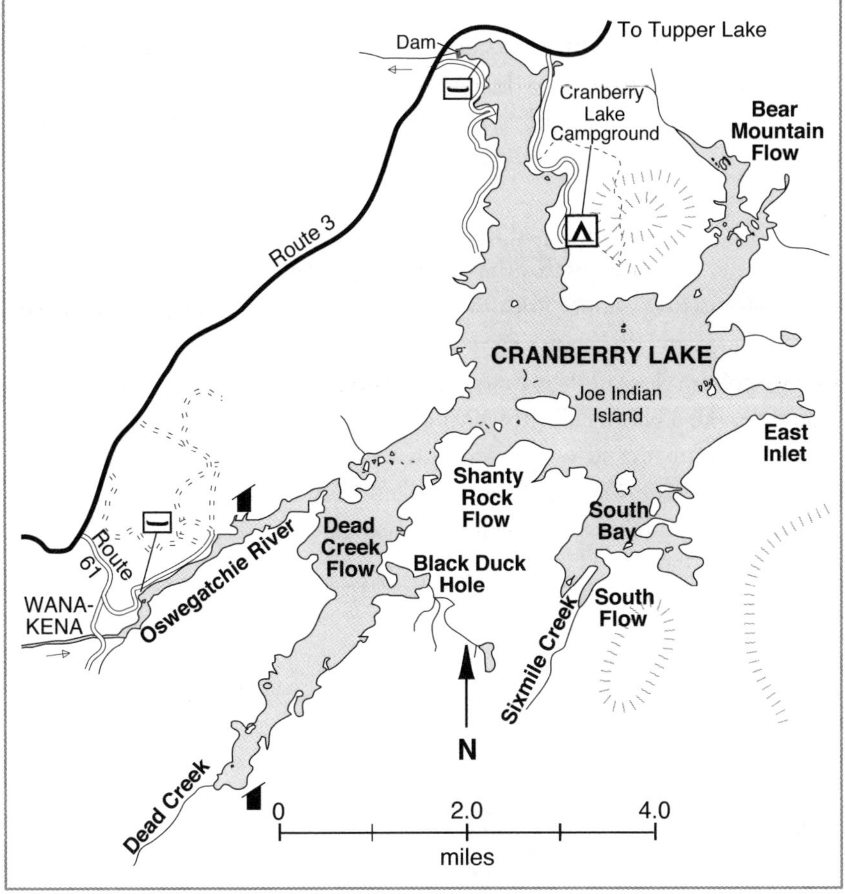

inkblot that runs to the edges of the map in all directions. While the two larger lakes attract hordes of big boats and personal watercraft, Cranberry attracts far fewer of these and about equal numbers of paddlers and motorboaters.

Cranberry's attraction lies in the protective islands and coves that shelter quietwater paddlers from the wind and in the 46 free water-accessible campsites scattered about the shore and islands. The extensive marshes of Bear Mountain Swamp, a network of hiking trails in the surrounding Five Ponds Wilderness Area (107,000 acres) and Cranberry Lake Wild Forest (26,000 acres), abundant wildlife, and the lake's relative seclusion combine to make Cranberry one of the Adirondacks' finest paddling destinations.

We prefer putting in on the quieter southwestern arm in Wanakena, where the Oswegatchie River East Branch enters the lake, thereby avoiding the congestion and development that characterize the village and surrounding shoreline. The Wanakena arm also provides access to more sheltered coves and bays.

Here, hemlocks line the banks in places, sporting a conspicuous browse line where deer munch from the winter ice, particularly right across from the ranger school, which represents the last development on this section of Cranberry Lake; the state owns and protects three-quarters of the lakeshore and most of the surrounding hillsides.

On our early morning paddle, numerous great blue herons patrolled the shallow coves, and hermit thrushes sang from the understory. An osprey fished the quiet waters of Shanty Rock Flow, and two flocks of common mergansers tried to hide along the shores as we cruised by. Ring-billed gulls dive-bombed us if we got too close to their nests on bare granite boulders, and we watched a loon pair with a black, half-grown chick swimming between them.

Later, we picnicked on the smooth ledges surrounding the falls where Sixmile Creek enters South Flow and hiked back along the trail leading away from the falls, searching the marshes for beaver. None seemed to be out in the middle of the day.

Joe-pye weed is part of the sunflower family.

Granite boulders, some really huge, crowd the shoreline. Glacial erratics—boulders left behind thousands of years ago by retreating glaciers—form small islands, even out in the middle of the main lake. Spruce, hemlock, tamarack, red maple, yellow birch, aspen, and many other tree species cover the hills that recede off into the distance.

Marshy areas exist at the back of Black Duck Hole on the east side of Dead Creek Flow and much more extensively in Bear Mountain Flow. In Black Duck Hole, the eponymous ducks dabbled for abundant succulent underwater vegetation. A cavorting otter and a huge beaver lodge confirmed that this area has abundant wildlife. A fellow paddler who visits Cranberry frequently said that he often sees otters in the lake's southern portions.

You can travel back for a couple of miles into Bear Mountain Flow to a very long line of black spruce that mark the end of the marsh, and you probably will paddle alone here. We turned around at the second beaver dam.

Broad mats of red-tinged sundew cover the hummocks of Bear Mountain Flow, in as great a concentration as we have seen. As we carefully inspected these small, carnivorous plants, we could see the dew-like, sticky secretions on short stalks that crowd the outer margins of their rounded pads—their only leaves. Insects, attracted to the glistening secretions, become entrapped. A slight roll of the pad pushes the prey onto shorter stalks that contain digestive enzymes. Plant tissues incorporate the digested insects, supplementing the meager nutrients available in swamps and bogs.

Large patches of beautiful yellow-flowered bladderwort provided our biggest treat. Pushing gently on the long spur protruding from the rear of the flower opens the front two petals, revealing the interior reproductive parts. We often see yellow-flowered bladderwort and, more rarely, the purple-flowered species, particularly in shallow, stagnant water, with only the small bloom stalk above the surface. However, the bladderwort here (genus *Utricularia*) shared the hummocks with sphagnum and sundew. One of the few terrestrial bladderworts, these plants trap insects on dry land, with their bladders immersed in mud, functioning much the same way as their aquatic cousins.

We spent several hours back in Bear Mountain Flow and saw nary another paddler. Ducks, great blue herons, and kingfishers kept us company. This was the last part of Cranberry Lake that we explored, and the memory of the wonderful sights and sounds of the marsh helped ease the long paddle back to the Wanakena access.

70 | Five Falls, Rainbow Falls, and Blake Falls Reservoirs

You will see wildlife, especially birds, on each of these reservoirs, but we encountered higher numbers and more diversity on Blake Falls. Look for bald eagle, wild turkey, beaver, deer, kingfisher, merganser, and woodland avian species.

Location: Colton, Parishville
Maps: *New York Atlas & Gazetteer*, Map 20: D1, D2, D3, E2, E3; USGS Carry Falls Reservoir, Rainbow Falls, Stark, Sylvan Falls
Area: Five Falls Reservoir, 106 acres; Rainbow Falls Reservoir, 739 acres; Blake Falls Reservoir, 642 acres
Time: All day
Habitat Type: Wooded reservoirs
Fish: Smallmouth bass, northern pike, walleye (see fish advisories, Appendix C; see specific advisory, health.ny.gov/environmental/outdoors/fish/health_advisories)
Camping: Appendix A (59)
Take Note: Private campground on Blake Falls Reservoir

GETTING THERE

Five Falls Access. From Potsdam at the junction of Route 56/Pierrepont Avenue and Main Street, go 13.8 miles south on Route 56, turn left on Snell Road, and then take an immediate left on Three Falls Lane/Raquette River Road. Go 2.6 miles (16.4 miles) to the access on the left. (44° 31.720′ N, 74° 50.556′ W)

From Tupper Lake, head west on Route 3. At the junction with Route 56, go 18.5 miles north on Route 56, turn right on Snell Road, and follow as above.

Rainbow Falls Access. From Five Falls, continue 1.5 miles (17.9 miles) to the access on the left. (44° 30.873′ N, 74° 49.276′ W)

Blake Falls Access. From Rainbow Falls, continue 4.7 miles (22.6 miles) to the access on the left. (44° 28.129′ N, 74° 45.808′ W)

WHAT YOU'LL SEE

On the northwestern edge of Adirondack Park, a series of seven reservoirs drowns the Raquette River rapids to provide electric power. What was once a beautiful wilderness river—second longest in the state after the Hudson—succumbed to people's continuing thirst for power. Thankfully, Brookfield

TRIP 70: FIVE FALLS, RAINBOW FALLS, AND BLAKE FALLS RESERVOIRS

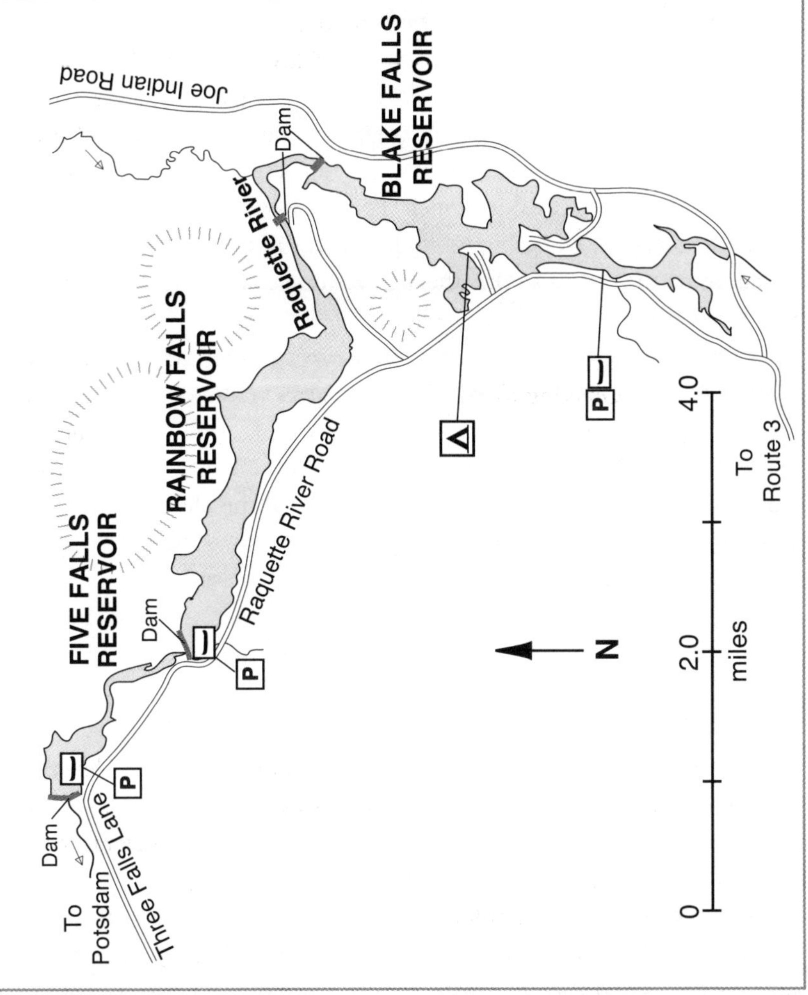

Power allows public use of these waters. We include here three connected intermediate reservoirs. If you have limited time, we suggest visiting Blake Falls, the nicest of the three.

Five Falls Reservoir

Small, quiet Five Falls Reservoir receives little attention. If chaos reigns on the others, we suggest paddling here. Where the main body necks down as you paddle around to thc right from the access, note the rock formations near shore that extend out into the water, making passage difficult during times of low water.

The forested shoreline contains a wide variety of tree species, including aspen—both big-tooth and quaking—paper and yellow birches, red maple, red and white pines, northern white cedar, hemlock, and several others. A relatively open understory hosts a large fern population.

We recognize aspen, a member of the willow family, by its smooth, pale green or yellow bark. In a light breeze, its leaves quake. It grows in association with pine and other conifers, and its golden-yellow leaves in fall provide a beautiful contrast with the surrounding dark evergreens. Distinguish the two species by their leaves: quaking aspen (*Populus tremuloides*) has very fine teeth on its leaf margins, while big-tooth aspen (*Populus grandidentata*) has large serrations on the margins. Also, the big-tooth aspen trunk loses its smoothness as it grows larger.

Both species regenerate quickly after fire or other disturbance, serving as soil anchors. Quaking aspen also propagates readily by sending out root suckers, forming dense clones, all with the same genetic makeup. Taller species frequently crowd out quaking aspen. In the West, with less crowding, individual trees may live for only 100 years, but the clones can survive for thousands, placing aspen (or at least its roots) among the oldest species on Earth. Furthermore, some scientists believe that an aspen clone is actually a single organism, interconnected by the root system. That would make some Western clones the largest organisms in the world—far outweighing the biggest redwood, sequoia, or blue whale.

A few hundred species of wildlife—including moose, beaver, bear, elk, grouse, quail, and deer—rely on aspen for food from its bark, leaves, buds, flowers, and fruits. Coupled with the aspen's early successional, soil-holding character, this food production makes it one of the most important tree species in the North Country.

We spotted yellow warbler, black-throated green warbler, American redstart, and black-capped chickadee bustling among the branches, while song sparrow and wood thrush hunted insects along the ground. A deer snorted at us from the brush, and we searched in vain for the beaver that had fed on tender aspen branches. We enjoyed paddling among these shores with their rich mixture of conifer and deciduous trees, but it takes only a few hours to cover the entire reservoir.

Rainbow Falls Reservoir

Located between Five Falls and Blake Falls reservoirs, Rainbow Falls Reservoir takes much more time to explore. Despite the occasional houses along the southern shore, paddling here still provides a quietwater experience, especially

A majestic bald eagle clasps its perch in a hemlock on the south end of Blake Falls Reservoir.

early and late in the season. The broad expanse of water near the dam on the west end gives way to an island that blocks the view of many of the houses. At the east end, the reservoir takes an abrupt left turn as it heads toward Blake Falls Reservoir. The most beautiful area on the reservoir, this narrow arm sports forested shores and tall banks covered with lush vegetation, akin to that found at Five Falls.

Paper birch, very similar to aspen in ecological niche, grows in profusion, and beavers hack away at it just as they do to aspen on Five Falls Reservoir. In some sections, deer have created a conspicuous browse line by feeding heavily on lakeside branches.

Here, in addition to the birds we saw at Five Falls, we observed red-eyed vireo, belted kingfisher, common loon, two families of common merganser, spotted sandpiper, black duck, and ring-billed gull.

Blake Falls Reservoir

By all metrics the most scenic of the three reservoirs, Blake Falls Reservoir provided us with the best looks at wildlife, even though we paddled here in midafternoon. Plant species also appear in greater abundance, and the aquatic habitat includes marshes, absent in the other reservoirs.

A wild turkey hen and her brood greeted us as we approached the water. This magnificent game bird, standing more than 3 feet tall, once inhabited most of the forested parts of eastern North America, foraging on acorns, chestnuts, beechnuts, seeds, and insects. With the clearing of forests, loss of the American chestnut to chestnut blight, and unregulated hunting, the wild turkey had disappeared over much of its historic range. Reintroduced in many areas, this bird now ranges over large tracts of New York.

As we approached the southern end of the reservoir, we noticed two mature bald eagles. We searched for their nest but never found it. Eagle nests, made of sticks, may reach 6 or more feet in diameter. Adults mate for life and usually return to the same nest, adding a new layer each year. Eventually, the nest may reach 8 or more feet in depth and weigh up to a ton. Often built in dead trees that stand on partially rotted trunks, the nests make trees top-heavy, eventually bringing them down in windstorms.

As we returned to the access, we reflected on the differences among the three reservoirs. Although Five Falls and Rainbow Falls have relatively open understories filled with bracken and hay-scented ferns, Blake Falls has much more shrubbery. Its narrower channel lends it a more closed-in, riverlike feeling, making it seem smaller; indeed, because of peninsulas and meandering channels, from most locations it appears much smaller than the other two.

Back in Blake Falls' marshy areas—absent from the other two reservoirs—we found swamp rose and swamp milkweed growing among many other wetland species. More conifer species grow here as well, including some large tamaracks, spruces, balsam firs, and red and white pines. The lacy green foliage of hemlocks hanging out over the water shades the shoreline in several areas.

BLACKFLIES AND MOSQUITOES: SCOURGES OF THE NORTH

Anyone who has spent time in the Adirondacks knows these insects all too well. They can detract from outdoor fun in summer and can make most of June virtually off-limits to recreation in the state's northern reaches. Although it won't take away any of the itch, understanding these insects may help us accept them as part of the ecosystem we enjoy.

Blackflies

Blackflies belong to the family Simuliidae, and most species of concern belong to the genus *Simulium*. Scientists have identified more than 1,500 blackfly species, including 300 in North America. Only 10 to 15 percent of blackfly species suck blood from humans or domestic animals.

In areas of northern North America, blackflies lead to considerable livestock difficulties—mostly because cattle do not eat well when tormented by flies, but blackflies can actually cause enough blood loss to kill cattle. In parts of Alberta, Canada, mortality rates from blackflies range from 1 to 4 percent. Researchers have collected as many as 10,000 feeding blackflies from a single cow. Blackfly problems in North America, however, pale compared with problems in Africa and Central America, where the aptly named species *Simulium damnosum* has infected an estimated 20 million people with onchocerciasis, or river blindness (a disease caused by roundworms transmitted by the fly).

Blackflies begin their life cycle in streams and rivers. Females deposit eggs in the water, and emerging larvae attach to rocks, plants, and other surfaces. Larvae use two tiny, fanlike structures to sweep food particles into their mouths. Blackfly larvae can become so dense that they form a slippery, mosslike mat. A stretch of several hundred feet in a narrow stream can support more than a million larvae. In a river, the population can number in the multibillions per mile.

After a period of days or weeks, each larva builds a pupal case in which it metamorphoses into an adult blackfly. When ready to emerge, it splits open the case and rides to the water's surface in a bubble of oxygen that formed in the case.

Adult blackflies have one primary goal: to make more blackflies. Female blackflies seek the nourishing blood meal that they need to lay eggs. Only females bite (actually puncture and suck); pacifist males sip nectar from flowers and may be important blueberry pollinators. Blackflies rely heavily on eyesight to find prey, so they are active almost exclusively during daylight—and at temperatures above 50 degrees Fahrenheit. Some blackflies travel more than 50 miles in search of blood meals.

No blackfly species preys exclusively on humans. We are too new on the evolutionary chain to be a specific host to blackflies, which arose during the Jurassic period 180 million years ago. An estimated 30 to 45 species in North America feed on humans. One species (*Simulium euryadminiculum*) feeds only on loons.

Mosquitoes

Another insect nemesis is the ubiquitous mosquito, a member of the Culicidae family. Mosquito species number more than 3,400 worldwide, including 170 in North America. Three-quarters of the mosquito species in the United States and Canada belong to three genera: *Aedes* (78 species), *Culex* (29 species), and *Anopheles* (16 species).

Like blackfly larvae, mosquito larvae live an aquatic life. Unlike blackflies, most mosquitoes have adapted to still water. In any bog or salt marsh, you can find mosquito larvae wriggling about, ingesting algae and other organic matter that they filter out of water with brushlike appendages. Larvae molt several times as they grow and develop into pupae. Both larvae and pupae breathe through air tubes at the water's surface.

Adult mosquitoes live short lives—females about a month and males about a week. Their buzzing sound comes from their wings moving at about 1,000 beats per second. Females generate a higher-pitched whine that helps males locate them. You can recognize males by their bushier antennae, used to find females.

Both sexes feed on plant nectar as their primary energy source, but females of most mosquito species also require a blood meal to fuel egg production. Like the blackfly, a mosquito does not actually bite. Rather, she stabs through the victim's skin with six sharp stylets that form the proboscis center. Saliva flows into the puncture to keep the blood from coagulating. Most people have an allergic reaction to the saliva, resulting in swelling and itching. Upon repeated exposure to bites, one gradually builds immunity.

Although mainly just a nuisance in New York, mosquitoes cause more deaths in the tropics than any other animal. They carry more than 100 different diseases, including malaria, yellow fever, encephalitis, filariasis, dengue, and West Nile virus. The most destructive of these, malaria, kills about 1 million people a year, mostly children, and as many as 200 million people carry the disease. More recently, Zika virus has become a human scourge in the tropics and the southern United States, which harbor populations of host mosquitoes, *Aedes aegypti* and *Aedes albopictus*.

Southern latitudes have far greater mosquito species diversity (tropical areas can harbor as many as 150 different species in a square mile), but the numbers of individuals generally increase farther north. The Arctic, for example, has fewer than a dozen species, but adults can swarm so thickly they literally blacken the skies. In one experiment, several rugged Canadian researchers bared their torsos, arms, and legs to Arctic mosquitoes and reported as many as 9,000 bites per minute! At this rate, an unprotected person could lose half of the body's blood in two hours.

So, you see, we really don't have it so bad in New York. Most mosquitoes don't carry deadly diseases (despite occasional cases of mosquito-borne encephalitis and West Nile virus), and even in the Adirondacks in June, we have found it rare to get more than a thousand bites a minute.

Blackfly and Mosquito Control

Humans have tried many different strategies to control these pests. For mosquito control, people drained thousands of square miles of salt marsh during the 1930s and 1940s by building long, straight drainage ditches—many of which are still visible. As much as half of U.S. wetlands area has been lost during the last 200 years—partly for mosquito control and partly for development and agriculture. Along with eliminating habitat, people have used thousands of tons of pesticides in the battle against mosquitoes. DDT remained the chemical of choice for decades because of its supposed safety—a claim that proved tragically untrue. DDT and other deadly chlorinated-hydrocarbon pesticides were banned in 1973, and osprey, bald eagle, peregrine falcon, and other important bird species have made a comeback.

Today, most attention focuses on biological control of these insects, relying on natural enemies: viruses, protozoa, bacteria, fungi, and parasites. A bacterium generally known as Bti (*Bacillus thuringiensis* variety *israelensis*), discovered in 1977 in Negev Desert sand, has exhibited the most successful control. Gardeners use another variety of this bacterium for controlling cabbage loopers, corn borers, and other garden pests; foresters use it for gypsy moth control. Bti bacteria produce protein crystals that react with other chemicals in the insects' stomachs, producing a poison that kills larvae.

Although Bti currently enjoys high success rates, hidden problems could arise, just as with DDT, especially as bioengineers incorporate the Bti gene into plants. Widespread and indiscriminate spreading of the Bti protein could easily lead to pest resistance. Conservation biologists also worry that monarch butterflies, on their 1,000-plus-mile migrations to Mexico wintering grounds, will suffer huge mortality rates from feeding on Bti-engineered corn.

Protecting Yourself from Biting Insects

To protect yourself from biting insects, you could stay out of the woods in summer—maybe buy a good book on paddling and read it in the comfort of your home. As Henry David Thoreau wrote in *The Maine Woods*: "I was fortunate also in the season of the year, for in the summer myriads of black flies, mosquitoes, and midges, or, as the Indians call them, 'no-see-ums,' make traveling in the woods almost impossible; but now their reign was nearly over."

Staying home might be a good choice in June when clouds of blackflies and mosquitoes could be the most memorable part of an outing. Largely because of the lack of biting insects, autumn and May—during that narrow window between ice-out and the blackfly hatch—remain our favorite times for paddling the North Country. During all but the height of the blackfly season in June, however, these pests should not spoil your trip. Paddlers can often escape insects out on the water, where frequent breezes blow.

Proper clothing forms the most important line of defense. During blackfly season, wear long-sleeved, tight-knit shirts and pants with elastic cuffs, or tuck your pant legs into oversized socks. Blackflies land on your clothing and search for openings, such as at wrists, ankles, and necks. A mosquito-cloth headnet works well, but with a collared shirt, blackflies will usually find a route in. Cotton gloves can help, too.

Mosquitoes can penetrate soft clothing better than blackflies can, so choose more rugged materials for shirts and pants. Wearing two light shirts also works. Tight cuffs are not as important because mosquitoes usually fly directly to their dining table.

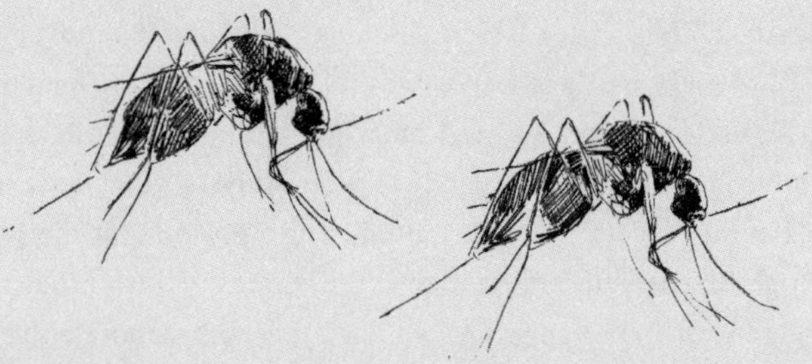

Insect repellents generally deter mosquitoes better than blackflies. DEET (N,N-diethyl-meta-toluamide) remains the chemical of choice in the North Country. Fortunately, one of our co-authors, a chemist, can actually pronounce this name. Unfortunately, he also knows enough about this chemical structure to be concerned about potential long-term toxicity to humans. Most repellents work by evaporating into the nearby air to clog insects' odor receptors, but because you have to keep slathering it on, we recommend clothing as the primary defensive strategy.

Because of the Zika virus's penetration into the United States, *Consumer Reports* released to the public results of its research on repelling *Aedes* and

Culex mosquitoes (found in the United States and Canada) in 2016. Here are the results, in hours of effectiveness, for the eight highest-rated products.

Product	Active Ingredient	Hours against Aedes	Hours against Culex	Hours against deer ticks
Sawyer Picaridin	Picaridin 20%	8	8	8.5
Ben's 30% DEET Wilderness Formula	DEET 30%	7.5	8	8.5
Repel Lemon Eucalyptus	Oil of Lemon Eucalyptus 30%	7	8	7
Repel Scented Family	DEET 15%	5	8	8.5
Natrapel 8 Hour	Picaridin 20%	8	8	6
Off! Deep Woods	DEET 25%	8	8	5
Coleman SkinSmart	IR3535	3	6	8
Avon Skin-So-Soft Bug Guard plus	Picaridin 10%	3	8	7

For information on chemical toxicity, see ewg.org/research/ewgs-guide-bug-repellents/repellent-chemicals.

Is There Anything Good about Blackflies and Mosquitoes?

In reviewing all of the problems with blackflies and mosquitoes, one wonders what might possibly be good about the little beasts. The answer lies in the role they play in aquatic ecosystems, where they provide a vital food source for a wide variety of animals. Many game fish rely on blackfly and mosquito larvae for part of their diets. One study found that blackfly larvae constitute as much as 25 percent of the brook trout diet. Even if blackfly and mosquito larvae do not provide a *direct* food source for our favorite game fish and waterfowl, chances are pretty good that they form a vital part of the food chain upon which these animals rely. If we appreciate angling for brook trout, listening to the call of the loon, or watching the stately great blue heron, we should recognize that these species might not be here without blackflies and mosquitoes.

71 | Coles Creek

Dammed-up Coles Creek offers several coves and miles of shoreline to explore. Tree diversity, especially on the eastern shore, is quite high. The marshy areas support many different wetland species, including great blue herons, kingfishers, and deer.

Location: Louisville, Waddington
Maps: *New York Atlas & Gazetteer*, Map 13: E8; USGS Chase Mills, Louisville
Area: 680 acres
Time: All day
Habitat Type: Shallow, marshy, dammed-up creek
Fish: Smallmouth bass, northern pike, walleye (see fish advisories, Appendix C)
Camping: Appendix A (54) (on-site)
Take Note: Farm fields line portions of the shore

GETTING THERE

From Ogdensburg at the junction of Route 37 and Trooper Snow Street, go 21.0 miles east on Route 37, and turn right on Coles Creek Road. Go 0.4 mile (21.4 miles) to the access on the left. (44° 53.059′ N, 75° 6.907′ W) Alternatively, continue 1.5 miles (22.9 miles) to the Coles Creek bridge access on the left. (44° 52.022′ N, 75° 5.887′ W)

From Massena at the junction of Route 37 and Main Street, go 11.8 miles west on Route 37, turn left on Coles Creek Road, and proceed as previously.

WHAT YOU'LL SEE

Coles Creek, flowing into the mighty Saint Lawrence River, has the distinction of being the northernmost body of water in this guidebook. A large earthen dam at its outlet backs up Coles Creek for several miles. Only tiny streams feed the impoundment's southern end, which should make Coles more a swamp than a flowage. Only about a mile away, Grass River drains a major portion of the northwestern Adirondacks, taking away much of the water in Coles Creek's environs. However, the magnitude of the northward-flowing water under the bridges and culverts surprised us, especially during low-water years.

The three causeways that bisect the creek have low culverts or low stone bridges, not high enough to paddle under. Carrying over the two roads and the

TRIP 71: COLES CREEK

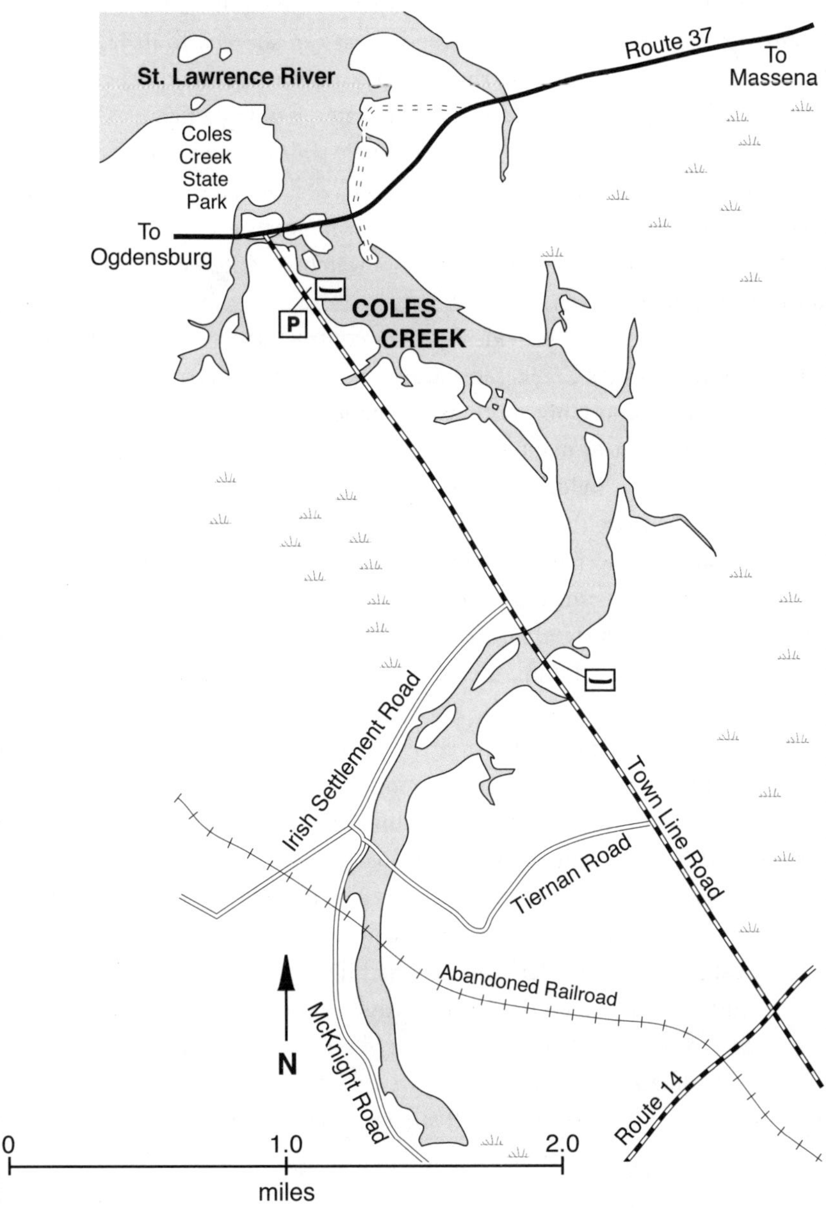

old railroad bed does not provide a challenge because the grades lie close to the water's surface. The several-mile-long waterway represents a real dichotomy: on the western shore, Canada geese and ring-billed gulls gambol in farmers' weedy fields, whereas the heavily wooded eastern shore with its jagged inlets has a much wilder feel. On one trip, a belted kingfisher guarded a cove with lacy green hemlock boughs bent low over the water, lending a primeval feeling of dark isolation. As we watched a painted turtle slide off a log into the stagnant, pea-green water, a great blue heron startled us as it bolted skyward, squawking away. We spotted these magnificent predators in nearly every cove and in many shallow, marshy locations. In two coves, we watched white-tailed deer drinking at the water's edge.

Tree-species diversity provides another contrast between the northern and southern ends of Coles Creek. Most everywhere, deciduous trees dominate. On the north, cottonwood, big-tooth aspen, paper and yellow birches, American beech, black gum, ash, maple, and basswood dot the shoreline; on the south, large conifers have made inroads into the hardwood realm. Surprisingly, tamarack seems to be the biggest tree on the south end, with fair numbers of white pine and northern white cedar. Ferns abound in the southern understory, and sumac surrounds the old railroad grade. Near the far southern shore, the water and surrounding land turn swampy, with large patches of cattail and more and more aquatic vegetation, including pondweed, yellow pondlily, bulrush, and more. Bullfrogs call from the grassy shore and from among the lily pads.

Because of the depth of most coves, paddling the complete shoreline of Coles Creek presents quite a challenge for a daylong trip. We paddled into all of the coves and around each island, finding great blue herons at every turn. As we emerged from the coves, the scene changed to common terns performing aerial acrobatics and common yellowthroats warbling in the underbrush. Loons dove for fish, and eastern wood-pewees sang in the woods. Signs of past beaver activity caused us to wonder why they had disappeared. Will another colony move in to harvest the bountiful hardwoods along the shore? Have conifers encroached on the southern end because of selective logging by beavers?

As we paddled back to the access, we noted another alien species starting its invasion: purple loosestrife. Will alien species crowd out the native species in these waters and shores? Only time will tell.

4 | WESTERN NEW YORK

This guidebook includes nineteen bodies of water in western New York. Compared with the Adirondacks just to the east, the area is very flat, so this section includes seventeen slow-flowing, mostly marshy creeks and rivers. Paddlers hoping to see lots of marshland species and diverse vegetation should get great satisfaction here. Outstanding examples include Crooked Creek, a tributary to the Saint Lawrence River; Clyde River, part of which flows through the Galen Marsh Wildlife Management Area; West River, which lies within the High Tor Wildlife Management Area; and Oak Orchard Creek, which flows through the Iroquois National Wildlife Refuge. Similar marshy creeks line the shores of Lake Ontario: the two Sandy Creeks of the Lakeview Wildlife Management Area; Deer Creek of the Deer Creek Wildlife Management Area; Sterling Valley Creek, which ends at Fair Haven Beach State Park; Mudge Creek, which feeds East Bay; and Salmon and West creeks, which flow into Braddock Bay.

Slow-flowing rivers include the Allegheny on the Pennsylvania border, the Seneca River and Erie Canal around Howland Island, Tonawanda Creek near Buffalo, and sections of the Indian and Genesee rivers. The famed Finger Lakes of western New York are mostly too large for quietwater paddling, but we do describe the two smallest: scenic, untrammeled Hemlock and Canadice lakes, which are well worth a visit; mostly, you can paddle in solitude here.

72 | Crooked Creek

Crooked Creek, true to its name, zigzags through the valley. This marshy stream harbors abundant marshland species, both plant and animal. Look for Bryozoa, a clean-water indicator, here. You will also see great blue heron, Canada goose, wood duck, common yellowthroat, and lots more. You might spot wild turkey and otter.

Location: Alexandria, Hammond
Maps: *New York Atlas & Gazetteer*, Map 25: A10; USGS Chippewa Bay, Redwood
Length: 7 miles one way
Time: All day
Habitat Type: Shallow, marshy creek
Fish: Largemouth bass, northern pike (see fish advisories, Appendix C)
Camping: Appendix A (51, 56, 58, 61, 62, 65, 69)
Take Note: Wind can make paddling treacherous on Chippewa Bay

GETTING THERE

Schermerhorn Landing Access. From Ogdensburg at the junction of Route 37 and State Street/Route 812, go 11.7 miles south on Route 37, and bear right on Route 12. Go 15.2 miles (26.9 miles) to Schermerhorn Landing on the right. (44° 24.696′ N, 75° 47.127′ W)

Route 12 Access. From Schermerhorn Landing, go 1.0 mile (27.9 miles) south on Route 12 to the access on the left, just before the bridge. (44° 24.136′ N, 75° 48.077′ W)

Route 1 Access. From Schermerhorn Landing, go 2.7 miles (29.6 miles) south on Route 12, and turn left on Scribby Road/Kring Point Road. Go 0.7

TRIP 72: CROOKED CREEK

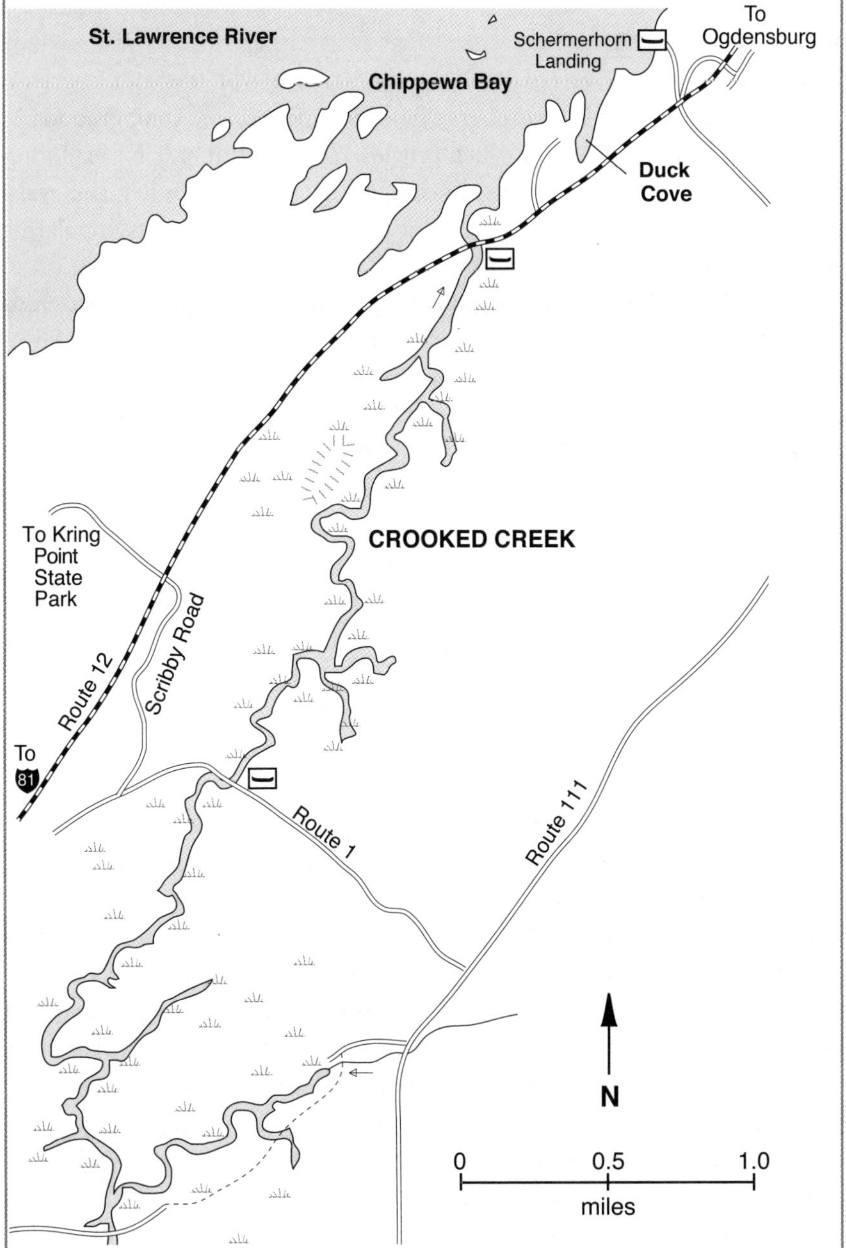

mile (30.3 miles), and turn left on Route 1. Continue 0.3 mile (30.6 miles) to the access on the left before the bridge. (44° 22.581′ N, 75° 49.150′ W)

WHAT YOU'LL SEE

Kring Point State Park, one of the first parks established on the Saint Lawrence River, dates back to 1898 and offers one of the most scenic campgrounds in the Thousand Islands region, which provides a wonderful base for exploring its streams and lakes. Half of the 108 camping sites front the water, and every site has a view of Goose Bay or the Saint Lawrence. Because of its popularity, we strongly recommend reservations.

More than 1,700 islands dot the Saint Lawrence, luring anglers from all over the East. Only seasoned paddlers should venture out on the river, however, because of truly huge wakes churned up by large pleasure craft and by commercial vessels traveling the Great Lakes. Ironsides Island—just north of Kring Point State Park and owned by The Nature Conservancy—once provided a home for the largest great blue heron rookery on the river. Dozens of treetop nests—some measuring 6 feet wide and 4 feet deep—dotted the island. The rookery peaked at more than 1,400 nests. However, heron rookeries come and go, and this one went to zero nests in the 2000s, likely the result of heron excrement killing trees, raccoon predation (a pair probably reached the island over the ice), and the large numbers of herons reducing nearby foraging success. But you will still see lots of great blue herons in the region's marshy areas.

We recommend turning your attention inland to some of the small streams and lakes. Crooked Creek, which winds its way through extensive marshland just on the other side of Route 12 from Kring Point State Park, remains one of our favorites. Three access points offer opportunities for trips of different lengths. We had two cars and did a one-way trip downstream to Schermerhorn Landing. We put in at the Route 1 bridge and paddled upstream for a little less than 3 miles, then paddled back downstream, under the Route 1 bridge, continuing down to Chippewa Bay. If you stop to explore side channels and study the plants and abundant wildlife, this leisurely trip will take most of a day.

Cattails become your constant companion, but many other plant species, both aquatic and terrestrial, crop up to keep things from getting boring. Pines appear beyond the marsh's fringe, along with large red oaks, but we focused more on the immediate vicinity. In one downstream section of the creek, tall cliffs—some rising 50 or 60 feet above the water—and massive slabs of pinkish rock add dramatic variety to an otherwise marshy paddle.

We found huge patches of Bryozoa, invertebrates in their own phylum (phyla include birds, mammals, reptiles, and so on). Bryozoa, in the genus *Pectinatella*, consist of huge, closely linked colonies of tiny individuals called zooids. The zooids have protruding hairs, or cilia, that sweep the water to snare passing microscopic protozoans, algae, and diatoms. The slimy, gelatinous colonies look somewhat like translucent pineapples. An indicator species, its welcome presence points to pollution-free water.

Besides the ubiquitous cattails, we found rafts of yellow pondlily, lots of American white waterlily, a fair amount of floating heart in the upper reaches, and frequent large patches of yellow-flowered bladderwort in the tea-colored water.

We watched a pair of red-tailed hawks circling lazily on afternoon thermals, rising skyward to get a better view of the surrounding fields. These rodent specialists have the widest range of all U.S. hawks, inhabiting every conceivable niche from desert to wet forest, sea level to mountaintop, coast to coast, and border to border. We also saw a few wild turkeys strutting in the fields.

Typical marsh species thrive here, including great blue herons, common yellowthroats, and abundant red-winged blackbirds. We very much enjoyed our lazy trip down the creek, and because of our pleasant experience, we really did not mind having to paddle the last little bit to Schermerhorn Landing out on crowded Chippewa Bay. If you plan a one-way trip ending at the landing and then get out onto the bay and find wind-whipped waves, we strongly suggest that you paddle back upstream to the Route 12 bridge and walk the 1.4 miles to Schermerhorn Landing to retrieve your second vehicle.

73 | Red Lake and Indian River

Slow-flowing Indian River and Red Lake offer a wonderful paddling opportunity through wild country with few houses and no roads. Marshy areas lead to tree-covered hillsides. Look for osprey, red-tailed hawk, great blue heron, wood duck, wild turkey, and woodland songbirds.

Location: Theresa

Maps: *New York Atlas & Gazetteer*, Map 25: B10, C10 and Map 26: B2; USGS Muskellunge Lake, Redwood

Area and Length: Red Lake, 366 acres; Indian River, 5 miles one way

Time: 5 hours

Habitat Type: Winding, slow-flowing river and shallow lake

TRIP 73: RED LAKE AND INDIAN RIVER

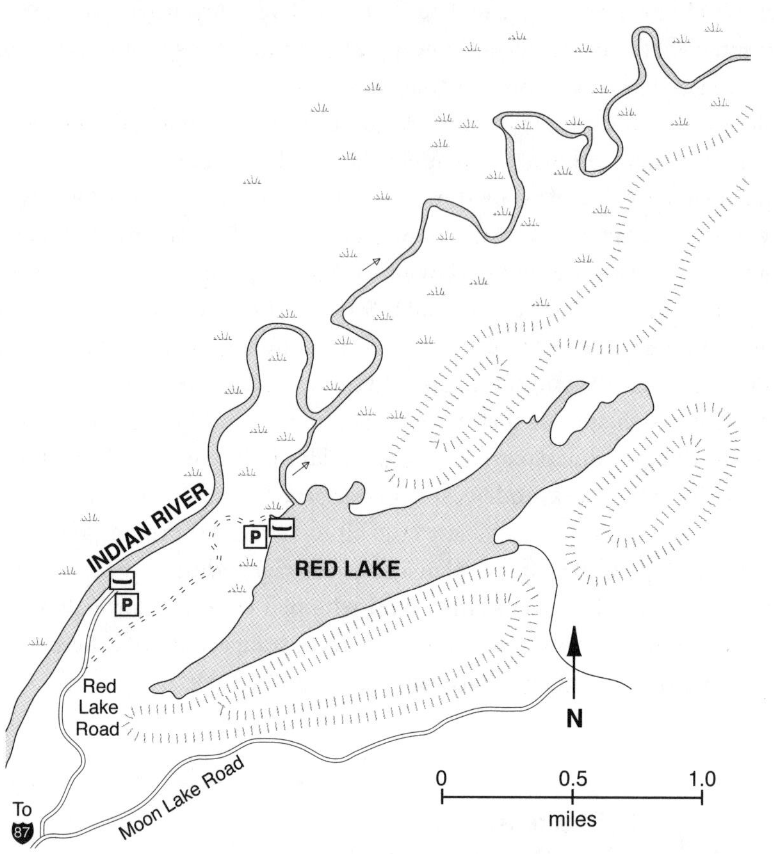

Fish: Largemouth and smallmouth bass, northern pike, walleye (see fish advisories, Appendix C; see specific advisory, health.ny.gov/environmental/outdoors/fish/health_advisories)
Camping: Appendix A (51, 56, 58, 61, 62, 65, 69)
Take Note: Stay off Indian River during high water

GETTING THERE

From I-81, Exit 49, go 4.7 miles east on Routes 411 and 26 to Theresa, and turn left on Commercial Street. Go 0.1 mile (4.8 miles), and turn left on Bridge Street, follow it for 0.2 mile (5.0 miles), and turn left on Red Lake Road. Go 3.7 miles (8.7 miles), and at the fork, bear left for 0.1 mile (8.8 miles) to Indian River (44° 15.886′ N, 75° 45.646′ W), or bear right for 1.0 mile (9.7 miles) to Red Lake. (44° 16.231′ N, 75° 44.809′ W)

WHAT YOU'LL SEE

Red Lake

When we visited, a great blue heron stood near the access where pickerelweed, bulrush, and grasses crowd the shoreline. Along much of the lake's southeastern side, extensive cliffs rise up from the water 100 feet or more. Many areas drip with polypody fern, lichens, and thick moss. On the more exposed cliff faces, look for the delicate, bell-like lavender flowers of harebell, which can establish itself in the tiniest of cracks. Scarlet cardinal flower—always a favorite—grows in rocky soil closer to the water.

On less steep banks, a diverse mix of conifers and deciduous trees—from northern white cedar to species usually found farther south, such as shagbark hickory and white oak—have taken hold. Hemlock, white pine, paper birch, basswood, white ash, silver and sugar maples, and red oak also appear. High species diversity occurs here because it represents a transition between the high elevation of the Adirondacks and the low-lying Saint Lawrence floodplain.

Just northwest of the access, water from Red Lake flows slowly through a broad, deep outlet channel, passing between a marsh and a small hill, flowing for less than a half-mile into Indian River. Thick vegetation covers the banks, but surprisingly little floating vegetation occurs in the channel.

Indian River

Flowing northeast toward Black Lake and the Saint Lawrence, the river channel meanders extensively. Minimal midsummer current makes paddling in both directions fairly easy. In spring and after heavy rainfall, water levels rise quickly, as Indian River and its tributaries drain a sizable portion of the western Adirondacks. After a steady rain, the river can rise a few feet in less than 24 hours. At high water, the river spreads out, providing access to bottomland, but current makes it more dangerous and difficult, if not impossible, to paddle in both directions.

Thick aquatic vegetation lines the waterway. Pickerelweed dominates in most areas, with patches of arrowhead mixed in. Cardinal flower and swamp milkweed grow in abundance, along with buttonbush, which sports spherical white flower clusters and sycamore-like seedpods.

Along a 5-mile stretch, we passed several beaver lodges, including a massive one with lots of cuttings. As we rounded a bend, a group of turkey vultures erupted into flight. They had been feeding on the bloated carcass of a huge snapping turtle. The vultures' broad wings wafted essence of long-dead turtle onto the river as we beat a hasty retreat from the malodor.

Crimson cardinal flower blooms along the banks of the Indian River.

We saw red-tailed hawk, osprey, kingfisher, yellow warbler, common yellowthroat, white-throated sparrow, great blue heron, eastern phoebe, eastern wood-pewee, red-winged blackbird, grackle, and ring-billed gull. Painted turtles sought a few rays of sunlight on a mostly overcast afternoon, and mussel shells littered the river's bottom and shoreline.

74 | Black River Bay

Shallow Black River Bay on Lake Ontario presents a great place to paddle, observe wildlife, and study plants—at least when it's not windy. Muskellunge Bay and the creek area by Doane Road are less susceptible to wind. You will likely see waterfowl, great blue heron, marsh wren, kingfisher, and osprey, as well as Caspian, common, and—if you're lucky—rare black terns.

Location: Brownsville, Hounsfield
Maps: *New York Atlas & Gazetteer*, Map 25: E7 and Map 33: A6, A7; USGS Dexter, Sackets Harbor
Area: 1,350 acres
Time: 4 hours to all day
Habitat Type: Shallow, marshy bay
Fish: Largemouth and smallmouth bass, northern pike (see fish advisories, Appendix C)
Camping: Appendix A (63, 67, 70)
Information: Dexter Marsh Wildlife Management Area, dec.ny.gov/outdoor/40663.html
Take Note: Wind can make paddling treacherous on the main bay

GETTING THERE

Muskellunge Creek Access. From Watertown Public Square, go 7.5 miles west on Route 3/Arsenal Street, and turn right (north) on Route 180. Go 1.5 miles (9.0 miles) to the access on the left. (43° 58.634′ N, 76° 2.910′ W)

Military Road Access. From the junction of Route 3/Arsenal Street and Route 180, go 1.2 miles (8.7 miles) north on Route 180, and turn left on Military Road. Go another 1.2 miles (9.9 miles) to the access on the right. (43° 57.960′ N, 76° 4.216′ W)

TRIP 74: BLACK RIVER BAY

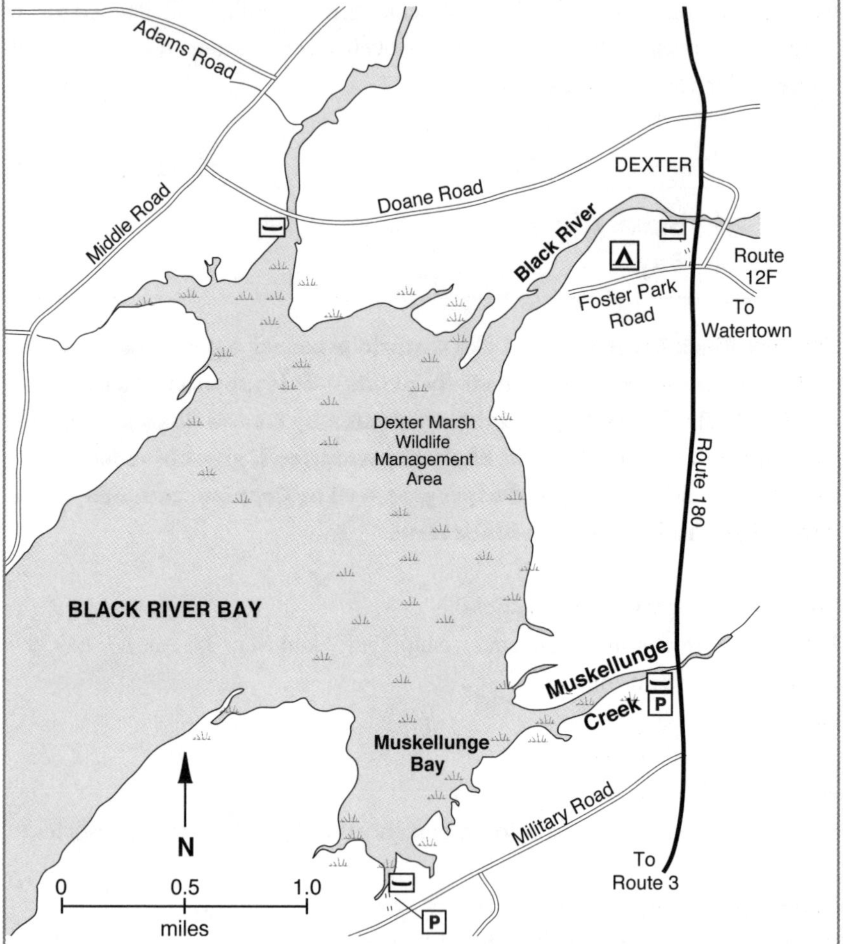

WHAT YOU'LL SEE

Shallow, marshy Dexter Marsh Wildlife Management Area protects Black River Bay from development. The northernmost wildlife management area on Lake Ontario's eastern shore, Dexter harbors many plants and animals—and few paddlers.

We launched at sunup from the private campground on Black River, paddling southwest down to the bay. After clearing the campground, we passed a few small islands with beautiful fractured rock formations and eventually emerged onto Black River Bay, with Lake Ontario in the background. We were totally unprepared for the unfolding sight. Water shimmering on the horizon made it impossible to judge distance over the glass-like surface that lay before us. Caspian terns diving for fish barely made ripples. Rarely do we confront a body of water this large under such calm conditions.

When we paddled here in July, a high-pressure cell had stalled over the eastern Great Lakes, providing crystal-clear skies and, more importantly, absolutely windless conditions. However, in summer, afternoon breezes blowing eastward off Lake Ontario can whip up formidable waves that surge unimpeded into Black River Bay, making boating treacherous. Under windy conditions, we strongly recommend sticking to more protected Muskellunge Bay.

Along Black River Bay's northern edge, a northern water snake (*Nerodia sipedon*) swam along with us for a short distance before retreating into the cattails. Huge carp periodically startled us as they thrashed in the shallow, muddy water.

Much of the Muskellunge Bay section, particularly the southern end, contains intermittent dense stands of cattail that protect wildlife (and paddlers) from wind-driven waves. Here we found a dozen great blue herons fishing the shallows and several nesting black terns. When we got too close to one of the small cattail islands, three or four black terns dive-bombed us until we retreated quite a distance.

On the bay's eastern end, cattail-covered islands give way to willow-clad shores. Here, among the trees, we listened to the eastern wood-pewee's *pee-o-wee*; the tufted titmouse's whistled *peet-er, peet-er, peet-er*; and the cardinal's *bir-dee, bir-dee, bir-dee*. Beaver had dined recently on felled willow. A crow-sized pileated woodpecker made an undulating flight over the water in front of us, alighting in a dead tree. But the real attraction remained the marsh.

We found diminutive yellow pondlily (*Nuphar microphyllum*), with leaves less than 5 inches long and flowers less than an inch across. Floating heart (*Nymphoides cordata*), an aquatic gentian with small heart-shaped leaves and little white flowers, choked the channel in protected areas. Acres of white and yellow waterlilies, plants that do not grow in water deeper than 4 feet, confirmed the bay's shallowness.

Clumps of arrowhead and yellow-flowered bladderwort, especially along Muskellunge Creek, added to the interesting plant life. We saw as many as five great blue herons fishing at once, and ducks scurried into the cattails as we approached. Spotted sandpipers bobbed along the shore, and barn swallows skimmed the water's surface for a morning drink. As we watched a cormorant trying to deal with a fish way too large to swallow, marsh wrens in the cattails serenaded us. We spent most of the morning exploring the entire shoreline of the bay's south end, a great place for quietwater paddlers to study plants and wildlife.

75 | Lakeview Wildlife Management Area: North and South Colwell Ponds, Goose Pond, Floodwood Pond, and Lakeview Pond

If you love marshes, this is the place to visit: the largest continuous wetland left along the shores of Lake Ontario. It harbors many interesting plants, including all four New York species of yellow pondlily, and tons of wildlife. You will see many bird species here, including osprey, black tern, kingfisher, common yellowthroat, yellow warbler, wood duck, and more. Also look for muskrat, otter, and deer.

Location: Ellisburg
Maps: *New York Atlas & Gazetteer*, Map 32: C5, D5; USGS Ellisburg, Henderson
Area: 3,461 acres in the wildlife management area
Time: 5 hours to all day
Habitat Type: Shallow, marshy ponds; small, wooded streams
Fish: Largemouth bass, northern pike, Chinook salmon (fall), steelhead trout (spring) (see fish advisories, Appendix C)
Camping: Appendix A (A 67, 68, 70)
Information: Lakeview Wildlife Management Area, dec.ny.gov/outdoor/41213.html
Take Note: 10 HP limit (shallow, weedy ponds make it very difficult to use motors)

GETTING THERE

Colwell Ponds Access. From I-81, Exit 37, go 0.3 mile west on Harwood Drive, and turn right on North Main Street. Go 0.1 mile (0.4 mile), and turn left on Ellisburg Street. Go 0.5 mile (0.9 mile), and turn left on Hadley Road. Continue 2.9 miles (3.8 miles), and turn right on Route 3. After 3.6 miles (7.4 miles), turn left on Montario Point Road, go 0.7 mile (8.1 miles), and turn right to the access by the tower. (43° 41.827′ N, 76° 11.635′ W)

South Sandy Creek Access. Continue 1.1 miles (8.5 miles) north on Route 3 from Montario Point Road to the access on the left. (43° 42.610′ N, 76° 10.925′ W)

Lakeview Pond Access. Continue 3.3 miles (11.8 miles) north on Route 3 from South Sandy Creek, and turn left on Pierrepont Place. Go 0.5 mile (12.3 miles) to the access. (43° 45.119′ N, 76° 12.166′ W)

TRIP 75: LAKEVIEW WILDLIFE MANAGEMENT AREA

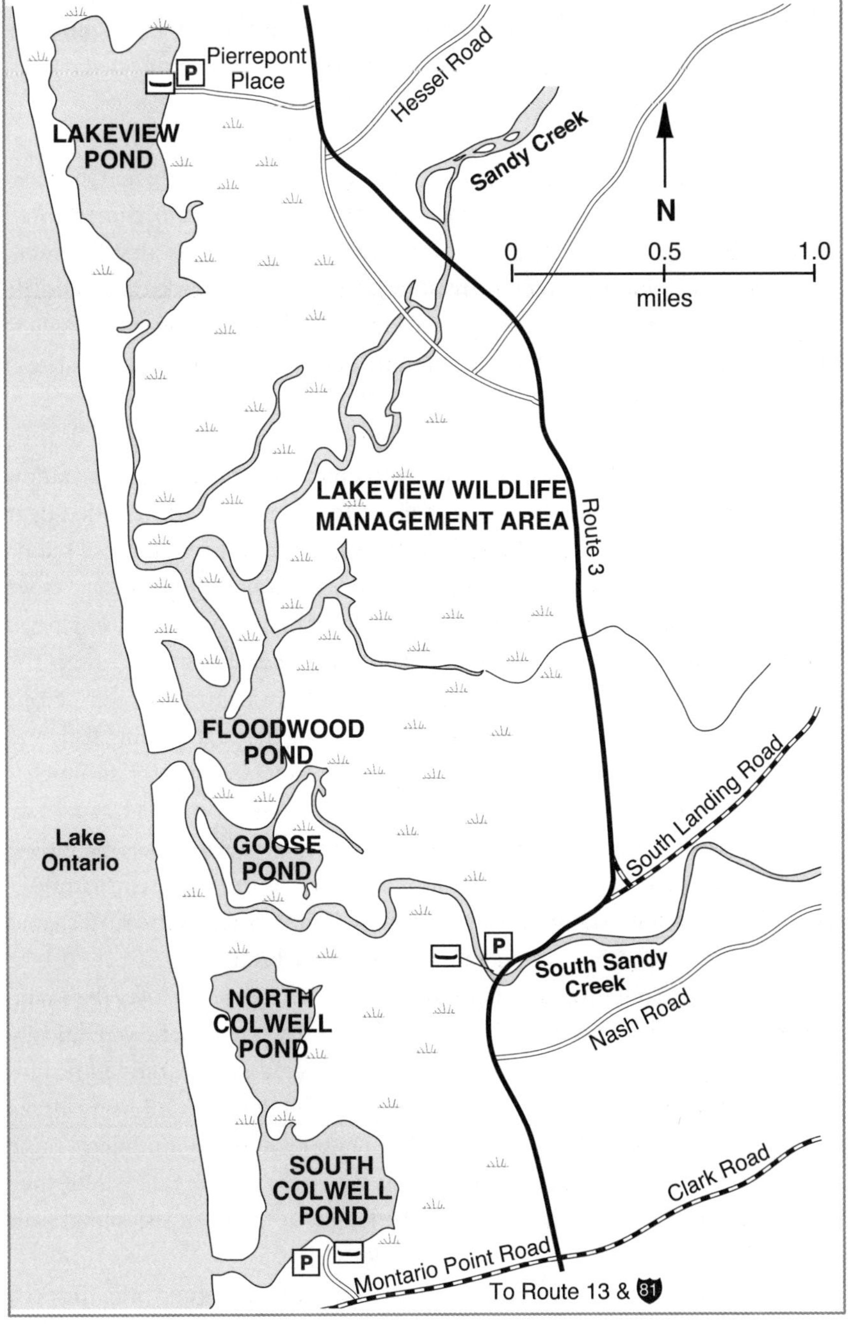

WHAT YOU'LL SEE

Paddlers may enter the Lakeview Wildlife Management Area on the south, southeast, or north. The southern entrance provides access to only South and North Colwell ponds. The other two—one on South Sandy Creek and the other on Lakeview Pond—provide access to a series of interconnected creeks, sloughs, and ponds.

On your way to South Colwell Pond off Montario Point Road, stop at the lookout tower on the right, and enjoy the view out over the marsh. Most of Lake Ontario's eastern shore harbors wetlands. Although shortsighted humans drained some of these wetlands for agriculture and development, large pockets remain protected by a series of six state parks and wildlife management areas. The expanse you see from the lookout tower—Lakeview Wildlife Management Area—represents the most extensive of these remaining wetlands.

We paddled North and South Colwell ponds in mid-June, a perfect time for wildlife viewing. Trees cover the barrier dunes, and narrow-leaved cattails ring the ponds, providing protected habitat for numerous white-tailed deer and multihued wood ducks. Because little water flows through these scenic ponds, later in the year they become choked with aquatic vegetation. As we paddled the shoreline in early morning, flocks of male wood ducks exploded into the air with their high-pitched cries, and deer crashed through the cattails after we interrupted their morning drink. In contrast, green herons sat patiently on low perches over the water, waiting to spear passing fish, and great blue herons stood stock-still out in the water, waiting for somewhat larger passing fish.

Even in early summer, aquatic plants crowded the water's surface, including an extensive patch of water crowfoot—a member of the buttercup family—with small white flowers projecting just an inch or two above the surface and threadlike leaves evenly spaced along the submerged stalks.

As we paddled out through a light morning mist hanging low over the water, a huge caddis fly hatch was on. Millions of tiny all-white flies flew erratically over the surface in a primordial mating ritual. As the sun rose, the caddis flies headed for the filtered light making its way through tall trees. Caddis fly larvae build underwater structures of small twigs or stones and feed on microscopic underwater plants and animals that drift by. When they hatch into adults, they can be identified by the wings running the length of their bodies, folded over their backs like tents.

As we watched black terns dart about catching caddis flies and other insects, we also noticed the pond's surface change from glass-smooth to wind-rippled.

As the sun heats the land, warm air rises. To replace the rising mass, cooler replacement air drifts in from Lake Ontario, quietly at first, but building in strength throughout the morning and early afternoon. Toward evening, as the sun sets, the wind dies again and drifts toward calm.

After about an hour, we somewhat reluctantly left the terns and headed to South Sandy Creek. With two cars, paddlers could travel from the north end of Lakeview Pond down through Floodwood and Goose Ponds and up South Sandy Creek to the access. When winds are out of the south, you might want to paddle this route in the opposite direction. With winds off Lake Ontario—the usual state of affairs—coastal dunes provide some protection from the wind, and travel direction becomes less important.

If you desire solitude, we recommend putting in at South Sandy Creek and paddling downstream into Goose Pond. Large willows and huge box elders crowd the water; several deadfalls—called "structure" by anglers—provide habitat for fish and turtles. We had no problem paddling around them. We were, however, surprised to find a muskrat sitting out on a deadfall, watching us as we glided by.

Resist the temptation to bypass Goose Pond, a wild, wonderful place to study aquatic plants and ducks in solitude. Yellow pondlily mats the surface, interrupted by clumps of very narrow-leaved arrowhead and patches of

The lookout tower provides a view of Lake Ontario and the flat coastal plain of the Lakeview Wildlife Management Area.

pickerelweed. Cattails, providing cover for hidden marsh wrens singing their melodious songs, encircle the pond. We watched black terns skim the water's surface while ducks fed near the edges and deer cautiously crept out for a drink.

Floodwood Pond has more open water than Goose Pond but still boasts its share of aquatic plants. As you paddle north out of Floodwood, watch carefully for a narrow channel heading west that leads to Lakeview Pond. Yellow pondlilies cover this long, straight channel, providing outstanding habitat for pike, bass, turtles, and frogs.

We spent some time here trying to sort out the four resident species of *Nuphar*, or yellow pondlily. We distinguished the two larger-flowered (1.5 to 2.5 inches wide), larger-leaved (8 to 15 inches long) species by how the leaf lobes grow from the submerged stalks. In *Nuphar advena*, the lobes diverge at about a 45-degree angle, while the lobes on *N. variegata* cross each other. The third species, *N. microphyllum*, as its name suggests, has small leaves (less than 5 inches long) and tiny flowers (less than an inch wide). The fourth species, *N. rubrodiscum*, the most difficult to identify, has leaves 5 to 8 inches long, flowers 1 to 1.5 inches wide, stigma with more than 10 rays (fewer than 10 in *N. microphyllum*), and leaf notch about half the midrib length (two-thirds in *N. microphyllum*). In practice, the last two species gave us fits, perhaps because *N. rubrodiscum* may be a hybrid of *N. microphyllum* and another *Nuphar* species.

Returning from Lakeview Pond, you could turn left (northeast) onto Sandy Creek and travel to North Landing to the string of camps and houses on the island where the creek divides. Given the huge expanse of wetland wilderness waiting for exploration, we would skip the populated area of Sandy Creek. If you do paddle up Sandy Creek, on the way back, watch for the relatively wide human-made connector that leads into the top of Floodwood Pond. When you get to the pilings at the end of the connector, a left turn (northeast) takes you up into the far reaches of the marsh, whereas a right turn (south-southwest) takes you back down toward Goose Pond.

76 | Deer Creek Marsh

Because relatively few people paddle here, the wildlife remains somewhat unwary. You'll likely see waterfowl, great blue heron, snapping turtle, beaver, muskrat, and deer, along with a large variety of aquatic vegetation.

Location: Richland
Maps: *New York Atlas & Gazetteer*, Map 32: E5 and Map 46: A5; USGS Pulaski
Area and Length: 1,771 acres in the wildlife management area; Deer Creek, 2.5 miles one way
Time: 3 hours
Habitat Type: Shallow, slow-flowing creek
Fish: Largemouth and smallmouth bass, northern pike (see fish advisories, Appendix C)
Camping: Appendix A (13, 68)
Information: Deer Creek Marsh Wildlife Management Area, dec.ny.gov/outdoor/68686.html
Take Note: No motors

GETTING THERE

From Pulaski at the junction of Route 5/Lake Street and Jefferson Street, head 3.1 miles west on Route 5, and turn right on Route 3. Go 1.4 miles (4.5 miles) to the access on the left. Hike 120 yards down to the water. (43° 35.387′ N, 76° 10.329′ W)

WHAT YOU'LL SEE

Deer Creek meanders through one of the extensive marshes that line the shores of eastern Lake Ontario. Fortunately, many of these marshes enjoy protection from development by inclusion in six state parks or wildlife management areas. Although the creek affords a view of only a tiny portion of Deer Creek Wildlife Management Area, we found that the accessible property abounds with wildlife. True to the creek's name, a deer drank from the water as we paddled along; upon spotting us, it bounded off through the thick cattails, flashing its white tail at us in annoyance.

TRIP 76: DEER CREEK MARSH

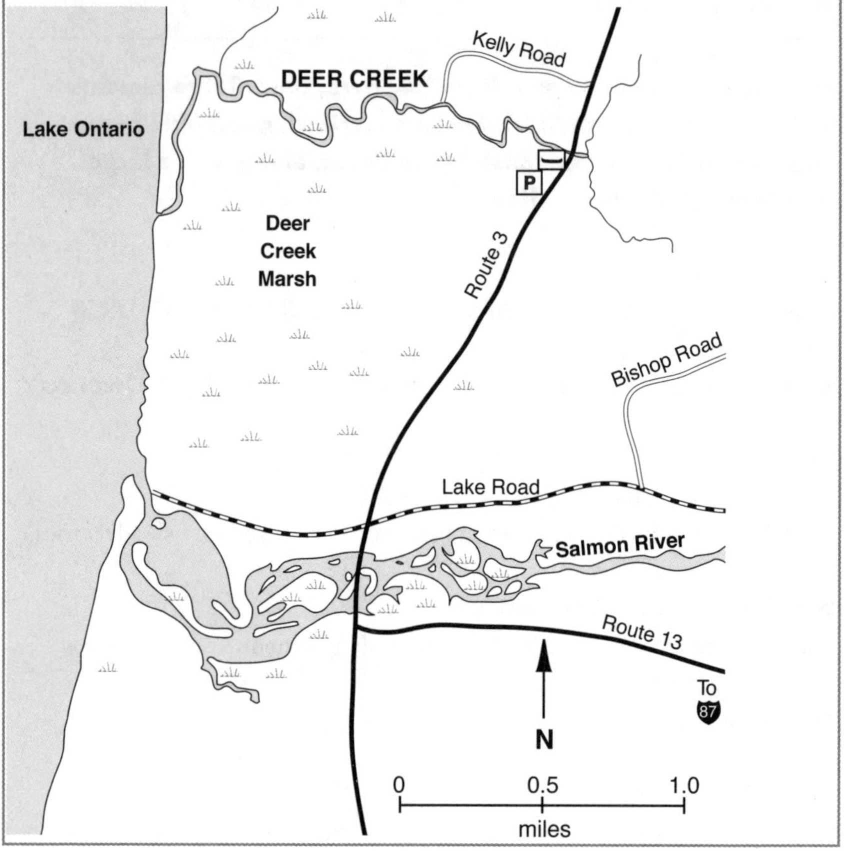

Because Deer Creek remains unobtrusive—sometimes with no outlet to the lake—not many people boat here, compared with the heavy fishing and recreational use of Salmon River, just to the south. Thus, wildlife has not become nocturnal. When we paddled here in June, we saw at least a dozen muskrats harvesting grass in the late-afternoon sun; one sat out in plain view and watched us with a wary eye as we paddled by. On our return trip, we surprised a beaver cutting alder branches along the shore. After staring at us for a few moments, it slid into the water as we glided by. Apparently deciding that we did not belong in its environs, it whacked the water vigorously with its tail, sending showers into the air in front of us.

Numerous female snapping turtles—some certainly weighing 25 or 30 pounds—had climbed out onto the soft banks to lay eggs. As we rounded a bend, we spotted one excavating a nest near the top of a huge beaver lodge.

Although we tried not to disturb her, she spotted us and, amazingly, simply let go and rolled like a rock, tumbling snout over tail down the side of the lodge, ending with a large splash in the water.

Snapping turtles inhabit freshwater marshes and streams from southern Canada to the Gulf Coast and from the Atlantic to the Rockies. They usually climb out on land only to lay eggs; rarely do they bask like other turtles. If you have confronted a big snapper on land—they can reach 60 pounds—you probably know they act aggressively and will snap at anything nearby with a powerful bite that can easily sever fingers. Surprisingly, they remain docile in water; if stepped on, they just retract their heads into their shells. Indeed, some people hunt them by walking barefoot in muddy areas, feeling with their toes for the carapace's saw-toothed rear edge, and then yanking the turtle out of the water by its long tail. Having no firsthand knowledge of this technique, we are not advocating it and should not be held responsible for any mishaps! (For more on snapping turtles, see "Snapping Turtle: Hidden Dweller of the Pond," on page 43.)

We also saw great blue herons patiently stalking the shallows. At one point, we observed three of these majestic birds in the air at once. A veery called from the woods, and a rufous-sided towhee piped up from the brush. Marsh wrens, occasionally popping into sight, sang melodies from the reeds, and a female mallard ushered her brood into the protection of the surrounding marsh. Red-winged blackbirds, by all odds the most common marsh bird, dangled from cattail stems as we slipped by.

Down by Lake Ontario, spotted sandpipers ran along the tall barrier dunes; a colony of bank swallows had carved nest cavities into the steeper sides of the dunes. Invading cottonwoods struggled to hold the dunes together, warding off erosion caused by rain and the harsh winter winds from the lake. The creek's "outlet" turned out to be an exposed sandbar—littered with the tiny shells of dead invasive zebra mussels. These bars build up because winds from the west blow on most days across Lake Ontario's shallow end, carrying along sand and the rest of the lake bottom to deposit along shore, choking off channels and forming dunes. New channels get cut both by large storms off the lake and by inland runoff after major rains. We no longer wondered why no current flowed on Deer Creek.

The creek itself presents a study in contrasts. Alternately flowing by alders and oaks, through narrow then wide channels, past cattail swamps and coastal sand dunes, it provides a rich habitat diversity for plants, the basis of the food chain. Besides alder and white oak, we saw jewelweed with its delicate leaves, mighty hemlocks, clumps of yellow iris, and a huge assortment of aquatic

A sandbar temporarily keeps Deer Creek from flowing into Lake Ontario. Occasional storms alternately open and close access to the lake.

vegetation. This and other wildlife management areas and lakeshore parks in western New York contain the largest variety of waterlilies in the United States outside of Florida, including two subspecies with white flowers and four species with yellow flowers.

Instead of paddling directly back to the access, we continued upstream, passing under the Route 3 bridge. As we did, a raft of nesting barn swallows exploded out from under the bridge. We could continue only a little way upstream, out into farm country, before the creek became impassable, but we did see a couple of broods of Canada geese and wood ducks above the bridge. As we paddled back to the access, the waning sun reflected on the placid water, and we reflected on the incredible amount of wildlife that we had seen in this biologically rich area.

77 | Sterling Valley Creek/ The Pond

Usually, you will have this wildlife paradise to yourself, although you might encounter the occasional personal watercraft or motorboat. We recommend paddling in spring or fall to avoid having to navigate through mats of aquatic vegetation. You should see great blue heron, waterfowl, beaver, muskrat, and deer.

Location: Sterling
Maps: *New York Atlas & Gazetteer*, Map 45: C9, C10; USGS Fair Haven
Length: 7 miles one way
Time: 5 hours
Habitat Type: Shallow, marshy streams
Fish: Largemouth bass, northern pike (see fish advisories, Appendix C)
Camping: Appendix A (17) (on-site)
Information: Fair Haven Beach State Park, parks.ny.gov/parks/12
Take Note: Motors allowed

GETTING THERE

Farden Road Access. From Oswego at the junction of Route 104/West Seneca Street and Washington Boulevard, go 4.2 miles west on Route 104, and stay straight on Route 104A where Route 104 goes left. Go 3.5 miles (7.7 miles), and bear right on Old State Road/Route 122. Go 0.1 mile (7.8 miles), and jog right on McFarland Road. Follow it for 1.4 miles (9.2 miles), and curve left on Farden Road. Go 0.1 mile (9.3 miles) to the canoe access on the left. (43° 22.011′ N, 76° 39.002′ W)

Fair Haven Beach State Park Access (fee). Proceed as above to the junction of Route 104A and Old State Road. Continue 5.3 miles (13.0 miles) on Old State Road, and turn right on State Park Road. Go 1.8 miles (14.8 miles) to the access on the right. (43° 20.578′ N, 76° 41.853′ W)

WHAT YOU'LL SEE

Sterling Valley Creek drains the hills east and south of Fair Haven Beach State Park. The tributaries flow together into Sterling Valley near the end of their journey to Lake Ontario, spilling out over an extensive marsh. This marsh—and many like it along Lake Ontario's broad plain—provides wonderful habitat for fish and waterfowl. Although the waterfowl back in the tules try to escape

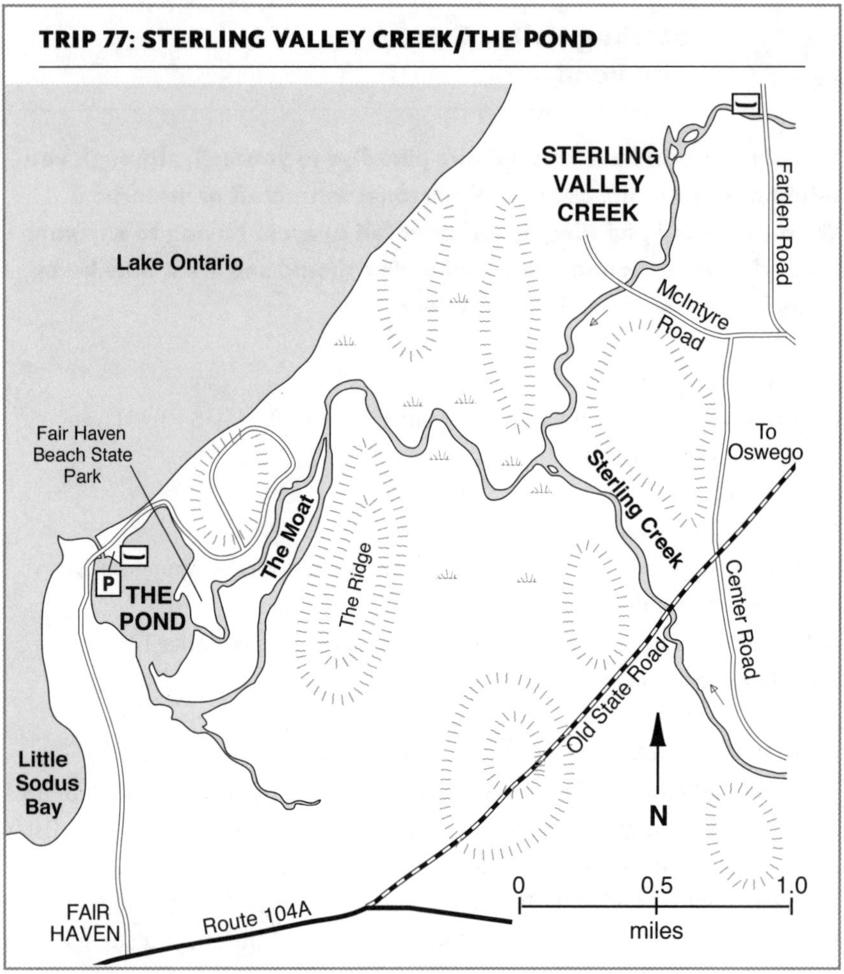

human notice, particularly the beautiful wood duck and ring-necked duck, those inhabiting The Pond have grown quite used to human presence. Signs suggest that feeding the abundant Canada geese and mallards will cost you more than the price of the food.

When we visited, several broods of mallard and Canada goose munched away on the abundant vegetation. Out in the middle of The Pond, a common moorhen grazed on fanwort floating in the surface film. The moorhen resembles its relative the American coot, except that it has a red bill, whereas the coot has a white one. Members of the rail family, they both swim and graze on aquatic plants, just like ducks. Yellow pondlily spread out in great mats, and duckweed—one of the smallest of all flowering plants—had started to fill in any available open water. By summer's end, paddling here can be a challenge.

The Moat, an impenetrable swamp filled with downed trees and duckweed, provides abundant habitat for numerous wood ducks. As you paddle up Sterling Valley Creek, an island ringed with cattails separates The Moat from the creek. We suggest that you paddle back through one of the several cuts through the island—particularly on the northern end—to the edge of The Moat. Here we watched wood ducks feeding on aquatic vegetation and turtles basking on logs.

Back on Sterling Valley Creek, we saw many ring-necked ducks and common mergansers. Barn swallows swooped over the water's surface, alternately catching insects on the wing and dipping for a drink. Red-winged blackbirds sang from the cattails, their weight bending the slender stalks, and kingbirds darted out from streamside perches to catch some of the all-too-abundant insect life.

Along the creek, ramshackle cabins with boat docks askew lined the banks for a short way on the right. After clearing these, we paddled through an idyllic swamp to a fork where Sterling Creek veers right into farm country and becomes impassable as it nears Old State Road. Sterling Valley Creek continues several miles through the valley.

As we studied a beaver lodge with fresh cuttings and watched muskrats feeding on grasses, two personal watercraft roared up this narrow creek. They create awful noise, leave a huge wake, and drive wildlife to cover. We should ban

A delicate, iridescent green damselfly folds its wings vertically over its back, in contrast with dragonflies, which hold their wings out to the side.

them from streams and ponds, as has been done in other states. If they want to roar around Lake Ontario, fine, but they have no business on small waterways, such as Sterling Valley Creek.

Paddling back to the access as the sun set, passing huge willows, red oaks, paper birches, and hemlocks, we wondered about the fate of this wildlife paradise. Disruptive recreation should be banned in habitats such as this.

78 | East Bay

You will usually paddle alone among the cattails on the small, marshy creeks, although you may encounter motors out on the bay. The creeks are shallow but harbor a lot of wildlife, including Canada goose, wood duck, muskrat, and beaver.

Location: Huron
Maps: *New York Atlas & Gazetteer*, Map 45: D7; USGS East Bay
Area and Length: 290 acres; 6 miles one way on creeks
Time: 4 hours
Habitat Type: Shallow, marshy creeks
Fish: Largemouth bass, northern pike (see fish advisories, Appendix C)
Camping: Appendix A (17)
Take Note: Novice paddlers should avoid Lake Ontario

GETTING THERE

From the junction of Main Street/Route 143 and Lake Avenue in Wolcott, go 1.0 mile west on Route 143, and turn right, then left on Route 155/Lummisville Road. Go 3.9 miles (4.9 miles), and turn right on East Bay Road. Go 2.2 miles (7.1 miles) to the access on the right. (43° 16.600′ N, 76° 54.361′ W)

Another access is on nearby Slaght Road. (43° 16.374′ N, 76° 54.145′ W)

WHAT YOU'LL SEE

You will see many animals—including great blue heron, marsh wren, wood duck, kingfisher, Canada goose, beaver, muskrat, and painted turtle—in East Bay's long, winding inlet channels. For a birder, botanist, or photographer, the bay's marshland provides tremendous opportunity for exploration.

TRIP 78: EAST BAY

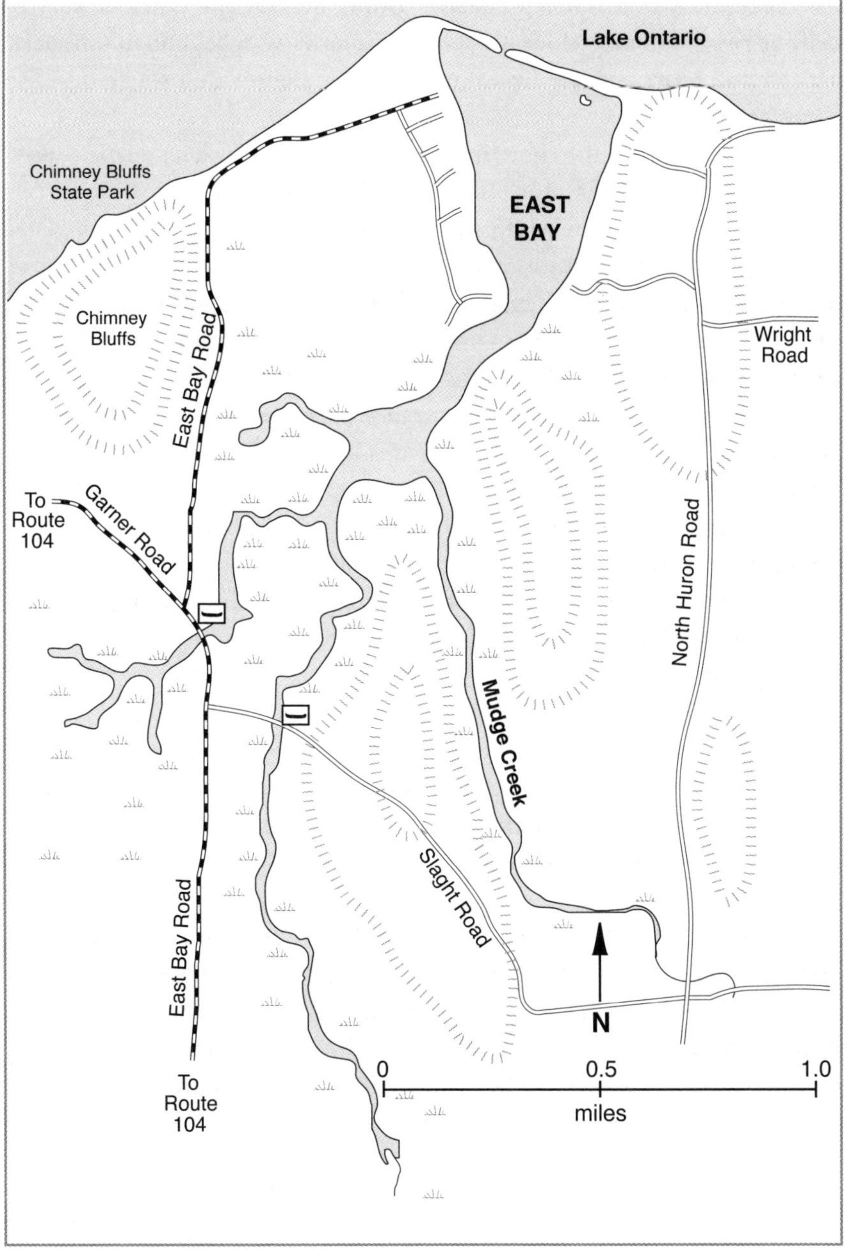

Several slow-flowing inlet creeks meander through extensive cattail marshes. From the East Bay Road access, paddle toward the main bay and then take the arm to the left (west). Visiting here in late June, we spotted delicate rose pogonia orchids hidden among ferns on sphagnum hummocks. This orchid bears a single flower on a slender stem with a single oval leaf about halfway up.

Cattails dominate the shoreline and waterlilies the water's surface. Both yellow pondlily and the more common tuberous waterlily grow here. Two subspecies of American white waterlily occur in this region: *Nymphaea odorata* subspecies *odorata* and *Nymphaea odorata* subspecies *tuberosa*. Although guidebooks list them separately, taxonomists have recently lumped them into one species. *Tuberosa* pads have green undersides and the flowers have green sepals, and both are often quite large; the usually smaller *odorata* pads have purple-tinged undersides and sepals. East Bay had some of the biggest *tuberosa* we have seen, with leaves as wide as 17 inches across and stems a half-inch thick.

Interestingly, after blooming, the flower gets pulled underwater by a coiling action of the stem, which protects the seed head and permits the seeds to ripen over a period of three or four weeks. After ripening, the seed head, or aril, breaks free and floats to the surface, where it gradually decomposes and releases its seeds to the pond bottom.

Here, you will also see arrowhead, pickerelweed, nettle, alder, blue flag, morning glory, swamp loosestrife—a native cousin of the pesky invasive purple loosestrife that has taken over wetlands throughout the eastern United States—duckweed, fanwort, and bladderwort. Where the land rises from the water, deciduous trees dominate: red oak, basswood, beech, sassafras, red maple, and yellow birch, to mention a few.

We saw the most birdlife in Mudge Creek, including several dozen wood ducks. Usually you see them flying away far ahead, because they spook very easily, but by paddling quietly, you can sometimes get quite close. The wood duck now abounds in North American marshes, after nearly suffering extermination at the turn of the century, saved by the Migratory Waterfowl Act, which protects migrating birds except during carefully timed waterfowl hunting seasons. The wood duck got a further boost beginning in 1940 with the construction of nesting boxes—a practice begun in Massachusetts after most dead trees used for nesting got knocked down by a 1938 hurricane.

As we paddled up Mudge Creek, an armada of about 75 adult and immature Canada geese surprised us around a bend. Upon spotting us, they began bobbing their heads in concern, a comical spectacle that had the desired effect.

After watching the geese for about 10 minutes, we turned around and left them in peace.

We also saw huge carp, surface feeding amid the waterlilies, humped backs extending out of the water an inch or more. We drifted over almost on top of one particularly large individual—and got a great look. It finally noticed us and took off, its wake imparting a noticeable rock to our boat.

We saw the most beaver activity in the inlet creek extending farthest south, upstream from the Slaght Road access. Late in the day, we spotted four beaver and several lodges.

East Bay's northern end suffers from development, and you may encounter water-skiers and personal watercraft. When we visited, we paddled through the breachway onto Lake Ontario, but two excavators—one antique quietly rusting in the shade of a willow—provided evidence that the breachway may close occasionally. On a calm day, paddling out onto Ontario and around the point to the west offers a real treat for experienced paddlers.

Chimney Bluffs, about a mile down the shoreline from the breachway, contains a remarkable geologic feature that definitely rates a visit—either by water in very calm conditions or by East Bay Road. Dramatic, 150-foot-tall, eroding reddish sandstone spires look more like they belong in Utah or Arizona. Some knife-edge ridges and spires run so thin you wonder how they still stand. You can walk or paddle the shore along Chimney Bluffs or explore above by trails.

On our paddles in New York, we often see female mergansers herding their broods.

79 | Seneca River (Howland Island)

This section of the Seneca River circles Howland Island, part of the 50,000-acre Montezuma Wetlands Complex. Abundant wildlife will accompany you here: osprey, numerous waterfowl species, great blue heron, kingfisher, muskrat, beaver, and woodland songbirds. Many bald eagles patrol the skies.

Location: Conquest
Maps: *New York Atlas & Gazetteer*, Map 59: A9, A10, B9, B10; USGS Montezuma
Area and Length: 7,500 acres in Northern Montezuma Wildlife Management Area; 10-mile loop
Time: 5 hours
Habitat Type: Shallow, slow-flowing river
Fish: Largemouth and smallmouth bass, northern pike (see fish advisories, Appendix C; see specific advisory, health.ny.gov/environmental/outdoors/fish/health_advisories)
Camping: Appendix A (16)
Information: Northern Montezuma Wildlife Management Area, dec.ny.gov/outdoor/31112.html; Montezuma National Wildlife Refuge, fws.gov/refuge/montezuma
Take Note: Shallow water in drought years; avoid during waterfowl hunting season

GETTING THERE

Haiti Island Access. From the junction of Route 38/Canal Street and Rochester Street in Port Byron, go 3.0 miles north on Route 38 to the access on the left. (43° 4.711′ N, 76° 38.697′ W)

Carncross Road Access. From the Haiti Island access, continue 1.4 miles north on Route 38, and turn left on Route 23/Spring Lake Road. Go 4.0 miles (5.4 miles), and turn left on Savannah Spring Lake Road/Town Line Road. Go 1.1 miles (6.5 miles), and bear right on 39 Road. Go 0.4 mile (6.9 miles), and turn left back onto Savannah Spring Lake Road. Follow this road for 2.1 miles (9.0 miles), and turn left on Carncross Road. Go 0.7 mile (9.7 miles) to the access on the left, just before the bridge. (43° 4.702′ N, 76° 42.236′ W)

TRIP 79: SENECA RIVER (HOWLAND ISLAND)

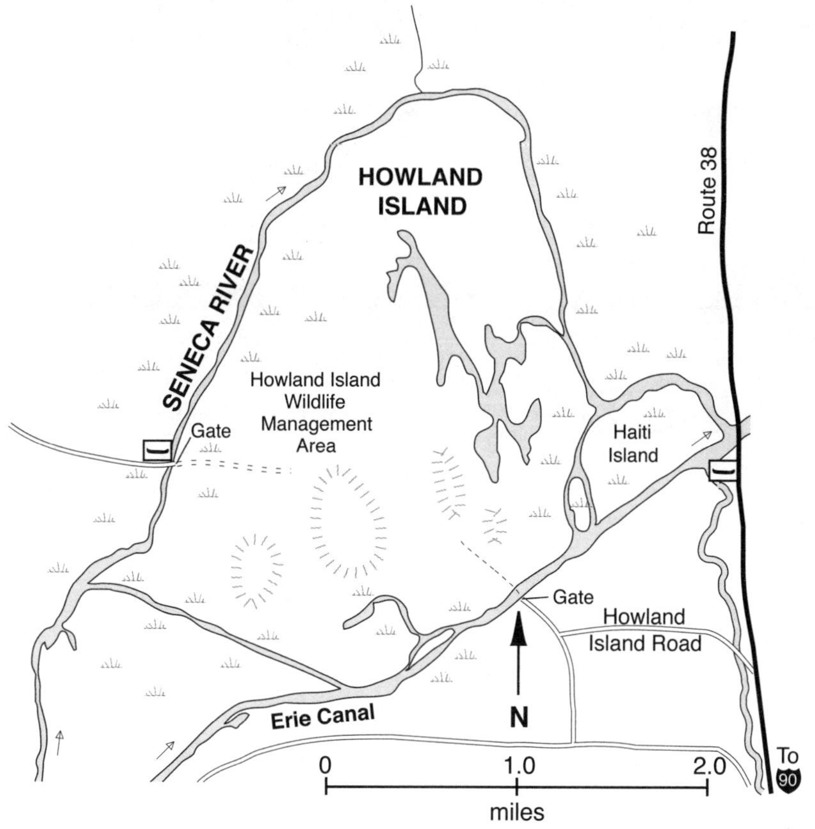

WHAT YOU'LL SEE

The Erie Canal takes a shortcut across a deep Seneca River bend, neatly enclosing the Howland Island Wildlife Management Area and providing a wonderful 10-mile loop trip. Although you may encounter a few motorboats on the canal, most stay off the Seneca. Portions of the river, particularly the long stretch that heads southwest to northeast, suffer from siltation. When we paddled here in a drought year, we hit bottom with every paddle stroke for a few miles. In wetter years, the higher water level should provide sufficient depth. In summer, you may also encounter large mats of duckweed or invasive European water chestnut.

Under calm conditions, toss a coin to choose your travel direction, but if the wind blows from the west or northwest, we suggest traveling counterclockwise. The western half of the loop, in contrast with the heavily wooded eastern half,

Canada geese abound at Howland Island Wildlife Management Area.

has low banks and few trees to block the wind. We tried to paddle clockwise into a stiff northwest wind and regretted that choice.

Although we thought that the day would bring mostly a study of plants, given that we started late in the morning, when most birds and mammals rest, instead it brought us special looks at two monarchs: the great blue heron, monarch of the marsh, and the bald eagle, monarch of the skies.

Ducks and geese abound in this marshy paradise, but rarely have we seen as many stately great blue herons. Although we did not keep count, we must have seen more than a dozen, standing knee-deep in water, patiently waiting to harpoon passing fish. If this were not sufficient inducement to paddle here, we also spotted two bald eagles. The first one—a mature adult with white head and tail—soared effortlessly on huge, broad wings.

The second bird, judging from the white flecking on the underside, must have been a second- or third-year bird. First-year birds remain almost completely brown, but older birds turn progressively whiter on the head and tail, reaching full adult plumage in four to five years. This bird, soaring ever higher, seemed totally oblivious to the raucous harassment from several crows trying to drive it from their territory. The attacking crows seemed sparrow-sized compared with the massive eagle.

Forty years ago, such a sight almost never occurred. DDT—introduced in the 1940s to control mosquitoes and other pests—and its breakdown products accumulated in the environment and caused reproductive failure in eagles, osprey, and peregrine falcons. The eagle has traveled a long road to recovery in New York, from no successful hatchings for many years before 1976 to producing only three young in 1987, to fledging 30 birds from 19 nests in 1995, 112 birds from 92 nests in 2005, and 244 birds from 173 nests in 2010. In 2017, there were 323 nests. In 2019, there were six active nests in Montezuma National Wildlife Refuge alone. Because of the amazing success in New York and elsewhere, the U.S. Fish and Wildlife Service removed the nation's symbol from the Endangered Species List and placed it on the list of threatened species—a good start.

Despite the bald eagle success, shortsighted economic interests continue to press for weakening of the Endangered Species Act. We believe that most people would much rather see an eagle doing aerial battle with crows, a peregrine falcon stooping on a pigeon, and a California condor floating with the clouds than see some favored business get the green light to destroy the preferred habitat of an endangered species for short-term economic gain for a few individuals. We all pay for such largesse by living in an altered environment very much less beautiful, interesting, and wild. Those who enjoy the outdoors—be they quietwater paddlers, hikers, sportsmen, or sportswomen—should make their voices heard: a strong Endangered Species Act will help preserve the environment for future generations.

Lots more awaits you on your paddle around Howland Island. In addition to beaver activity, we saw a groundhog—eating leaves in a tree! Admittedly, the tree trunk had bent to a low angle, but this nonetheless raises questions about the name "groundhog."

We never tired of paddling through huge patches of American white waterlily on the north side, nor of the chattering call of kingfishers as they fled before us. Great crested flycatchers darted off their streamside perches to snatch insects that fluttered on the breeze, and dozens of wood ducks provided dramatic sparkles of color. If you hear what sounds like a robin calling from the higher foliage, take a close look. It easily could be a beautiful rose-breasted grosbeak; we saw several along the way. We are fortunate that we can paddle such a wonderful wildlife area.

80 | Clyde River

Woods border one side of the slow-flowing Clyde River, while fields border much of the rest, except for the northern section. Because downed timber and aquatic vegetation can impede your progress, we recommend paddling at times of high water. You will see waterfowl, great blue heron, kingbird, oriole, and other woodland birds.

Location: Galen
Maps: *New York Atlas & Gazetteer*, Map 59: B6, B7; USGS Lyons
Length: 10.5 miles one way
Time: 5 hours
Habitat Type: Small, shallow stream
Fish: Largemouth and smallmouth bass, northern pike (see fish advisories, Appendix C)
Camping: Appendix A (16)
Take Note: Snags and aquatic vegetation make for slow going.

GETTING THERE

From I-90, Exit 41, head 2.9 miles north on Route 414, and turn left on Strang Road. Go 2.0 miles (4.9 miles), and turn left on Turnpike Road. Go 2.0 miles (6.9 miles), and turn right on River Road. Follow it for 1.7 miles (8.6 miles) to the first of several accesses. (43° 2.783′ N, 76° 55.222′ W) The best access is the last one (11.1 miles). (43° 4.415′ N, 76° 54.532′ W)

WHAT YOU'LL SEE

Forgotten by time, the Clyde River gave up much of its water and its character to the Erie Canal. Portions of it still run along with the canal. We do not cover those sections here because they include channelized water and too much boat traffic. Instead, we focus on the headwaters of the Clyde, if they can be called such. With almost no flow, the river collects snags and mountains of aquatic vegetation as summer wears on. Still, something primeval beckons one to paddle the Clyde.

One shore parallels River Road, and the other shore marks the beginning of deep, dark, brushy forests with towering trees and hanging vines. Fields and occasional cottages line the eastern shore, making the western shore vastly more

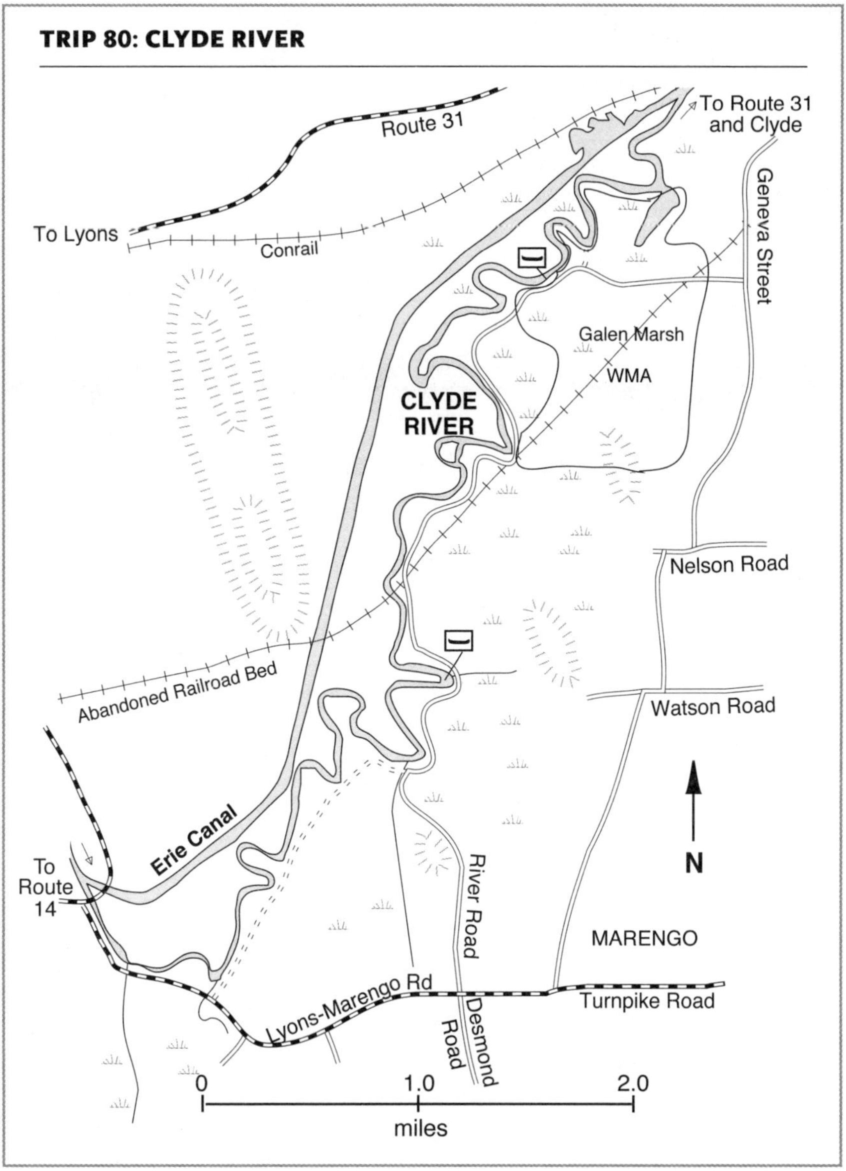

interesting. Paddling the Clyde up and back, we found ourselves clinging to the western shore, except where drowned logs dictated detouring to the other side.

Vultures circled lazily overhead as great blue herons fished the productive waters. From the northern access, we paddled about 5 miles upstream and back down without seeing any other fishers besides birds and turtles; and the turtles were taking a break, basking on logs. While tree swallows skimmed the surface to drink, bullfrogs called from the lily pads. We stopped to photograph colorful

A tiger swallowtail perches on the leaves and flowers of a streamside hawthorn.

Baltimore orioles hanging from branches as they stooped to suck nectar from flowers with their narrow, pointed bills. Kingbirds patrolled the water, fluttering about to catch moths and other insects on the wing.

The dark swamp water harbored many fish that darted away, seeking cover under acres of floating vegetation. Along the far bank, ferns and swamp roses fought for light under a canopy of tall silver maple, ash, shagbark hickory, white oak, basswood, and many others. Hawthorn, with showy clusters of white flowers, bloomed along both banks. Back in the woods, eastern wood-pewees sang *pee-o-whee*, and veeries whistled their cascading, flutelike notes. Many more bird species announced their territories, including gray catbird, northern cardinal, yellow warbler, common yellowthroat, eastern phoebe, mourning dove, red-winged blackbird, rose-breasted grosbeak, great crested flycatcher, and American goldfinch.

It took quite a while to reconcile the two banks of the river, one with development, the other an impenetrable jungle. We can only wonder what this wonderful swamp must have contained in precolonial times. Because people have forgotten this waterway, you probably will paddle here alone, perhaps joined by an occasional angler. Often, that fisher is the great blue heron.

81 | West River

Marshy West River, part of the High Tor Wildlife Management Area, abounds in both aquatic vegetation and wildlife. You will see more wildlife paddling upstream. We were able to closely observe wood duck, muskrat, snapping and painted turtles, and great blue heron. You will see lots of waterfowl and possibly beaver.

Location: Italy
Maps: *New York Atlas & Gazetteer*, Map 74: A1, A2, B1, B2; USGS Middlesex
Length: 3.5 miles one way
Time: 4 hours
Habitat Type: Slow-flowing stream through a wide swamp
Fish: Largemouth and smallmouth bass (see fish advisories, Appendix C)
Camping: Appendix A (19, 23)
Information: High Tor Wildlife Management Area, dec.ny.gov/outdoor/24439.html
Take Note: At times—particularly in summer—mats of aquatic vegetation impede paddling

GETTING THERE

From the junction of Routes 245 and 21 in Naples, go 4.2 miles east on Route 245, and turn left on Sunnyside Road. Go 0.1 mile (4.3 miles) to the access on the left. (42° 39.383′ N, 77° 19.869′ W) There's a trailer access closer to the lake. (42° 39.066′ N, 77° 20.378′ W)

WHAT YOU'LL SEE

The Department of Environmental Conservation protects West River, which flows—pretty much imperceptibly—into the south end of Canandaigua Lake. Part of the 6,800-acre High Tor Wildlife Management Area, the stream contains two portions, both worth exploring. When the wind has turned the surfaces of big lakes to foaming froth, paddle here instead.

Putting in at the Sunnyside Road access, stay to the right (east) and head upstream under two bridges, into the heart of the High Tor Wildlife Management Area and, more importantly, away from motorboats. Travel sinewy West River upstream about 2 weed-choked miles before you reach the first beaver dam. We did not explore beyond the dam, although it looked as though paddlers

TRIP 81: WEST RIVER

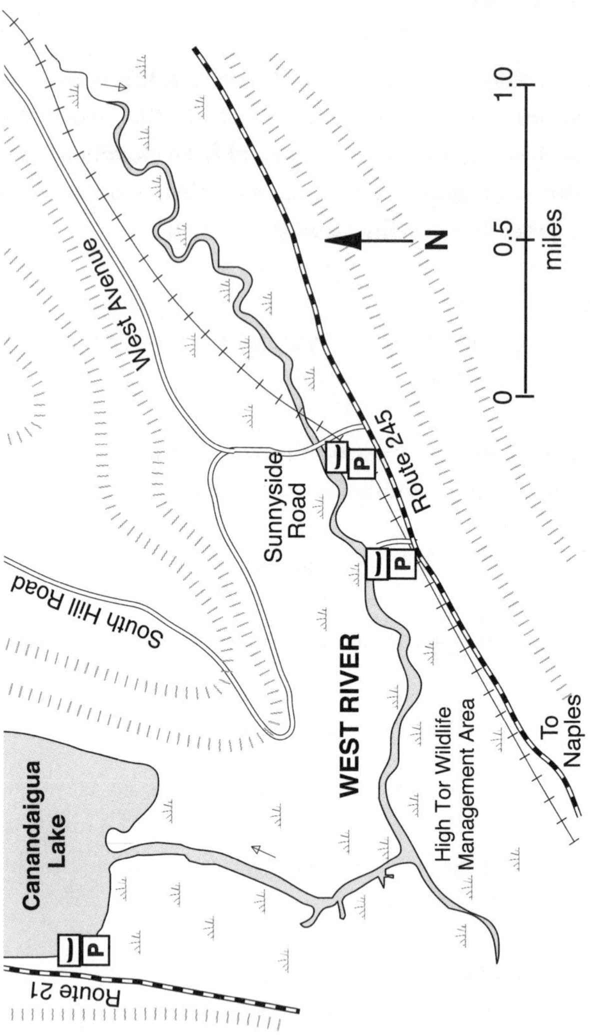

could go quite a bit farther. The structure provided the first inkling that we were paddling upstream, given the seemingly nonexistent current.

A sea of aquatic vegetation covers the waterway from bank to bank, even where the river is 100 feet across. Large mats of duckweed, a minuscule, stemless, flowering plant, float above the underwater vegetation. Tuberous American white waterlilies and yellow pondlilies occur in profusion out in the water, with arrowhead lining the shore. Extensive cattail stands course through the shallows, broken occasionally by clumps of dwarf silver maple, alder, large willow hanging out over the water, and lower-growing vegetation. We found large clusters of beautiful pink swamp rose, yellow iris, swamp milkweed, and many other flowering plants.

But wildlife provides the real attraction. Evidence of beaver activity appeared everywhere, and we saw muskrat both swimming and harvesting grasses. Turtles poked their heads up through the vegetation seemingly every few feet; we surprised several huge snapping turtles, which dove for cover under the boat. We saw great blue heron, green heron, kingfisher, great crested flycatcher, eastern phoebe, red-winged blackbird, and more than 100 ducks, mostly wood ducks. A Canada goose family grazed the shoreline. Two young great horned owls sat on a log hanging out over the water. If you are lucky, you may catch sight of the small, brightly colored hooded merganser; it competes with the wood duck for cavity nesting sites.

Because this river represents a very wild, truly productive environment, we strongly discourage paddling upstream from the hand-carry access during nesting season (before July 1). We paddled here in mid-July. Downstream is OK at any time.

Downstream from the hand-carry access, motorboats maintain an open channel. We suggest avoiding this area on summer weekends. Although

The slow-moving, marshy West River flows into the south end of Canandaigua Lake.

vegetation along the lower river remains pretty much the same as above the access, wildlife appears with less frequency, no doubt driven away by boat traffic. You can also see layered farms on the hillsides off in the distance, whereas above the bridges we saw no development.

At the hand-carry access, a plaque reads "Nundawao. Legendary site of the first Seneca Indian Village just across the river. This was the birthplace of the Seneca, members of the Iroquois nation."

82 | Hemlock Lake and Canadice Lake

We enjoy paddling on the only two undeveloped Finger Lakes. Like the others, they lie on a north-south axis and can funnel wind, making paddling treacherous. But in calm conditions, it's a pleasure to paddle these wild shores. Look for bald eagle, osprey, red-tailed hawk, and woodland songbirds. Plant and animal marshland species inhabit Springwater Creek at Hemlock Lake's south end.

Location: Canadice, Conesus, Livonia
Maps: *New York Atlas & Gazetteer*, Map 57: E8 and Map 73: A8, A9; USGS Honeoye, Springwater
Area: Hemlock Lake, 1,800 acres; Canadice Lake, 650 acres
Time: All day
Habitat Type: Deep, long, water-supply reservoirs
Fish: Largemouth and smallmouth bass; pickerel; landlocked salmon (Hemlock); brown, lake, and rainbow trout (see fish advisories, Appendix C; see specific advisory, health.ny.gov/environmental/outdoors/fish/health_advisories)
Camping: Appendix A (23)
Take Note: North or south winds can make paddling treacherous; a required self-service permit (free) is available at Hemlock Lake

GETTING THERE

Hemlock Lake Northern Access. From I-390, Exit 14, in Rochester, head 22.4 miles south on Route 15A, and turn right on Rix Hill Road. Follow signs to the self-service permit station. To reach the northern access, go 1.2 miles (23.6 miles) south on East Lake Road. (42° 45.767′ N, 77° 36.675′ W)

TRIP 82: HEMLOCK LAKE AND CANADICE LAKE

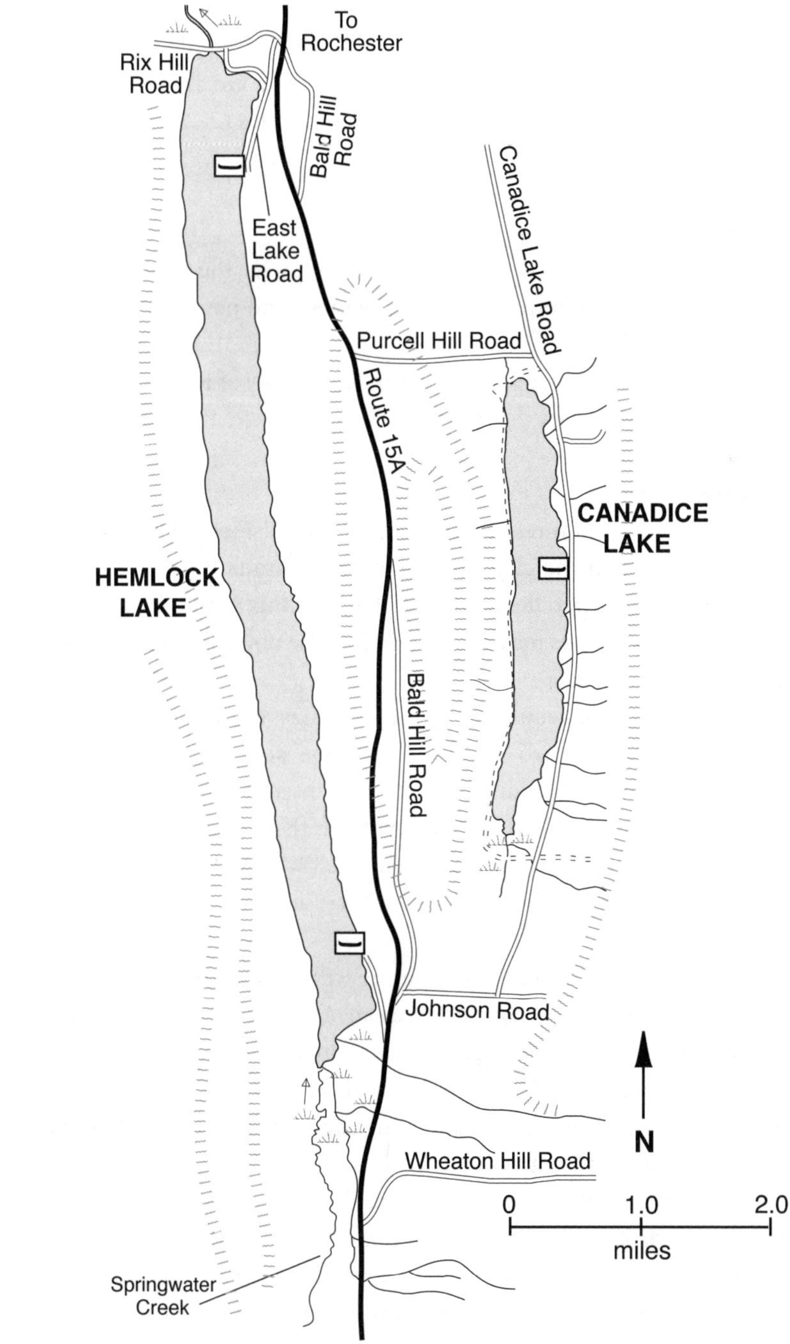

Southern Access. From the Rix Hill Road, continue 7.7 miles (30.1 miles) south on Route 15A, and turn sharply back right onto the access road. (42° 40.691′ N, 77° 35.591′ W)

Canadice Lake Access. From Rix Hill Road, go 2.5 miles (24.9 miles) south on Route 15A, and turn left on Purcell Hill Road. Go 1.4 miles (26.3 miles), and turn right on Canadice Lake Road. Go 1.4 miles (27.7 miles) to the access on the right. (42° 43.446′ N, 77° 33.867′ W)

WHAT YOU'LL SEE

Hemlock and Canadice lakes stand out as rare jewels, the only Finger Lakes not ringed by roads or dominated by development and personal watercraft. Alas, preservation did not result from farsighted conservation efforts but because the lakes serve as water-supply reservoirs for the city of Rochester, which limits access and controls uses.

Hemlock Lake

Only a couple of structures mar the view of the hillsides surrounding Hemlock Lake, and although the city allows motors, it limits boats to 16 feet and to 10 HP. A picnic area perches on the north end of this 8-mile-long, north-south-oriented lake, but boats may not go north of the northern access (about a mile from the northern end).

After getting the required permit, you may want to travel down to the southern access for two reasons: first, the southern section, including Springwater Creek and marsh, offers more interesting paddling; second, the prevailing summer winds usually blow from the south, which protects those waters somewhat from wind. However, when winds blow from any direction, we suggest that you paddle nearby West River at the south end of Canandaigua Lake (see trip 81).

Rochester imposes some rules that we will not recount here, except for one that relates to water quality: you must clean off your boat to prevent introducing invasives, such as zebra mussel, a Eurasian import that arrived in the Great Lakes region in the ballasts of ships. These very destructive bivalves have reproduced prolifically in the Great Lakes, attaching themselves in many deep clusters to water intakes and other marine structures, eventually clogging water passages.

While giving out warnings we should mention that, although this is an unspoiled lake, thirsty Rochester does draw down the level in summer, revealing ugly barren shores, especially in dry years. In wet years, the level may remain quite high even in the middle of July. If you know people in Rochester, ask them

Flowering dogwood blooms in spring on the hillsides surrounding Hemlock and Canadice lakes.

to help preserve the lake by installing low-flow toilets and showerheads and sink aerators and by using water judiciously.

Hardwoods, such as aspen, willow, red and white oaks, walnut, and sycamore, dominate the Hemlock Lake shoreline. Pines, mostly red, appear here and there, and a well-developed understory fights for light along the shore. Surprisingly, the quite-clear water harbors a relatively large amount of submerged aquatic vegetation, even out in the open lake. The Springwater Creek marsh at the south end consists of a wide expanse of cattails, grasses, and waterlilies. During times of high water, you can paddle down into it quite a way. It starts far over on the western shore and continues south.

When we paddled here, we saw ring-billed gull, a nesting red-tailed hawk pair, spotted sandpiper bobbing on rocks, belted kingfisher, eastern phoebe, great crested flycatcher, and tons of tree and barn swallows skimming the water's surface, snatching up airborne insects. You may also see the main attraction, a nesting pair of bald eagles.

Canadice Lake

Much of what we said about Hemlock remains true for Canadice. According to local anglers, even a modest breeze can kick up rollers on Canadice. Because it has a north-south orientation with steep hillsides all around, winds get funneled up and down the lake, even when they blow from off-axis directions.

Canadice, slightly more than 3 miles long and less than a half-mile wide, nestles in a deep valley, ringed with forested hillsides rising more than 1,000 feet above the lake's surface. A lone house appears near the northern shore, the only development visible from the water. Drawdown reveals a rock-filled shore instead of exposed muddy banks, making the view a lot less ugly here than at Hemlock. Although a road travels down the eastern lakeshore, it contains only very light local traffic.

While crows and red and gray squirrels harassed a perched red-tailed hawk, fish jumped out in the open water, rising for a late-May fly hatch. A few anglers searched for the lunker trout that inhabit the depths. We were content to absorb the sight of dogwood blooming on the hillsides and the songs of Baltimore orioles and black-throated green warblers emanating from the treetops. Heart-shaped leaves of bankside cottonwoods rattled in the light breeze as we peered into the undergrowth, trying to glimpse veery, common yellowthroat, and other ground-dwelling songbirds.

We enjoyed our early season paddle here, thankful that Rochester had not drawn the water down appreciably. Given the proximity to lakes infested with zebra mussels—Conesus, Canandaigua, Keuka, Seneca, and Ontario—we wondered how long it would take for Canadice and Hemlock to become infested with the destructive bivalves. Will the warnings about zebra mussels at the access have any effect on their appearance here? Can the larvae hitchhike on the legs of long-legged waders such as the great blue heron? We all will have to wait to see how this plays out here and in our other favorite waters.

83 | Mendon Ponds

Mendon Ponds Park provides many recreational and educational opportunities for families. You won't paddle alone here, so we recommend an early morning excursion to avoid the crowds. You will surely see Canada geese, great blue herons, eastern kingbirds, common yellowthroats, and swallows, as well as diverse aquatic vegetation.

Location: Mendon
Maps: *New York Atlas & Gazetteer*, Map 57: B9; USGS Pittsford

TRIP 83: MENDON PONDS

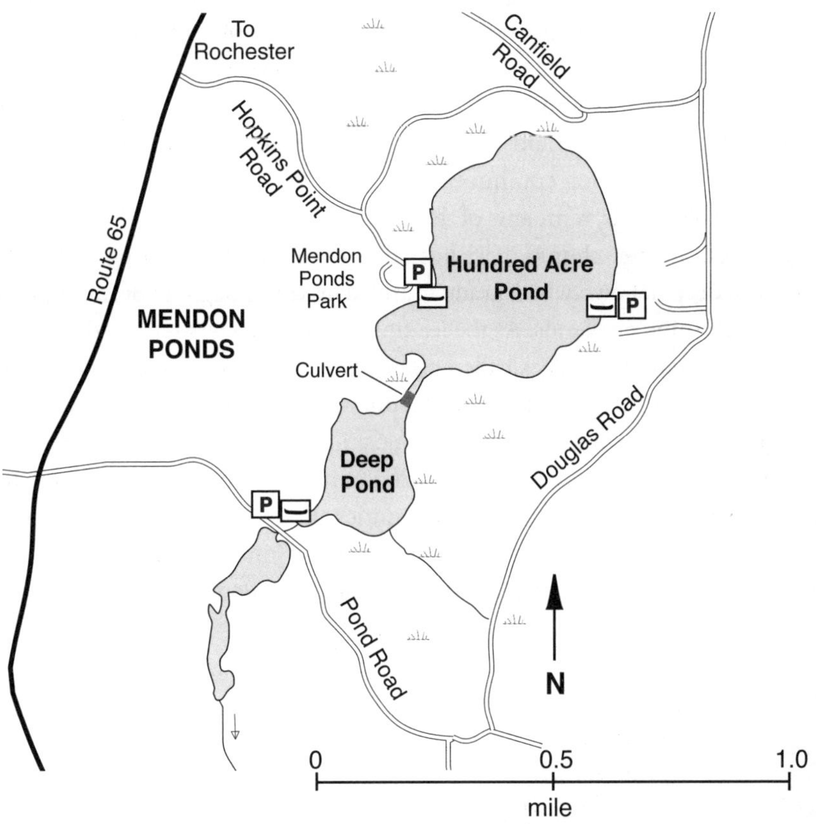

Area: Hundred Acre Pond, 120 acres; Deep Pond, 30 acres
Time: 2 hours
Habitat Type: Small, shallow ponds
Information: Mendon Ponds Park, monroecounty.gov/parks-mendonponds.php
Take Note: No motors

GETTING THERE

From Rochester, go south on Route 65 for 0.6 mile past the bridge over I-90, and turn left on Canfield Road. Go 1.1 miles (1.7 miles), and turn right on Douglas Road. Go 0.7 mile (2.4 miles) to the access on the right. (43° 1.588′ N, 77° 33.722′ W)

WHAT YOU'LL SEE

Mendon Ponds Park lies close to Rochester, just a mile south of the New York State Thruway. Although not a wilderness environment, it provides a wonderful opportunity for family recreation and a place to teach children about plants, wildlife, and canoeing. The 1,000-acre wetland area has much to teach both adults and children about climate cycles and geology. The surrounding bog, underlaid with peat, provides an outstanding example of the rare kettle hole bog community.

Kettle hole ponds, remnants of the last Ice Age, formed as glaciers retreated and left behind huge chunks of ice buried in glacial till. The melting ice formed kettles, or deep hollows, which gradually filled in with sphagnum over thousands of years, forming peatlands. As the leading edges of glaciers retreated, they left behind low sediment ridges called eskers, which are in Mendon Ponds Park and many other areas of the North Country. Eskers formed when under-ice rivers flowed through glacial cracks, depositing sediment along their borders.

The park rents canoes at the Hundred Acre Pond access site off Route 65; other recreation and picnicking opportunities abound. Launch your boat from the canoe rental facility or the opposite shore on Hundred Acre Pond or from the southwest corner of Deep Pond, off Route 65 on Pond Road.

Acres of American white waterlily dominate the south end of Hundred Acre Pond, a kettle hole left by a melting glacier at the end of the last Ice Age.

During our mid-July visit, anglers told us that in some summers the waters become completely choked with aquatic vegetation. Clearly, with ever-increasing accumulations of dead plant material during each annual cycle, the ponds march inexorably toward becoming filled-in bogs, where a floating mat of sphagnum supports bog specialists, adapted to acidic conditions. Eventually, trees encroach as the bog fills in, the added plant material eventually squeezing out the water.

Norway spruce, red pine, silver maple, ash, oak, and other trees grow well back from the water, with occasional willows on the shore. Cattails cover the banks in shallow water, and arrowhead grows in huge patches where cattails have not yet crowded it out.

We saw ducks, great blue herons, red-winged blackbirds, and common yellowthroats. A hermit thrush called from the dense undergrowth, and several species of swallow skimmed the water's surface to get a drink on a sweltering July day. Eastern kingbirds patrolled the airways, performing the excellent service of snaring deerflies. Large flocks of Canada geese simultaneously mowed the grass and fertilized it, probably saving park staff a great deal of work.

As we approached the carry into Deep Pond at the southern end of Hundred Acre Pond, a huge beaver lodge and lots of beaver activity greeted us. Entering the more secluded Deep Pond from Hundred Acre Pond should be a breeze; just paddle through the culvert that separates them. However, the beaver here must have been really hard up for running water, because they had chosen to dam up this culvert, thus requiring us to carry up and over the embankment.

We tried to paddle into the southeastern cove on Deep Pond but couldn't penetrate more than 50 feet, because yellow pondlily and American white waterlily, along with arrowhead, some rushes, and a few cattails, choked the waterway. In this more secluded area, we watched turtles bask and enjoyed the beauty of swamp rose and swamp milkweed. It's hard to believe such tranquil surroundings exist on the very outskirts of Rochester.

84 | Genesee River Gorge

You'll know you're paddling in an urban environment here, but just barely. Upstream from Turning Point Park, the Genesee River flows through a gorge, which keeps most urban noises at bay. Streamside vegetation harbors a surprising amount of wildlife—many bird species and turtles. You might see beaver, especially in early morning or evening.

Location: Rochester
Maps: *New York Atlas & Gazetteer*, Map 43: D8, E8; USGS Rochester East, Rochester West
Length: 4 miles one way
Time: 3 hours
Habitat Type: Wide, deep, slow-flowing river
Camping: Appendix A (28)
Take Note: Motorboats dominate the downstream section

GETTING THERE

From the junction of State and Main streets in Rochester, go 5.2 miles north on State Street/Lake Avenue, and turn right on Boxart Street at the sign for Turning Point Park. Continue 0.4 mile (5.6 miles) to the parking area inside the gate (check closing time). Carry 0.25 mile to the river; a portage cart works fine. (43° 13.647′ N, 77° 37.064′ W)

WHAT YOU'LL SEE

The Genesee River's lower section, from Genesee Dock at Turning Point Park to the spectacular falls 4 miles upstream (south), offers a wonderful morning or afternoon paddle within Rochester's city limits. The river—wide and deep for most of this section—really surprised us, given its urban setting. Ships ply these waters—indeed, a cement tanker had docked just north of the park when we visited—but most boat traffic stays north of Turning Point Park and heads out onto Lake Ontario.

The river's high banks help paddlers feel remarkably separated from the surrounding city. You go under a few bridges—including Route 104—and what appears to be a piped aqueduct, pass a large water treatment plant on the right, and glimpse a few large buildings and smokestacks. But mostly you paddle isolated

TRIP 84: GENESEE RIVER GORGE

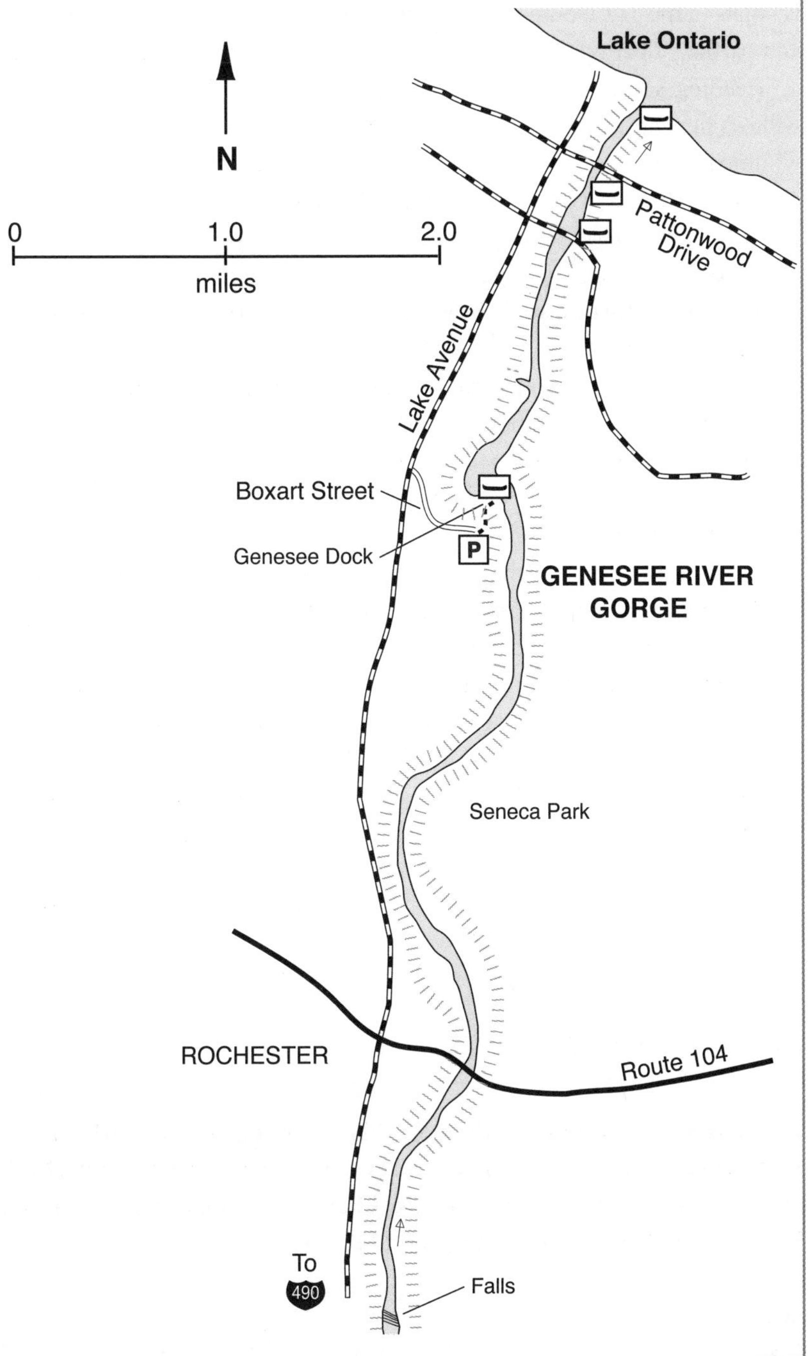

from the urban congestion a quarter-mile to the east or west. The canyon walls somehow muffle the noise as well; we felt quite alone here—albeit we paddled very late in the day. However, the occasional rusting engine block, shopping cart, and partially floating tire reminded us that civilization lingered not far away.

Heading south, the initially marshy shores grow thick with cattails, with willows here and there. On higher terrain, deciduous trees dominate: red and white oaks, basswood, maple, walnut, and sassafras. In some areas, tall, red sandstone cliffs probably serve the local kingfishers well. When we paddled here in late June, large carp spawned at the water's surface—sometimes you can paddle quite close and get a good view of these huge fish. We also saw snapping turtles, painted turtles, and a beaver during our upstream exploration.

Eventually, the marsh gives way to a more abrupt shoreline, rising steeply from the river. About 4 miles from the put-in, you pass an island on the left, the current picks up, and you have to dodge protruding rocks. Depending on flow, you may be able to continue paddling upstream, or you can beach your boat and walk along the shoreline. A wide cirque of red cliffs appears ahead, and around the bend to the left, in the distance, the northernmost falls on the river roars. Although not quite as dramatic as Upper Falls (a little farther south), this one tumbles a greater distance, providing a spectacular sight. Water cascades over a broad brim, dropping approximately 150 feet into a widened section of the gorge.

We did not paddle north of Turning Point Park. Closer to Lake Ontario, high banks disappear, development encroaches, and powerboats dominate the water—not our idea of a good time. We prefer watching beaver forage on cattails as dusk approaches, studying basking painted turtles through binoculars, and spotting herons fishing the marsh. You can almost forget that New York's third-largest city churns away above you.

85 | Buck Pond

Perched on the edge of Rochester, this wildlife preserve harbors large numbers of birds and other species. In and among the diverse plant species, look for osprey, bald eagle, black tern, wood duck, great blue heron, marsh wren, mute swan, and lots more.

Location: Greece

Maps: *New York Atlas & Gazetteer*, Map 43: D7, D8; USGS Braddock Heights

TRIP 85: BUCK POND

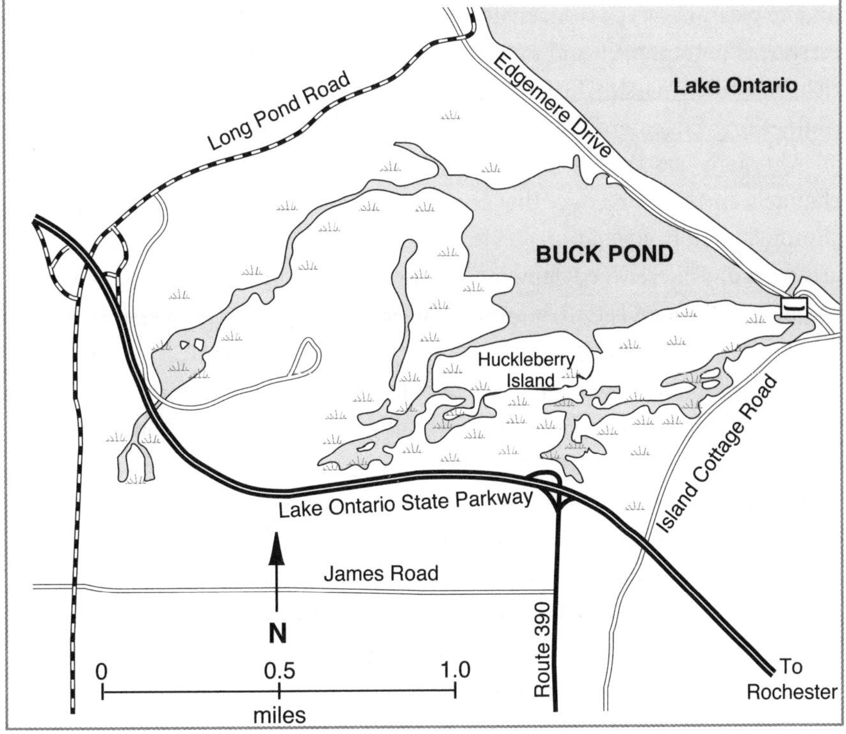

Area: 550 acres
Time: 3 hours
Habitat Type: Cattail swamp
Fish: Largemouth bass, northern pike, pickerel, walleye (see fish advisories, Appendix C)
Camping: Appendix A (28)
Information: Braddock Bay Wildlife Management Area, dec.ny.gov /outdoor/24428.html
Take Note: Novice paddlers should not venture out onto Lake Ontario

GETTING THERE

From Rochester at the junction of Pattonwood Drive/Lake Ontario State Parkway and Lake Avenue, go 0.9 mile west on the Parkway, and turn right on Greenleaf Road. Go 0.8 mile (1.7 miles), and turn left on Beach Avenue. Follow for 0.3 mile (2.0 miles), and then continue straight on Edgemere Drive. Go 1.6 miles (3.6 miles) to the access on the left behind the guardrail. (43° 16.772′ N, 77° 39.339′ W)

WHAT YOU'LL SEE

Backed up against Lake Ontario and only a few miles from Rochester, Buck Pond offers a pleasant escape from civilization. Although most of the marsh lies within earshot of automobiles and motorboats, you will feel alone here exploring the rich, bird-filled marsh. The few buildings on the northeastern shore and vacation traffic along Edgemere Drive do not spoil the pond's wild character.

Although less than a mile across, Buck Pond offers long, winding inlet channels and hidden coves that could occupy you for several hours. By early summer, marsh vegetation—cattail, bulrush, bur-reed, swamp loosestrife, arrowhead, pickerelweed, fanwort, duckweed, waterlily—chokes the shallower channels. Although cattail dominates the shoreline, this rich diversity provides for the needs of the marsh ecosystem's many animals. At the end of June, we could still paddle up the western inlet—where the current seemed nonexistent—and under the Lake Ontario State Parkway, although thick plant growth impeded our progress in a few places.

Paddling around Huckleberry Island to the west was harder, but it's well worth the effort. Open water gradually disappears amid the thick cattail stands as you pass the island and head southwest. Watch for a stately great blue heron or osprey perched on the dead tree overlooking the marsh from Huckleberry Island. We saw several dozen wood ducks, observed great blue herons fishing, happened on a secretive, rarely seen least bittern amid the cattails, and enjoyed the song of the marsh wrens—we even glimpsed one slipping in and out of its hidden nest woven of cattail leaves.

Thick vegetation, mostly cattails, dominates the winding channels of Buck Pond.

The least accessible section extends east from the access and around to the south and southwest along Island Cottage Road. Although we could not get through the thick waterlilies here, we watched a dozen black terns swooping and diving for small fish in the shallows. This uncommon species, the only tern that is mostly black, also has silvery wings; it nests on freshwater marshes. To protect its young, please keep your distance.

In addition to birdlife, we saw lots of painted turtles, particularly in the westernmost section; watched huge carp splashing at the water's surface; and caught fleeting glimpses of a few lunker largemouth bass. Indeed, the fishing looked excellent.

Paddling in spring before cattail emergence, you can see more of the marshy inlets and coves, and without the floating and submerged vegetation, you can explore a much larger area, possibly making your way around Huckleberry Island.

On a day when the wind barely rippled the surface, we used the opportunity to paddle under the Edgemere Drive bridge and onto Lake Ontario. (You may have to carry your boat over a narrow sandbar.) Ontario, although smallest of the Great Lakes, ranks fourteenth largest in the world, nearly as big as New Jersey. It feels more like the ocean than a freshwater lake. Along the shore, note the quantity of zebra mussel shells. This recently introduced nuisance species continues to wreak havoc throughout the Great Lakes.

CARNIVOROUS PLANTS: THE TABLE IS TURNED

Carnivorous plants thrive in New York's marshes, and their meat-eating adaptations make them one of nature's true wonders. Carnivory in plants apparently resulted from convergent evolution, the development of similar traits among unrelated species. Plant families on nearly every continent have some carnivorous species, with two common characteristics: they live in mineral-poor soils, supplementing soil nutrients with animal nutrients, and they use modified leaves to trap food.

Two capture strategies have evolved: active and passive. The Venus flytrap, which grows in sandy soils along the Carolina coast, uses an active capture strategy. A few others have adopted active strategies, including bladderworts (genus *Utricularia*), which form dense mats in shallow marshes. Bladderwort leaves consist of minute bladders that ingest and digest insect larvae and other organisms.

Passive capture strategies have taken two main paths. Pitcher plants—*Sarracenia purpurea*—collect rainwater in funnel-shaped leaves, and enzymes digest insects that fall into the leaves. Sundews (genus *Drosera*) form sticky pads with enzymes that digest insects.

Although bladderworts, pitcher plants, and sundews capture prey in different ways, they all have the same reason for doing so: in nutrient-poor marshes, absorbing minerals from insects and other organisms gives them a selective advantage over other plants. Tea-colored bog water, laden with organic acids from decaying vegetation, washes out minerals. Although carbon dioxide and water remain plentiful, nitrogen, phosphorus, potassium, and other important elements get leached out or bound up in underlying layers of sphagnum and peat.

Bladderwort

Bladderwort grows in shallow waters or in shoreline muck. Small yellow or purple snapdragon-like flowers lead on short stalks to carnivorous underwater bladders that form dense, feathery mats, bearing hundreds of tiny (0.02 to 0.1 inch long), bulbous traps that make up the plant's leaves. Bladders have two concave sides and a trapdoor. When a small organism bumps into the door's guard hairs, the bladder's sides pop out, and the door swings open, sucking in the hapless critter. This occurs in 0.002 second, followed by slow digestion by plant enzymes.

Mosquito larvae form the bulk of the bladderwort's diet, but the plant also ingests other larvae, rotifers, protozoans, and small crustaceans. With large prey, such as a tadpole, the door closes around the organism, and the plant digests only part of it. The next time the hairs get triggered, the plant ingests more of the organism, eventually sucking it all in.

Several bladderwort species grow in New York; two species have purple flowers, and as many as ten species have yellow flowers. Watch for the small blossoms protruding a few inches above the water's surface.

Pitcher Plant

The northern pitcher plant grows from British Columbia to Nova Scotia, southward through the Great Lakes region, and down the eastern coastal plain, crossing the Florida panhandle to the Mississippi River. Its pitcher-shaped leaves, initially green in spring, turn purple in fall. The plants bloom in June and July, and single reddish flowers, borne on stout stalks, tower a foot or more above the pitcher cluster.

The curved "pitchers" recline, allowing rain to fall into their open hoods. Stiff, downward-pointing hairs in the pitcher's throat keep insects that fall in from climbing back out, and its narrow funnel leaves little room for airborne escape. Upper pitcher walls sport a waxy coating, making for slippery footing. A combination of plant and bacterial enzymes degrades the trapped insects, and their nutrients pass easily through the lower pitcher's unwaxed surface.

Pitcher plant

Sundew

Sundew grows mainly in sphagnum bogs from Alaska to Northern California, across the Canadian Rockies and plains, through the Great Lakes, north throughout Labrador, south to Chesapeake Bay, and down through the Appalachians. The same plant grows in Europe, and four species occur in New York, including roundleaf sundew *(Drosera rotundifolia)*, the most common.

Sundew plants average about 3 inches across and 1 inch tall, with leaves modified into flattened oval pads, covered with red, stalked glands. Longer glands secrete a sticky fluid, while shorter glands secrete digestive enzymes. Attracted to the plant's nectar-like secretions, insects become trapped and are then digested by the enzymes. The flowers—usually white—hover well above the plant's leaves, borne on slender stalks. To find sundew, watch for the tiny glistening drops on their traps. Look carefully on sphagnum mats for reddish rosettes. You should also see several small insects in various stages of digestion.

86 | Salmon Creek and West Creek

The clear water of these small, marshy streams beckons paddlers away from the noise and congestion of Braddock Bay. Upstream lands between the creeks are part of Braddock Bay Wildlife Management Area. You will see ducks, moorhens, great blue herons, black terns, and other marshland species.

Location: Greece, Parma
Maps: *New York Atlas & Gazetteer*, Map 43: D6, D7; USGS Braddock Heights, Hilton
Length: 6 miles one way
Time: 3 hours
Habitat Type: Shallow, marshy creeks
Fish: Largemouth bass, northern pike (see fish advisories, Appendix C)
Camping: Appendix A (28)
Information: Braddock Bay Wildlife Management Area, dec.ny.gov /outdoor/24428.html
Take Note: Avoid the main part of Braddock Bay because of overcrowding and motors

GETTING THERE

From Rochester at the junction of Pattonwood Drive/Lake Ontario State Parkway and Lake Avenue, go 7.9 miles west on the Parkway, and exit for Manitou Beach Road. Go 0.2 mile (8.1 miles), and turn left on Manitou Beach Road/Route 261. Follow for 1.1 miles (9.2 miles), and bear left on Route 261. Continue 0.6 mile (9.8 miles) to the access at Docksiders Pub. (43° 18.312′ N, 77° 44.913′ W)

WHAT YOU'LL SEE

Braddock Bay, an inlet of Lake Ontario, lies just a few miles east of Rochester. Thirty or so creeks flow into Lake Ontario, starting at Braddock Bay and ending at Round Pond, 4 miles to the southeast, drawing from at least 150 square miles of flat coastal plain. The associated wetlands have regional significance. Indeed, the state protects 2,125 acres as the Braddock Bay Wildlife Management Area, covering most of the marshes north of the Lake Ontario Parkway, from Rose Marsh on the west to Buck Pond on the east.

TRIP 86: SALMON CREEK AND WEST CREEK

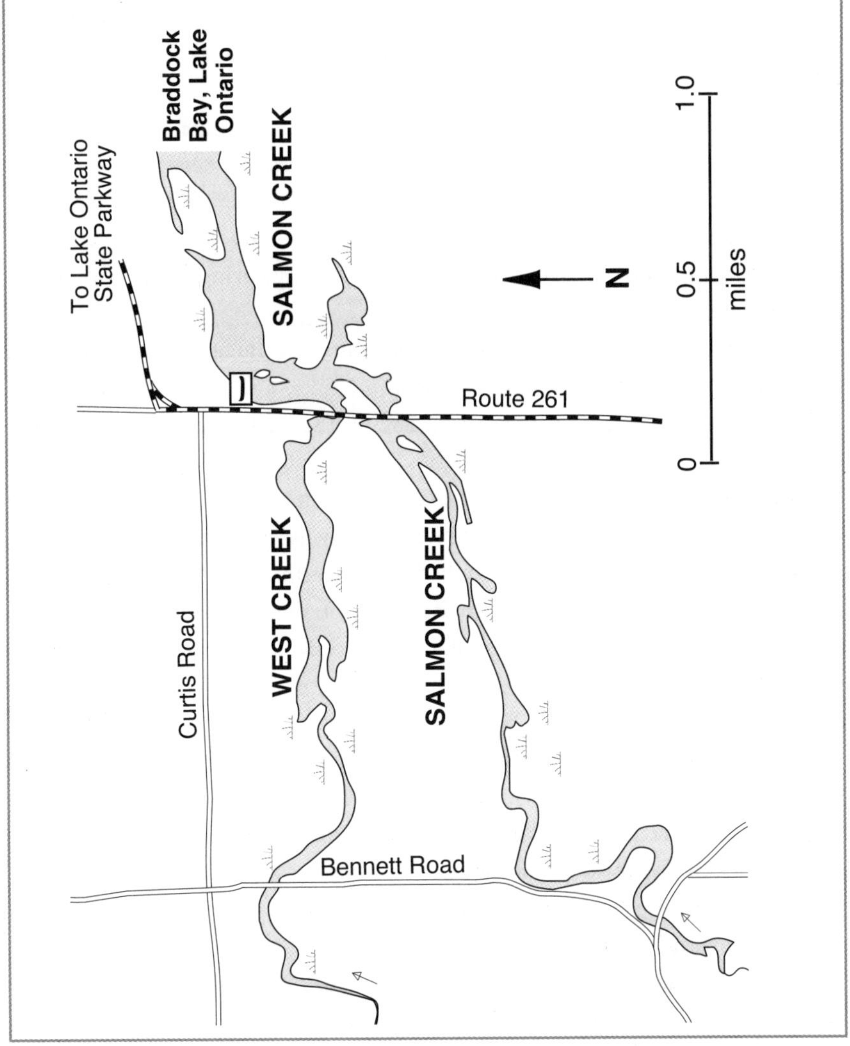

Unfortunately, protection does not extend to most of Braddock Bay, which bristles with crowded marinas, development, large boats, and the dreaded personal watercraft. Any paddler who heads out into the bay on a July or August weekend risks getting run over or swamped. Fortunately, an alternative exists. Paddlers can enjoy two relatively unspoiled Braddock Bay tributaries—West Creek and Salmon Creek—or nearby Buck Pond (see trip 85).

From the access, paddle south a short distance, and cross under Route 261, which puts you on West Creek; the bridge over Salmon Creek lies a few hundred feet farther south. Try to time your passage so no cars cross the bridges while you are underneath, because the noise can be quite loud, especially on Salmon Creek. These low-clearance bridges exclude most boats other than canoes and kayaks. Further, weeds choke the two creeks so that props on motors would foul instantly.

Cattails dominate the marshes surrounding West Creek, and pickerelweed and acres of waterlilies crowd the channel. We watched several red-winged blackbirds chase a red-tailed hawk from the cattails where it was looking for a meal. Hawks appear in abundance, especially during migration. In 1987, observers counted more than 100,000 raptors during spring migration, which peaks in late April.

Tree species include towering Norway spruces, huge willows, and ash. Grapevines drape the vegetation along the banks, and sumac appears here and there. Flocks of cedar waxwings and several species of swallows patrol the waterway, picking off insects borne of these fertile waters, while great blue herons fish the shallows. Painted turtles dive for cover as you approach, and if you paddle in the morning, acres of American white waterlily flowers will greet you.

You can paddle upstream through clear water and undisturbed habitat for about a mile and a half, all the way to the bridge on Bennett Road. After that, the creek gets too shallow. If you have time, return downstream, go back under the Route 261 bridge, turn south for a few hundred feet, recross under Route 261, and paddle up Salmon Creek. While you are out in the south end of Braddock Bay, explore the extensive marsh, teeming with wildlife. If you get too close to the tiny islands where black terns nest, they will dive-bomb your boat. After one warning, we steered clear and watched them glide effortlessly over the water. A mostly black bird with silvery wings, this tern has become increasingly rare over most of its breeding range, which stretches from coast to coast in the northern United States and Canada.

Salmon Creek has more water than West Creek, and consequently, aquatic vegetation does not choke the main channel nearly as much. The longer Salmon also has more side channels to explore and fewer cattails, which can get boring after a while. You can paddle upstream almost to the high school before riffles block your way. Common moorhens take a break from grazing on aquatic plants to scurry into the cattails as you approach. Kingfishers fly upstream from perch to perch, announcing your presence as they go. The unusual box elder, the only maple with a three-leaflet compound leaf, hangs out over the water in many places. Thick vines drape the shoreline vegetation, and, like a vine, a rope swing dangles from a hemlock over the water, inviting you to drop into the 7-foot-deep pool on sultry summer days.

87 | Oak Orchard Creek

Paddling here is best in spring and fall. During summer, sometimes abundant aquatic vegetation makes for slow going. This wildlife paradise offers opportunities to see bald eagle, osprey, waterfowl, great blue heron, kingfisher, and common yellowthroat. You might also see beaver and deer, especially in early morning or evening.

Location: Alabama, Shelby
Maps: *New York Atlas & Gazetteer*, Map 55: A9, A10; USGS Knowlesville, Medina, Oakfield
Length: 6 miles one way
Time: 5 hours
Habitat Type: Shallow, marshy, slow-flowing stream
Fish: Smallmouth bass, northern pike (see fish advisories, Appendix C)
Camping: Appendix A (27, 29, 36)
Information: Iroquois National Wildlife Refuge, fws.gov/refuge/iroquois; Oak Orchard and Tonawanda wildlife management areas, dec.ny.gov /outdoor/24442.html
Take Note: No motors

GETTING THERE

Iroquois National Wildlife Refuge Visitor Center. From I-90, Exit 48A, go 7.4 miles north on Route 63, and turn left on Casey Road. Go 0.7 mile (8.1 miles) to the visitor center. (43° 6.739′ N, 78° 24.212′ W)

Oak Orchard Creek Access. From the junction of Route 63 and Casey Road, go less than 0.1 mile (7.5 miles) north on Route 63, and turn right on Roberts Road. Go 2.6 miles (10.1 miles), and turn left on Knowlesville Road. Continue 1.4 miles (11.5 miles) to the access on the left, just before the bridge. (43° 7.187′ N, 78° 19.492′ W)

WHAT YOU'LL SEE

If you want a truly wonderful wildlife experience in western New York, go to the Oak Orchard area in spring or fall when thousands of migrating geese, ducks, and swans descend on three wildlife refuges surrounding the creek. More than 100,000 Canada geese have landed here during spring migration. In the mid-1980s, the bald eagle also returned to the Iroquois refuge, and in 1994, a pair

TRIP 87: OAK ORCHARD CREEK

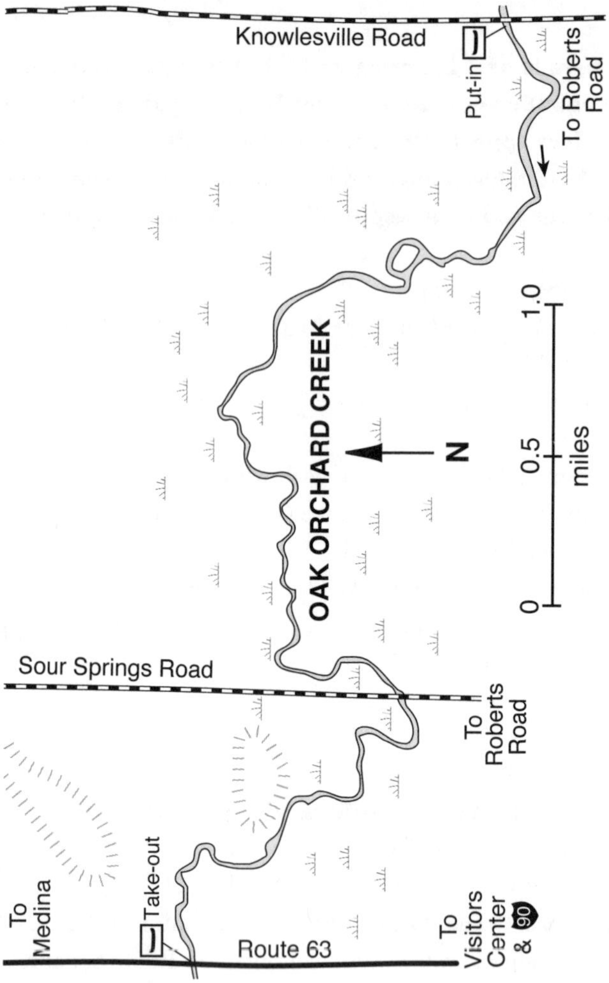

nested within sight of the visitor center and fledged three young, an extraordinary event. Since the first edition of this book in 1996, at least twenty more eagles have fledged there. In the last ten years, nests blew down, and eagles constructed new ones. In 2005, three nests produced an astounding seven eaglets.

The refuges include two state-owned wildlife management areas, Oak Orchard to the east and Tonawanda to the west, with Iroquois National Wildlife Refuge (NWR) sandwiched in between—a total of 20,000 acres of protected wetlands. Oak Orchard Creek meanders from east to west through

Oak Orchard Wildlife Management Area (WMA) and Iroquois NWR before turning north and heading for Lake Ontario. The section included here flows through Iroquois NWR.

Paddle west from Knowlesville Road, the dividing line between Oak Orchard WMA and Iroquois NWR. One might be tempted to use two cars and to make this a one-way trip. We advise against this except during high water or in spring before aquatic plants choke the channel, making it difficult to paddle the full distance. Check stream conditions at the visitor center before embarking on such an adventure; some sections may be impassable or extremely slow. In mid-July, the lazy current allows tons of duckweed—a minuscule, free-floating, flowering plant—to clog the waterway, especially behind beaver dams and logjams, making travel exceedingly difficult. Still, despite the duckweed and downed trees, we love paddling here among myriad plants and birds and other animals.

As you leave the access, look for giant cottonwoods that send seed-carrying "cotton balls" on the wind, drifting out over the water. The creek starts out about 30 feet wide but widens to 40 to 50 feet across as tree-lined banks of willow, ash, and silver maple give way to dense stands of cattails. Occasional beaver lodges and a few dams dot the waterway. Wood ducks, coots, and other waterfowl scurry into the protective cattails as you pass, while common yellowthroats and hermit thrushes call from the dense undergrowth.

Canada geese keep a lookout for danger as their downy goslings feed on tender springtime shoots.

Beautiful stands of swamp rose and swamp milkweed grace the shores in places, and arrowhead and *Rumex* poke up from the shallows. During high water, side channels off the main creek flood the adjoining land, providing greater access to these very productive wetlands. Besides touring the area by boat, we recommend that you visit the waterfowl-viewing areas and trails at the refuge and the wildlife management areas if you are here in spring or fall.

88 | Tonawanda Creek

Slow-flowing Tonawanda Creek is a great paddling resource. You'll pass an occasional camp, and you will hear road noise in places, but you will also paddle through pleasant scenery and see lots of wildlife, including great blue heron, waterfowl, beaver, muskrat, deer, and songbirds galore. Be prepared to portage around logjams.

Location: Amherst, Clarence, Lockport, Newstead, Pendleton, Royalton
Maps: *New York Atlas & Gazetteer*, Map 54: A5, A6, A7, B4, B5, B6, B7; USGS Clarence Center, Tonawanda East, Wolcottsville
Length: 20 miles one way
Time: All day
Habitat Type: Slow-flowing stream
Fish: Largemouth and smallmouth bass, northern pike, walleye (see fish advisories, Appendix C)
Camping: Appendix A (27, 35, 36)
Take Note: Logjams may require carries on steep muddy banks

GETTING THERE

Route 270 Access. From South Lockport at the junction of Robinson Road and Route 78, go 1.5 miles west on Robinson Road, and turn left on Bear Ridge Road. Go 3.9 miles (5.4 miles), and turn left on Route 270. Follow for 1.8 miles (7.2 miles), and turn left on Tonawanda Creek Road. Access is on the left just after the turn. (43° 4.148′ N, 78° 46.217′ W)

Route 78 Access. From South Lockport at the junction of Robinson Road and Route 78, go 3.1 miles south on Route 78 to the access on the left, just before the bridge. (*Caution*: Heavy traffic can make this access point dangerous.) (43° 5.215′ N, 78° 41.825′ W)

TRIP 88: TONAWANDA CREEK

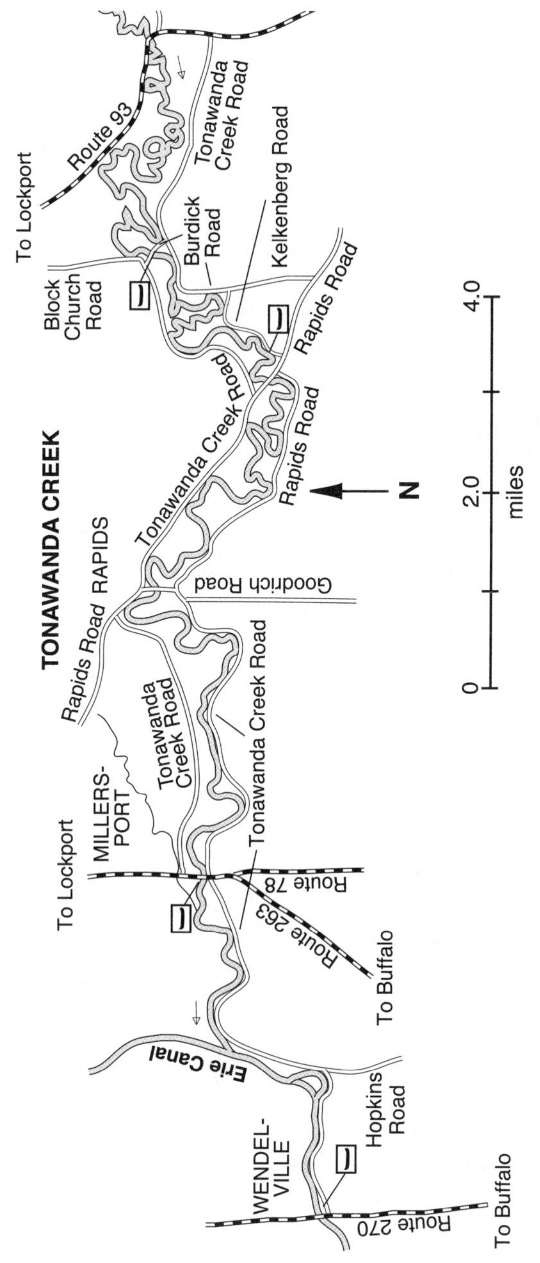

Kelkenberg Road Access. From its junction with Route 78, go 7.0 miles (10.1 miles) east on Tonawanda Creek Road South/Rapids Road, and turn right on Rapids Road. Go 0.2 mile (10.3 miles), turn left on Kelkenberg Road, and go 0.1 mile (10.4 miles) to the access on the left, just past the guardrail. (43° 4.374′ N, 78° 35.142′ W)

Burdick Road Access. From the Kelkenberg Road access, continue 1.0 mile (11.4 miles) east, and turn left on Burdick Road. Go 1.0 mile (12.4 miles), and turn left to remain on Burdick Road. Follow for 0.2 mile (12.6 miles) to the access on the left before the bridge. Carry through the grass to the creek. (43° 5.460′ N, 78° 33.817′ W)

WHAT YOU'LL SEE

Tonawanda Creek runs northward to Batavia from its source in Wyoming County south of Attica and then turns west, eventually emptying into the Niagara River just north of Buffalo. Before reaching the river, however, it joins the Erie Canal in Pendleton (near the downstream end of the section included here). Although some whitewater exists in the creek's upper reaches, the 20-mile section described in this book drops less than 1 foot per meandering mile, resulting in modest to no measurable current most of the time. In the upper reaches, houses do not crowd the banks and few motorboats ply these waters, but below Route 78 in Millersport development increases significantly.

A study in contrasts, Tonawanda Creek alternates between ferns and fields, camps and woodlots, wooded shores and muddy banks, clear sailing and annoying logjams. Beaver have contributed quite a bit to the logjams, some long-standing, judging by the jewelweed growing out of the logs. We recommend paddling upstream and downstream from one access point rather than using a shuttle, simply because you could find an impenetrable logjam surrounded by steep, muddy banks, forcing you to turn around.

Where tree density remains low, beautiful, aroma-laden honeysuckle alternates with iris and dame's rocket—a widespread escapee from cultivation. Willows lean out over the water, nearly closing the canopy. Wild grapevines drape much of the shoreline vegetation. Three maples grow in profusion, mostly silver maple, along with lesser amounts of red maple and box elder. Other common trees include ash, basswood, white oak, black walnut, and cottonwood.

We never tired of the songs of three dominant birds here: Baltimore oriole with its melodious treetop tune; red-winged blackbird calling *cong-ka-ree* from the tops of cattails; and the loud *witchety, witchety, witchety* from the diminutive common yellowthroat in the undergrowth, a small yellow warbler with a black mask across the eyes. Other birds we saw include cardinal, grackle, song sparrow, mallard, robin, gray catbird, mourning dove, bobolink, American goldfinch, crow, eastern phoebe, black-capped chickadee, house wren, and blue jay.

Turtles basked on the many logs we passed, while groundhogs munched on streamside grass. Raccoon tracks on the muddy banks told of nighttime foraging, and occasional discarded tires reminded us that many people view the nation's streams as more of a dump than a recreational asset. As a light rain began, runoff from the banks and agricultural fields turned the clear water clay-colored nearly instantly. One wonders where this huge silt burden eventually leads.

We also never tired of the creek's twists and turns, although much of the shoreline looked the same. The course straightened in the lower reaches, and we made more progress. We least enjoyed the last stretch between Millersport and Wendelville, particularly after the Erie Canal joined from the north.

Still, this whole reach provides enjoyable paddling and a wonderful resource for the quietwater enthusiast in an area with little else to offer. While glaciers carved out the Finger Lakes to the east and south and molded the Great Lakes, they left this area flat and without many waterways. So we should all remain thankful for Tonawanda Creek and do our best to keep it untrammeled for future generations.

89 | Buffalo River

This river in downtown Buffalo showcases ecological restoration practices that clean water and bring back fish and wildlife. Substantial urban renewal has occurred as well, making this area a good choice for exploring and for learning about the nation's industrial and commercial history. Expect to see Canada goose, mallard, and great blue heron. During spring and fall, this migration corridor attracts large numbers of bird species.

Location: Buffalo, West Seneca
Maps: *New York Atlas & Gazetteer*, Map 54: D3, D4; USGS Buffalo SE
Length: 6 miles one way
Time: Half day to all day
Habitat Type: Slow-flowing, industrial, channelized, polluted river undergoing ecological restoration
Fish: Unsafe to eat

TRIP 88: TONAWANDA CREEK

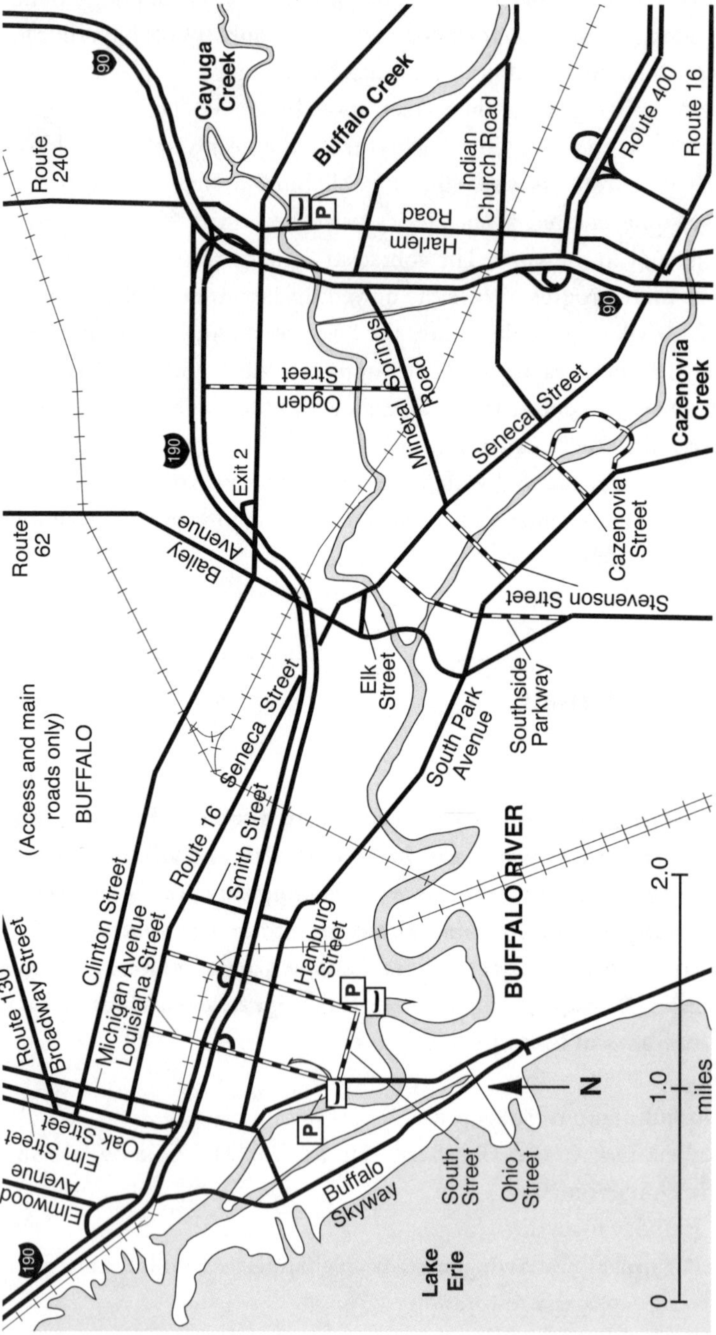

Camping: Appendix A (27, 35)
Information: Canoe, kayak rentals: Elevator Alley Kayak, elevatoralleykayak.com; BFLO Harbor Kayak, bfloharborkayak.com
Take Note: Avoid direct contact with the water; large boats ply this river, making it unsafe for novice paddlers and sometimes treacherous for small open boats

GETTING THERE

Mutual Riverfront Park Access. From I-90, go north 3.5 miles on I-190, and exit on Hamburg Street. Turn right (south), and go 0.7 mile (4.2 miles) to the access at the 90-degree turn to the right.

From downtown Buffalo, head south on I-190, and exit south on Louisiana Street. Go 0.6 mile, and turn left on Republic Street. Follow for 0.4 mile (1.0 mile), and turn right on Hamburg Street. Park along the street; carry your boat through the brick entry piers to the floating access (42° 51.858′ N, 78° 51.623′ W).

Ohio Street Kayak Launch Access. Follow directions as above to the Mutual Riverfront Park access, and turn right on South Street. Go 0.4 mile to the access, just after crossing Ohio Street (42° 51.921′ N, 78° 52.083′ W).

Harlem Road Access. (6.4 miles upstream from river mouth). From downtown Buffalo, head south on I-190, and take Exit 2. Turn left on Clinton Street, go 1.3 miles, and turn right on Harlem Road (Route 240). Go 0.2 mile (1.5 miles) to the access on the left, just over the bridge (42° 52.155′ N, 78° 47.221′ W).

WHAT YOU'LL SEE

A fascinating waterway, full of history, the Buffalo River also showcases the ecological restoration practices helping to transform some of our nation's most polluted waterways into healthy ecosystems. President Lyndon Johnson visited here in 1966 at the behest of a local jeweler and ardent conservationist, Stanley Spisiak. Appalled by the level of pollution, Johnson said, "Don't worry, I'll take care of it." This key visit played a large part in the eventual passing of the nation's Clean Water Act in 1972.

Starting in the 1970s, a public-private partnership of the U.S. Environmental Protection Agency, the Army Corps of Engineers, New York State's Department of Environmental Conservation, the City of Buffalo, Buffalo Niagara Waterkeeper, and Honeywell Corporation removed more than 1 million cubic yards of contaminated sediment from the Buffalo River. Extensive habitat restoration efforts carried out from 2013 to 2015 have helped to bring back wildlife, including fish.

Manipulated for human needs with dredging, riprap, creosote-soaked retaining walls, shipping piers, and buildings, the river's largely artificial channel has a certain beauty and a deep history that you can imagine as you paddle here. Buffalo—and especially the land immediately along the lower 4 miles of the Buffalo River—was once the grain capital of the world. For decades, ships traveled through the Great Lakes bringing wheat, corn, and oats from America's grain belt to Buffalo, unloading their cargo into massive concrete grain elevators that line the river's banks.

Here, Archer Daniels Midland, Cargill, Crosby Flour, and General Mills milled grain into flour and processed it into finished goods to be shipped east on the Erie Canal and, later, around the country by train and truck. You can see the names of these companies on buildings along the river. General Mills still operates a large mill here to make Cheerios and Lucky Charms—infusing the lower reaches of the river with the sweet aroma of toasted oats and sugar.

These American grain elevators influenced Swiss-French architect Le Corbusier (Charles-Édouard Jeanneret) and German architect Walter Gropius in their visions of modernist skyscrapers and vertical cities. Reinforced-concrete grain elevators lining the banks of the Buffalo River, built between 1900 and the 1930s, provided a key influence—for better or worse. For a detailed look at this architectural history, see Reyner Banham's *A Concrete Atlantis* (MIT Press, 1986).

Most grain elevators have fallen into disrepair, but their thick concrete and protection as historical structures means they will likely last for a long time. People have repurposed some into unique art spaces, breweries, tiki bars, recreation venues, and other facilities. One cluster of silos has been painted as a giant Labatt beer six-pack! You could spend some time exploring the lower river area—from your boat and on foot.

Upstream from the Mutual Riverfront Park and Ohio Street accesses lies the old Republic Steel factory, which turned iron ore from northern Minnesota into steel for an industrializing America. Tesla's 1.2-million-square-foot Gigafactory 2—where 800 workers manufacture solar modules and electrical components for Tesla battery systems—now occupies this cleaned-up site, once heavily polluted from decades of using the river as a waste repository.

You can paddle 6.4 miles up the river to the Harlem Road access in the suburb of West Seneca, just upstream of the I-90 overpass. This section of the river, although heavily developed, can provide a pleasant morning or afternoon of paddling. It passes under about a dozen bridges, and you will see the remains of others. Some drawbridges in the lower stretch allow larger ships to access the river.

A solo paddler in front of one of the massive abandoned grain silos on the Buffalo River.

Paddling downstream from Mutual Riverfront Park, just after passing under South Michigan Avenue, you'll see the Edward M. Cotter fireboat of the Buffalo Fire Department on the right. Built in 1900, it is believed to be the oldest fireboat still in active service.

Continuing downstream, after you pass KeyBank Center on the right (home of the National Hockey League's Buffalo Sabres) and go under the Buffalo Skyway, you will reach Canalside, Buffalo's waterfront redevelopment area, on the right. Here, on foot, you can explore a wide boardwalk, lawns, food vendors, interpretive materials about the Erie Canal, and more. The Buffalo Naval and Military Park displays several U.S. Navy ships and a submarine here.

The river empties into Lake Erie just downstream from these attractions. A Coast Guard station perches on the left, along with Buffalo Main Light (a lighthouse). Breakwaters installed to protect the waterfront keep the area fairly calm.

90 | Allegheny Reservoir

Huge Allegheny Reservoir offers hours of quiet paddling in its many nooks and crannies. The tree-lined shores harbor numerous songbirds, and you will see waterfowl everywhere. Wind can make paddling treacherous. If the wind crops up, take that as an opportunity to visit the Seneca-Iroquois National Museum.

Location: Cold Spring, Elko, South Valley
Maps: *New York Atlas & Gazetteer*, Map 86: C3, C4, D2, D3; USGS Little Valley, Redhouse, Steamburg
Area: 12,000 acres
Time: All day
Habitat Type: Large reservoir
Fish: Smallmouth bass, muskellunge, northern pike, walleye (see fish advisories, Appendix C)
Camping: Appendix A (1, 2) (on-site)
Take Note: Wind can make paddling the main reservoir treacherous; Seneca-Iroquois National Museum, senecamuseum.org; personal flotation devices (PFDs) must be worn in canoes and in boats 16 feet and under

GETTING THERE

From Route 17, Exit 18, go 3.6 miles south on Route 280 to Friends Boat Launch, Allegany State Park, on the right. (42° 3.520′ N, 78° 52.859′ W)

WHAT YOU'LL SEE

Located almost entirely within the Allegany Indian Territories, Allegheny Reservoir represents one of the few quietwater paddling resources in southwestern New York. A dam just over the border in Pennsylvania caused inundation of a many-mile stretch of the scenic Allegheny River. The river begins in Pennsylvania, swings northward and flows west through New York for about 50 miles, goes back into Pennsylvania through the reservoir, and eventually joins the Monongahela to form the Ohio River at Pittsburgh.

Portions of the reservoir's eastern shore belong to Allegany State Park, a huge park that includes a pleasant camping site, which fills up nearly every day of the summer, and two popular swimming areas: Quaker Beach on Quaker Lake, just a mile from the access, and Red House Beach on Red House Lake.

TRIP 90: ALLEGHENY RESERVOIR

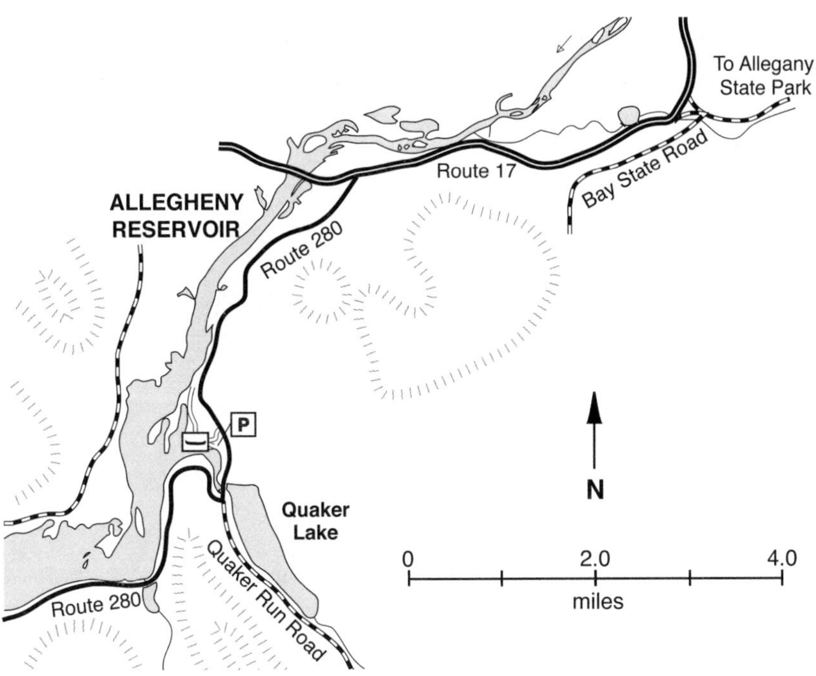

Leaving behind the droopy-branched Norway spruces and large white pines at the access, paddle into the cove on the left over to the Quaker Lake outfall to view the water cascading over the dam. Along the way, note the pine groves on the hillsides. Scrub vegetation, including lots of willow, grows down to the waterline along the left shore, and tall silver maples, white pines, hickories, oaks, and hemlocks climb the hills along the right.

Paddling back past the access, two coves appear on the right just before you get to the main reservoir. Willow dominates the shoreline here as well, with silver maple farther back and basswood and aspen on higher ground. The first cove to the right contains many camps and boats. A peninsula forms the far shore, but high water sometimes cuts it off, forming an island. The camp on the peninsula's high spot includes ducks, chickens, and mounds of trash. The second peninsula is a lot more attractive.

Moving out into the main reservoir, we noted that the shoreline in this area remains pretty much intact, punctuated only occasionally by camps. Wooded hillsides receding into the distance provide a scenic backdrop. Upon entering the reservoir, three choices immediately confront you: paddling upstream toward Salamanca, downstream toward Pennsylvania, or to the opposite shore. No matter which direction you choose, you should enjoy miles of scenery and plenty of wildlife.

Paddling here during high water in early July, we could barely detect any current on the main reservoir. A breeze, just sufficient to ripple the water's surface, blew us gently upstream, while a northern cardinal called from the dense undergrowth. American redstarts, acting more like flycatchers than warblers, darted out to snare insects on the wing. Barn and tree swallows skimmed the water's surface, doing their best to reduce the hordes of bugs produced by these productive waters.

Appendix A: Camping and Cabin Information

NEW YORK STATE PARKS AND NEW YORK STATE FOREST PRESERVES

Reservations

reserveamerica.com; 800-456-2267

Information

Office of Parks, Recreation and Historic Preservation
Empire State Plaza
Agency Building 1
Albany, NY 12238
General Information on State Parks: 518-474-0456, 518-486-1899 TDD; parks.ny.gov

New York State Department of Environmental Conservation
Public Affairs and Education
625 Broadway
Albany, NY 12233-4500
General Information: 518-457-3521
Campground and Cabin Information Only: 518-457-2500
Backcountry Camping: 518-402-9428
dec.state.ny.us/website/do/or2top.htm

Listing of State Parks by Region
Office of Parks, Recreation and Historic Preservation
State Park Campgrounds

ALLEGANY REGION—716-354-9101

1	NY Atlas 86:D3	Allegany: Quaker	716-354-2182	Rte. 17, Exit 18, 11 mi. w. of Salamanca
2	NY Atlas 86:C4	Allegany: Red House	716-354-9121	Rte. 17, Exit 19, 7 mi. w. of Salamanca
3	NY Atlas 69:D6	Lake Erie	716-792-9214	Rte. 5, 7 mi. w. of Dunkirk

CENTRAL REGION—315-492-1756

4	NY Atlas 80:B1	Betty & Wilbur Davis	607-547-8662	off Gatley Road, 2 mi. s. of Middlefield
5	NY Atlas 78:C1	Bowman Lake	607-334-2718	off Rte. 220, 8 mi. w. of Oxford
6	NY Atlas 93:B10	Chenango Valley	607-648-5251	Rte. 369, 12 mi. n. of Binghamton
7	NY Atlas 48:D4	Delta Lake	315-337-4670	Rte. 46, 6 mi. ne. of Rome
8	NY Atlas 79:B8	Gilbert Lake	607-432-2114	Rtes. 205 & 51, 12 mi. nw. of Oneonta
9	NY Atlas 64:E1	Glimmerglass	607-547-8662	4 mi. s. of Rte. 20, E. Springfield
10	NY Atlas 61:B8	Green Lakes	315-637-6111	Rtes. 290 & 5, 10 mi. e. of Syracuse
11	NY Atlas 78:B5	Hunts Pond	607-674-4017	off Rte. 8, 2 mi. n. of S. New Berlin
12	NY Atlas 94:B4	Oquaga Creek	607-467-4160	off Rte. 206, 11 mi. s. of Sidney
13	NY Atlas 46:A5	Selkirk Shores	315-298-5737	Rte. 3, 3 mi. w. of Pulaski
14	NY Atlas 48:E1	Verona Beach	315-762-4463	Rte. 13, 7 mi. nw. of Oneida

FINGER LAKES REGION—607-387-7041

15	NY Atlas 76:E1	Buttermilk Falls	607-273-5761	Rte. 13, 4 mi. s. of downtown Ithaca
16	NY Atlas 59:D9	Cayuga Lake	315-568-5163	Rte. 89, 3 mi. e. of Seneca Falls
17	NY Atlas 45:C9	Fair Haven Beach	315-947-5205	Rte. 104A, 2 mi. n. of Fair Haven
18	NY Atlas 76:A3	Fillmore Glen	315-497-0130	Rte. 38, 1 mi. s. of Moravia
19	NY Atlas 74:B4	Keuka Lake	315-536-3666	Rte. 54A, 6 mi. sw. of Penn Yan
20	NY Atlas 75:A9	Long Point	315-364-5637	Lake Road, 3 mi. s. of Aurora
21	NY Atlas 91:D9	Newtown Battlefiled	607-732-6067	Newtown Reservation Road, 6 mi. se. of Elmira
22	NY Atlas 75:A7	Sampson	315-585-6392	Rte. 96A, 11 mi. s. of E. Geneva
23	NY Atlas 73:C7	Stony Brook	585-335-5530	Rte. 36, 3 mi. s. of Dansville
24	NY Atlas 75:C10	Taughannock Falls	607-387-6739	Rte. 89, 8 mi. n. of Ithaca
25	NY Atlas 76:D1	Robert H. Treman	607-273-3440	Rte. 327, 5 mi. sw. of Ithaca
26	NY Atlas 75:E7	Watkins Glen	607-535-4511	Rte. 14, main entrance, village of Watkins Glen

GENESEE REGION—585-493-3600

27	NY Atlas 55:D8	Darien Lakes	585-547-9242	Harlow Rd., Darien Center
28	NY Atlas 42:C4	Hamlin Beach	585-964-2462	Lake Ontario St. Parkway, 25 mi. w. of Rochester
29	NY Atlas 42:C1	Lakeside Beach	585-682-4888	Lake Ontario St. Parkway, 35 mi. w. of Rochester
30	NY Atlas 72:A4	Letchworth	585-493-3600	I-390 Exit 7, 35 mi. s. of Rochester

LONG ISLAND REGION—631-669-1000

31	NY Atlas 112:D4	Heckscher	631-581-2100	Heckscher St. Parkway, E. Islip
32	NY Atlas 115:C8	Hither Hills	631-668-2554	Montauk Highway, Montauk
33	NY Atlas 113:A9	Wildwood	631-929-4314	N. Country Rd., Wading River

NIAGARA REGION—716-278-1770

34	NY Atlas 69:B10	Evangola	716-549-1802	Rte. 5, 27 mi. sw. of Buffalo, Irving
35	NY Atlas 40:D2	Four Mile Creek	716-745-3802	Rte. 18 or Robert Moses Parkway, 4 mi. ne. of Youngstown
36	NY Atlas 41:C8	Golden Hill	716-795-3885	Lower Lake Rd., off Rte. 269, Barker

PALISADES REGION—845-786-2701

37	NY Atlas 108:C2	Bear Mountain	845-786-2701	Rte. 202, 3 mi. s. of Rte. 202 bridge over Hudson River
38	NY Atlas 108:D1	Harriman: Beaver Pond	845-947-2792	Palisades Pkwy, Exit 16
39	NY Atlas 107:D10	Harriman: Sebago Cabins	845-351-2360	Palisades Pkwy, Exit 16

SARATOGA-CAPITAL REGION—518-584-2000

40	NY Atlas 83:B9	Cherry Plain	518-733-5400	Rte. 22, 7 mi. n. of Stephentown
41	NY Atlas 52:E5	Moreau Lake	518-793-0511	I-87, Exit 17S, S. Glens Falls
42	NY Atlas 81:C7	Max V. Shaul	518-827-4711	Rte. 30, 6 mi. s. of Middleburgh
43	NY Atlas 66:B4	Saratoga Spa	518-584-2535	Rte. 9, 2 mi. s. of Saratoga Springs
44	NY Atlas 82:B1	Thompson's Lake	518-872-1674	Rte. 157, 18 mi. w. of Albany

TACONIC REGION—845-889-4100

45	NY Atlas 108:A4	Clarence Fahnestock	845-225-7207	Rte. 301, off Taconic Parkway
46	NY Atlas 98:C5	Lake Taghkanic	518-851-3631	Rte. 82 at Taconic Parkway, 11 mi. s. of Hudson
47	NY Atlas 103:A7	Margaret Lewis Norrie	845-889-4646	Rte. 9, 4 mi. n. of Hyde Park
48	NY Atlas 99:E7	Rudd Pond	518-789-3059	off Rte. 22, 2 mi. n. of Millerton
49	NY Atlas 99:C7	Taconic: Copake Falls	518-329-3993	east of Rte. 22, Copake Falls

THOUSAND ISLANDS REGION—315-482-2593

50	NY Atlas 24:D4	Burnham Point	315-654-2324	Rte. 12E, 4 mi. e. of Cape Vincent
51	NY Atlas 25:B7	Canoe-Picnic Point	315-686-3048	access by boat only, Grindstone Island
52	NY Atlas 24:B2	Cedar Island	315-654-2522	access by boat only, Cedar Island
53	NY Atlas 24:C5	Cedar Point	315-654-2522	Rte. 12E, 6 mi. w. of Clayton
54	NY Atlas 13:E8	Coles Creek	315-388-5636	Rte. 37, 4 mi. e. of Waddington
55	NY Atlas 23:B8	Cumberland Bay	518-563-5240	Rte. 314, 1 mi. e. of Plattsburgh
56	NY Atlas 25:B8	Dewolf Point	315-482-2012	I-81, Exit 51, 2 mi. n. of Alexandria Bay
57	NY Atlas 18:C4	Eel Weir	315-393-1138	Rte. 812, 7 mi. s. of Ogdensburg
58	NY Atlas 25:B8	Grass Point	315-686-4472	Rte. 12, 1 mi. w. of I-81, Alexandria Bay
59	NY Atlas 20:D1	Higley Flow	315-262-2880	Rte. 56, 2 mi. e. of S. Colton
60	NY Atlas 18:D1	Jacques Cartier	315-375-6371	Rte. 12, 3 mi. w. of Morristown
61	NY Atlas 25:B8	Keewaydin	315-482-3331	Rte. 12, 1 mi. w. of Alexandria Bay
62	NY Atlas 25:A9	Kring Point	315-482-2444	Rte. 12, 6 mi. e. of Alexandria Bay
63	NY Atlas 24:E5	Long Point	315-649-5258	Rte. 12E, 8 mi. w. of Three Mile Bay
64	NY Atlas 23:C6	Macomb Reservation	518-643-9952	off Rte. 22B, 2 mi. w. of Schuyler Falls
65	NY Atlas 25:A8	Mary Island	315-482-9381	access by boat only, Alexandria Bay
66	NY Atlas 14:D1	Robert Moses	315-769-8663	off Rte. 37, 3 mi. n. of Massena
67	NY Atlas 32:B4	Robert G. Wehle	315-938-5302	Rte. 3, 23 mi. sw. of Watertown
68	NY Atlas 32:C5	Southwick Beach	315-846-5338	off Rte. 3, 2 mi. w. of Woodville
69	NY Atlas 25:B7	Wellesley Island	315-482-2722	I-81, Exit 51, 4 mi. w. of Alexandria Bay
70	NY Atlas 33:B6	Westcott Beach	315-646-2239	Rte. 3, 3 mi. w. of Sackets Harbor
71	NY Atlas 34:D4	Whetstone Gulf	315-376-6630	Rte. 26, 6 mi. s. of Lowville

Department of Environmental Conservation Forest Preserve Public Campgrounds Adirondacks

WARRENSBURG—518-623-1200

72	NY Atlas 38:D4	Eagle Point	518-561-7080	Rte. 9, 2 mi. n. of Pottersville
73	NY Atlas 52:B5	Hearthstone Point	518-668-5193	Rte. 9N, 2 mi. n. of Lake George Village
74	NY Atlas 52:C5	Lake George Battleground	518-668-3348	Rte. 9, 1/4 mi. s. of Lake George Village
75	NY Atlas 53:B6	Lake George Islands:		
		Glen Island	518-644-9696	Bolton Landing
		Long Island	518-656-9426	Cleverdale
		Narrow Island	518-499-1288	Huletts Landing
76	NY Atlas 52:C4	Luzerne	518-696-2031	Rte. 9N, 8 mi. sw. of Lake George Village
77	NY Atlas 39:C8	Rogers Rock	518-585-6746	Rte. 9N, 3 mi. n. of Hague

RAYBROOK—518-897-1309

78	NY Atlas 23:D8	Ausable Point	518-561-7080	Rte. 9, 12 mi. s. of Plattsburgh
79	NY Atlas 21:D10	Buck Pond	518-891-3449	off Rte. 86, 6 mi. n. of Gabriels
80	NY Atlas 31:E8	Crown Point	518-597-3603	off Rte. 9N, 8 mi. n. of Crown Point
81	NY Atlas 29:B7	Fish Creek Pond	518-891-4560	Rte. 30, 12 mi. e. of Tupper Lake
82	NY Atlas 38:A5	Frontier Town	518-532-9051	Rte. 9, 1 mi. s. of North Hudson
83	NY Atlas 37:A6	Lake Eaton	518-624-2641	Rte. 30, 2 mi. w. of Long Lake
84	NY Atlas 37A:10	Lake Harris	518-582-2503	Rte. 28N, 3 mi. n. of Newcomb
85	NY Atlas 31:D7	Lincoln Pond	518-942-5292	Rte. 7, 6 mi. s. of Elizabethtown
86	NY Atlas 21:D8	Meacham Lake	518-483-5116	Rte. 30, 19 mi. n. of Lake Clear Jct.
87	NY Atlas 30:B1	Meadowbrook	518-891-4351	Rte. 86, 2 mi. e. of Saranac Lake
88	NY Atlas 38:B5	Paradox Lake	518-532-7451	Rte. 74, 2 mi. e. of Severance

89	NY Atlas 39:B7	Putnam Pond	518-585-7280	off Rte. 74, 6 mi. w. of Ticonderoga
90	NY Atlas 29:B7	Rollins Pond	518-891-3239	Rte. 30, 12 mi. e. of Tupper Lake
91	NY Atlas 29:B9	Saranac Lake Islands	518-891-3170	Rte. 3, 5 mi. w. of Saranac Lake village
92	NY Atlas 38:A5	Scaroon Manor	518-494-2631	Rte. 9, 4 mi. n. of Pottersville
93	NY Atlas 30:E5	Sharp Bridge	518-532-7538	Rte. 9, 15 mi. n. of Schroon Lake
94	NY Atlas 22:E4	Taylor Pond	518-647-5250	Silver Lake Rd., 9 mi. nw. of Au Sable Forks
95	NY Atlas 30:A3	Wilmington Notch	518-946-7172	Rte. 86, 3.5 mi. w. of Wilmington

HERKIMER—315-866-6330

96	NY Atlas 36:D1	Alger Island	315-369-3224	Rte. 28, 8 mi. e. of Old Forge
97	NY Atlas 35:D10	Nicks Lake	315-369-3314	off Rte. 28, 1.5 mi. sw. of Old Forge

CANTON—315-265-3090

98	NY Atlas 28:C2	Cranberry Lake	315-848-2315	off Rte. 3, 1.5 mi. s. of Cranberry Lake Village

INDIAN LAKE—518-648-5616

99	NY Atlas 36:C3	Browns Tract Pond	315-354-4412	Rte. 28, 7 mi. e. of Eagle Bay
100	NY Atlas 36:C3	Eighth Lake	315-354-4120	Rte. 28, 5 mi. w. of Raquette Lake
101	NY Atlas 36:B5	Forked Lake	518-624-6646	off Rte. 30, 3 mi. w. of Deerland Village
102	NY Atlas 36:C4	Golden Beach	315-354-4230	Rte. 28, 3 mi. n. of Raquette Lake
103	NY Atlas 37:D7	Indian Lake Islands	518-648-5300	Rte. 30, 14 mi. n. of Speculator
104	NY Atlas 37:B7	Lake Durant	518-352-7797	Rt. 28, 2 mi. e. of Blue Mountain Lake
105	NY Atlas 37:E7	Lewey Lake	518-648-5266	Rte. 30, 14 mi. n. of Speculator
106	NY Atlas 36:D2	Limekiln Lake	315-357-4401	off Rte. 28, 3 mi. se. of Inlet
107	NY Atlas 36:B4	Tioga Point	315-354-4101	Raquette Lake

NORTHVILLE—518-863-4545

108	NY Atlas 65:A6	Caroga Lake	518-835-4241	Rte. 29A, 9 mi. nw. of Gloversville
109	NY Atlas 50:C5	Little Sand Point	518-548-7585	off Rte. 8, 3 mi. w. of Piseco
110	NY Atlas 51:B7	Moffitt Beach	518-548-7102	Rte. 8, 4 mi. w. of Speculator
111	NY Atlas 51:E9	Northampton Beach	518-863-6000	Rte. 30, 1.5 mi. s. of Northville
112	NY Atlas 50:C5	Point Comfort	518-548-7586	off Rte. 8, 4 mi. w. of Piseco
113	NY Atlas 51:C8	Sacandaga	518-924-4121	Rte. 30, 4 mi. s. of Wells

CATSKILLS

SCHENECTADY—518-357-2234

114	NY Atlas 95:C9	Bear Spring Mountain	607-865-6989	off Rte. 206, 5 mi. se. of Walton
115	NY Atlas 97:C9	Devil's Tombstone	845-688-7160	Rte. 214, 4 mi. s. of Hunter
116	NY Atlas 96:D3	Little Pond	845-439-5480	off Rte. 17, 14 mi. nw. of Livingston Manor
117	NY Atlas 98:B1	North/South Lake	518-589-5058	off Rte. 23A, 3 mi. ne. of Haines Falls

NEW PALTZ—845-256-3099

118	NY Atlas 96:E1	Beaverkill	845-439-4281	off Rte. 17, 7 mi. nw. of Livingston Manor
119	NY Atlas 97:D9	Kenneth L. Wilson	845-679-7020	off Rte. 28, 4 mi. e. of Mt. Tremper on Rt. 40
120	NY Atlas 96:E3	Mongaup Pond	845-439-4233	off Rte. 17, 3 mi. n. of DeBruce
121	NY Atlas 97:D7	Woodland Valley	845-688-7647	off Rte. 28, 6 mi. sw. of Phoenicia

SUFFOLK COUNTY PARKS WITH CAMPGROUNDS

EAST END

122	NY Atlas 115:B6	Cedar Point	631-852-7620	Cedar Point, 6 mi. n. of East Hampton
123	NY Atlas 113:C10	Cupsogue Beach	631-852-8111	Barrier island sw. of Westhampton Beach
124	NY Atlas 114:D1	Indian Island	631-852-3232	Rte. 105, Riverhead
125	NY Atlas 114:D2	Sears Bellows	631-852-8290	off Rte. 24 nw. of Hampton Bays
126	NY Atlas 114:E3	Shinnecock East (beach vehicle camping only)	631-852-8839	Sw. of Southampton on barrier spit
127	NY Atlas 115:B9	Theodore Roosevelt (beach vehicle camping only)	631-852-7879	E. side of Lake Montauk

WEST END

128	NY Atlas 112:B4	Blydenburgh (county residents only)	631-854-3712	S. edge of Smithtown between Rtes. 25 and 347
129	NY Atlas 113:B7	Cathedral Pines	631-852-5502	on Longwood Rd. n. of Yaphank
130	NY Atlas 113:D8	Smith Point	631-852-1340	on Fire Island at end of Wm. Floyd Pkwy.
131	NY Atlas 113:C8	Southaven	631-854-1414	on Carmans River just n. of Sunrise Hwy.

FEDERAL NATIONAL FORESTS AND SEASHORES

132	NY Atlas 113:D8	Fire Island National Seashore	631-687-4750	on Fire Island
133	NY Atlas 75:D8	Finger Lakes National Forest	607-546-4470	on County Rte. 2 ne. of Watkins Glen

NASSAU COUNTY CAMPGROUNDS

134	NY Atlas 112:D1	Battle Row	516-572-8690	Claremont Rd. in Old Bethpage
135	NY Atlas 117:A9	Nickerson Beach	516-571-7724	Lido Blvd., Long Beach

PASSPORTS & PASSES

Empire Passport: Provides yearlong vehicle entry to state parks and recreation areas. Purchase can be made at participating facilities or by mail from Office of Parks (see address on page 381).

Golden Park Program: Provides New York State residents 62 or older free entry on weekdays, holidays excluded; simply show New York driver's license or Nondriver Identification Card.

Access Pass: Provides New York State residents with permanent disabilities free entry to state parks and recreation areas. Purchase can be made by mail from Office of Parks (see address on page 381).

Appendix B: Further Reading

Armstrong, Kathie, and Chet Harvey, *Adirondack Mountain Club Canoe and Kayak Guide: East-Central New York State,* 1st revised ed., Adirondack Mountain Club, 2005

Banham, Reyner, *A Concrete Atlantis,* MIT Press, 1986

Brame, Rich, and David Cole, *NOLS Soft Paths: Enjoying the Wilderness without Harming It,* 4th ed., Stackpole Books, 2011

DeLorme Mapping Company, *New York Atlas & Gazetteer,* 11th ed., 2018

Ehling, William, *Canoeing Central New York,* Backcountry Publications, 1982

Freeman, Mark, *Adirondack Mountain Club Canoe Guide to Western and Central New York State,* Adirondack Mountain Club, 1994

Hutchinson, Derek, *Basic Book of Sea Kayaking,* 2nd ed., Falcon, 2007

Hutchinson, Derek, *The Complete Book of Sea Kayaking,* 6th ed., Falcon, 2018

Jacobson, Cliff, *Basic Essentials Canoeing,* 3rd ed., Falcon, 2007

Jamieson, Paul, *Adirondack Pilgrimage,* Adirondack Mountain Club, 1988

Jamieson, Paul, *The Adirondack Reader,* Adirondack Mountain Club, 3rd ed., 2009

Jamieson, Paul, and Donald Morris, *Adirondack Canoe Waters: North Flow,* 3rd ed., Adirondack Mountain Club, 1988

Jerome, Christine, *Adirondack Passage: The Cruise of the Canoe Sairy Gamp,* 3rd ed., Breakaway Books, 2013

Lanza, Michael, *Ultimate Guide to Backcountry Travel,* AMC Books, 1999

New York State Department of Environmental Conservation publications locator: dec.ny.gov/64.html

Proskine, Alec, *Adirondack Canoe Waters: South & West Flow,* 2nd ed., Adirondack Mountain Club, 1989

Roberts, Harry, and Steve Salins, *Basic Essentials Canoe Paddling,* 3rd ed., Falcon, 2006

Sears, George Washington, and Dan Brenan, *Canoeing the Adirondacks with Nessmuk: The Adirondack Letters of George Washington Sears,* 2nd ed., Syracuse University Press, 1993

Seidman, David, *The Essential Sea Kayaker,* 2nd ed., Ragged Mountain Press, 2000

Walter, George, *The Loomis Gang,* North Country Books, 1985

Appendix C: Fish Advisories

Information presented here is adapted from the U.S. Environmental Protection Agency and the New York State Department of Health 48-page brochure, *Health Advice on Eating Sportfish and Game*. See: health.ny.gov/publications/2800.pdf and epa.gov/choose-fish-and-shellfish-wisely.

Fish and other seafood, especially those fish whose oils are rich in omega-3 fatty acids, should be part of everyone's diet. Not all seafood is safe, however, mainly because mercury, a very toxic metal, accumulates in some game fish. Generally, the larger the fish and the closer to the top of the food chain, the more mercury. Also, for some waters, PCBs and dioxins are also a concern. Those waters are listed separately below. If you have specific questions, see the New York State *Health Advice* brochure.

PCBs, dioxins, and pesticides accumulate in the fat of fish. To reduce the amount of these toxins, skin your fish and remove fat, which tends to lie along the belly, back, and midline.

Healthy Sport Fish and Seafood for the Whole Family

- Atlantic mackerel
- Sea-run smelt
- Farm-raised and wild-caught salmon
- Canned salmon
- Hatchery-reared trout
- Perch
- Sardines
- Tilapia
- Mussels, clams, oysters, and scallops
- Light canned tuna
- Haddock, hake, cod, and pollock
- Flounder, sole, and plaice
- Lobster (but not the tomalley), shrimp, crab
- Imitation crab and lobster
- Fish sticks

Recommendation is that everyone eat two meals per week from this list.

Sport Fish with Eating Limits

- Striped bass
- Bluefish
- Tuna, albacore and yellowfin
- Halibut
- Mahi mahi

Limits for pregnant and nursing women and children under age 15: one meal per month. Limits for everyone else: one meal per week.

Sport Fish with Very Strict Eating Limits

All other fish, including:

- Largemouth and smallmouth bass
- Northern pike and pickerel
- Walleye and perch larger than 10 inches
- Swordfish, shark, marlin, king mackerel, and tilefish
- Bigeye tuna

Limits for pregnant and nursing women and children under age 15: do NOT eat these fish. Limits for everyone else: one meal per month.

Advisories for Pregnant Women and Children under 15 Years Old

Pregnant and nursing women and children under age 15 should not eat fish from many of the state's waters. Others should follow the guidelines listed above. Further, specific bodies of water suffer greatly from toxic chemicals. We have noted in the entries for those waters that you probably should not eat the fish.

List of Waterways

About AMC in New York

The Appalachian Mountain Club's Mohawk Hudson and New York–North Jersey chapters have more than 1,000 members and offer hundreds of trips each year. Well-trained and dedicated leaders guide hiking, paddling, skiing, and climbing excursions. The chapters are also active in trail work, conservation projects, and instructional programs promoting outdoor activities. You can learn more about these chapters by visiting outdoors.org/chapters. To view a list of AMC activities in New York and other parts of the Northeast, visit trips.outdoors.org.

New York is also home to the Stephen & Betsy Corman AMC Harriman Outdoor Center, located at Breakneck Pond in Harriman State Park. The Center is open to the public, and offers common space for outdoor programs, waterfront access to 64-acre Breakneck Pond, a dining hall, and group meeting space. Accommodations include group and family cabins, tent platforms, and three-sided shelters, offering a range of overnight experiences.

About the Authors

ALEX WILSON is an avid canoeist and naturalist and a widely published writer on energy, building technology, and environmental issues. He lives in Dummerston, Vermont. **JOHN HAYES**, now retired, is the former director of sustainability at Pacific University in Oregon and former professor of environmental science at Marlboro College in Vermont. Besides paddling all over New England, New York, Pennsylvania, and New Jersey, he has paddled in the Pacific Northwest, in Minnesota's Boundary Waters, in the Okefenokee Swamp in Georgia, across the Everglades, and in Belize. In all, he has canoed and kayaked more than 5,000 miles.

AMC Book Updates

AMC Books strives to keep our guidebooks as up-to-date as possible to help you plan safe and enjoyable adventures. If we learn after publishing a book that relevant trails have been relocated or route or contact information has changed, we will post the updated information online. Before you hit the trail, visit outdoors.org/books-maps and click the "Book Updates" tab.

While hiking or paddling, if you notice discrepancies with the trip descriptions or maps, or if you find any other errors in this book, please let us know by submitting them to amcbookupdates@outdoors.org or to Books Editor, c/o AMC, 10 City Square, Boston, MA 02129. We will verify all submissions and post key updates each month. AMC Books is dedicated to being a recognized leader in outdoor publishing. Thank you for your participation.